High School Host Club

Vol. 1

Bisco Hatori

Ouran High School

Host Club™

Vol.1

CONTENTS

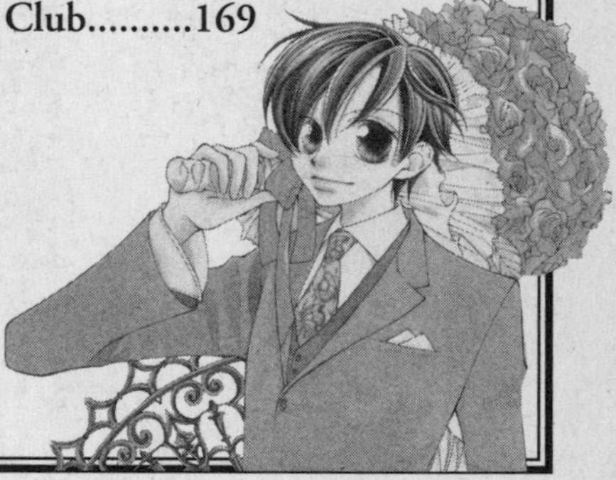

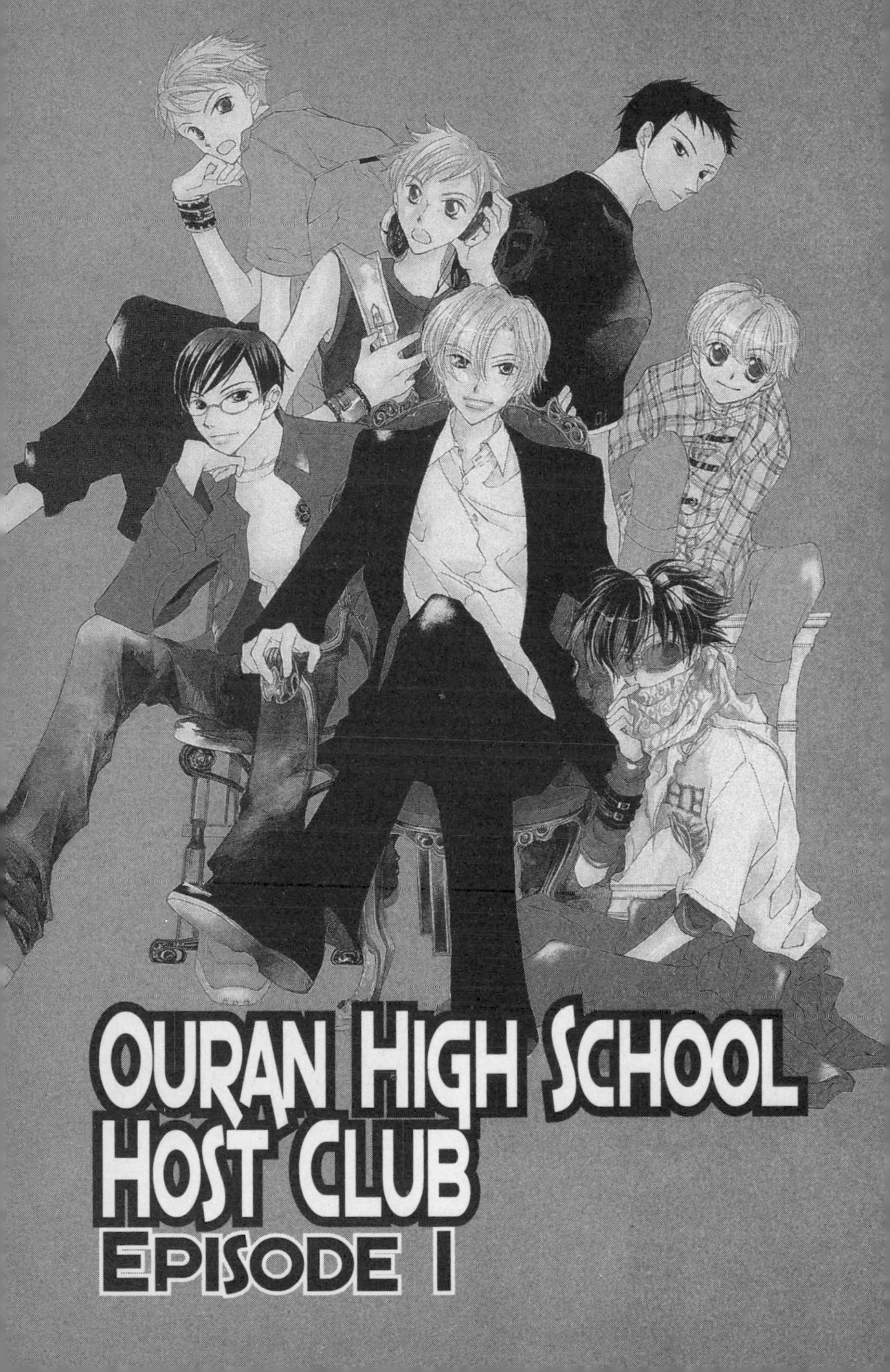

OURAN HIGH SCHOOL HOST CLUB

EPISODE 1

EXTRA MANGA

THE ELEGANT HOST CLUB EXPERIENCE

BISCO ☆ HATORI

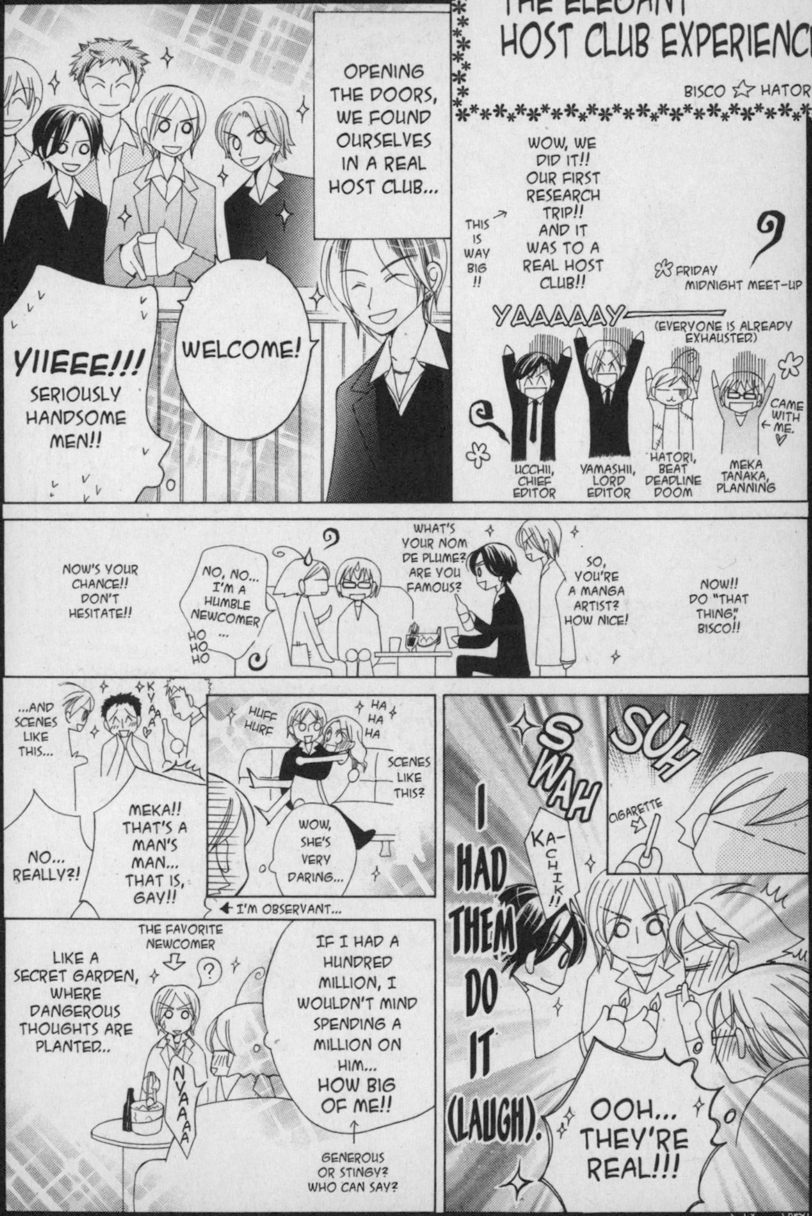
WOW, WE DID IT!! OUR FIRST RESEARCH TRIP!! AND IT WAS TO A REAL HOST CLUB!!
THIS IS WAY BIG !!
FRIDAY MIDNIGHT MEET-UP
YAAAAAY—
(EVERYONE IS ALREADY EXHAUSTED)
CAME WITH ME.
UCCHII, CHIEF EDITOR
YAMASHII, LORD EDITOR
HATORI, BEAT DEADLINE DOOM
MEKA TANAKA, PLANNING
OPENING THE DOORS, WE FOUND OURSELVES IN A REAL HOST CLUB...
WELCOME!
YIIEEE!!! SERIOUSLY HANDSOME MEN!!
NOW!! DO "THAT THING," BISCO!!
SO, YOU'RE A MANGA ARTIST? HOW NICE!
WHAT'S YOUR NOM DE PLUME? ARE YOU FAMOUS?
NO, NO... I'M A HUMBLE NEWCOMER ...
HO HO HO
NOW'S YOUR CHANCE!! DON'T HESITATE!!
SUH
CIGARETTE
SWAH
KA-CHIK!!
I HAD THEM DO IT (LAUGH).
OOH... THEY'RE REAL!!!
HA HA HA
HUFF HUFF
SCENES LIKE THIS?
WOW, SHE'S VERY DARING...
← I'M OBSERVANT...
KYAAA
...AND SCENES LIKE THIS...
MEKA!! THAT'S A MAN'S MAN... THAT IS, GAY!!
NO... REALLY?!
IF I HAD A HUNDRED MILLION, I WOULDN'T MIND SPENDING A MILLION ON HIM... HOW BIG OF ME!!
GENEROUS OR STINGY? WHO CAN SAY?
THE FAVORITE NEWCOMER
LIKE A SECRET GARDEN, WHERE DANGEROUS THOUGHTS ARE PLANTED...
NYAAAA

TO EVERYONE AT THE CLUB, THANK YOU FOR YOUR COOPERATION!!! THANKS, MEKA.

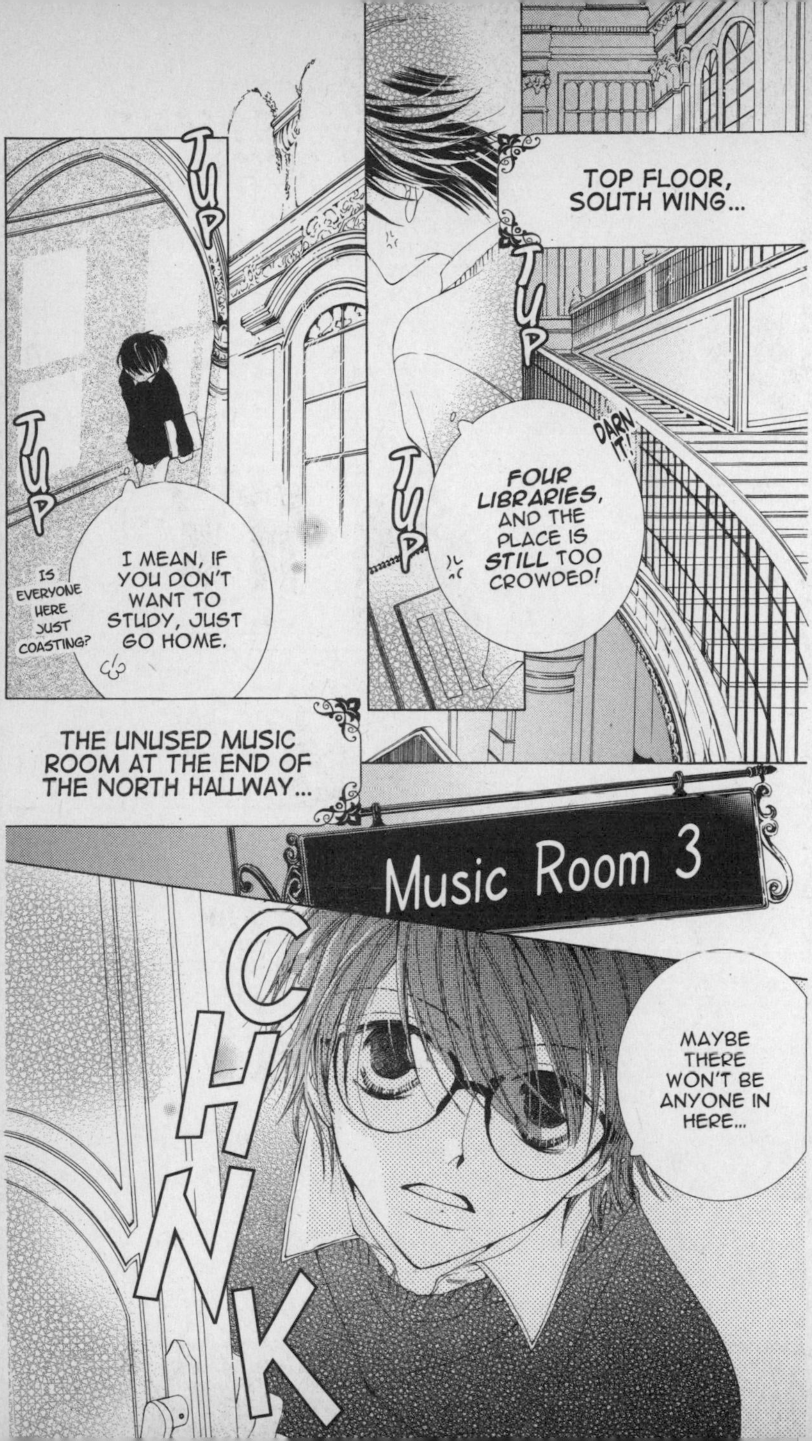

TOP FLOOR, SOUTH WING...
TUP
TUP
DARN IT!
FOUR LIBRARIES, AND THE PLACE IS STILL TOO CROWDED!
TUP
TUP
I MEAN, IF YOU DON'T WANT TO STUDY, JUST GO HOME.
IS EVERYONE HERE JUST COASTING?
THE UNUSED MUSIC ROOM AT THE END OF THE NORTH HALLWAY...
Music Room 3
MAYBE THERE WON'T BE ANYONE IN HERE...
CHUNK

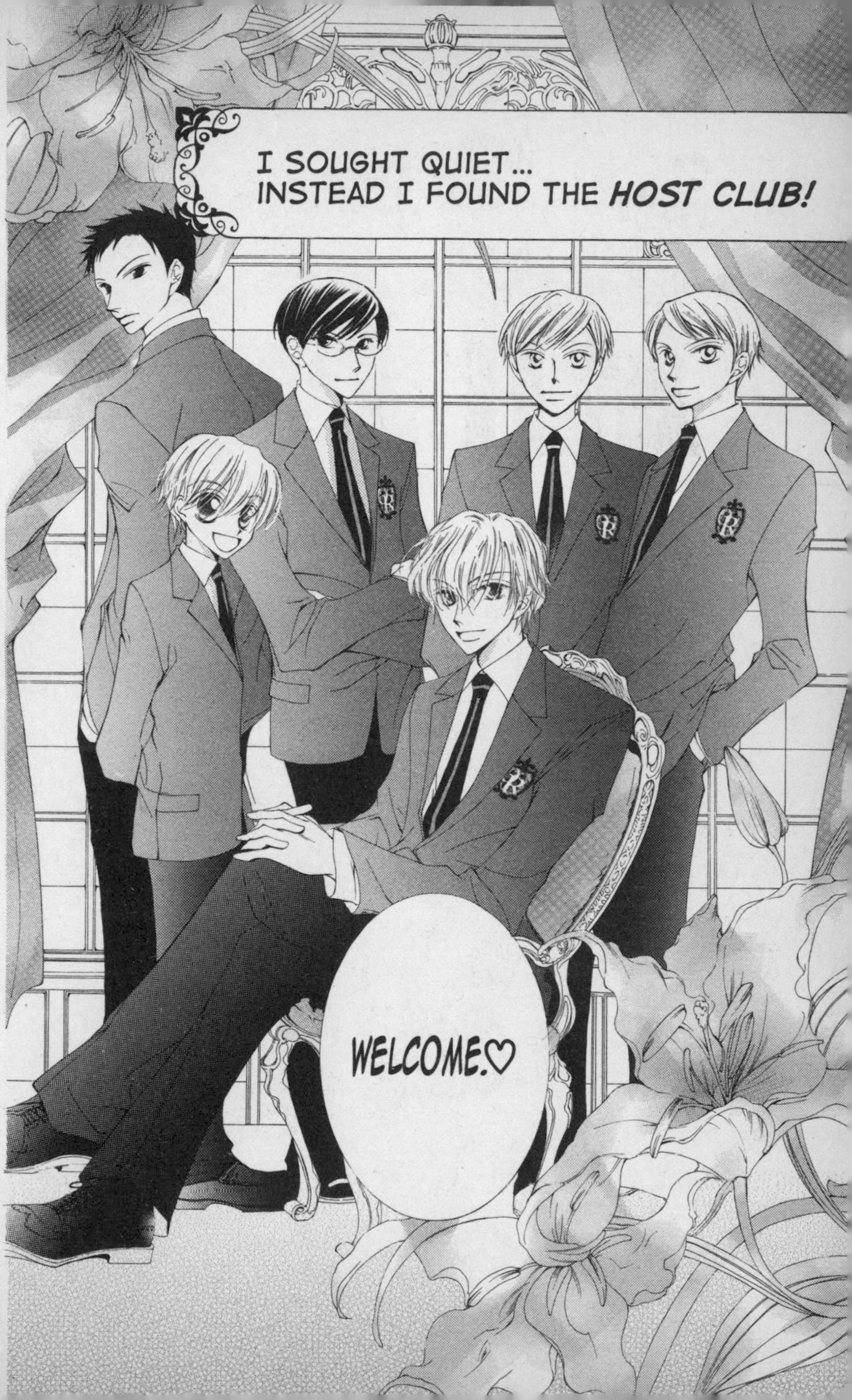
I SOUGHT QUIET...
INSTEAD I FOUND THE HOST CLUB!
WELCOME.♡

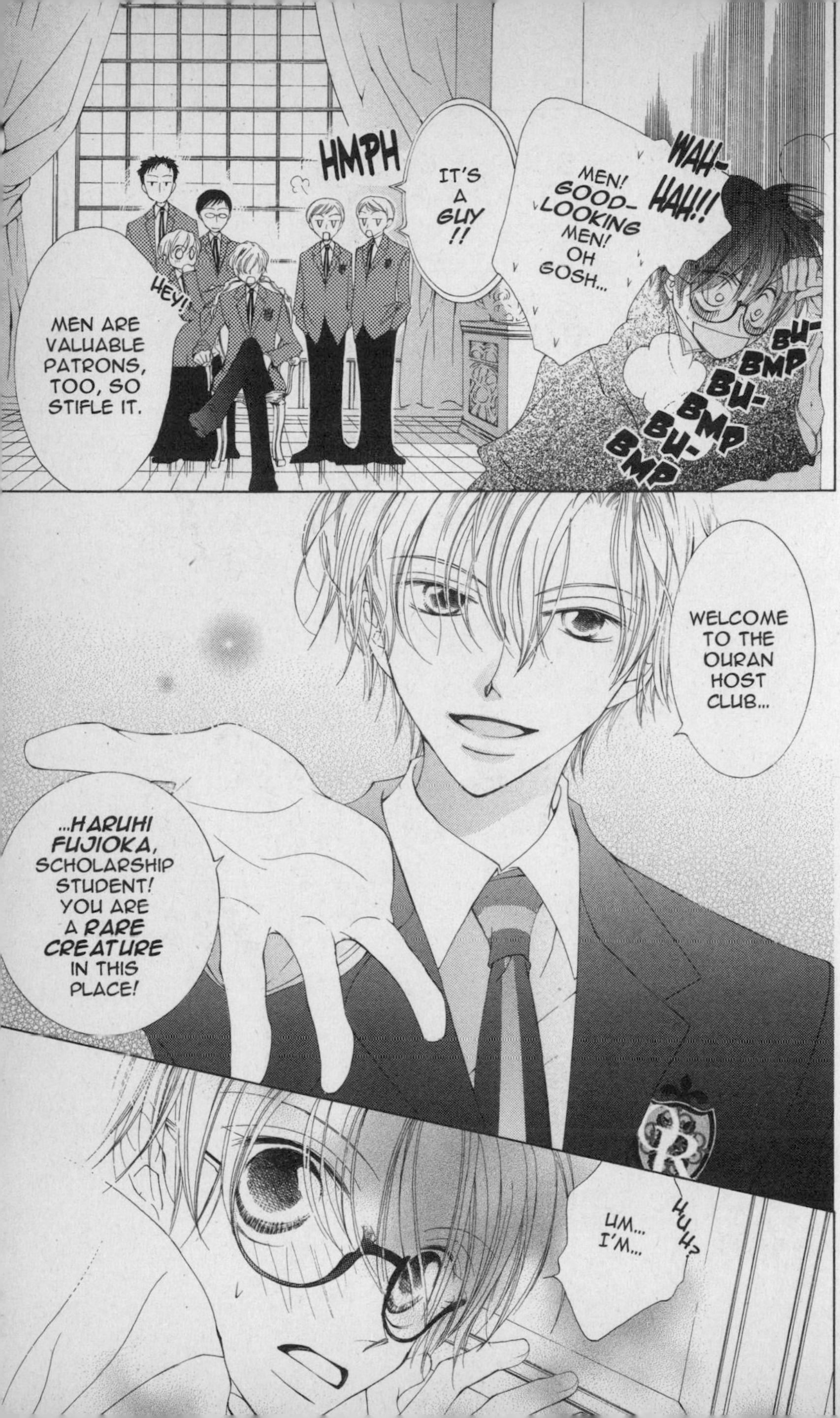
WAH-HAH!!
MEN! GOOD-LOOKING MEN! OH GOSH...
BU-BMP BU-BMP BU-BMP
IT'S A GUY!!
HMPH
HEY!!
MEN ARE VALUABLE PATRONS, TOO, SO STIFLE IT.
WELCOME TO THE OURAN HOST CLUB...
...HARUHI FUJIOKA, SCHOLARSHIP STUDENT! YOU ARE A RARE CREATURE IN THIS PLACE!
HUH?
UM... I'M...

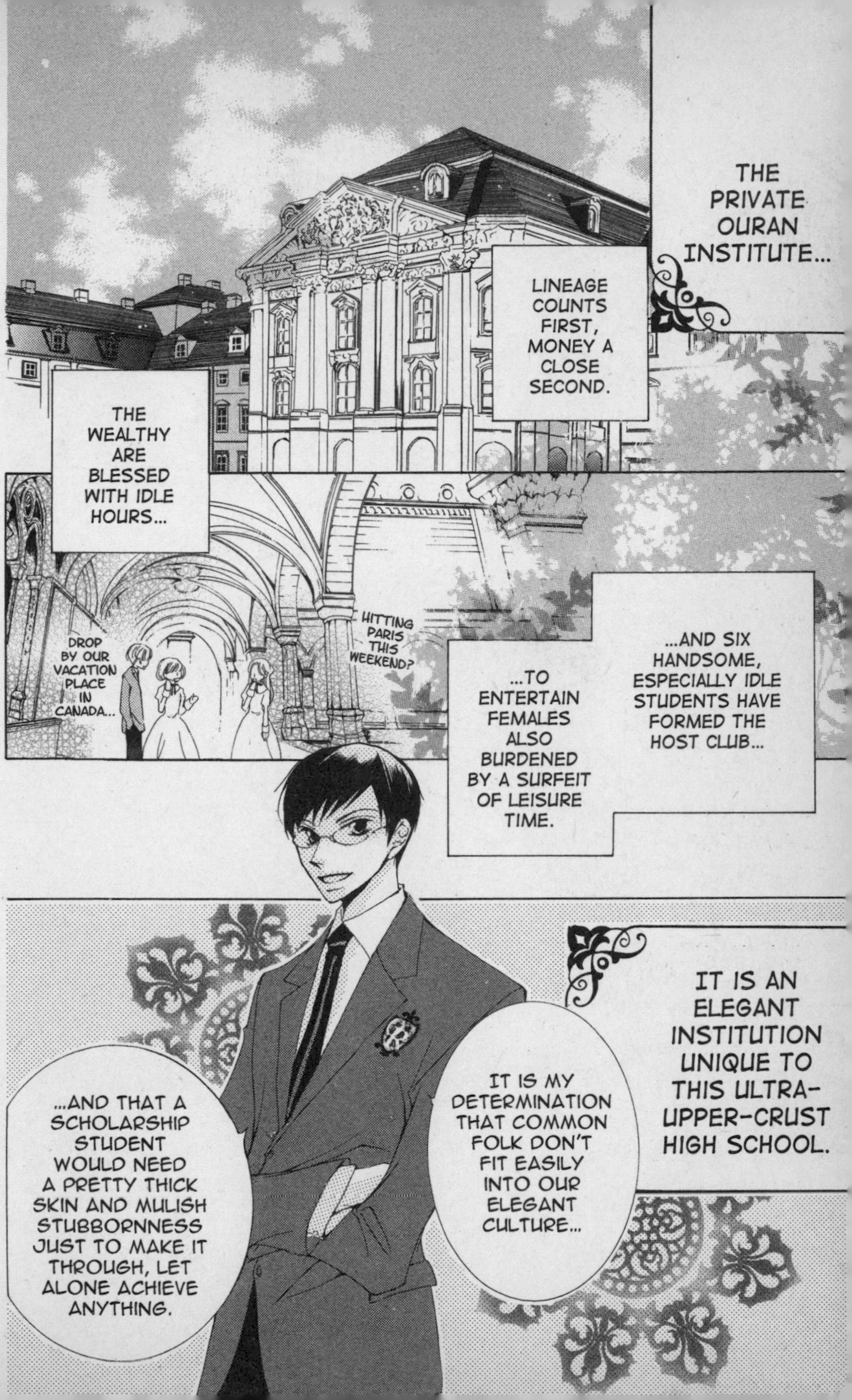
THE PRIVATE OURAN INSTITUTE...
LINEAGE COUNTS FIRST, MONEY A CLOSE SECOND.
THE WEALTHY ARE BLESSED WITH IDLE HOURS...
...AND SIX HANDSOME, ESPECIALLY IDLE STUDENTS HAVE FORMED THE HOST CLUB...
...TO ENTERTAIN FEMALES ALSO BURDENED BY A SURFEIT OF LEISURE TIME.
HITTING PARIS THIS WEEKEND?
DROP BY OUR VACATION PLACE IN CANADA...
IT IS AN ELEGANT INSTITUTION UNIQUE TO THIS ULTRA-UPPER-CRUST HIGH SCHOOL.
IT IS MY DETERMINATION THAT COMMON FOLK DON'T FIT EASILY INTO OUR ELEGANT CULTURE...
...AND THAT A SCHOLARSHIP STUDENT WOULD NEED A PRETTY THICK SKIN AND MULISH STUBBORNNESS JUST TO MAKE IT THROUGH, LET ALONE ACHIEVE ANYTHING.

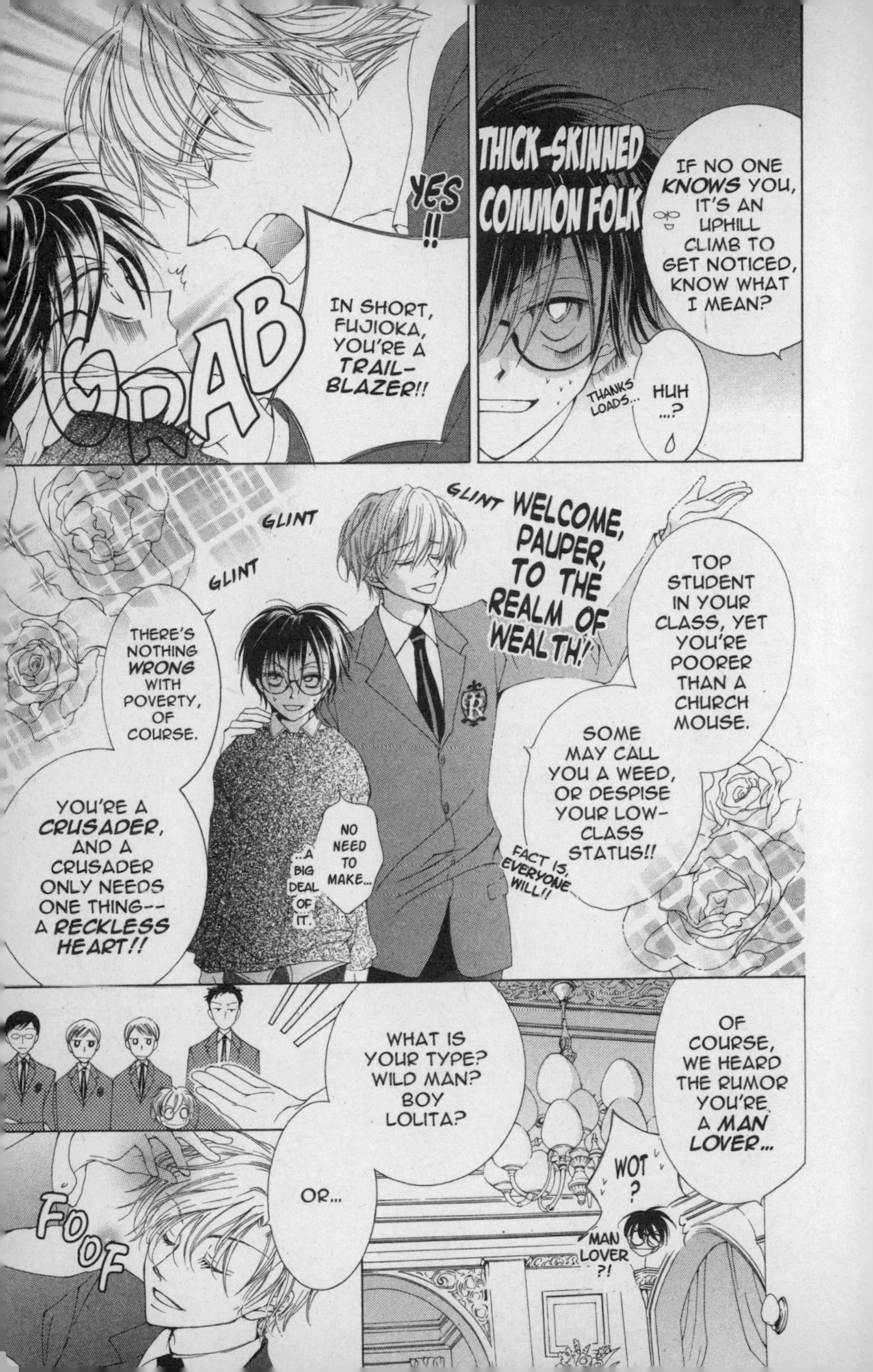
THICK-SKINNED COMMON FOLK
IF NO ONE KNOWS YOU, IT'S AN UPHILL CLIMB TO GET NOTICED, KNOW WHAT I MEAN?
HUH ...?
THANKS LOADS...
YES!!
IN SHORT, FUJIOKA, YOU'RE A TRAIL-BLAZER!!
GRAB
GLINT
WELCOME, PAUPER, TO THE REALM OF WEALTH!
TOP STUDENT IN YOUR CLASS, YET YOU'RE POORER THAN A CHURCH MOUSE.
SOME MAY CALL YOU A WEED, OR DESPISE YOUR LOW-CLASS STATUS!!
FACT IS, EVERYONE WILL!!
GLINT
GLINT
THERE'S NOTHING WRONG WITH POVERTY, OF COURSE.
NO NEED TO MAKE...
...A BIG DEAL OF IT.
YOU'RE A CRUSADER, AND A CRUSADER ONLY NEEDS ONE THING--A RECKLESS HEART!!
OF COURSE, WE HEARD THE RUMOR YOU'RE A MAN LOVER...
WOT?
MAN LOVER?!
WHAT IS YOUR TYPE? WILD MAN? BOY LOLITA?
OR...
FOOF

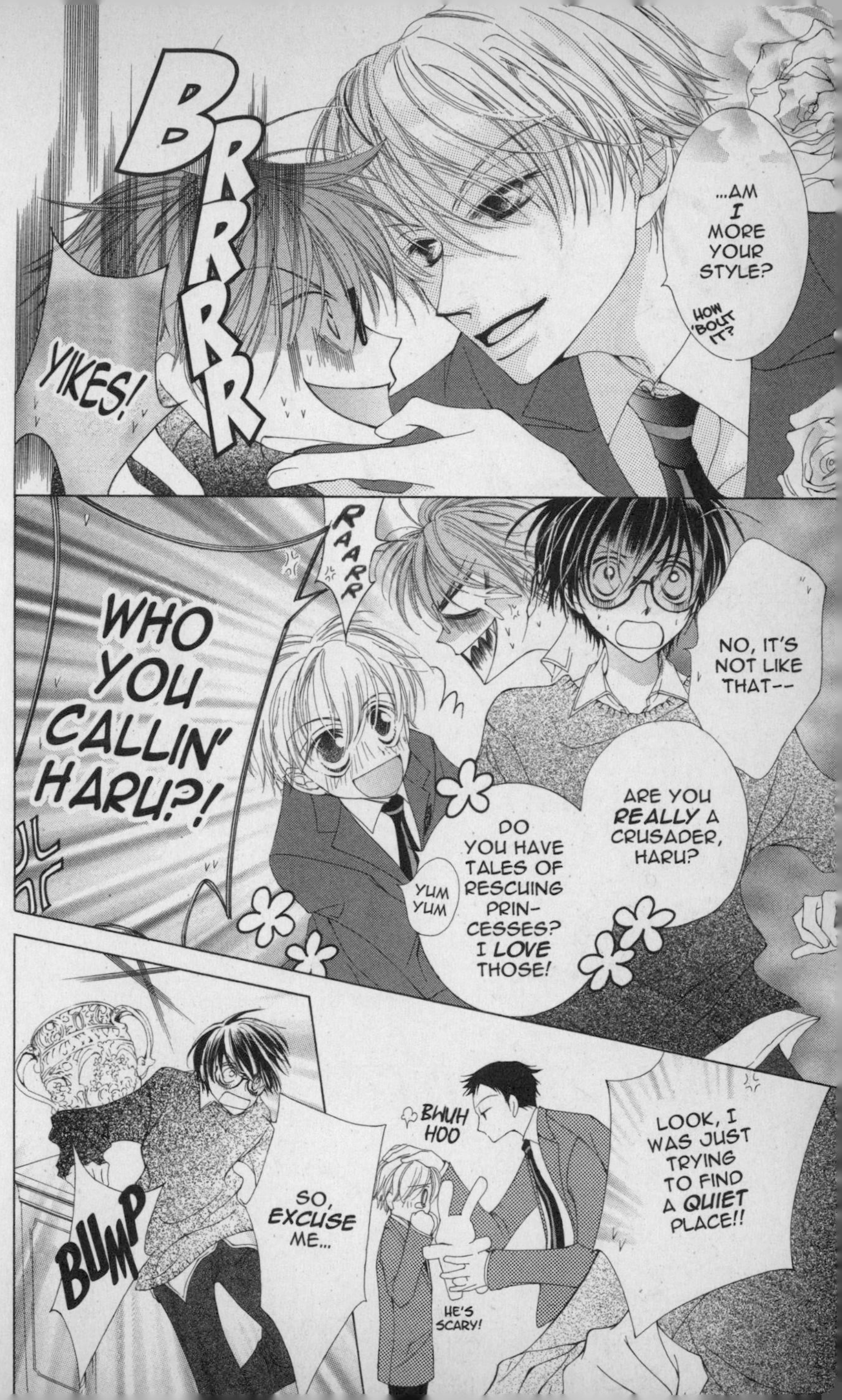
...AM I MORE YOUR STYLE?
HOW 'BOUT IT?
BRRRR
YIKES!
NO, IT'S NOT LIKE THAT--
ARE YOU REALLY A CRUSADER, HARU?
DO YOU HAVE TALES OF RESCUING PRIN- CESSES? I LOVE THOSE!
YUM YUM
RAAARR
WHO YOU CALLIN' HARU?!
LOOK, I WAS JUST TRYING TO FIND A QUIET PLACE!!
BWUH HOO
HE'S SCARY!
SO, EXCUSE ME...
BUMP

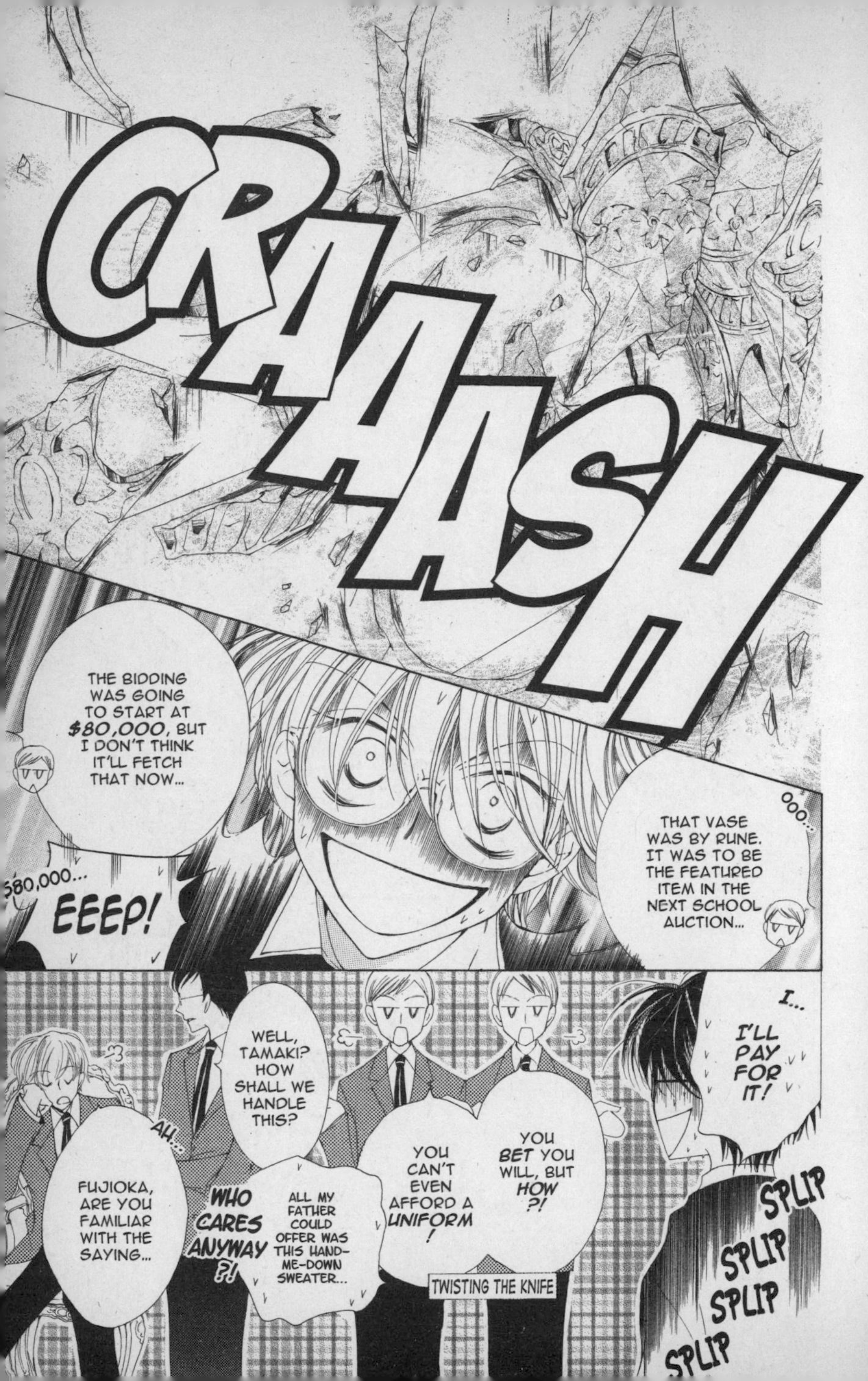
CRAAASH
OOO...
THAT VASE WAS BY RUNE. IT WAS TO BE THE FEATURED ITEM IN THE NEXT SCHOOL AUCTION...
THE BIDDING WAS GOING TO START AT $80,000, BUT I DON'T THINK IT'LL FETCH THAT NOW...
$80,000...
EEEP!
I...
I'LL PAY FOR IT!
SPLIP SPLIP SPLIP SPLIP
YOU BET YOU WILL, BUT HOW?!
YOU CAN'T EVEN AFFORD A UNIFORM!
TWISTING THE KNIFE
WELL, TAMAKI? HOW SHALL WE HANDLE THIS?
ALL MY FATHER COULD OFFER WAS THIS HAND-ME-DOWN SWEATER...
WHO CARES ANYWAY?!
AH...
FUJIOKA, ARE YOU FAMILIAR WITH THE SAYING...

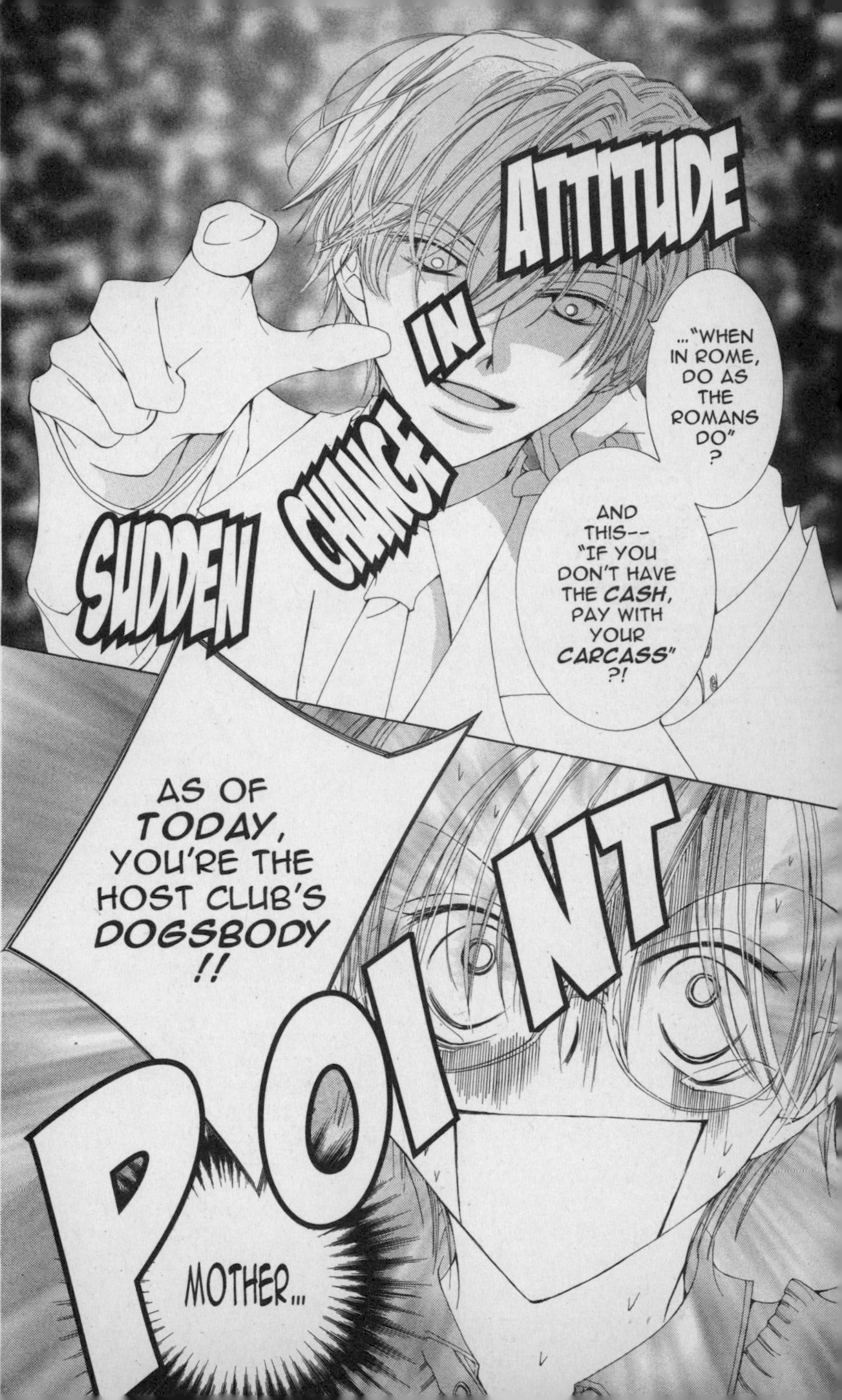
..."WHEN IN ROME, DO AS THE ROMANS DO"?
AND THIS-- "IF YOU DON'T HAVE THE *CASH*, PAY WITH YOUR *CARCASS*"?!
SUDDEN CHANGE IN ATTITUDE
AS OF *TODAY*, YOU'RE THE HOST CLUB'S *DOGSBODY*!!
POINT
MOTHER...

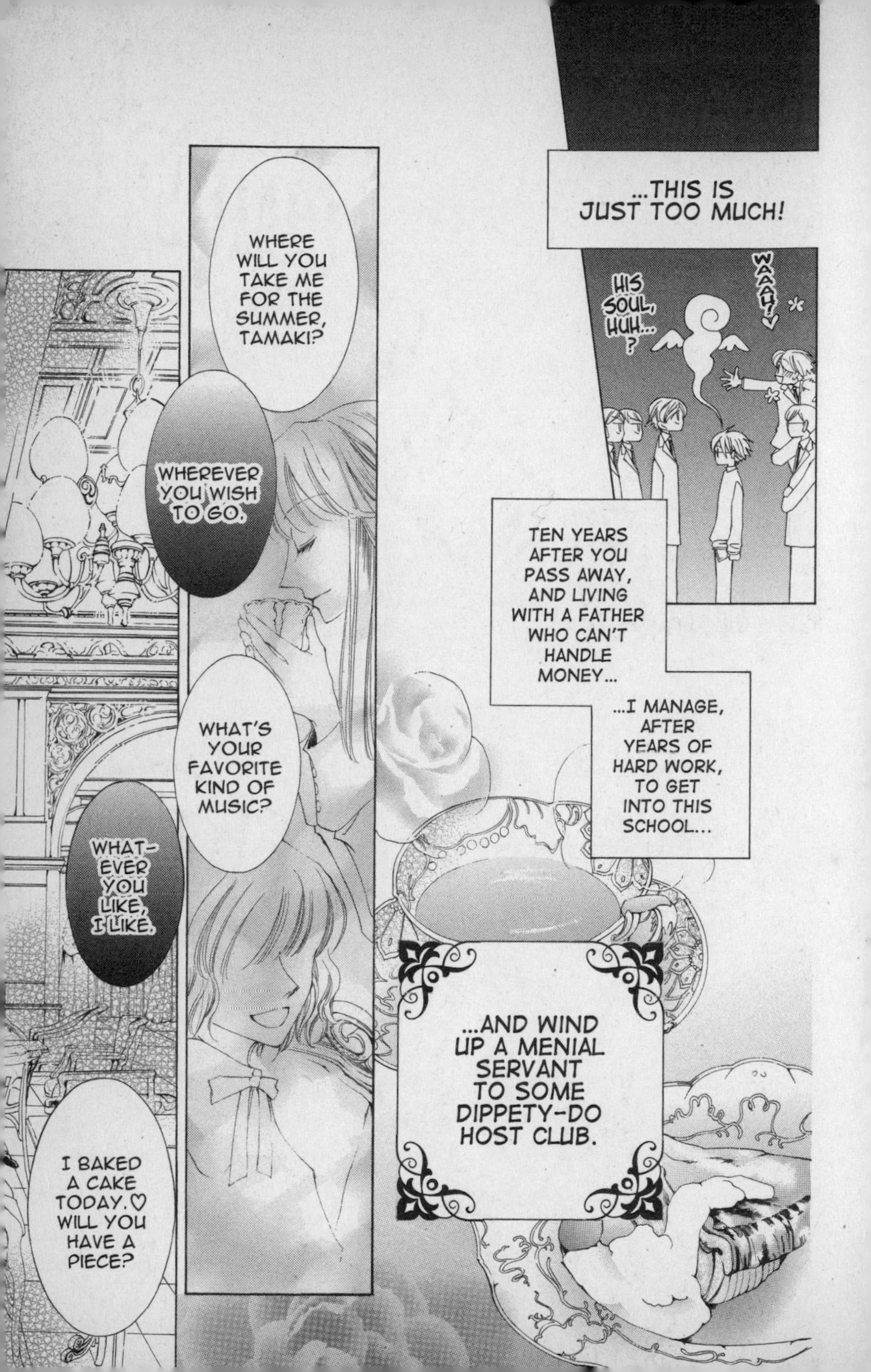
...THIS IS JUST TOO MUCH!
WAAAH!
HIS SOUL, HUH...?
TEN YEARS AFTER YOU PASS AWAY, AND LIVING WITH A FATHER WHO CAN'T HANDLE MONEY...
...I MANAGE, AFTER YEARS OF HARD WORK, TO GET INTO THIS SCHOOL...
...AND WIND UP A MENIAL SERVANT TO SOME DIPPETY-DO HOST CLUB.
WHERE WILL YOU TAKE ME FOR THE SUMMER, TAMAKI?
WHEREVER YOU WISH TO GO.
WHAT'S YOUR FAVORITE KIND OF MUSIC?
WHAT-EVER YOU LIKE, I LIKE.
I BAKED A CAKE TODAY.♡ WILL YOU HAVE A PIECE?

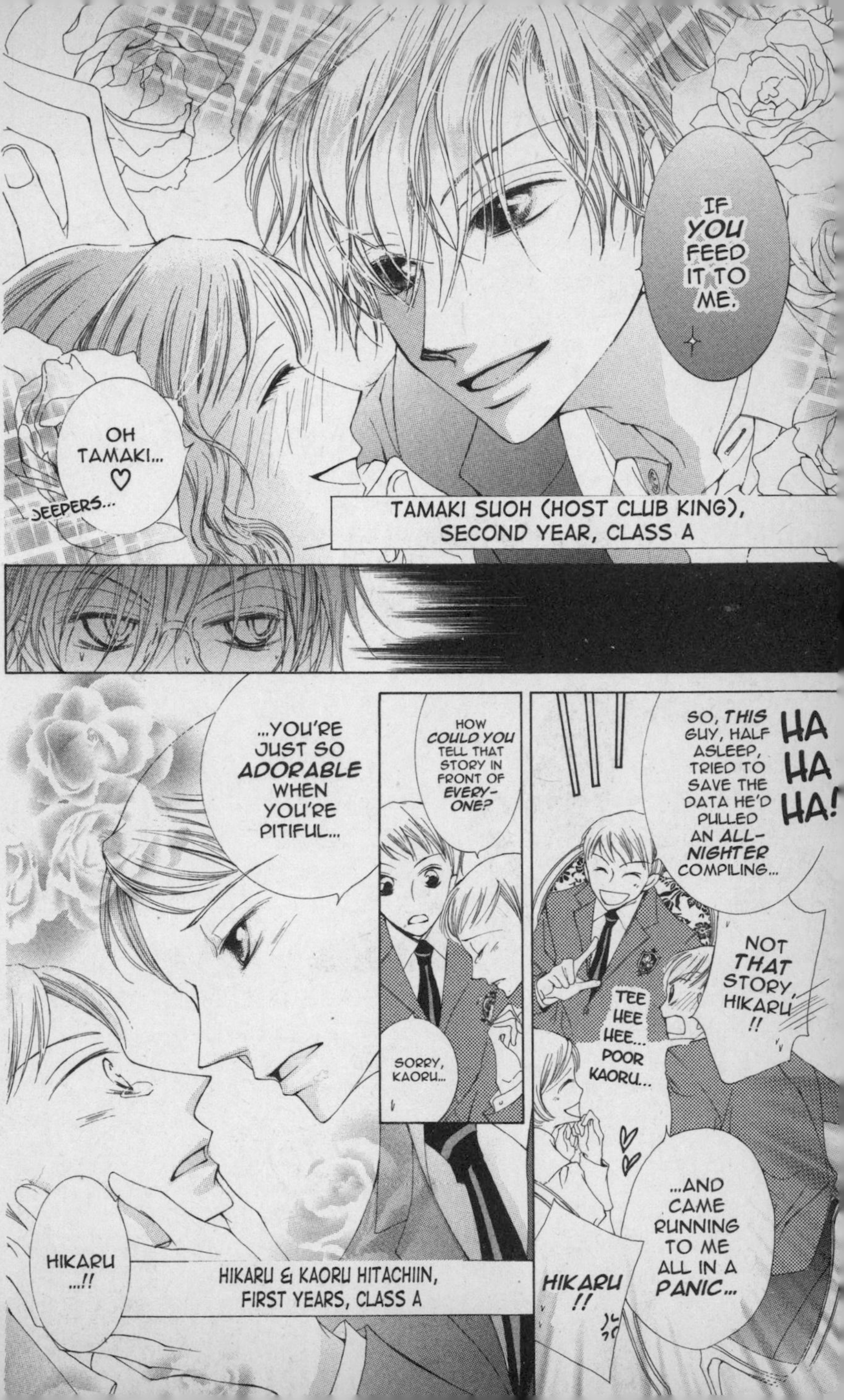
IF YOU FEED IT TO ME.
OH TAMAKI... ♡
EEPERS...
TAMAKI SUOH (HOST CLUB KING), SECOND YEAR, CLASS A
SO, THIS GUY, HALF ASLEEP, TRIED TO SAVE THE DATA HE'D PULLED AN ALL-NIGHTER COMPILING...
HA HA HA!
NOT THAT STORY, HIKARU!!
TEE HEE HEE... POOR KAORU...
...AND CAME RUNNING TO ME ALL IN A PANIC...
HIKARU!!
HOW COULD YOU TELL THAT STORY IN FRONT OF EVERYONE?
SORRY, KAORU...
...YOU'RE JUST SO ADORABLE WHEN YOU'RE PITIFUL...
HIKARU ...!!
HIKARU & KAORU HITACHIIN, FIRST YEARS, CLASS A

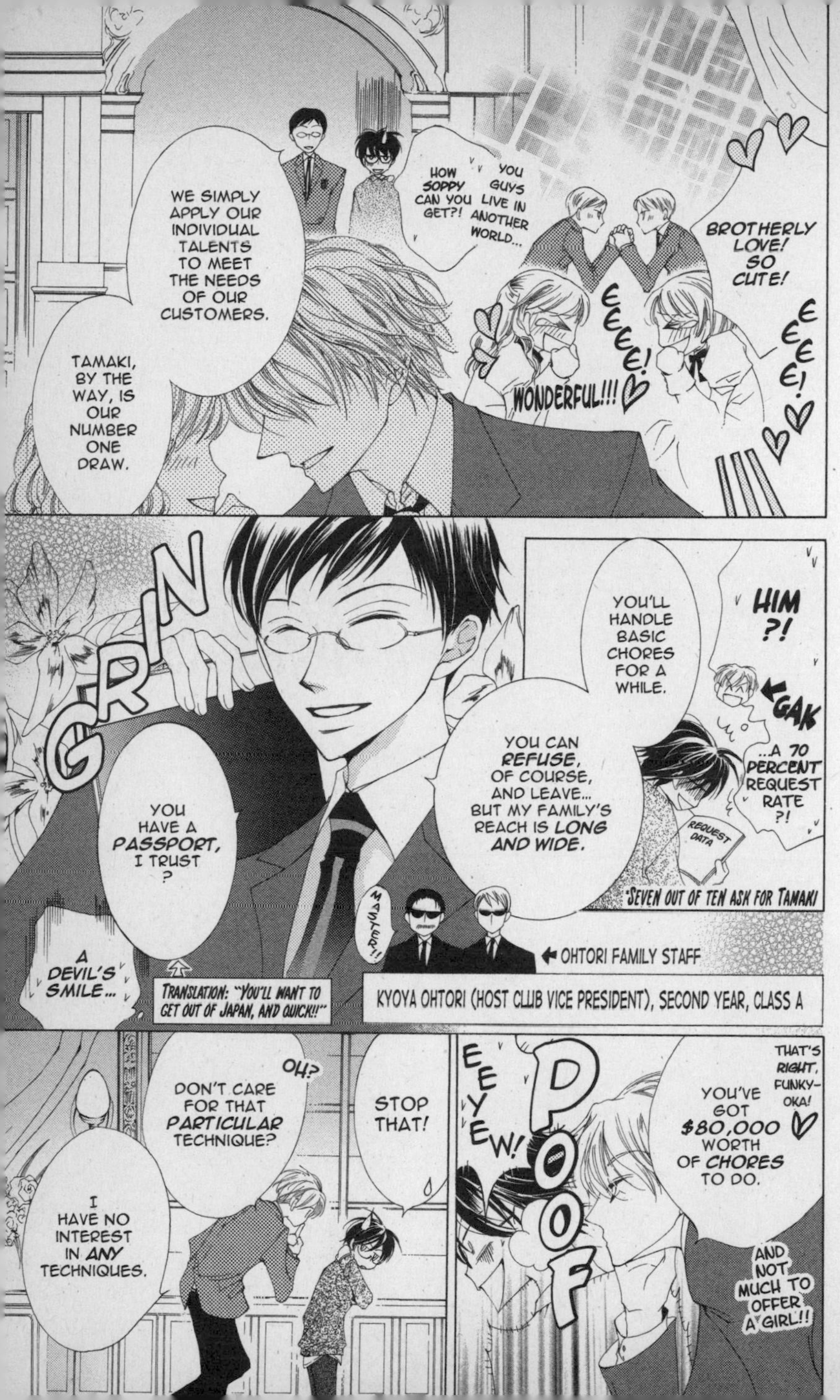
BROTHERLY LOVE! SO CUTE!
EEEE!
EEEE!
WONDERFUL!!!
YOU GUYS LIVE IN ANOTHER WORLD...
HOW SOPPY CAN YOU GET?!
WE SIMPLY APPLY OUR INDIVIDUAL TALENTS TO MEET THE NEEDS OF OUR CUSTOMERS.
TAMAKI, BY THE WAY, IS OUR NUMBER ONE DRAW.
HIM?!
GAK
...A 70 PERCENT REQUEST RATE?!
REQUEST DATA
*SEVEN OUT OF TEN ASK FOR TAMAKI
YOU'LL HANDLE BASIC CHORES FOR A WHILE.
YOU CAN REFUSE, OF COURSE, AND LEAVE... BUT MY FAMILY'S REACH IS LONG AND WIDE.
GRIN
YOU HAVE A PASSPORT, I TRUST?
MASTER!!
OHTORI FAMILY STAFF
KYOYA OHTORI (HOST CLUB VICE PRESIDENT), SECOND YEAR, CLASS A
TRANSLATION: "YOU'LL WANT TO GET OUT OF JAPAN, AND QUICK!!"
A DEVIL'S SMILE...
THAT'S RIGHT, FUNKY-OKA!
YOU'VE GOT $80,000 WORTH OF CHORES TO DO.
POOF
EEYEW!
AND NOT MUCH TO OFFER A GIRL!!
STOP THAT!
OH? DON'T CARE FOR THAT PARTICULAR TECHNIQUE?
I HAVE NO INTEREST IN ANY TECHNIQUES.

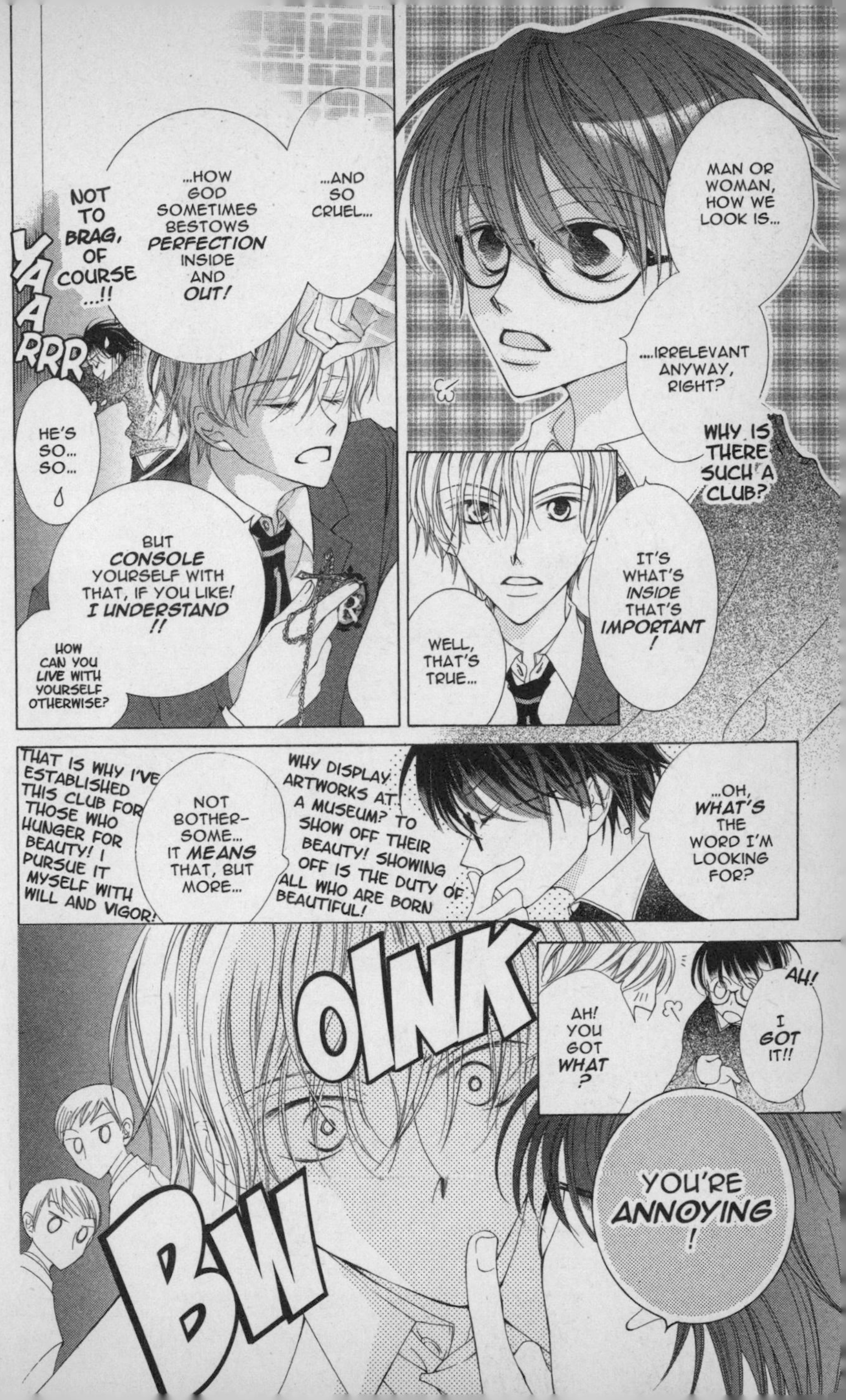
MAN OR WOMAN, HOW WE LOOK IS...
....IRRELEVANT ANYWAY, RIGHT?
WHY IS THERE SUCH A CLUB?
IT'S WHAT'S INSIDE THAT'S IMPORTANT!
WELL, THAT'S TRUE...
...AND SO CRUEL...
...HOW GOD SOMETIMES BESTOWS PERFECTION INSIDE AND OUT!
NOT TO BRAG, OF COURSE ...!!
YAARRR
HE'S SO... SO...
BUT CONSOLE YOURSELF WITH THAT, IF YOU LIKE! I UNDERSTAND!!
HOW CAN YOU LIVE WITH YOURSELF OTHERWISE?
...OH, WHAT'S THE WORD I'M LOOKING FOR?
WHY DISPLAY ARTWORKS AT A MUSEUM? TO SHOW OFF THEIR BEAUTY! SHOWING OFF IS THE DUTY OF ALL WHO ARE BORN BEAUTIFUL!
NOT BOTHER-SOME... IT MEANS THAT, BUT MORE...
THAT IS WHY I'VE ESTABLISHED THIS CLUB FOR THOSE WHO HUNGER FOR BEAUTY! I PURSUE IT MYSELF WITH WILL AND VIGOR!
AH! I GOT IT!!
AH! YOU GOT WHAT?
OINK
YOU'RE ANNOYING!
BW

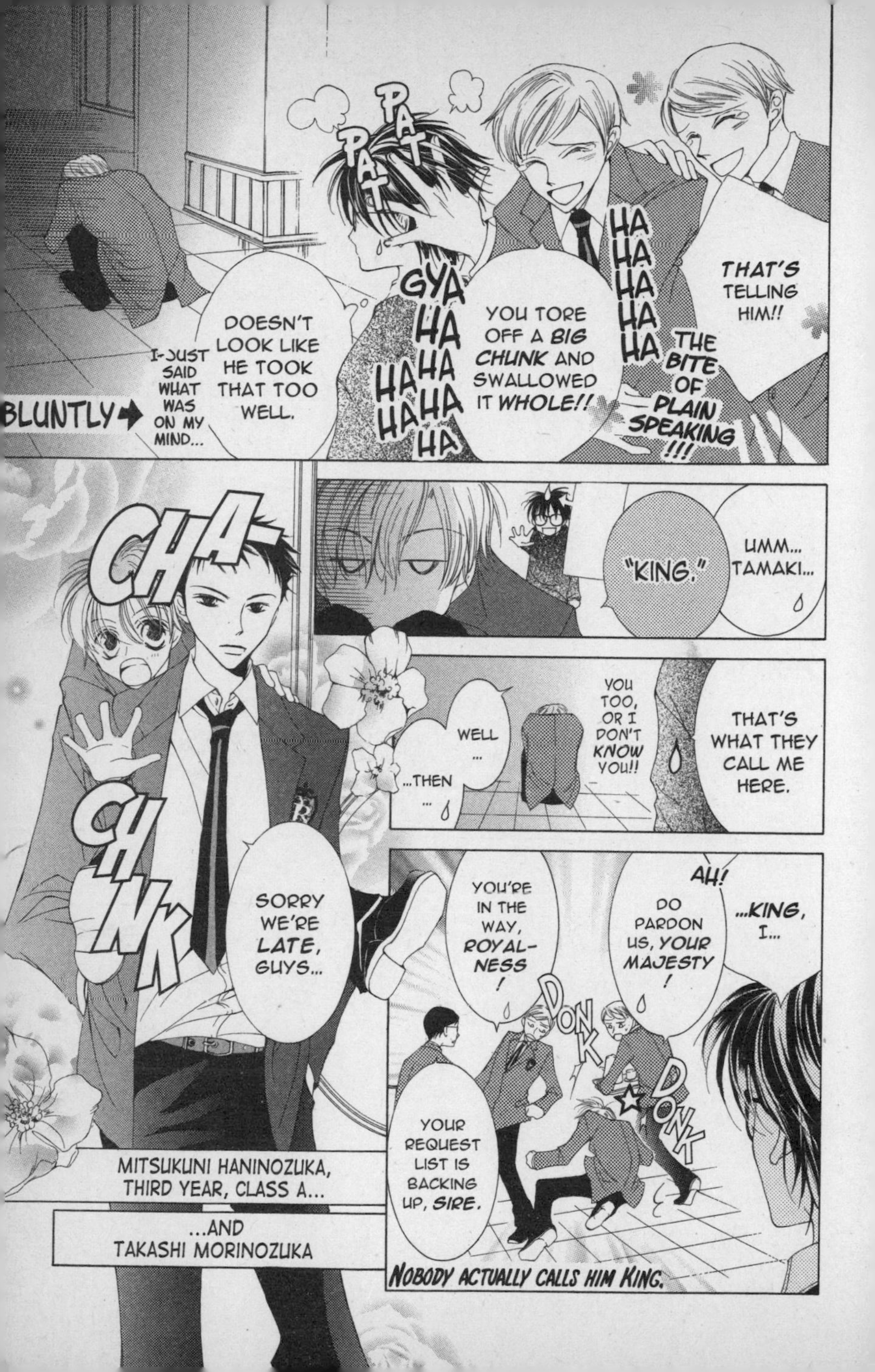

THAT'S TELLING HIM!!
THE BITE OF PLAIN SPEAKING!!!
HA HA HA HA HA HA
YOU TORE OFF A **BIG CHUNK** AND SWALLOWED IT **WHOLE!!**
PAT PAT PAT
GYA HA HA HA HA HA HA HA HA
DOESN'T LOOK LIKE HE TOOK THAT TOO WELL.
I-JUST SAID WHAT WAS ON MY MIND...
BLUNTLY
UMM... TAMAKI...
"KING."
THAT'S WHAT THEY CALL ME HERE.
YOU TOO, OR I DON'T **KNOW** YOU!!
WELL ... ...THEN ...
...**KING**, I...
AH!
DO PARDON US, **YOUR MAJESTY**!
YOU'RE IN THE WAY, **ROYAL-NESS**!
DONK DONK
YOUR REQUEST LIST IS BACKING UP, **SIRE**.
NOBODY ACTUALLY CALLS HIM KING.
CHA-CHUNK
SORRY WE'RE **LATE**, GUYS...
MITSUKUNI HANINOZUKA, THIRD YEAR, CLASS A...
...AND TAKASHI MORINOZUKA

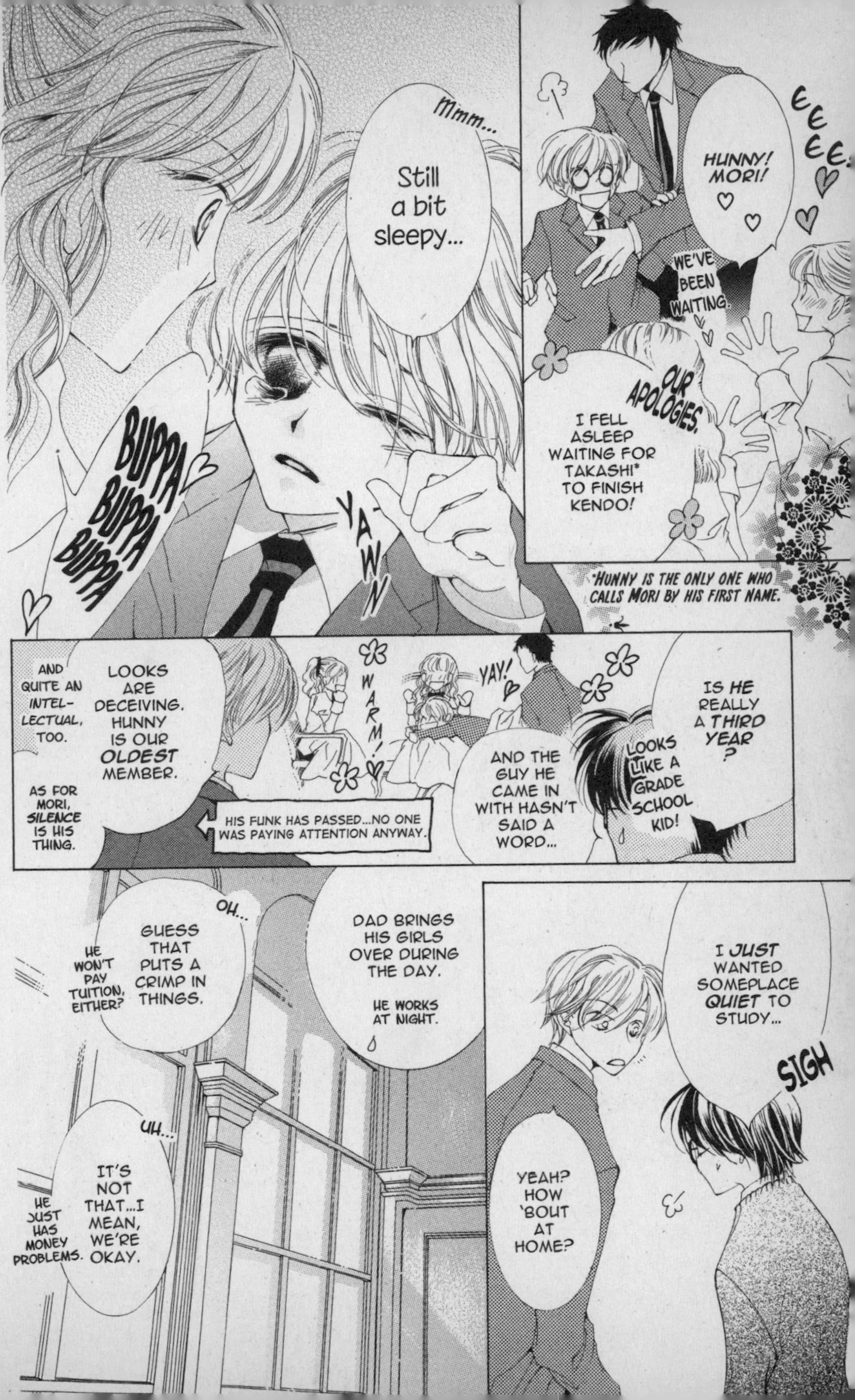
EEEE!
HUNNY! MORI!
WE'VE BEEN WAITING.
OUR APOLOGIES.
I FELL ASLEEP WAITING FOR TAKASHI* TO FINISH KENDO!
Mmm...
Still a bit sleepy...
YAWN
BUPPA BUPPA BUPPA
*HUNNY IS THE ONLY ONE WHO CALLS MORI BY HIS FIRST NAME.
IS HE REALLY A THIRD YEAR?
LOOKS LIKE A GRADE SCHOOL KID!
AND THE GUY HE CAME IN WITH HASN'T SAID A WORD...
YAY!
WARM!
LOOKS ARE DECEIVING. HUNNY IS OUR OLDEST MEMBER.
AND QUITE AN INTEL-LECTUAL, TOO.
AS FOR MORI, SILENCE IS HIS THING.
HIS FUNK HAS PASSED...NO ONE WAS PAYING ATTENTION ANYWAY.
I JUST WANTED SOMEPLACE QUIET TO STUDY...
SIGH
YEAH? HOW 'BOUT AT HOME?
DAD BRINGS HIS GIRLS OVER DURING THE DAY.
HE WORKS AT NIGHT.
OH...
GUESS THAT PUTS A CRIMP IN THINGS.
HE WON'T PAY TUITION, EITHER?
UH...
IT'S NOT THAT...I MEAN, WE'RE OKAY.
HE JUST HAS MONEY PROBLEMS.

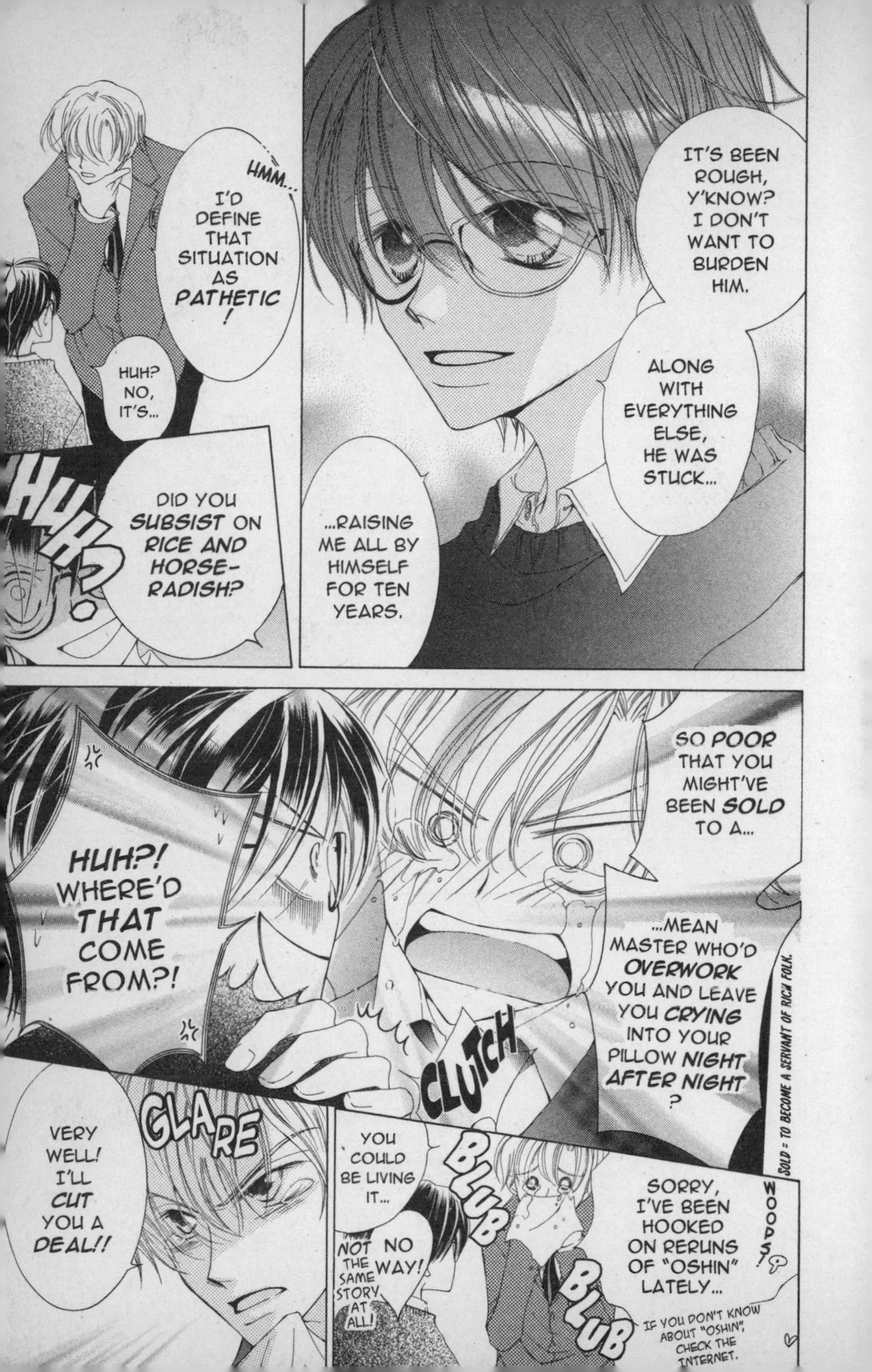
IT'S BEEN ROUGH, Y'KNOW? I DON'T WANT TO BURDEN HIM.
ALONG WITH EVERYTHING ELSE, HE WAS STUCK...
...RAISING ME ALL BY HIMSELF FOR TEN YEARS.
HMM...
I'D DEFINE THAT SITUATION AS PATHETIC!
HUH? NO, IT'S...
HUH?!
DID YOU SUBSIST ON RICE AND HORSE-RADISH?
SO POOR THAT YOU MIGHT'VE BEEN SOLD TO A...
...MEAN MASTER WHO'D OVERWORK YOU AND LEAVE YOU CRYING INTO YOUR PILLOW NIGHT AFTER NIGHT?
HUH?! WHERE'D THAT COME FROM?!
CLUTCH
SOLD = TO BECOME A SERVANT OF RICH FOLK.
SORRY, I'VE BEEN HOOKED ON RERUNS OF "OSHIN" LATELY...
WOODS!
BLUB
BLUB
YOU COULD BE LIVING IT...
NO WAY!
NOT THE SAME STORY AT ALL!
IF YOU DON'T KNOW ABOUT "OSHIN," CHECK THE INTERNET.
GLARE
VERY WELL! I'LL CUT YOU A DEAL!!

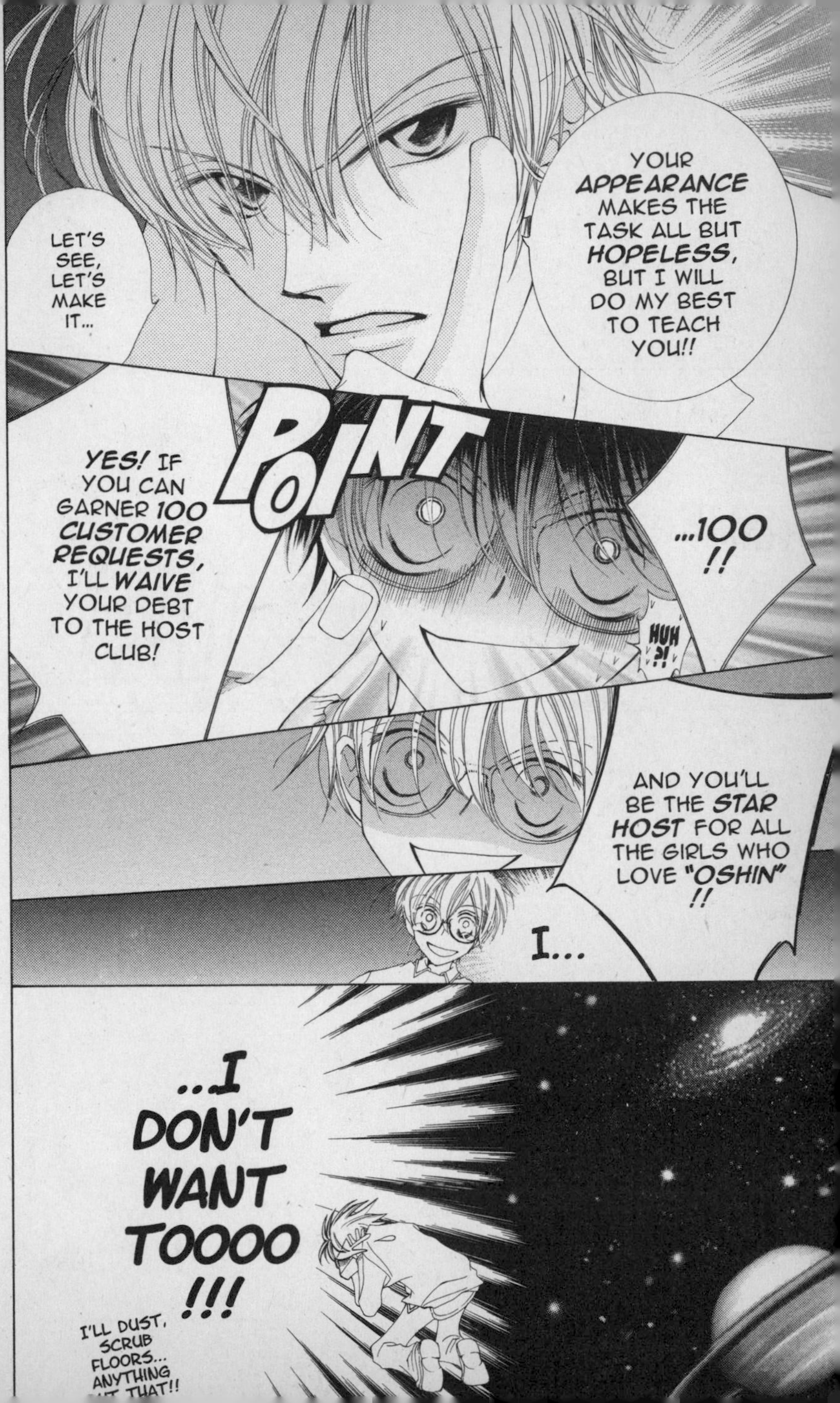
YOUR APPEARANCE MAKES THE TASK ALL BUT HOPELESS, BUT I WILL DO MY BEST TO TEACH YOU!!
LET'S SEE, LET'S MAKE IT...
POINT
YES! IF YOU CAN GARNER 100 CUSTOMER REQUESTS, I'LL WAIVE YOUR DEBT TO THE HOST CLUB!
...100 !!
HUH ?!
AND YOU'LL BE THE STAR HOST FOR ALL THE GIRLS WHO LOVE "OSHIN" !!
I...
...I DON'T WANT TOOOO !!!
I'LL DUST, SCRUB FLOORS... ANYTHING
THAT!!

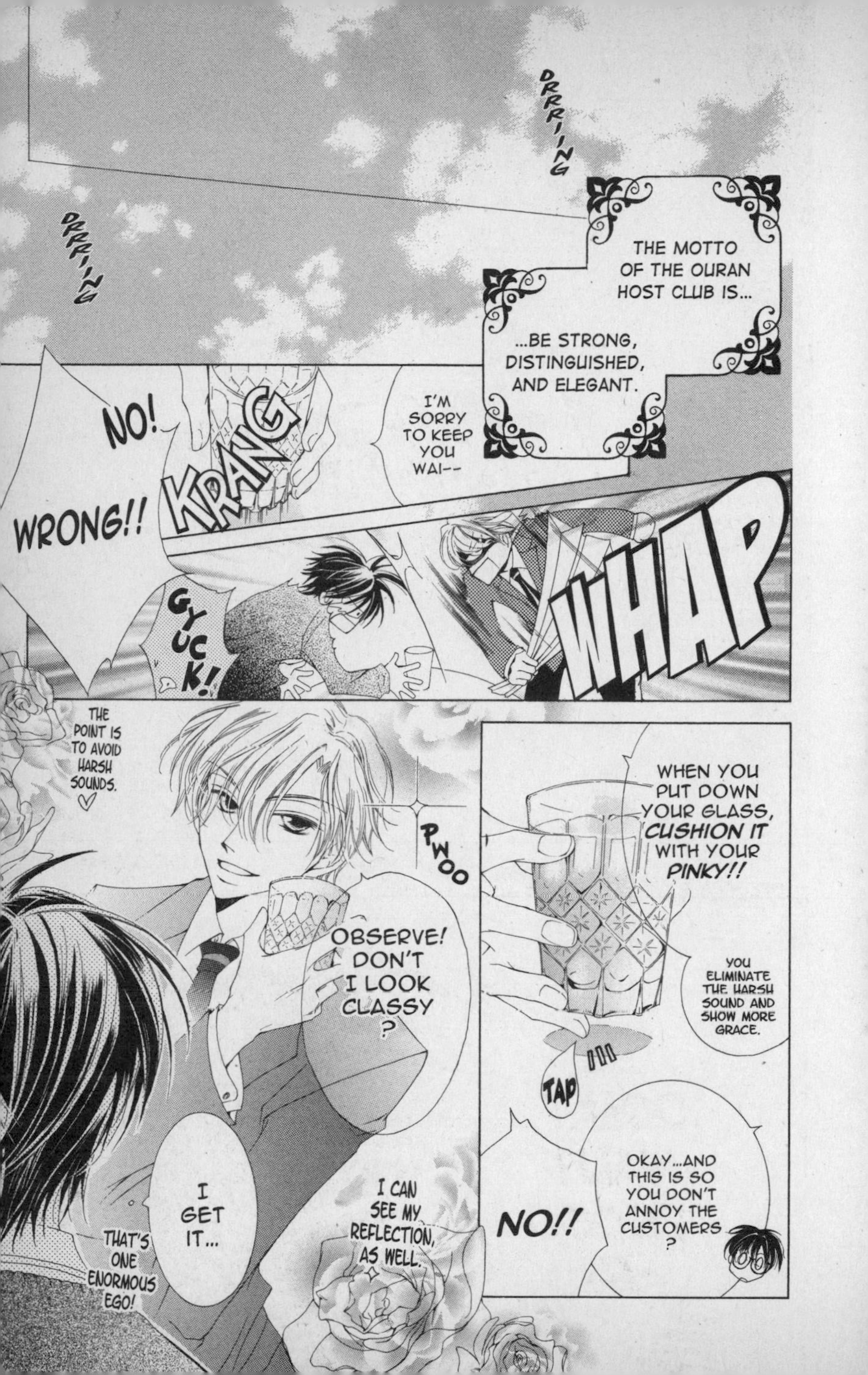
DRRRIING
DRRRIING
THE MOTTO OF THE OURAN HOST CLUB IS...
...BE STRONG, DISTINGUISHED, AND ELEGANT.
I'M SORRY TO KEEP YOU WAI--
KRANG
NO!
WRONG!!
WHAP
GYUCK!
WHEN YOU PUT DOWN YOUR GLASS, CUSHION IT WITH YOUR PINKY!!
YOU ELIMINATE THE HARSH SOUND AND SHOW MORE GRACE.
TAP
OKAY...AND THIS IS SO YOU DON'T ANNOY THE CUSTOMERS?
NO!!
PWOO
OBSERVE! DON'T I LOOK CLASSY?
THE POINT IS TO AVOID HARSH SOUNDS.♡
I CAN SEE MY REFLECTION, AS WELL.
I GET IT...
THAT'S ONE ENORMOUS EGO!

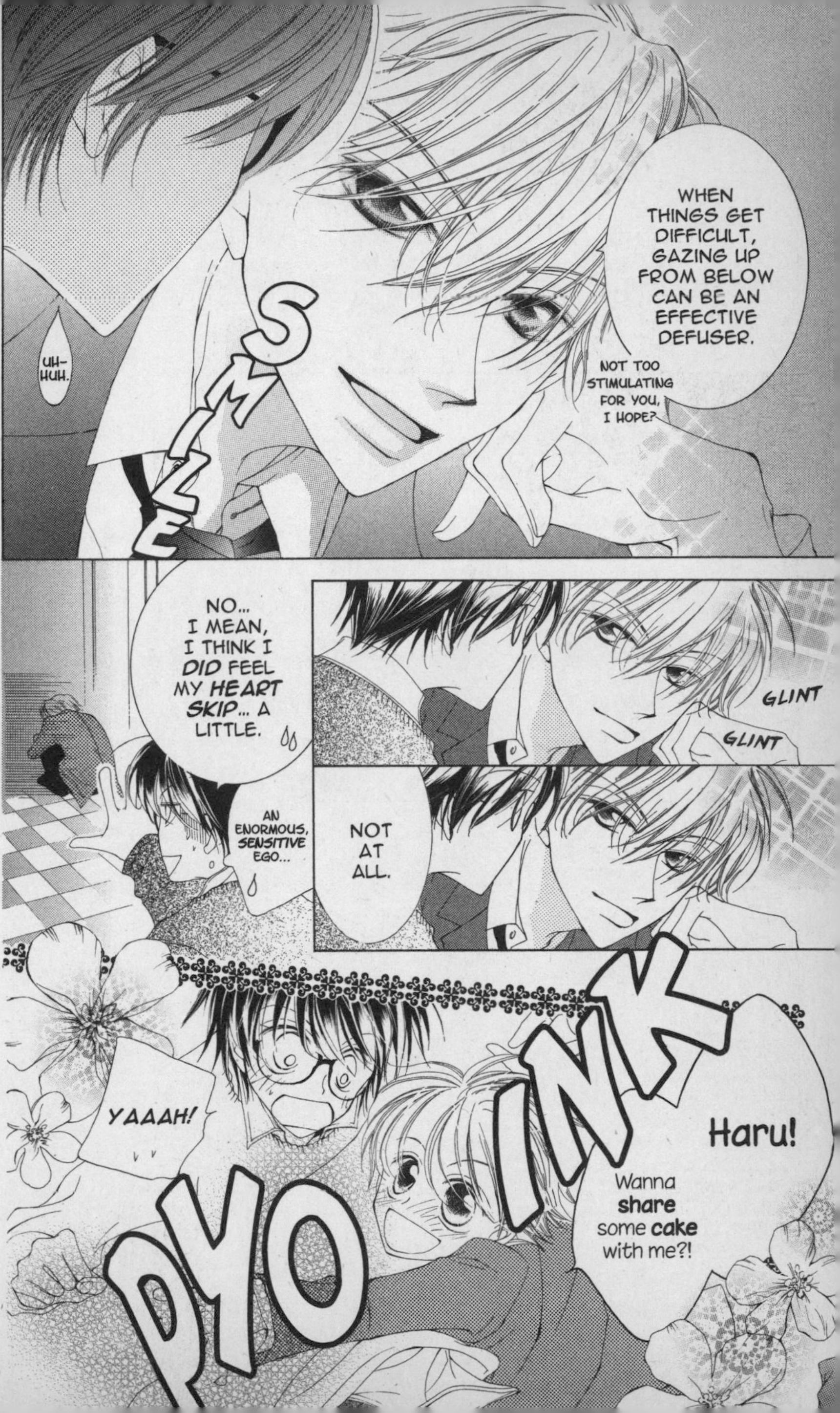
WHEN THINGS GET DIFFICULT, GAZING UP FROM BELOW CAN BE AN EFFECTIVE DEFUSER.
NOT TOO STIMULATING FOR YOU, I HOPE?
SMILE
UH-HUH.
GLINT
GLINT
NOT AT ALL.
NO... I MEAN, I THINK I *DID* FEEL MY **HEART SKIP**... A LITTLE.
AN ENORMOUS, **SENSITIVE** EGO...
Haru!
Wanna **share** some **cake** with me?!
PYOINK
YAAAH!

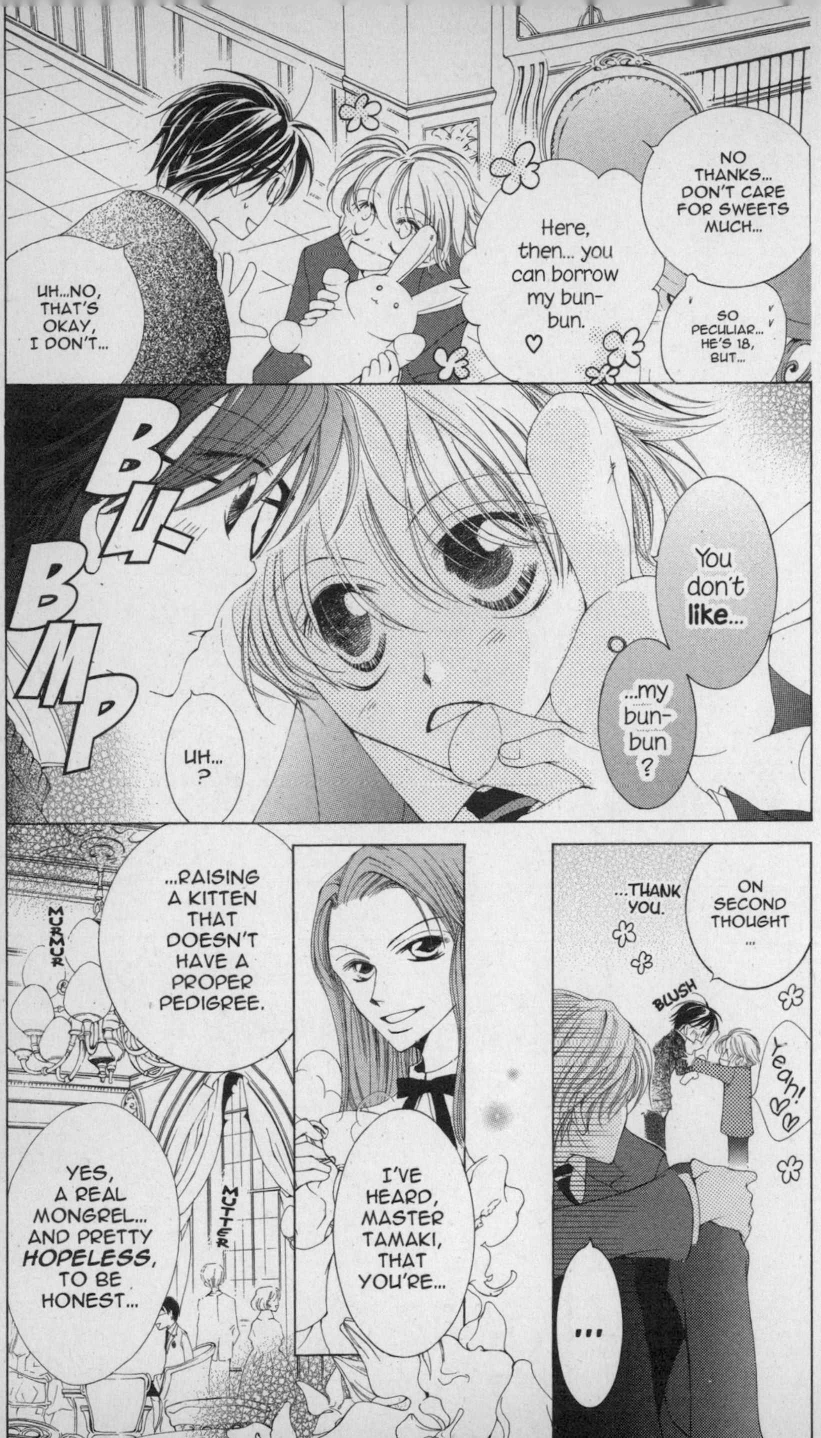
NO THANKS... DON'T CARE FOR SWEETS MUCH...
SO PECULIAR... HE'S 18, BUT...
Here, then... you can borrow my bun-bun. ♡
UH...NO, THAT'S OKAY, I DON'T...
You don't **like**...
...my bun-bun?
BU-BUMP
UH...?
ON SECOND THOUGHT...
...THANK YOU.
BLUSH
Yeah! ♡♡
...
I'VE HEARD, MASTER TAMAKI, THAT YOU'RE...
...RAISING A KITTEN THAT DOESN'T HAVE A PROPER PEDIGREE.
MURMUR
YES, A REAL MONGREL... AND PRETTY *HOPELESS*, TO BE HONEST...
MUTTER

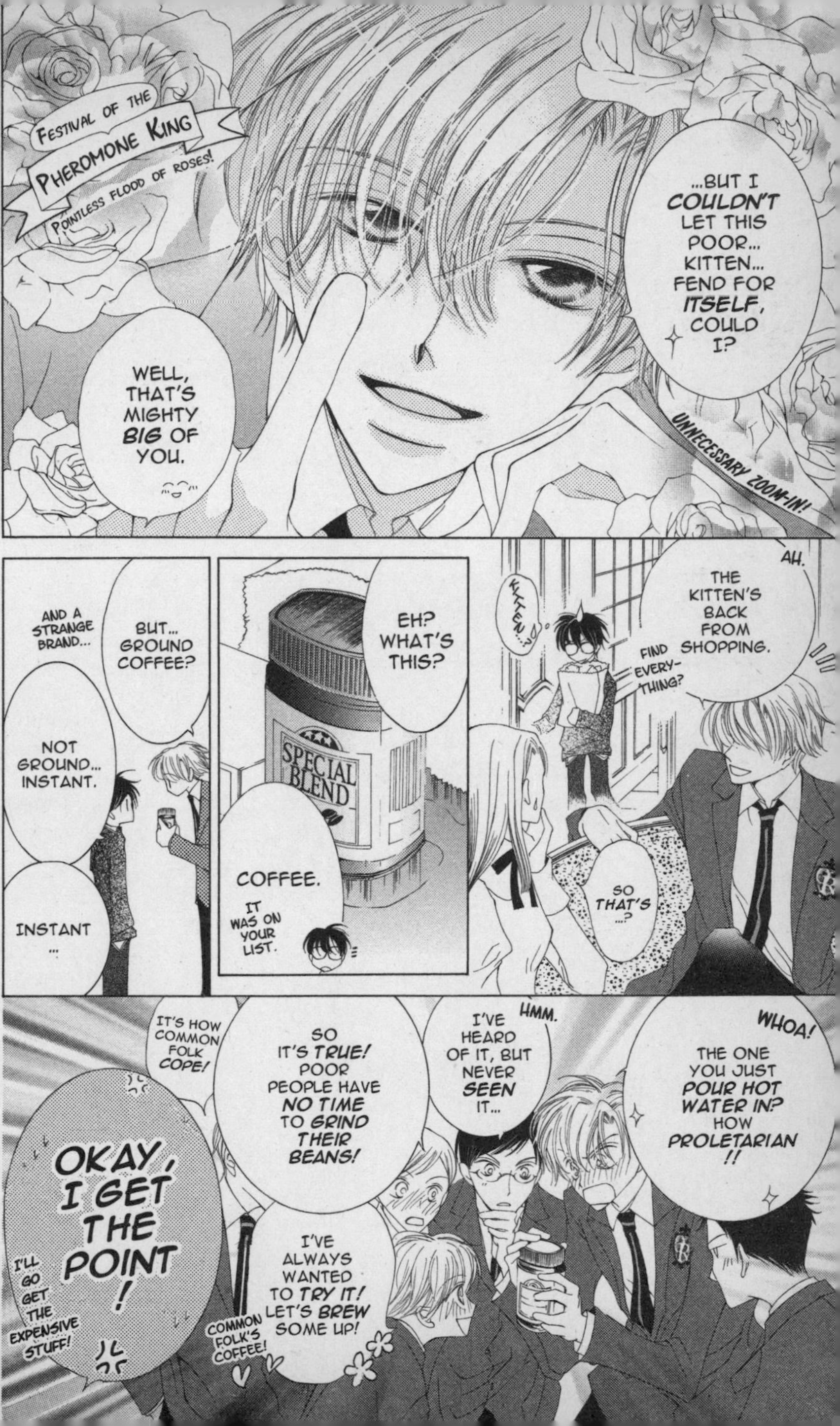
...BUT I COULDN'T LET THIS POOR... KITTEN... FEND FOR ITSELF, COULD I?
FESTIVAL OF THE PHEROMONE KING
POINTLESS FLOOD OF ROSES!
UNNECESSARY ZOOM-IN!
WELL, THAT'S MIGHTY BIG OF YOU.
AH.
THE KITTEN'S BACK FROM SHOPPING.
FIND EVERYTHING?
KITTEN...?
SO THAT'S ...?
EH? WHAT'S THIS?
SPECIAL BLEND
COFFEE.
IT WAS ON YOUR LIST.
BUT... GROUND COFFEE?
AND A STRANGE BRAND...
NOT GROUND... INSTANT.
INSTANT ...
WHOA!
THE ONE YOU JUST POUR HOT WATER IN? HOW PROLETARIAN!!
HMM.
I'VE HEARD OF IT, BUT NEVER SEEN IT...
SO IT'S TRUE! POOR PEOPLE HAVE NO TIME TO GRIND THEIR BEANS!
IT'S HOW COMMON FOLK COPE!
I'VE ALWAYS WANTED TO TRY IT! LET'S BREW SOME UP!
COMMON FOLK'S COFFEE!
OKAY, I GET THE POINT!
I'LL GO GET THE EXPENSIVE STUFF!

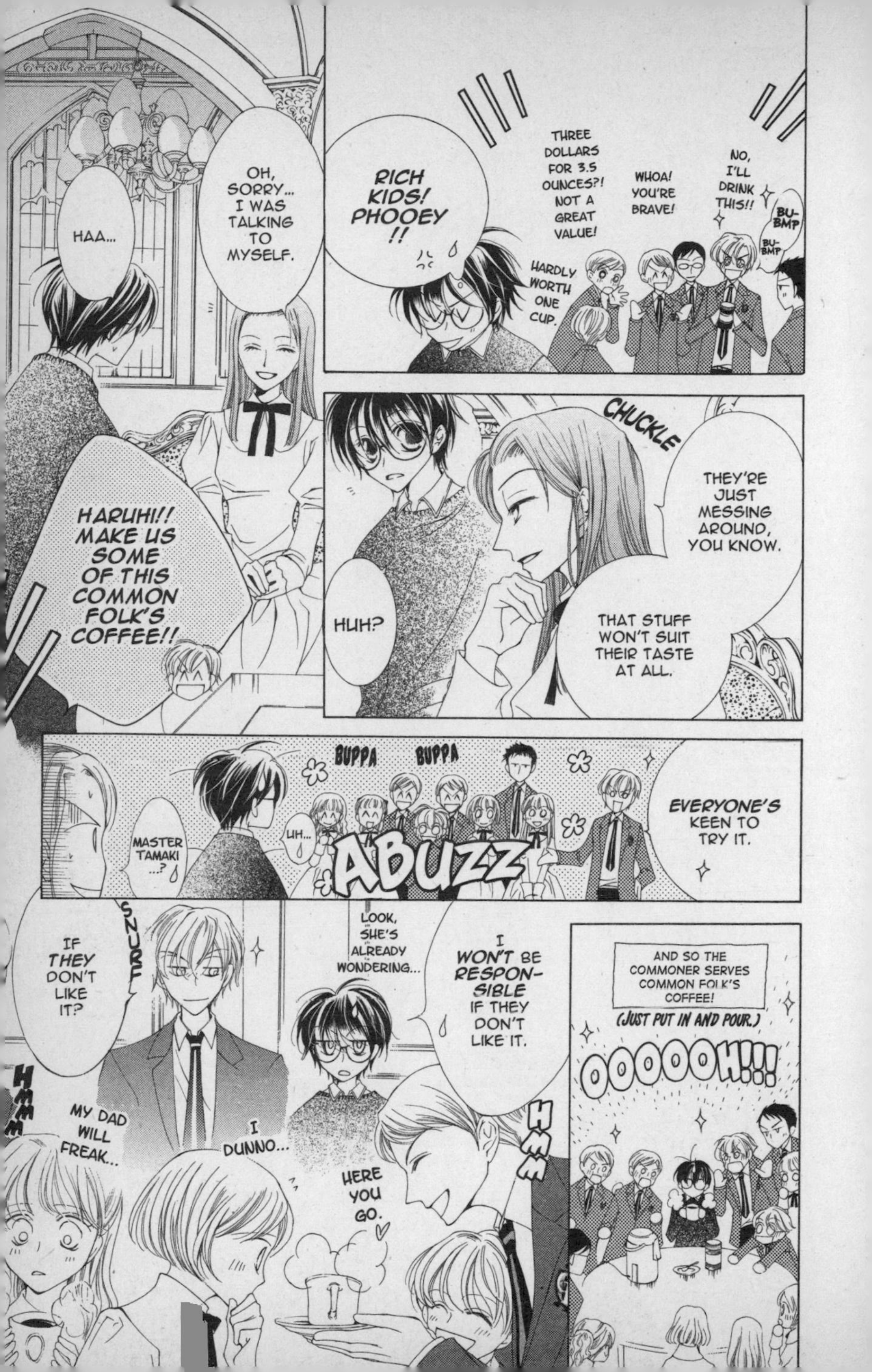
BU-BMP
BU-BMP
NO, I'LL DRINK THIS!!
WHOA! YOU'RE BRAVE!
THREE DOLLARS FOR 3.5 OUNCES?! NOT A GREAT VALUE!
HARDLY WORTH ONE CUP.
RICH KIDS! PHOOEY!!
CHUCKLE
THEY'RE JUST MESSING AROUND, YOU KNOW.
THAT STUFF WON'T SUIT THEIR TASTE AT ALL.
HUH?
OH, SORRY... I WAS TALKING TO MYSELF.
HAA...
HARUHI!! MAKE US SOME OF THIS COMMON FOLK'S COFFEE!!
EVERYONE'S KEEN TO TRY IT.
BUPPA
BUPPA
ABUZZ
UH...
MASTER TAMAKI ...?
AND SO THE COMMONER SERVES COMMON FOLK'S COFFEE!
(JUST PUT IN AND POUR.)
OOOOOH!!!
I WON'T BE RESPONSIBLE IF THEY DON'T LIKE IT.
LOOK, SHE'S ALREADY WONDERING...
IF THEY DON'T LIKE IT?
SNURF
HMM
HERE YOU GO.
I DUNNO...
MY DAD WILL FREAK...
HMM

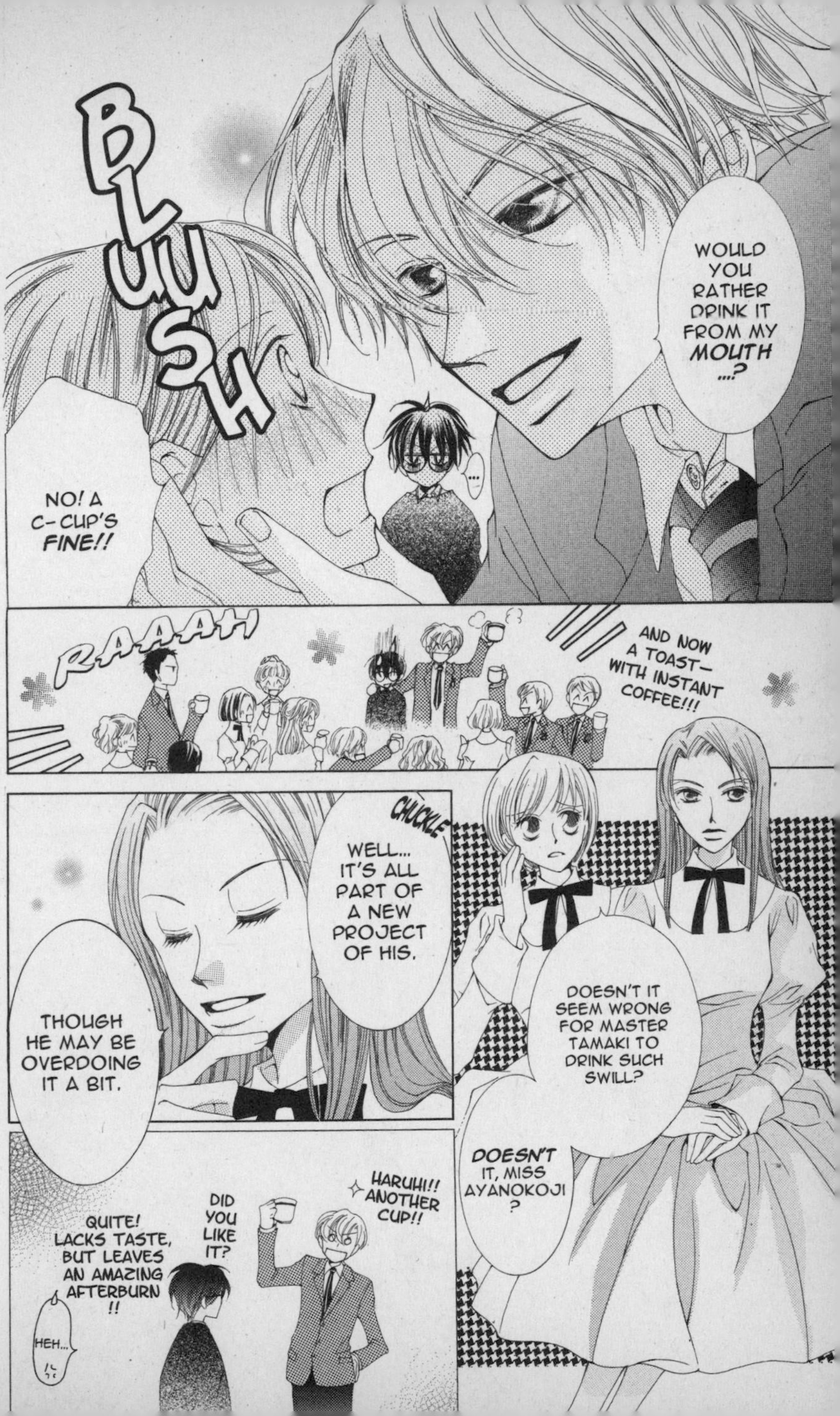
WOULD YOU RATHER DRINK IT FROM MY MOUTH ...?
BLUSH
...
NO! A C-CUP'S FINE!!
AND NOW A TOAST— WITH INSTANT COFFEE!!!
RAAAAH
DOESN'T IT SEEM WRONG FOR MASTER TAMAKI TO DRINK SUCH SWILL?
DOESN'T IT, MISS AYANOKOJI?
CHUCKLE
WELL... IT'S ALL PART OF A NEW PROJECT OF HIS.
THOUGH HE MAY BE OVERDOING IT A BIT.
HARUHI!! ANOTHER CUP!!
DID YOU LIKE IT?
QUITE! LACKS TASTE, BUT LEAVES AN AMAZING AFTERBURN!!
HEH...

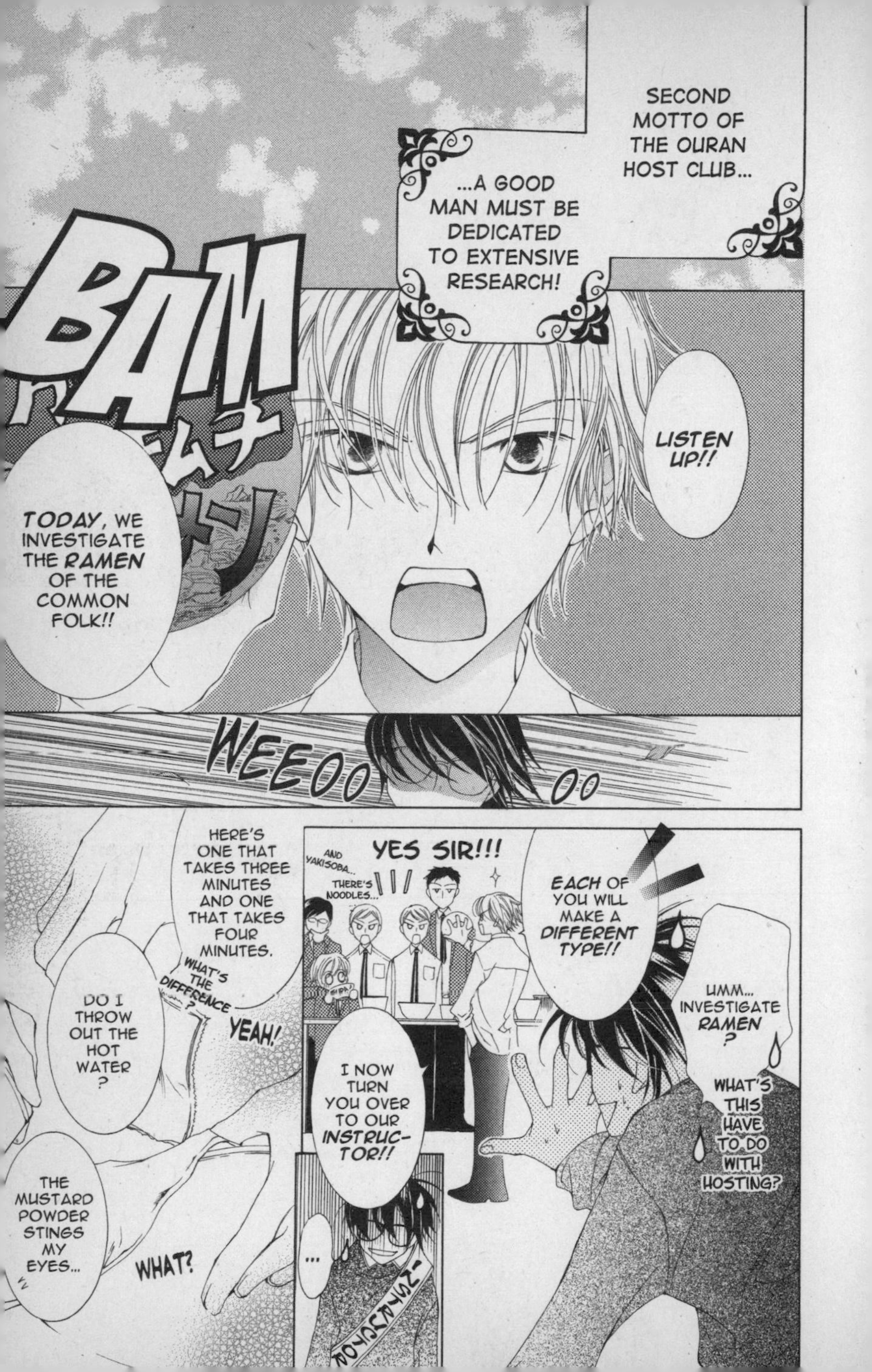
SECOND MOTTO OF THE OURAN HOST CLUB...
...A GOOD MAN MUST BE DEDICATED TO EXTENSIVE RESEARCH!
BAM
LISTEN UP!!
TODAY, WE INVESTIGATE THE RAMEN OF THE COMMON FOLK!!
WEEOO OO
EACH OF YOU WILL MAKE A DIFFERENT TYPE!!
UMM... INVESTIGATE RAMEN?
WHAT'S THIS HAVE TO DO WITH HOSTING?
YES SIR!!!
AND YAKISOBA...
THERE'S NOODLES...
I NOW TURN YOU OVER TO OUR INSTRUCTOR!!
...
HERE'S ONE THAT TAKES THREE MINUTES AND ONE THAT TAKES FOUR MINUTES.
WHAT'S THE DIFFERENCE?
YEAH!
DO I THROW OUT THE HOT WATER?
THE MUSTARD POWDER STINGS MY EYES...
WHAT?

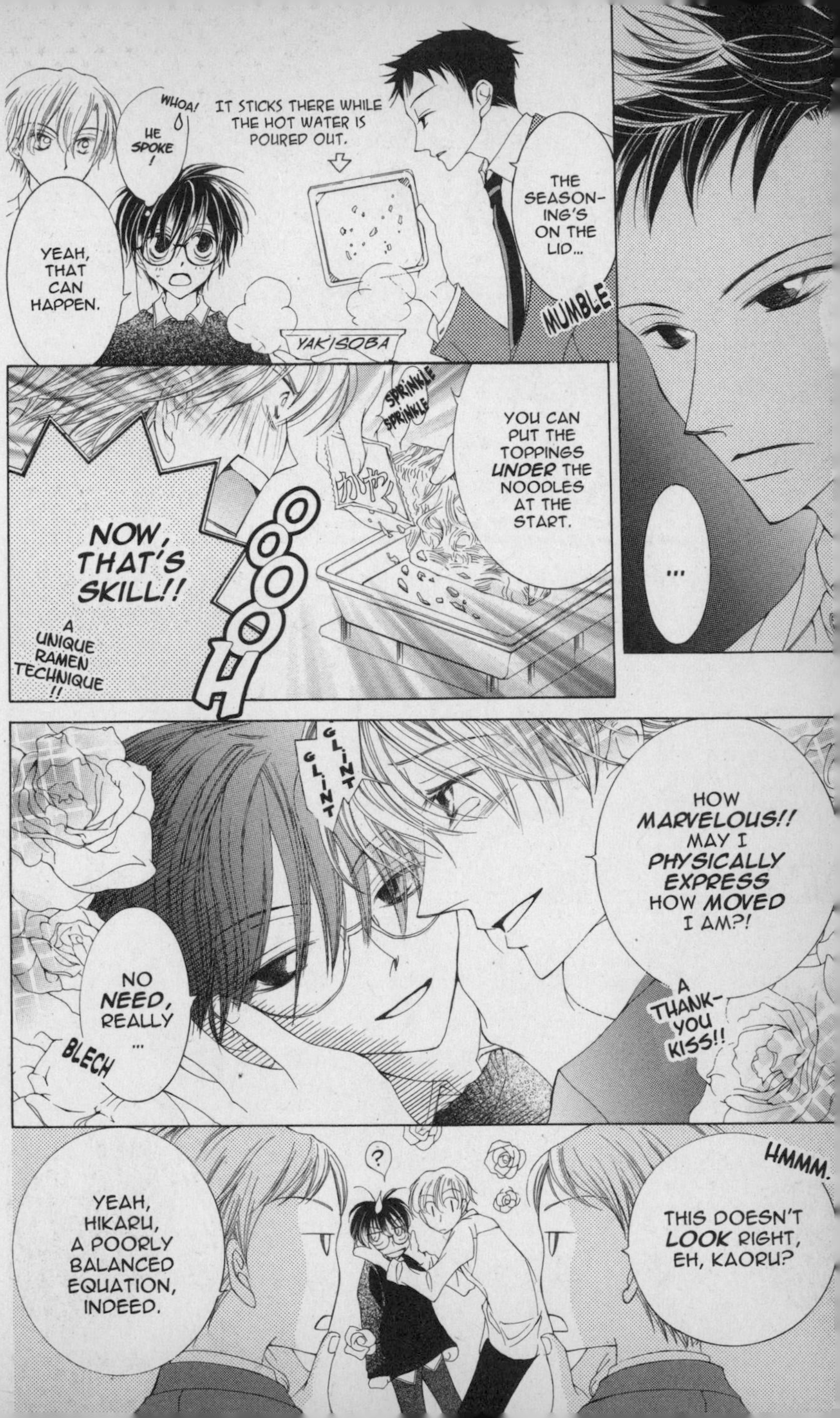
...
THE SEASONING'S ON THE LID...
MUMBLE
IT STICKS THERE WHILE THE HOT WATER IS POURED OUT.
YAKISOBA
WHOA! HE SPOKE!
YEAH, THAT CAN HAPPEN.
YOU CAN PUT THE TOPPINGS UNDER THE NOODLES AT THE START.
SPRINKLE SPRINKLE
かやく
OOOOOH
NOW, THAT'S SKILL!!
A UNIQUE RAMEN TECHNIQUE!!
HOW MARVELOUS!! MAY I PHYSICALLY EXPRESS HOW MOVED I AM?!
A THANK-YOU KISS!!
GLINT GLINT
NO NEED, REALLY ...
BLECH
HMMM.
THIS DOESN'T LOOK RIGHT, EH, KAORU?
?
YEAH, HIKARU, A POORLY BALANCED EQUATION, INDEED.

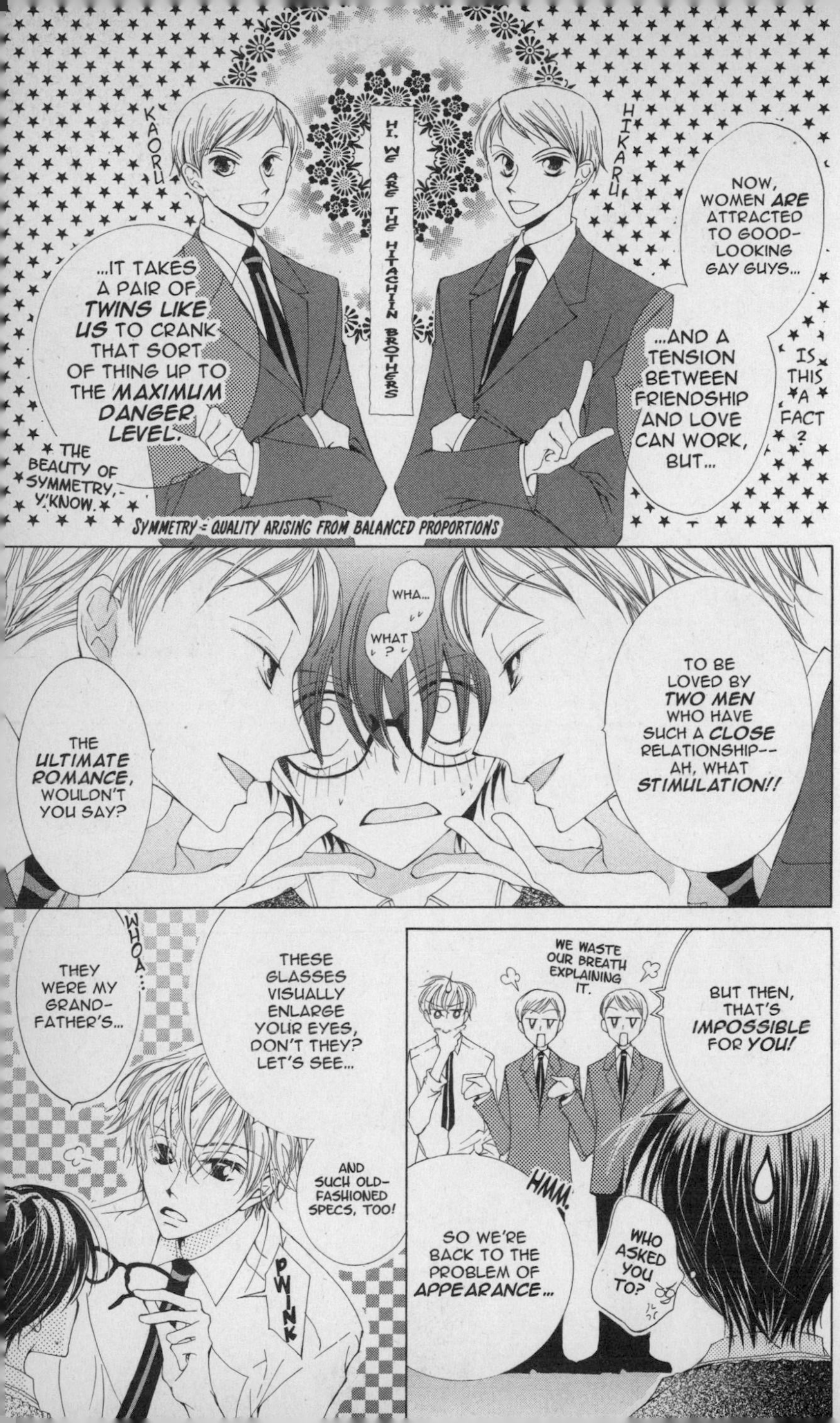
HIKARU
NOW, WOMEN ARE ATTRACTED TO GOOD-LOOKING GAY GUYS...
...AND A TENSION BETWEEN FRIENDSHIP AND LOVE CAN WORK, BUT...
IS THIS A FACT?
HI, WE ARE THE HITACHIIN BROTHERS
KAORU
...IT TAKES A PAIR OF TWINS LIKE US TO CRANK THAT SORT OF THING UP TO THE MAXIMUM DANGER LEVEL.
THE BEAUTY OF SYMMETRY, Y'KNOW.
SYMMETRY = QUALITY ARISING FROM BALANCED PROPORTIONS
TO BE LOVED BY TWO MEN WHO HAVE SUCH A CLOSE RELATIONSHIP--AH, WHAT STIMULATION!!
WHA...
WHAT?
THE ULTIMATE ROMANCE, WOULDN'T YOU SAY?
BUT THEN, THAT'S IMPOSSIBLE FOR YOU!
WE WASTE OUR BREATH EXPLAINING IT.
WHO ASKED YOU TO?
HMM.
SO WE'RE BACK TO THE PROBLEM OF APPEARANCE...
THESE GLASSES VISUALLY ENLARGE YOUR EYES, DON'T THEY? LET'S SEE...
WHOA...
THEY WERE MY GRANDFATHER'S...
AND SUCH OLD-FASHIONED SPECS, TOO!
PWINK

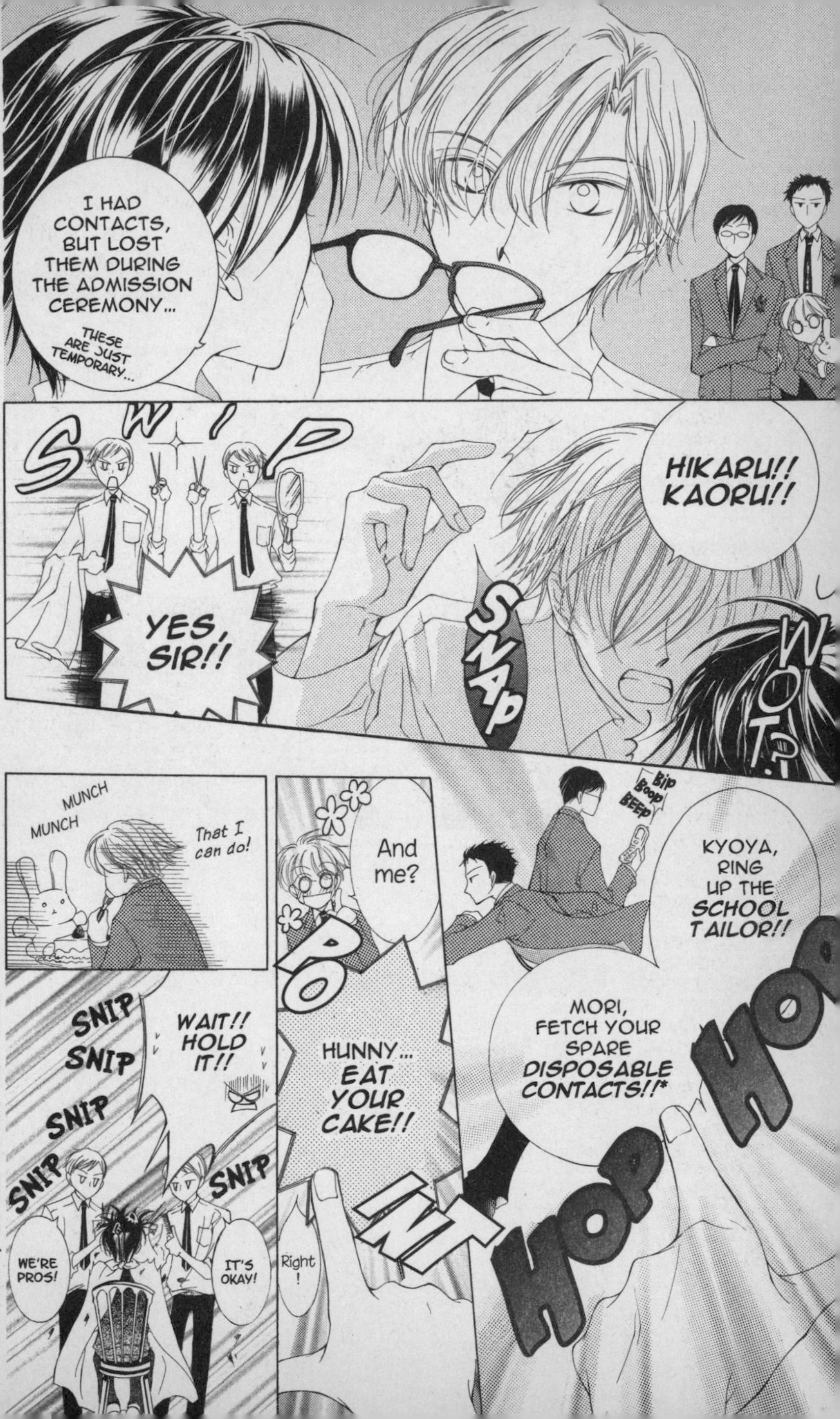
I HAD CONTACTS, BUT LOST THEM DURING THE ADMISSION CEREMONY...
THESE ARE JUST TEMPORARY...
HIKARU!! KAORU!!
WOT?!
SNAP
YES, SIR!!
SWIP
KYOYA, RING UP THE SCHOOL TAILOR!!
Bip Boop BEEP
MORI, FETCH YOUR SPARE DISPOSABLE CONTACTS!!*
HOP HOP
And me?
POINT
HUNNY... EAT YOUR CAKE!!
Right!
MUNCH MUNCH
That I can do!
WAIT!! HOLD IT!!
SNIP SNIP SNIP SNIP SNIP
WE'RE PROS!
IT'S OKAY!

*FOR THE RECORD, DISPOSABLE CONTACTS AREN'T ONE-SIZE-FITS-ALL.

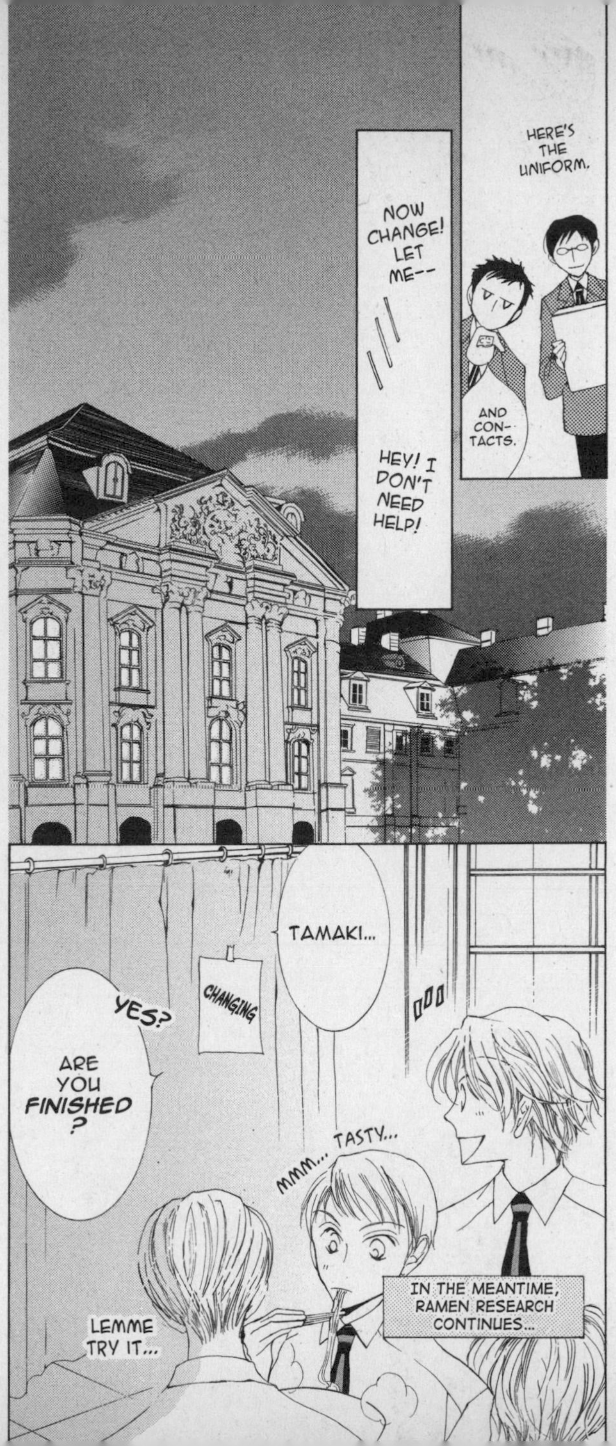
HERE'S THE UNIFORM.
AND CON-TACTS.
NOW CHANGE! LET ME--
HEY! I DON'T NEED HELP!
TAMAKI...
CHANGING
YES?
ARE YOU FINISHED?
IN THE MEANTIME, RAMEN RESEARCH CONTINUES...
MMM... TASTY...
LEMME TRY IT...

1

HELLO EVERYONE!! THIS IS BISCO HATORI. THANKS A LOT FOR BUYING AND READING "OURAN HIGH SCHOOL HOST CLUB"!!

"OURAN HIGH SCHOOL HOST CLUB"... HOW DO YOU LIKE THIS TITLE? (LAUGH). OH, BY THE WAY, THE "HOST BU [THE JAPANESE CHARACTER FOR CLUB]" IS READ AS "HOST CLUB [KURABU]" ONLY IN THE TITLE. THIS IS BECAUSE I THINK IT FLOWS BETTER, AND MAKES IT "AT LEAST SOUND SOMEWHAT COOL" (A FUTILE EFFORT, I SUPPOSE). NOW THAT I'LL BE PRODUCING THIS SERIES FOR A WHOLE YEAR, I'M STARTING NOT TO CARE EITHER WAY ANYMORE (LAUGH). DESENSITIZATION IS SCARY...

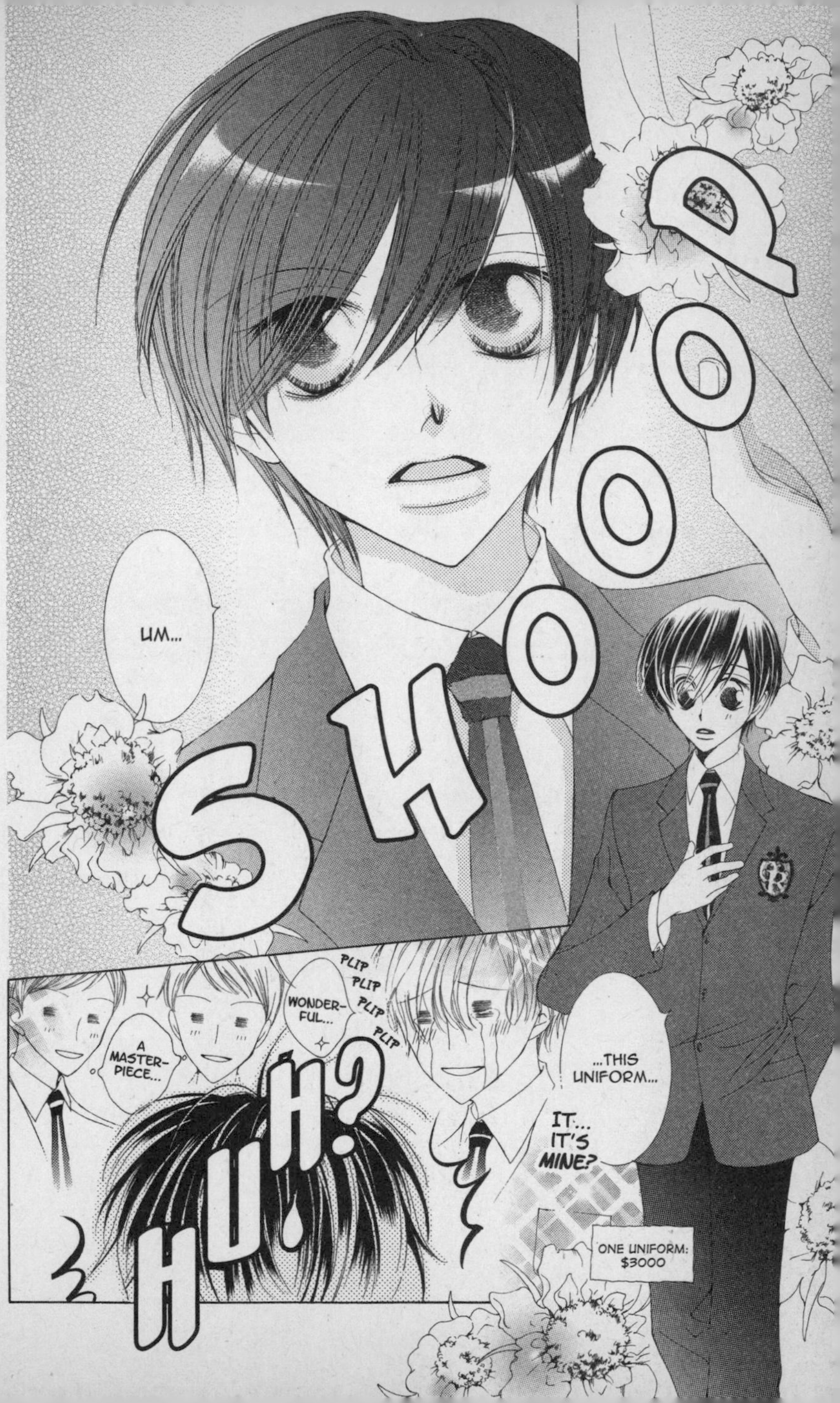
SHOOOP
UM...
...THIS UNIFORM...
IT... IT'S MINE?
ONE UNIFORM: $3000
PLIP PLIP PLIP PLIP
WONDERFUL...
A MASTERPIECE...
HUH?

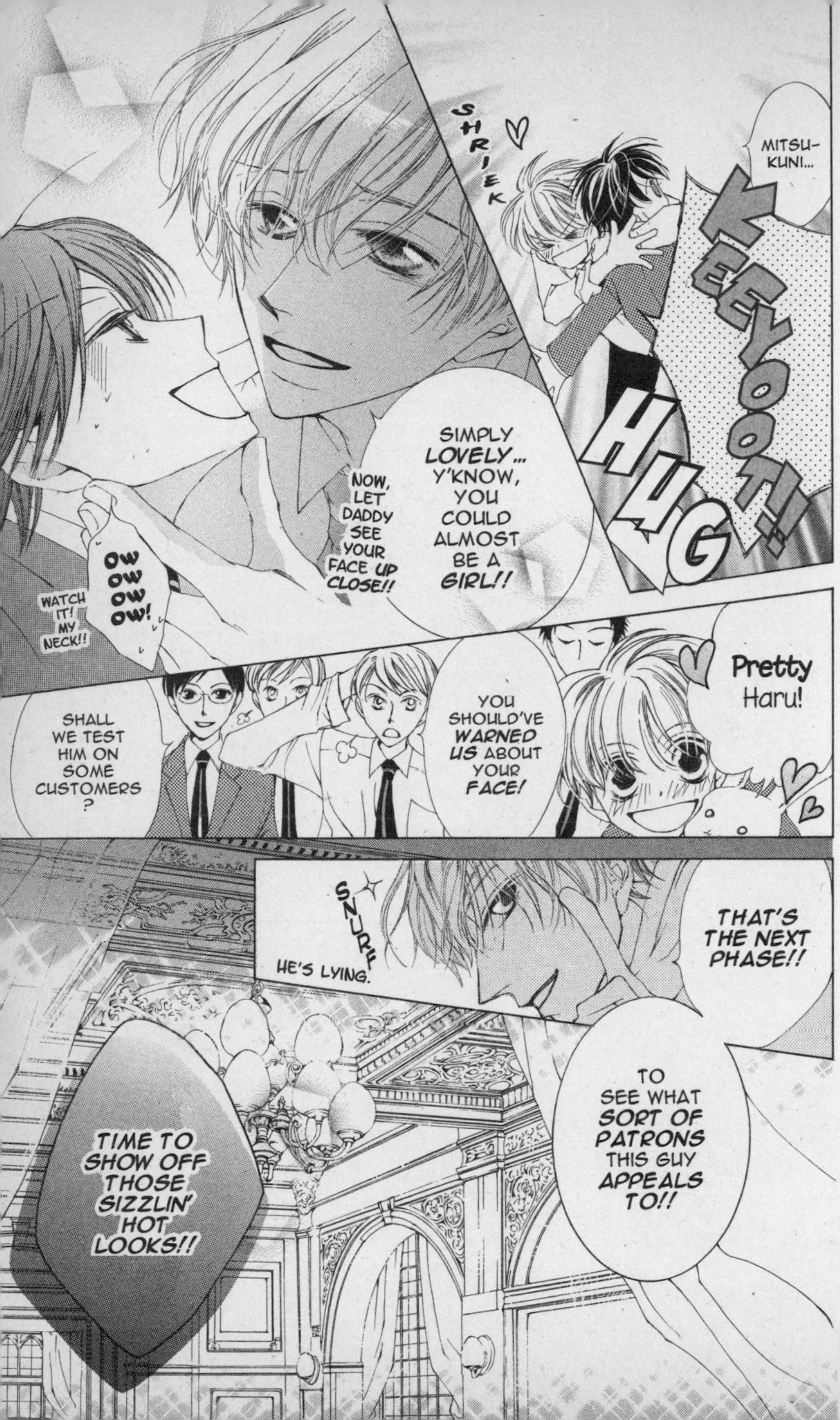
MITSU-KUNI...
KEEYOOT!!
HUG
SHRIEK
SIMPLY LOVELY... Y'KNOW, YOU COULD ALMOST BE A GIRL!!
NOW, LET DADDY SEE YOUR FACE UP CLOSE!!
OW OW OW OW!
WATCH IT! MY NECK!!
Pretty Haru!
YOU SHOULD'VE WARNED US ABOUT YOUR FACE!
SHALL WE TEST HIM ON SOME CUSTOMERS?
THAT'S THE NEXT PHASE!!
SNURF
HE'S LYING.
TO SEE WHAT SORT OF PATRONS THIS GUY APPEALS TO!!
TIME TO SHOW OFF THOSE SIZZLIN' HOT LOOKS!!

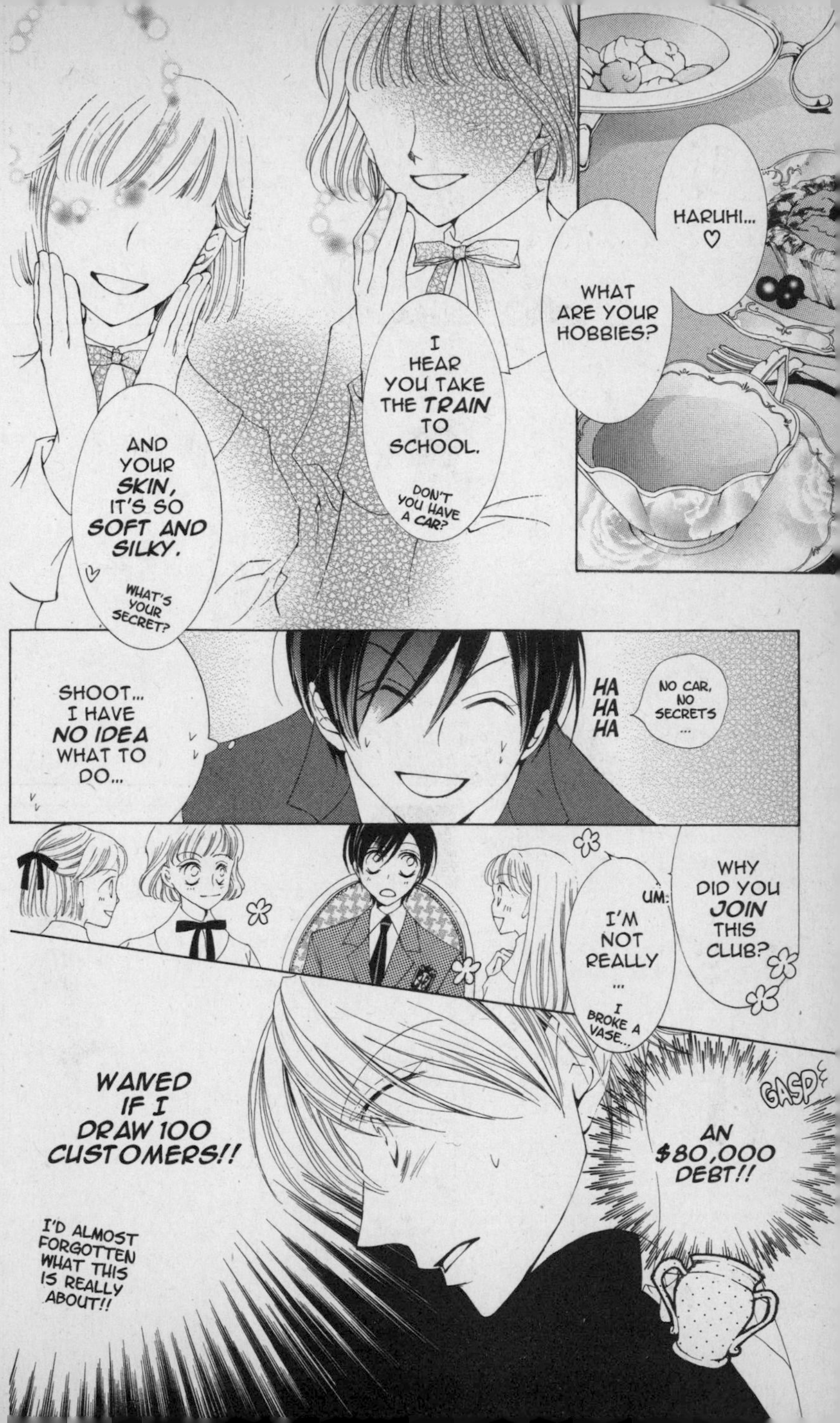
HARUHI... ♡
WHAT ARE YOUR HOBBIES?
I HEAR YOU TAKE THE TRAIN TO SCHOOL.
DON'T YOU HAVE A CAR?
AND YOUR SKIN, IT'S SO SOFT AND SILKY. ♡
WHAT'S YOUR SECRET?
HA HA HA
NO CAR, NO SECRETS...
SHOOT... I HAVE NO IDEA WHAT TO DO...
WHY DID YOU JOIN THIS CLUB?
UM: I'M NOT REALLY...
I BROKE A VASE...
GASP
AN $80,000 DEBT!!
WAIVED IF I DRAW 100 CUSTOMERS!!
I'D ALMOST FORGOTTEN WHAT THIS IS REALLY ABOUT!!

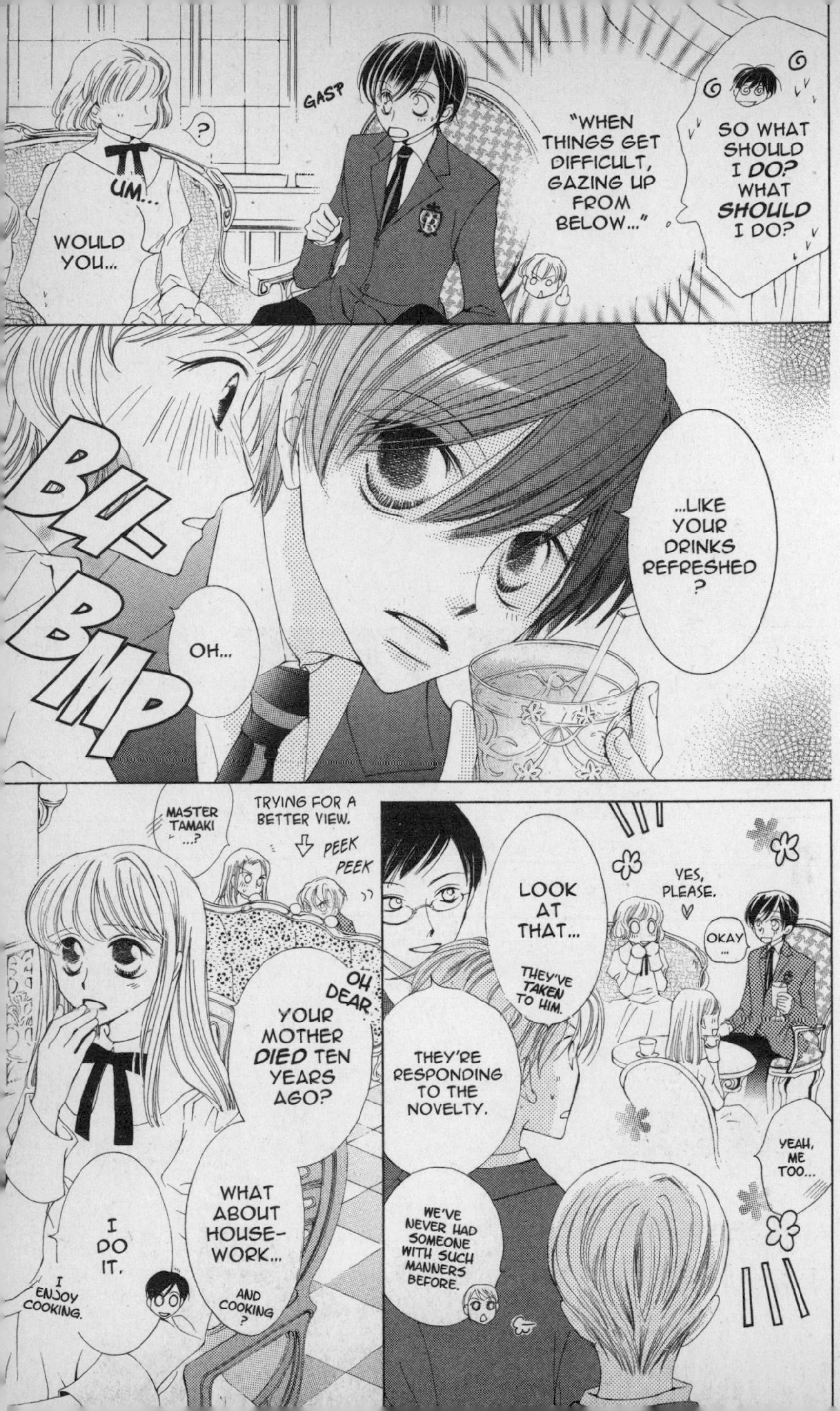
SO WHAT SHOULD I DO? WHAT SHOULD I DO?
"WHEN THINGS GET DIFFICULT, GAZING UP FROM BELOW..."
GASP
?
UM...
WOULD YOU...
...LIKE YOUR DRINKS REFRESHED?
OH...
BU-BUMP
YES, PLEASE.
OKAY...
LOOK AT THAT...
THEY'VE TAKEN TO HIM.
THEY'RE RESPONDING TO THE NOVELTY.
YEAH, ME TOO...
WE'VE NEVER HAD SOMEONE WITH SUCH MANNERS BEFORE.
TRYING FOR A BETTER VIEW.
PEEK PEEK
MASTER TAMAKI ...?
OH DEAR
YOUR MOTHER DIED TEN YEARS AGO?
WHAT ABOUT HOUSE-WORK...
AND COOKING?
I DO IT.
I ENJOY COOKING.

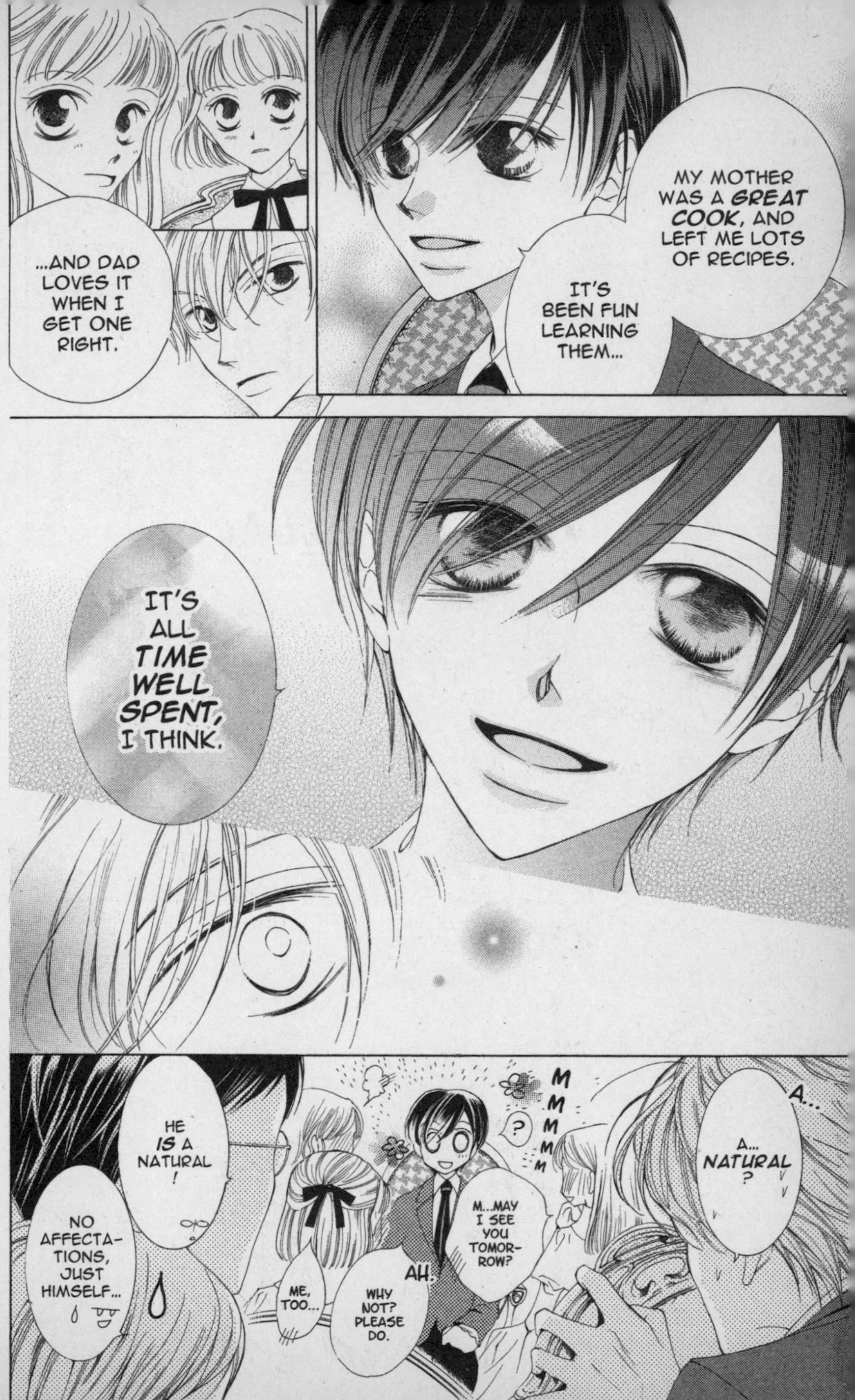
MY MOTHER WAS A *GREAT COOK*, AND LEFT ME LOTS OF RECIPES.
IT'S BEEN FUN LEARNING THEM...
...AND DAD LOVES IT WHEN I GET ONE RIGHT.
IT'S ALL *TIME WELL SPENT*, I THINK.
A...
A... **NATURAL**?
MMMMMMM
?
M...MAY I SEE YOU TOMORROW?
AH.
WHY NOT? PLEASE DO.
ME, TOO...
HE *IS* A NATURAL!
NO AFFECTATIONS, JUST HIMSELF...

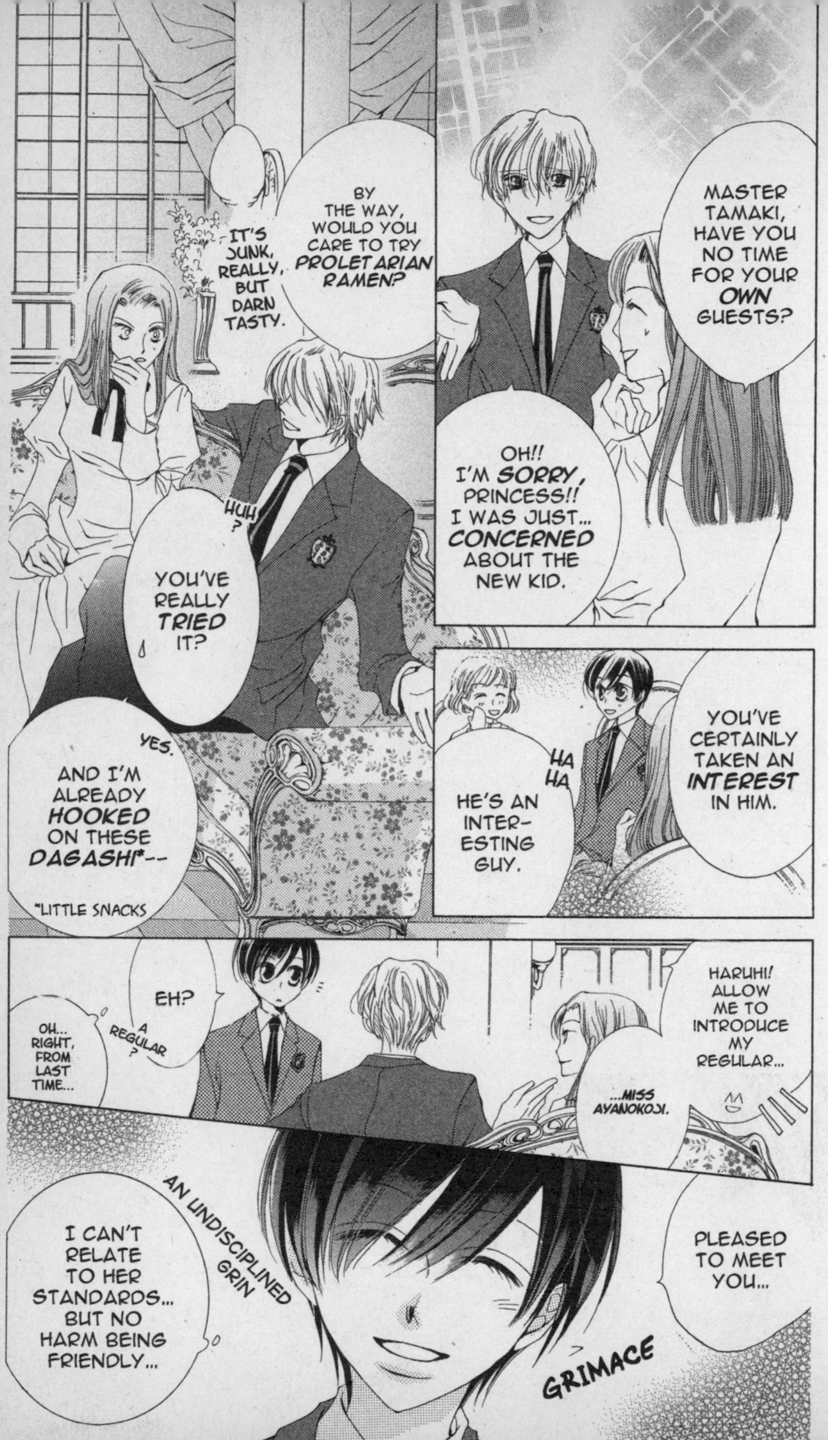

MASTER TAMAKI, HAVE YOU NO TIME FOR YOUR OWN GUESTS?
OH!! I'M SORRY, PRINCESS!! I WAS JUST... CONCERNED ABOUT THE NEW KID.
YOU'VE CERTAINLY TAKEN AN INTEREST IN HIM.
HA HA
HE'S AN INTERESTING GUY.
BY THE WAY, WOULD YOU CARE TO TRY PROLETARIAN RAMEN?
IT'S JUNK, REALLY, BUT DARN TASTY.
HUH?
YOU'VE REALLY TRIED IT?
YES.
AND I'M ALREADY HOOKED ON THESE DAGASHI*--
*LITTLE SNACKS
HARUHI! ALLOW ME TO INTRODUCE MY REGULAR...
...MISS AYANOKOJI.
EH?
A REGULAR?
OH... RIGHT, FROM LAST TIME...
PLEASED TO MEET YOU...
GRIMACE
AN UNDISCIPLINED GRIN
I CAN'T RELATE TO HER STANDARDS... BUT NO HARM BEING FRIENDLY...

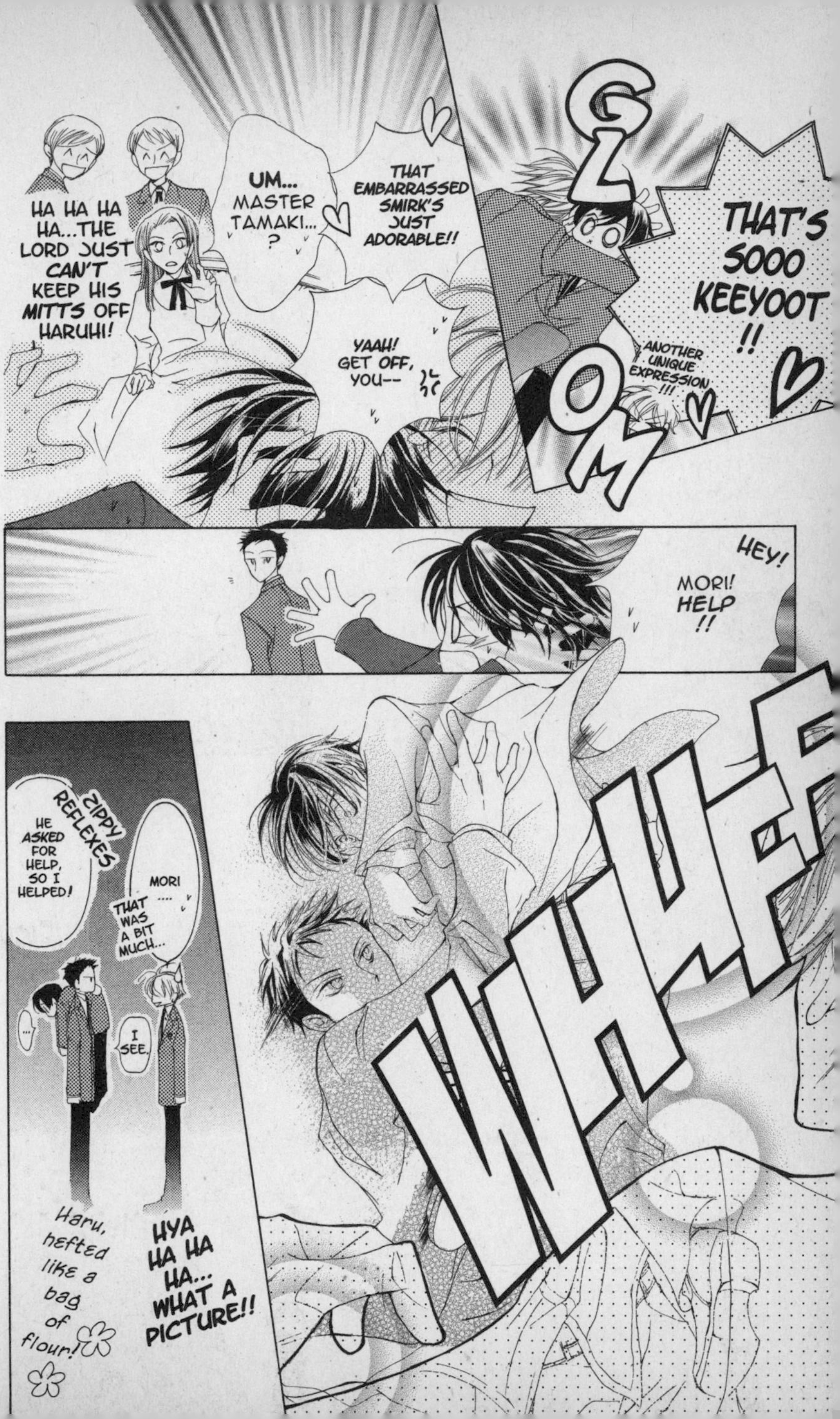
GLOMP
THAT'S SOOO KEEYOOT!!
ANOTHER UNIQUE EXPRESSION!!!
THAT EMBARRASSED SMIRK'S JUST ADORABLE!!
UM... MASTER TAMAKI...?
YAAH! GET OFF, YOU--
HA HA HA HA...THE LORD JUST CAN'T KEEP HIS MITTS OFF HARUHI!
HEY!
MORI! HELP!!
MORI.... THAT WAS A BIT MUCH...
HE ASKED FOR HELP, SO I HELPED!
ZIPPY REFLEXES
...
I SEE.
HYA HA HA HA... WHAT A PICTURE!!
Haru, hefted like a bag of flour!

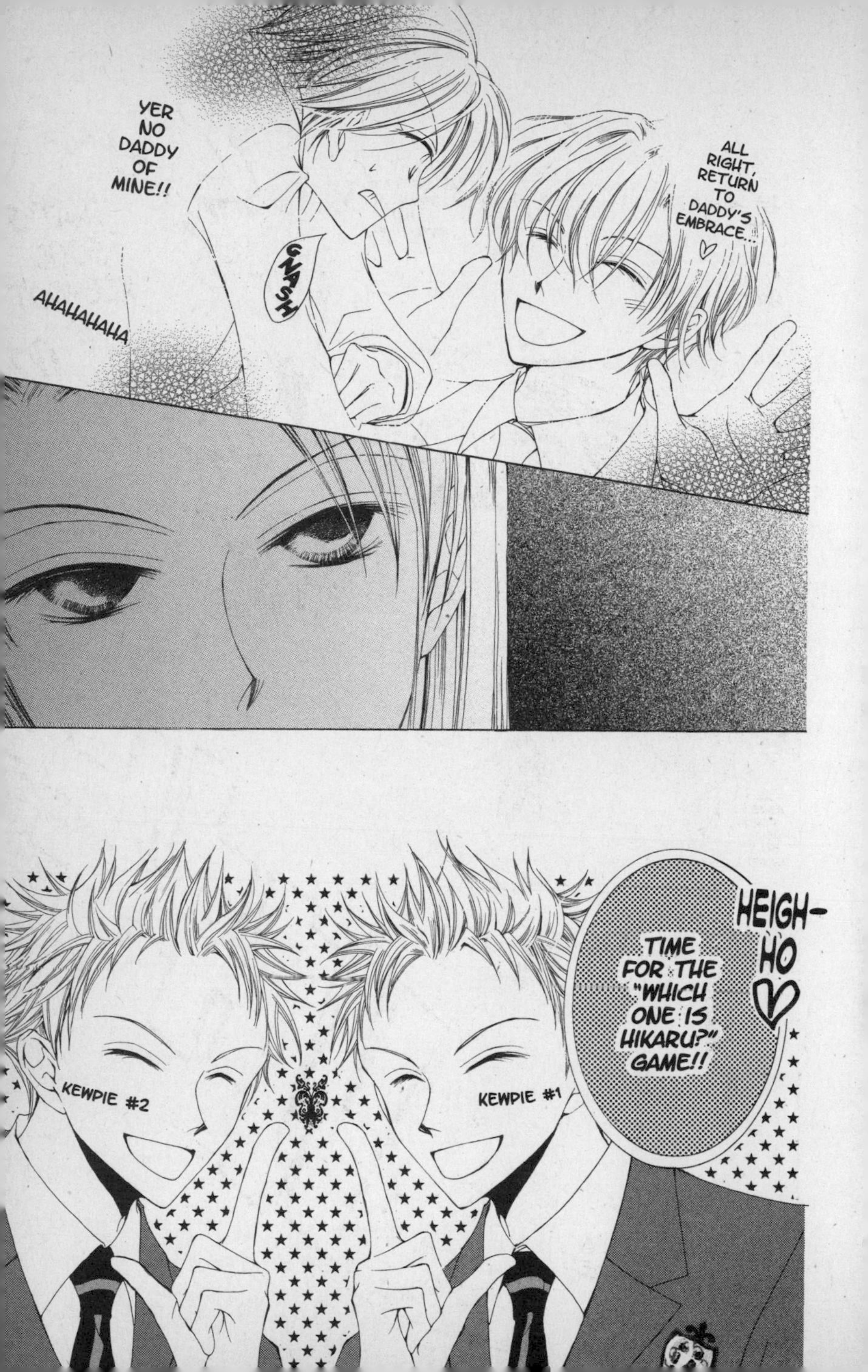
ALL RIGHT, RETURN TO DADDY'S EMBRACE... ♡
YER NO DADDY OF MINE!!
GNASH
AHAHAHAHA
HEIGH-HO ♡
TIME FOR THE "WHICH ONE IS HIKARU?" GAME!!
KEWPIE #1
KEWPIE #2

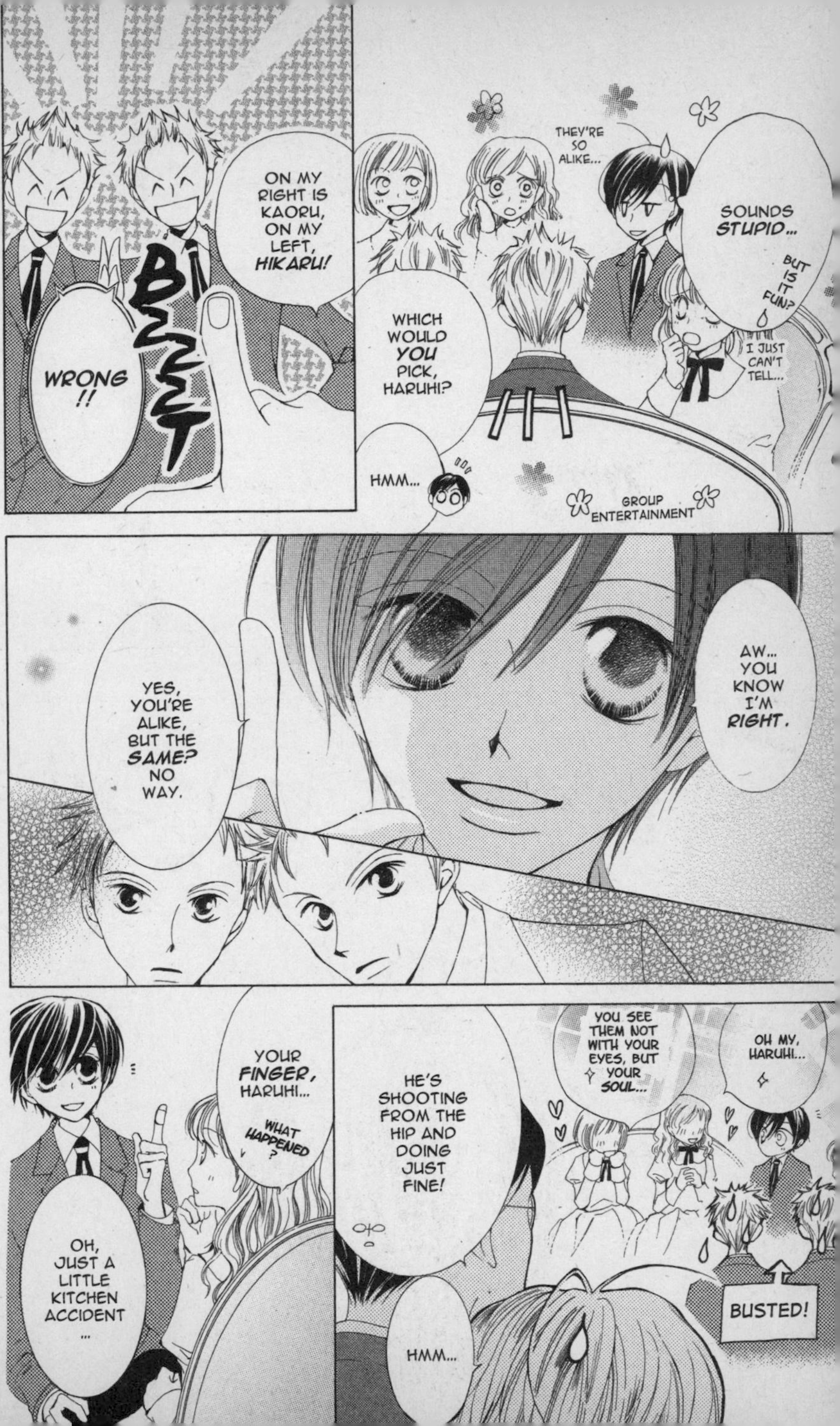
SOUNDS STUPID...
BUT IS IT FUN? I JUST CAN'T TELL...
THEY'RE SO ALIKE...
WHICH WOULD YOU PICK, HARUHI?
HMM...
GROUP ENTERTAINMENT
ON MY RIGHT IS KAORU, ON MY LEFT, HIKARU!
BZZZT
WRONG!!
AW... YOU KNOW I'M RIGHT.
YES, YOU'RE ALIKE, BUT THE SAME? NO WAY.
OH MY, HARUHI...
YOU SEE THEM NOT WITH YOUR EYES, BUT YOUR SOUL...
HE'S SHOOTING FROM THE HIP AND DOING JUST FINE!
BUSTED!
HMM...
YOUR FINGER, HARUHI...
WHAT HAPPENED?
OH, JUST A LITTLE KITCHEN ACCIDENT...

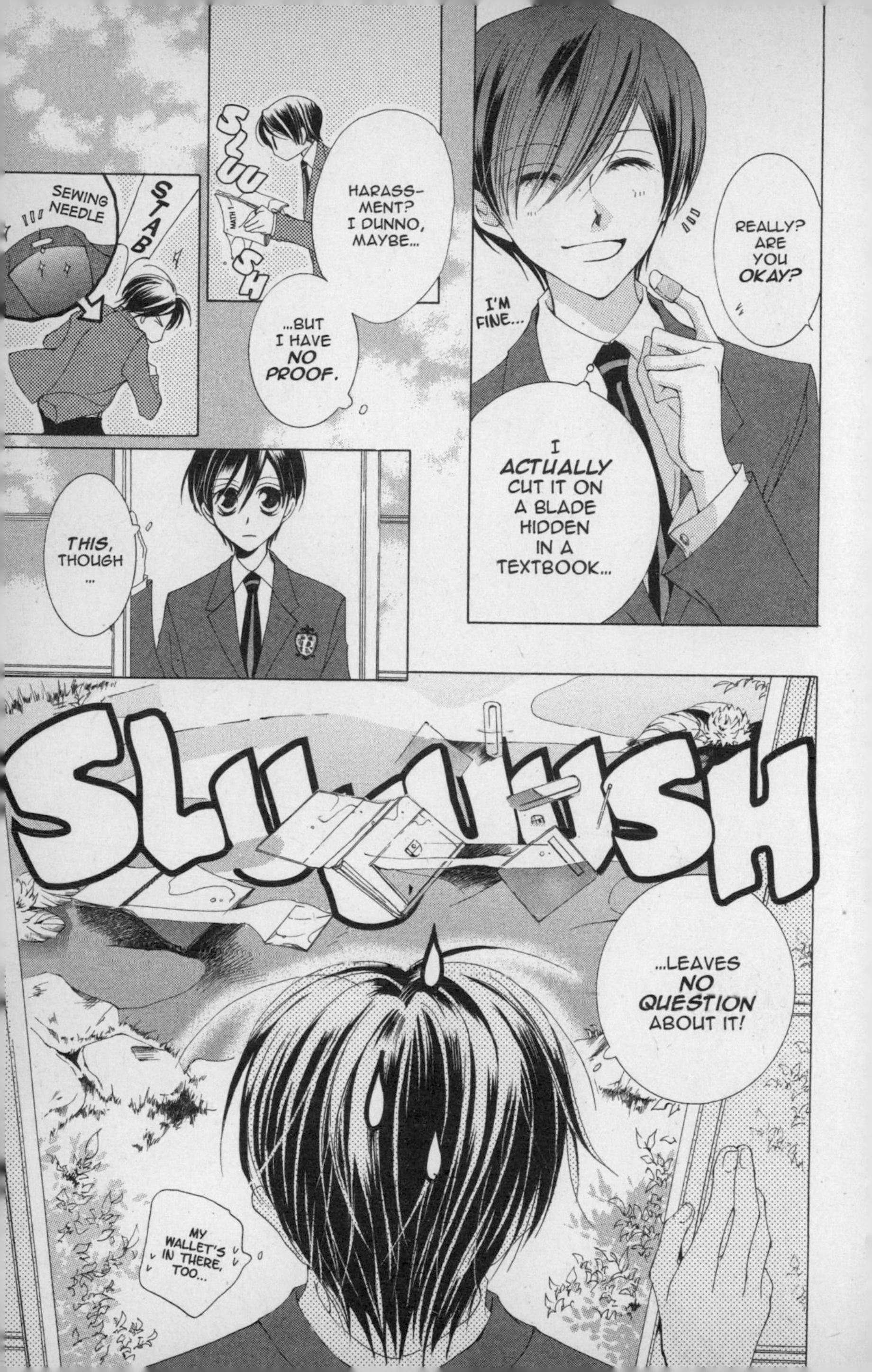
REALLY? ARE YOU OKAY?
I'M FINE...
I ACTUALLY CUT IT ON A BLADE HIDDEN IN A TEXTBOOK...
SLUUSH
HARASS-MENT? I DUNNO, MAYBE...
...BUT I HAVE NO PROOF.
SEWING NEEDLE
STAB
THIS, THOUGH ...
SLUUSH
...LEAVES NO QUESTION ABOUT IT!
MY WALLET'S IN THERE, TOO...

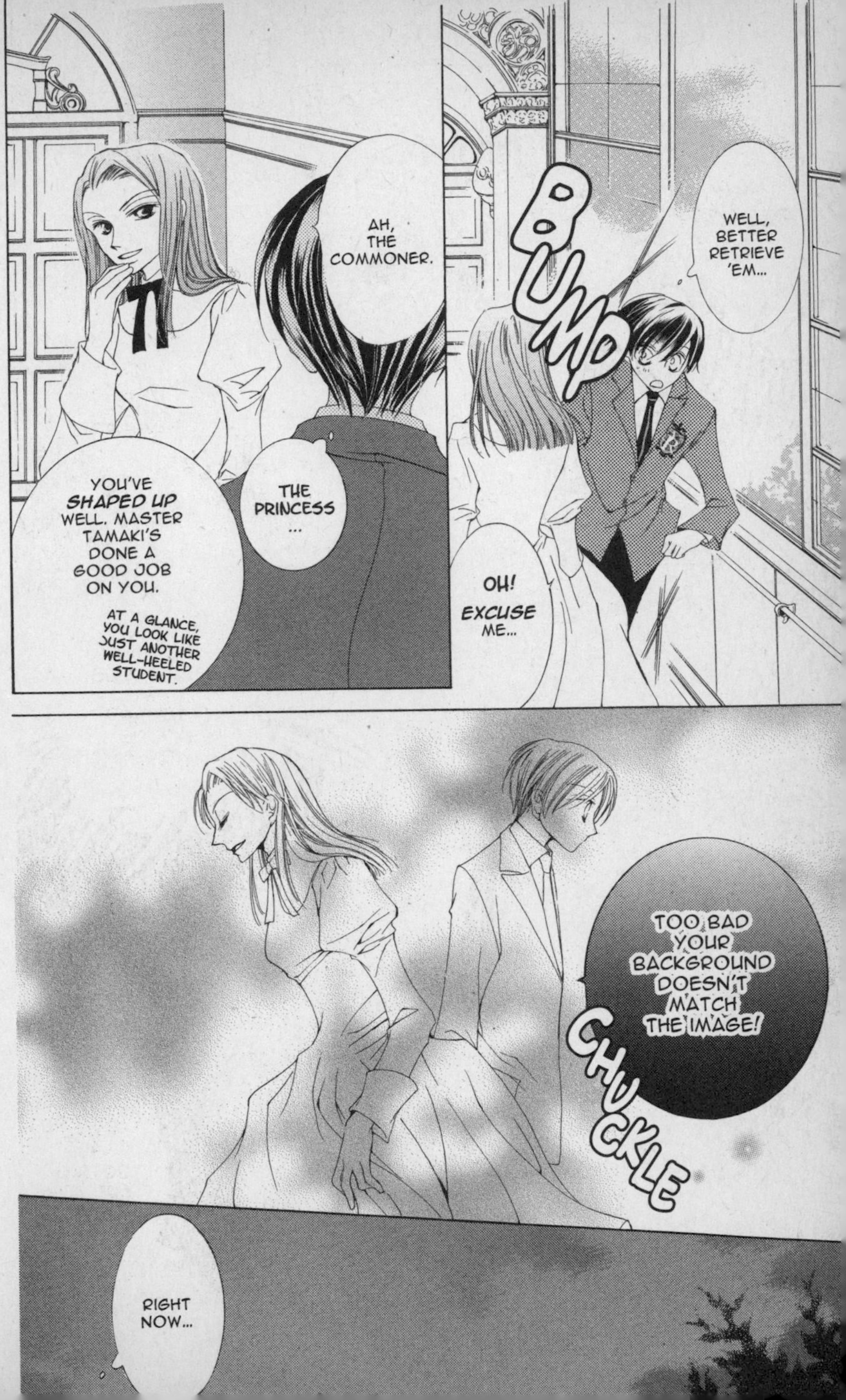
WELL, BETTER RETRIEVE 'EM...
BUMP
OH! EXCUSE ME...
AH, THE COMMONER.
THE PRINCESS ...
YOU'VE SHAPED UP WELL. MASTER TAMAKI'S DONE A GOOD JOB ON YOU.
AT A GLANCE, YOU LOOK LIKE JUST ANOTHER WELL-HEELED STUDENT.
TOO BAD YOUR BACKGROUND DOESN'T MATCH THE IMAGE!
CHUCKLE
RIGHT NOW...

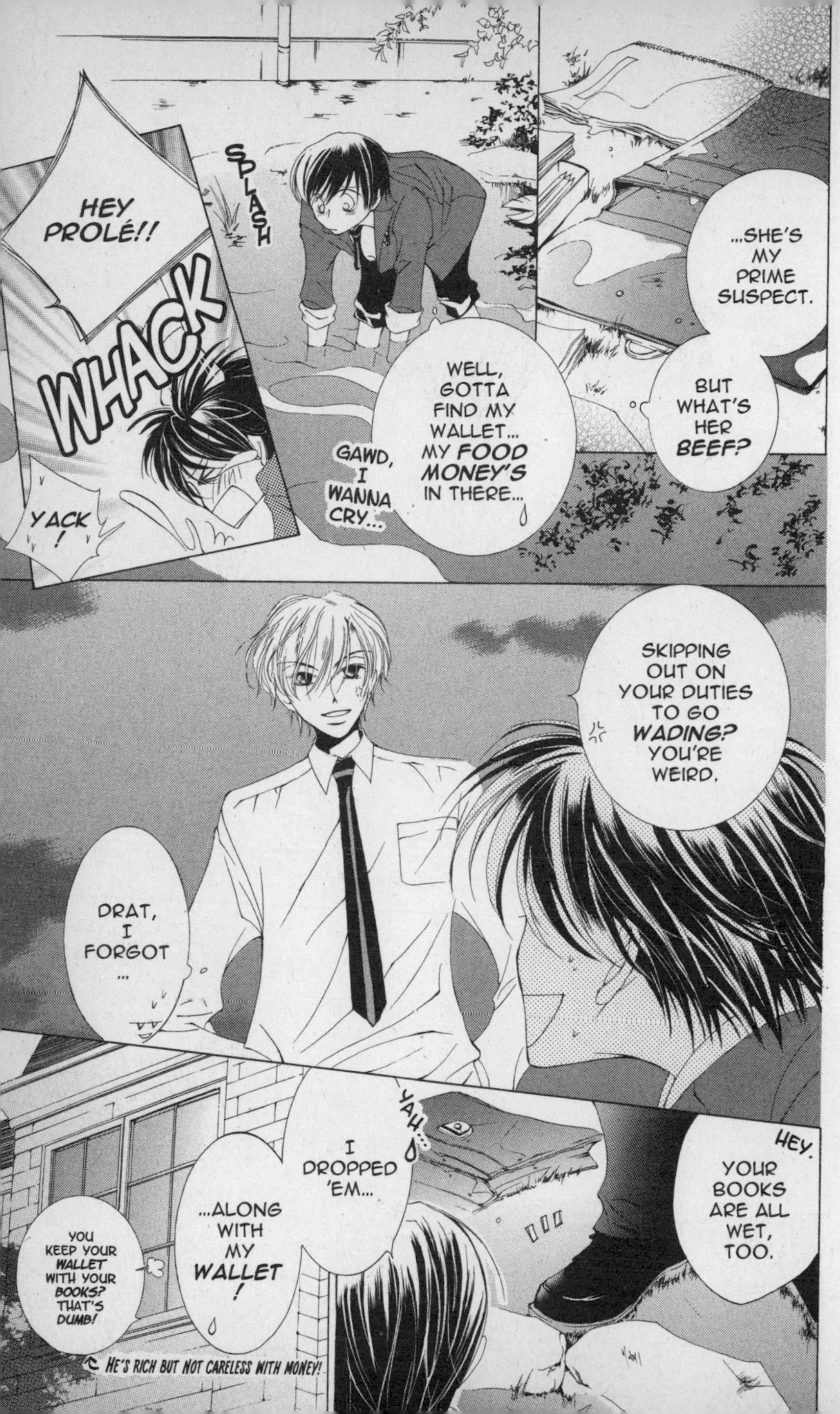
...SHE'S MY PRIME SUSPECT.
BUT WHAT'S HER BEEF?
SPLASH
WELL, GOTTA FIND MY WALLET... MY FOOD MONEY'S IN THERE...
GAWD, I WANNA CRY...
HEY PROLÉ!!
WHACK
YACK!
SKIPPING OUT ON YOUR DUTIES TO GO WADING? YOU'RE WEIRD.
DRAT, I FORGOT...
HEY. YOUR BOOKS ARE ALL WET, TOO.
YAH...
I DROPPED 'EM...
...ALONG WITH MY WALLET!
YOU KEEP YOUR WALLET WITH YOUR BOOKS? THAT'S DUMB!
HE'S RICH BUT NOT CARELESS WITH MONEY!

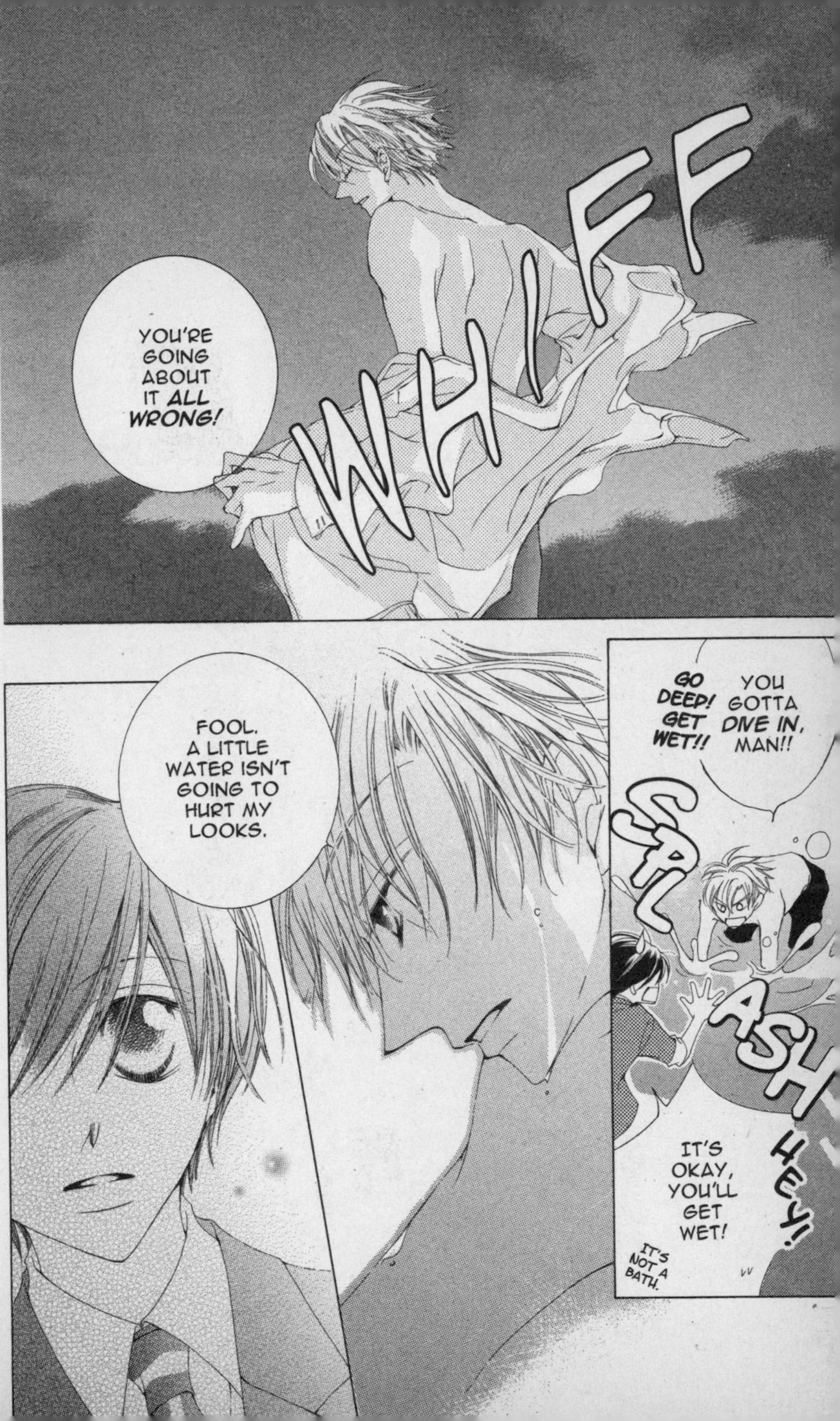
YOU'RE GOING ABOUT IT ALL WRONG!
WHIFF
YOU GOTTA DIVE IN, MAN!!
GO DEEP! GET WET!!
SPLASH
HEY!
IT'S OKAY, YOU'LL GET WET!
IT'S NOT A BATH.
FOOL. A LITTLE WATER ISN'T GOING TO HURT MY LOOKS.

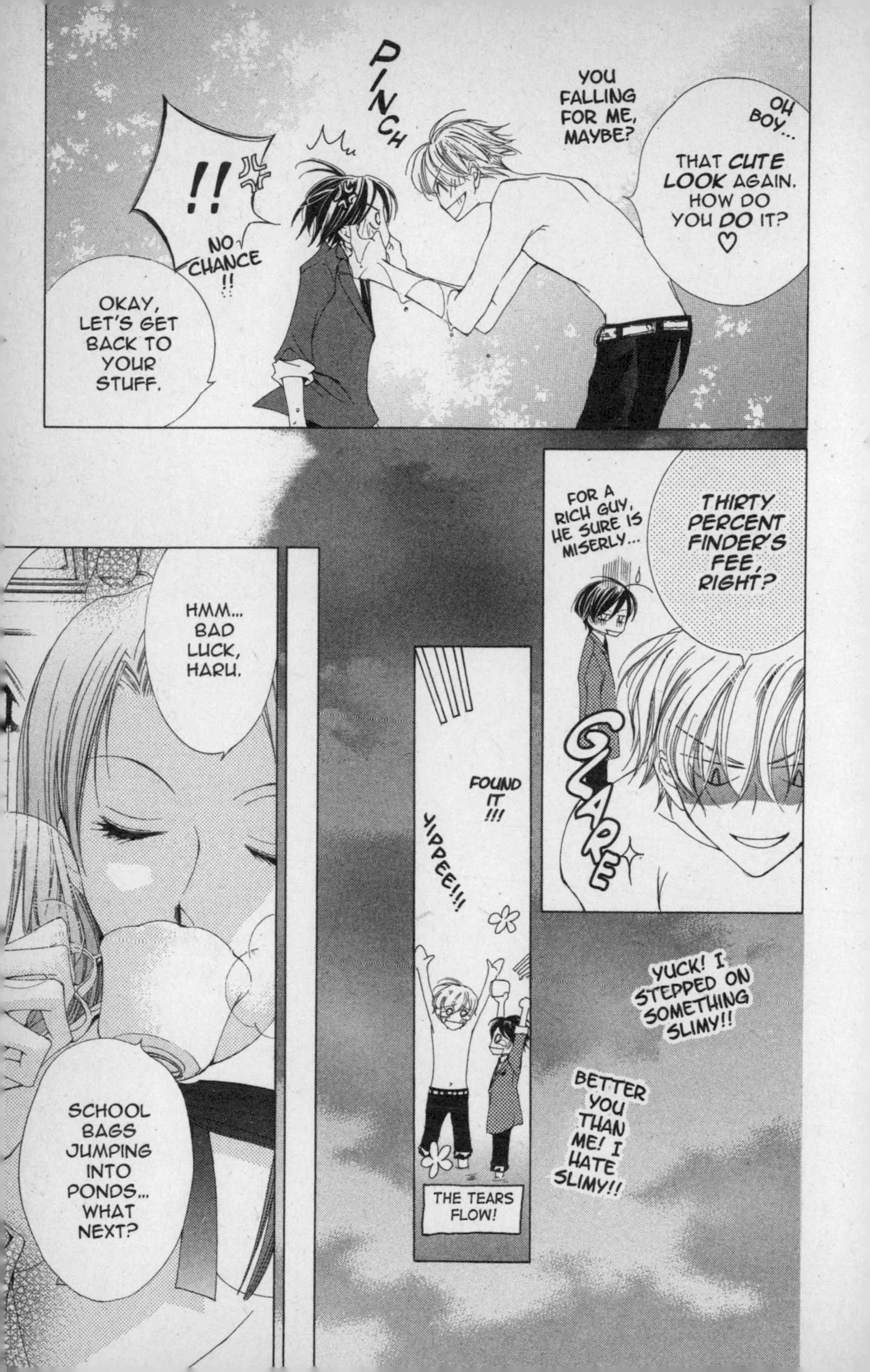
OH BOY...
THAT CUTE LOOK AGAIN. HOW DO YOU DO IT? ♡
YOU FALLING FOR ME, MAYBE?
PINCH
!!
NO CHANCE !!
OKAY, LET'S GET BACK TO YOUR STUFF.
THIRTY PERCENT FINDER'S FEE, RIGHT?
FOR A RICH GUY, HE SURE IS MISERLY...
GLARE
YUCK! I STEPPED ON SOMETHING SLIMY!!
BETTER YOU THAN ME! I HATE SLIMY!!
FOUND IT !!!
YIPPEE!!!
THE TEARS FLOW!
HMM... BAD LUCK, HARU.
SCHOOL BAGS JUMPING INTO PONDS... WHAT NEXT?

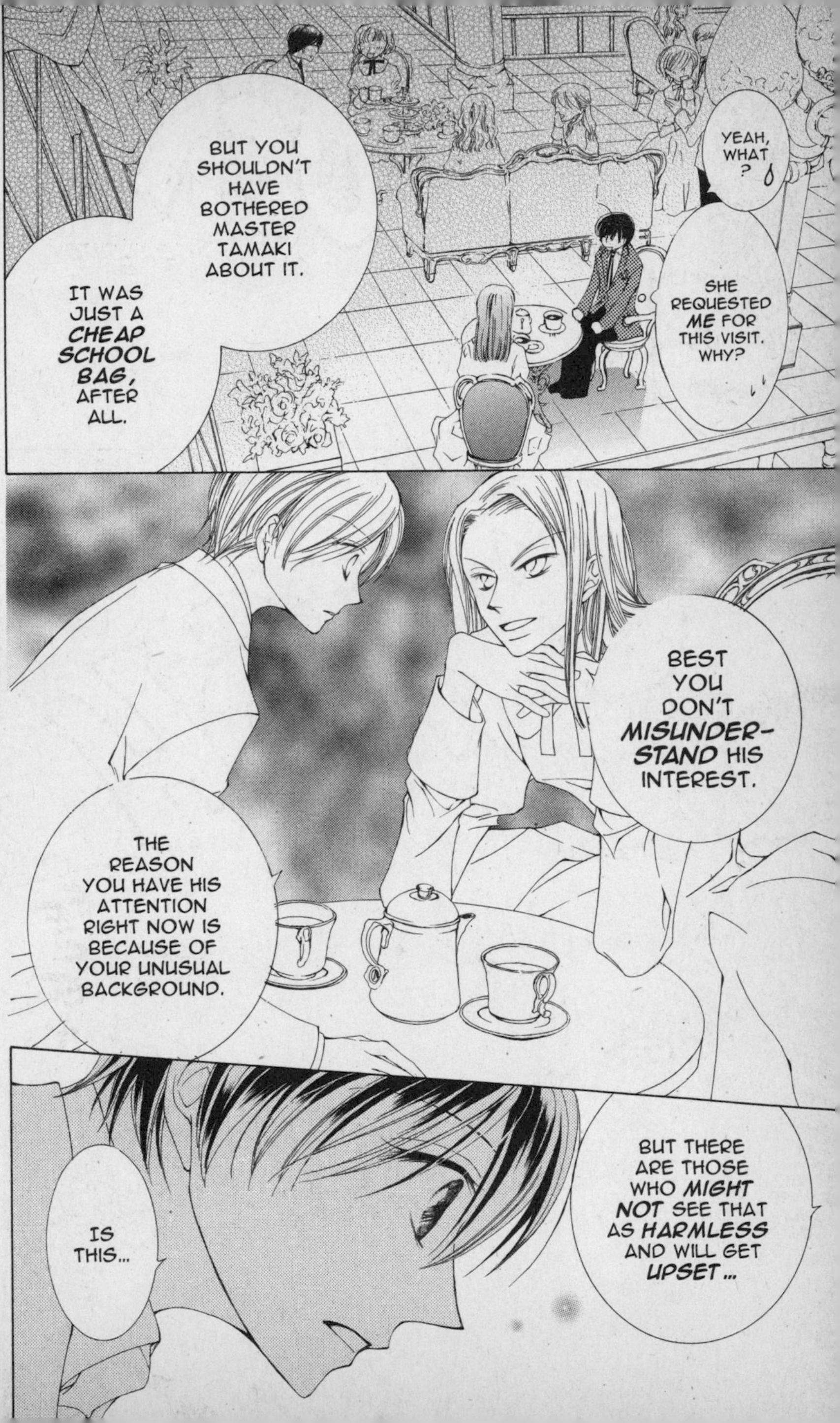
YEAH, WHAT?
SHE REQUESTED *ME* FOR THIS VISIT. WHY?
BUT YOU SHOULDN'T HAVE BOTHERED MASTER TAMAKI ABOUT IT.
IT WAS JUST A ***CHEAP SCHOOL BAG***, AFTER ALL.
BEST YOU DON'T ***MISUNDERSTAND*** HIS INTEREST.
THE REASON YOU HAVE HIS ATTENTION RIGHT NOW IS BECAUSE OF YOUR UNUSUAL BACKGROUND.
BUT THERE ARE THOSE WHO ***MIGHT NOT*** SEE THAT AS ***HARMLESS*** AND WILL GET ***UPSET***...
IS THIS...

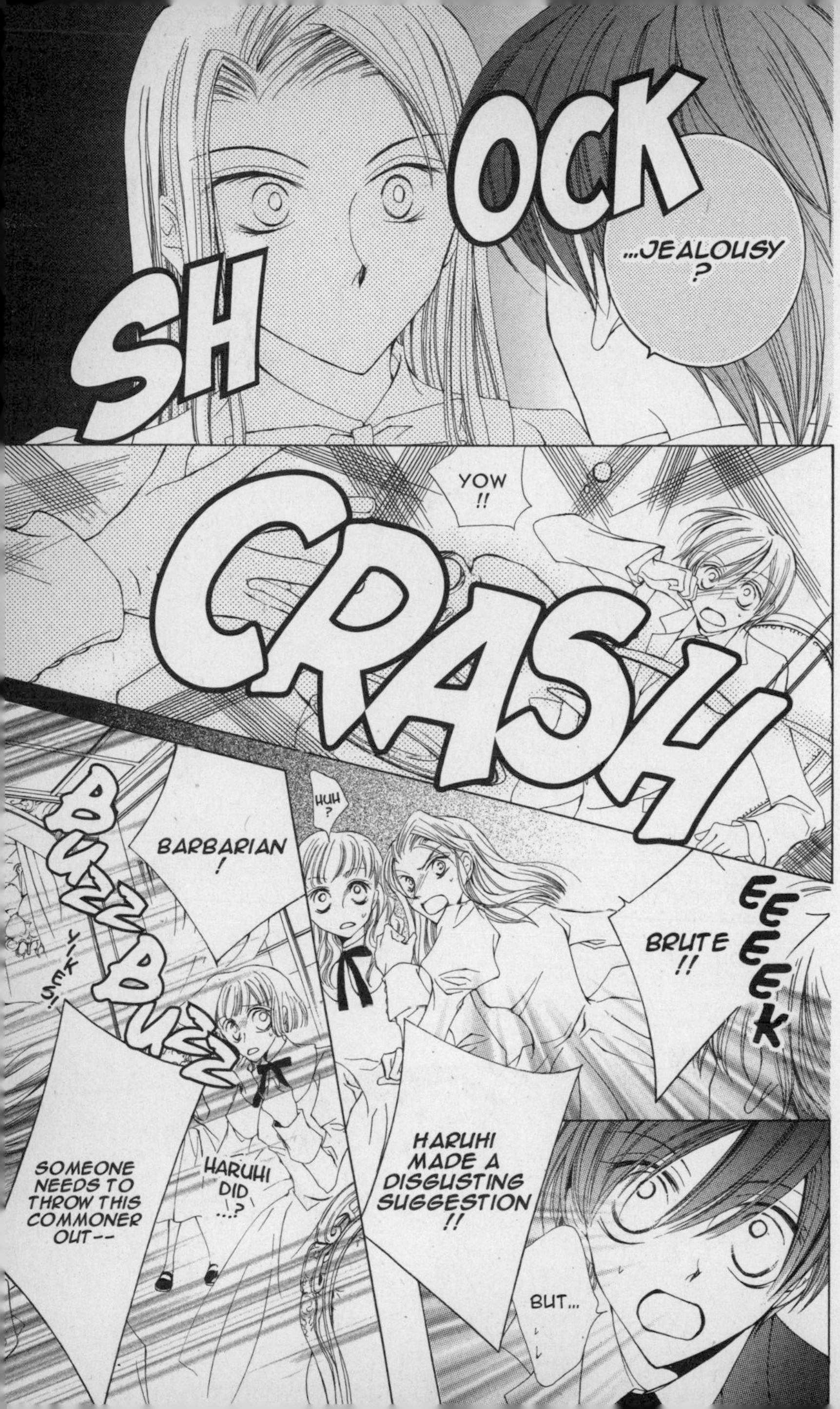
OCK
...JEALOUSY?
SH
YOW!!
CRASH
EEEEEK
BRUTE!!
HUH?
BARBARIAN!
BUZZ BUZZ
YIKES!!
HARUHI MADE A DISGUSTING SUGGESTION!!
HARUHI DID...?
SOMEONE NEEDS TO THROW THIS COMMONER OUT--
BUT...

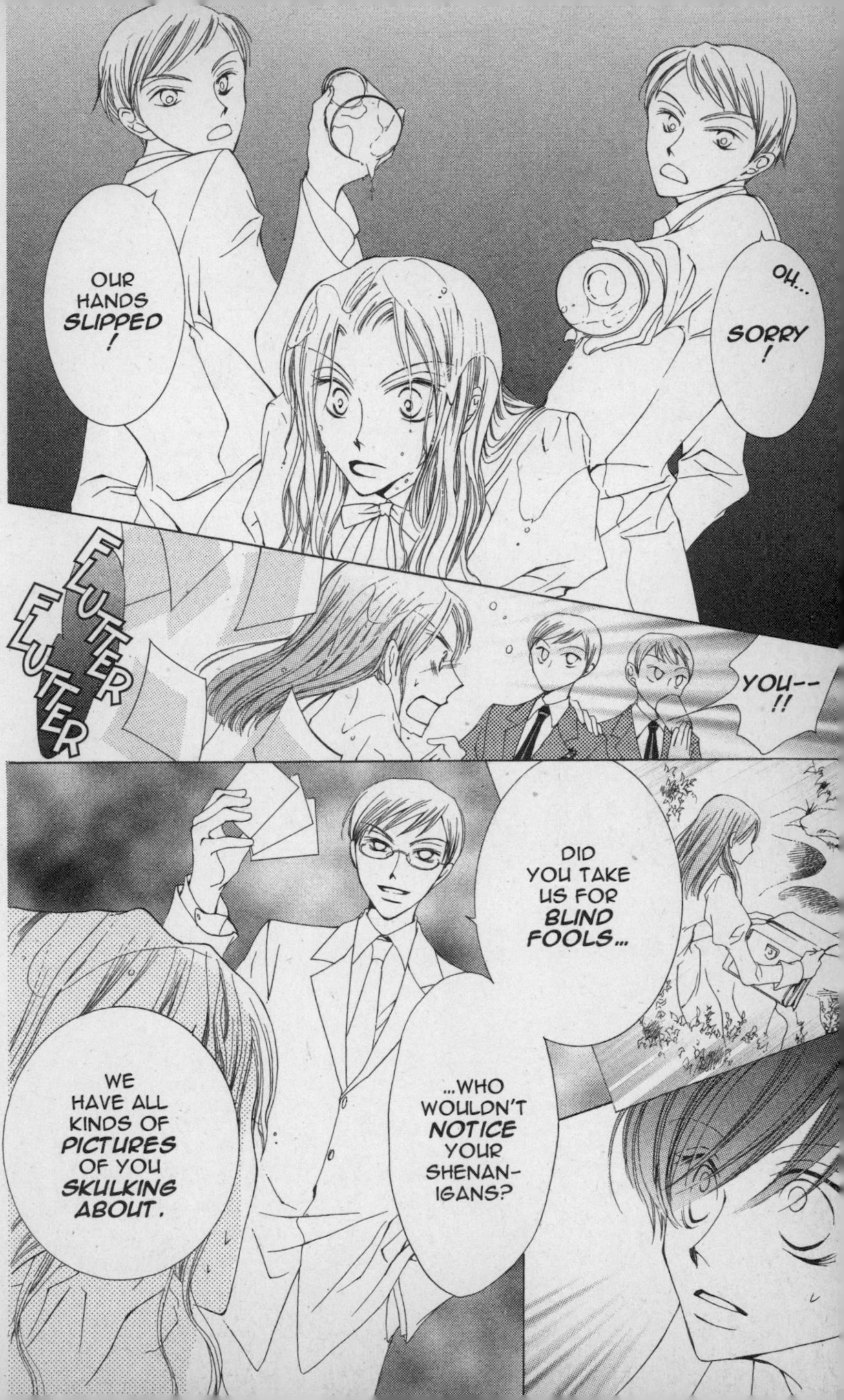
OH... SORRY!
OUR HANDS SLIPPED!
YOU-- !!
FLUTTER FLUTTER
DID YOU TAKE US FOR BLIND FOOLS...
...WHO WOULDN'T NOTICE YOUR SHENAN-IGANS?
WE HAVE ALL KINDS OF PICTURES OF YOU SKULKING ABOUT.

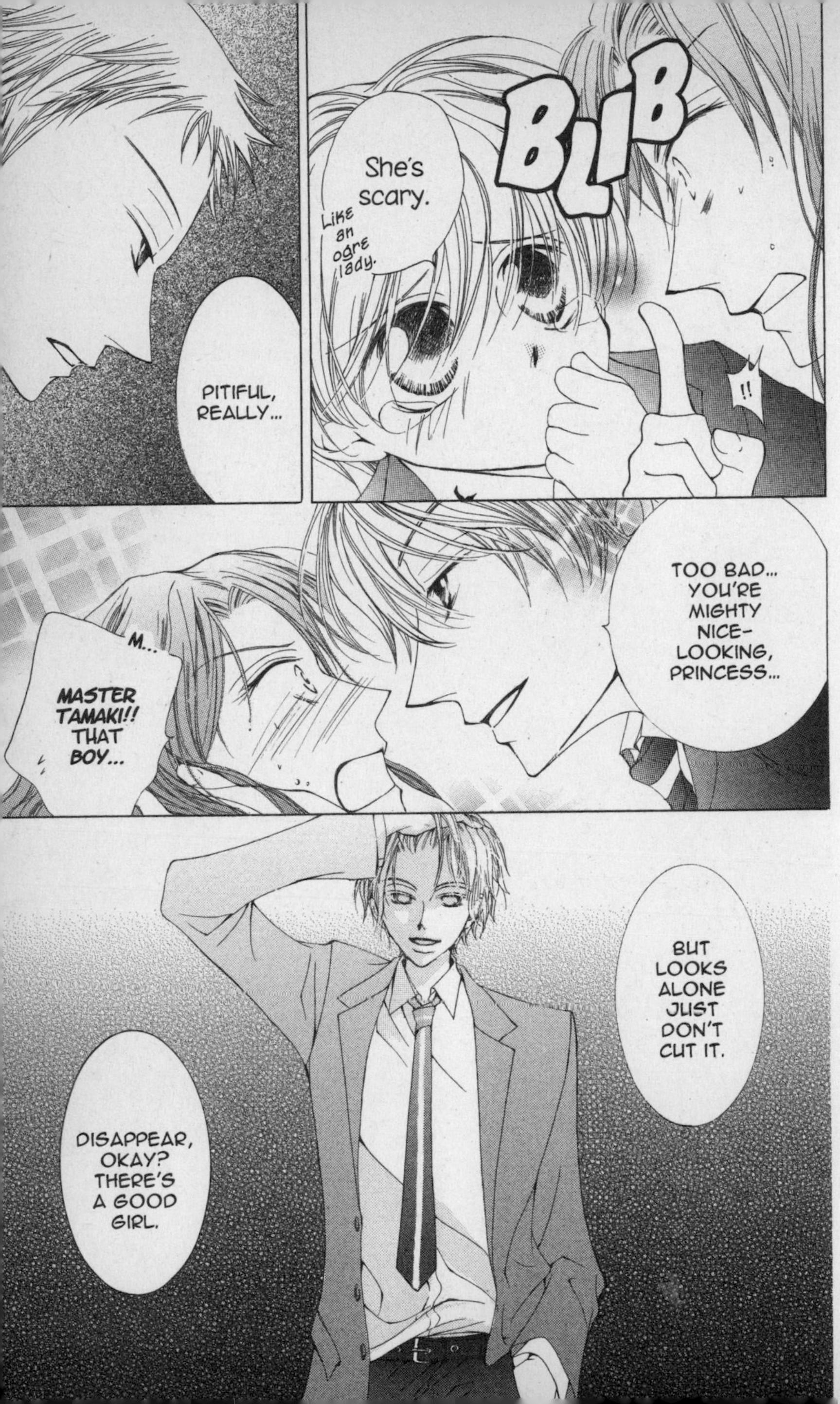
BLIB
She's scary.
Like an ogre lady.
!!
PITIFUL, REALLY...
TOO BAD... YOU'RE MIGHTY NICE-LOOKING, PRINCESS...
M... MASTER TAMAKI!! THAT BOY...
BUT LOOKS ALONE JUST DON'T CUT IT.
DISAPPEAR, OKAY? THERE'S A GOOD GIRL.

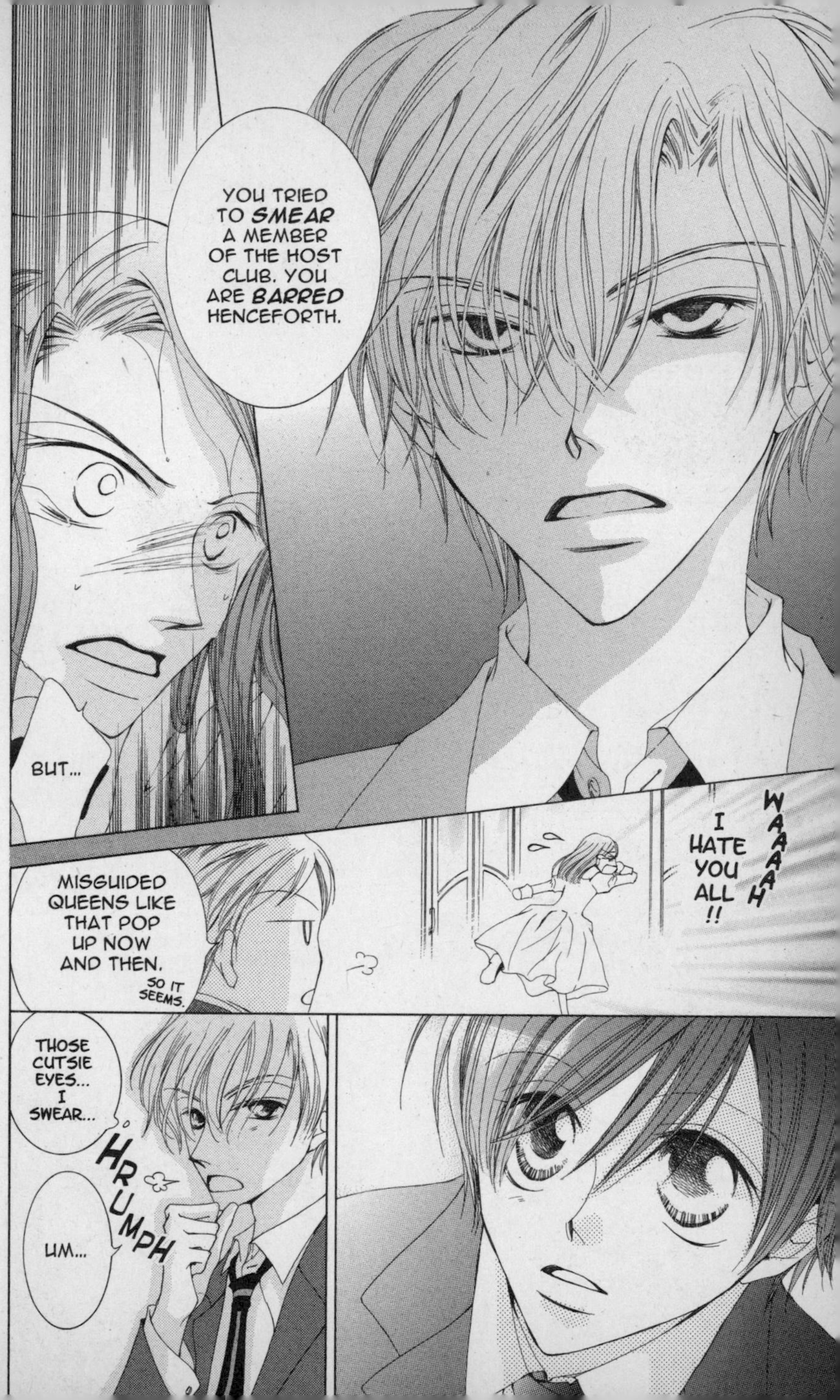
YOU TRIED TO SMEAR A MEMBER OF THE HOST CLUB. YOU ARE BARRED HENCEFORTH.
BUT...
WAAAAAH
I HATE YOU ALL!!
MISGUIDED QUEENS LIKE THAT POP UP NOW AND THEN.
SO IT SEEMS.
THOSE CUTSIE EYES... I SWEAR...
HRUMPH
UM...

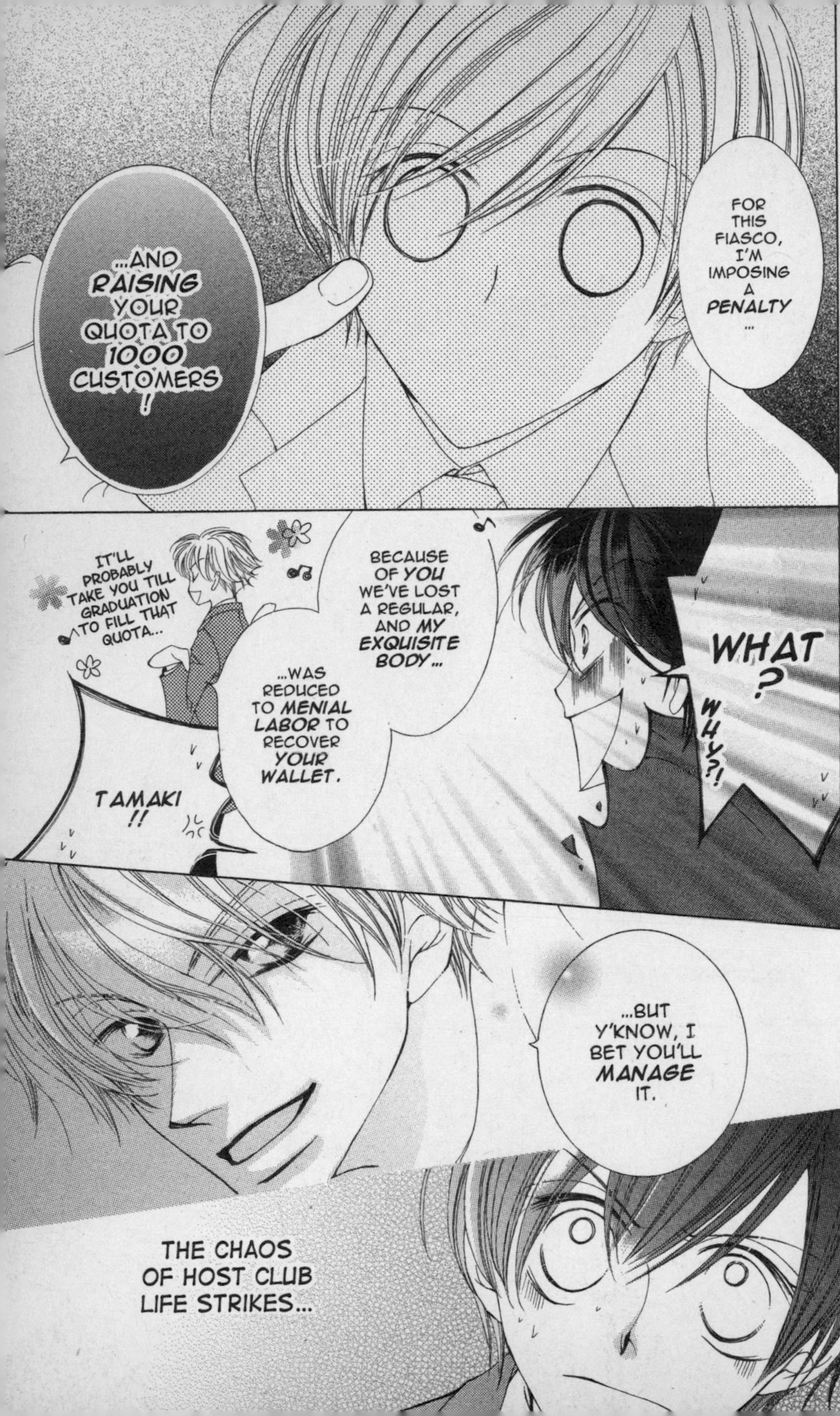
FOR THIS FIASCO, I'M IMPOSING A PENALTY...
...AND RAISING YOUR QUOTA TO 1000 CUSTOMERS!
WHAT?
WHY?!
BECAUSE OF YOU WE'VE LOST A REGULAR, AND MY EXQUISITE BODY...
...WAS REDUCED TO MENIAL LABOR TO RECOVER YOUR WALLET.
IT'LL PROBABLY TAKE YOU TILL GRADUATION TO FILL THAT QUOTA...
TAMAKI!!
...BUT Y'KNOW, I BET YOU'LL MANAGE IT.
THE CHAOS OF HOST CLUB LIFE STRIKES...

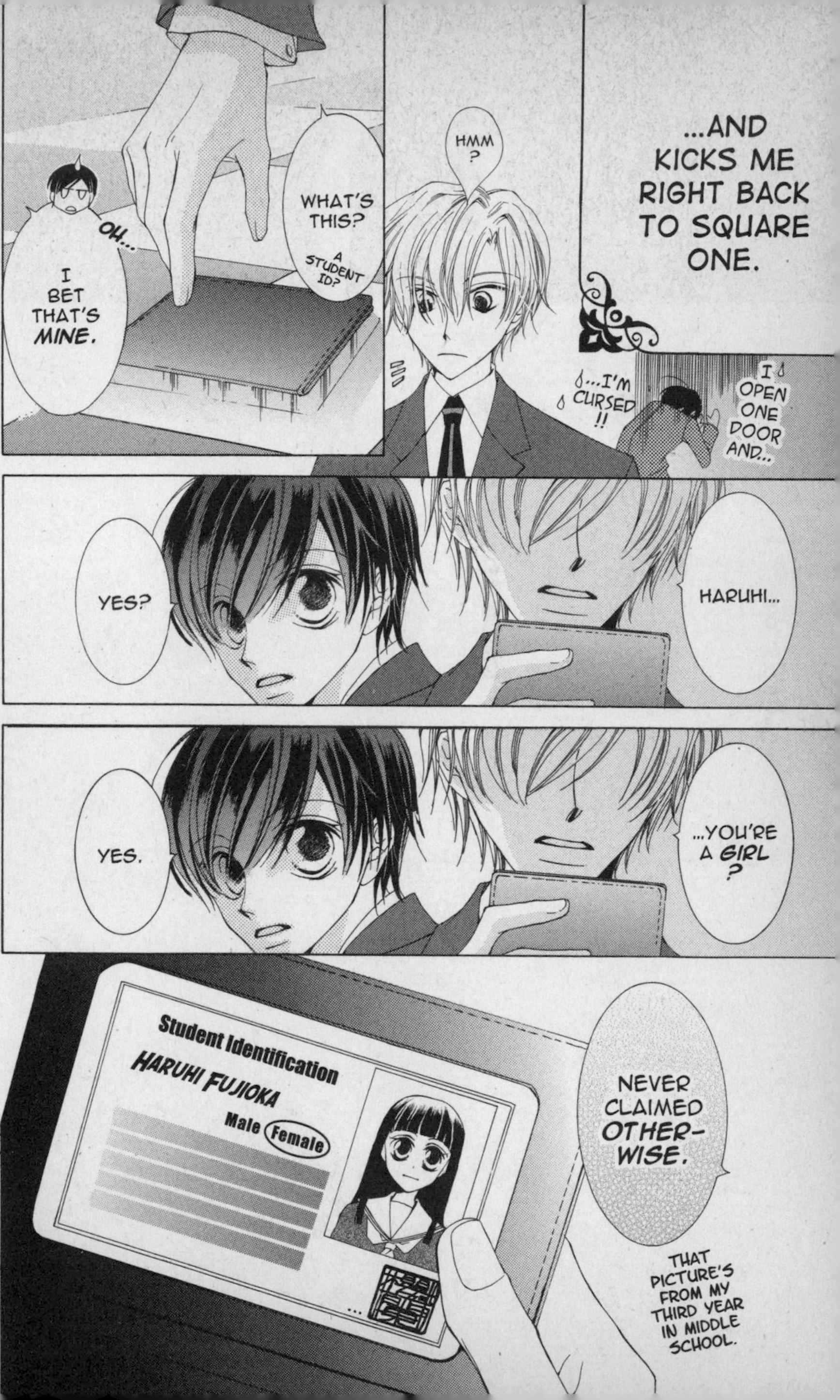
...AND KICKS ME RIGHT BACK TO SQUARE ONE.
I OPEN ONE DOOR AND...
...I'M CURSED!!
HMM?
WHAT'S THIS?
A STUDENT ID?
OH...
I BET THAT'S MINE.
HARUHI...
YES?
...YOU'RE A GIRL?
YES.
Student Identification
HARUHI FUJIOKA
Male Female
NEVER CLAIMED OTHERWISE.
THAT PICTURE'S FROM MY THIRD YEAR IN MIDDLE SCHOOL.

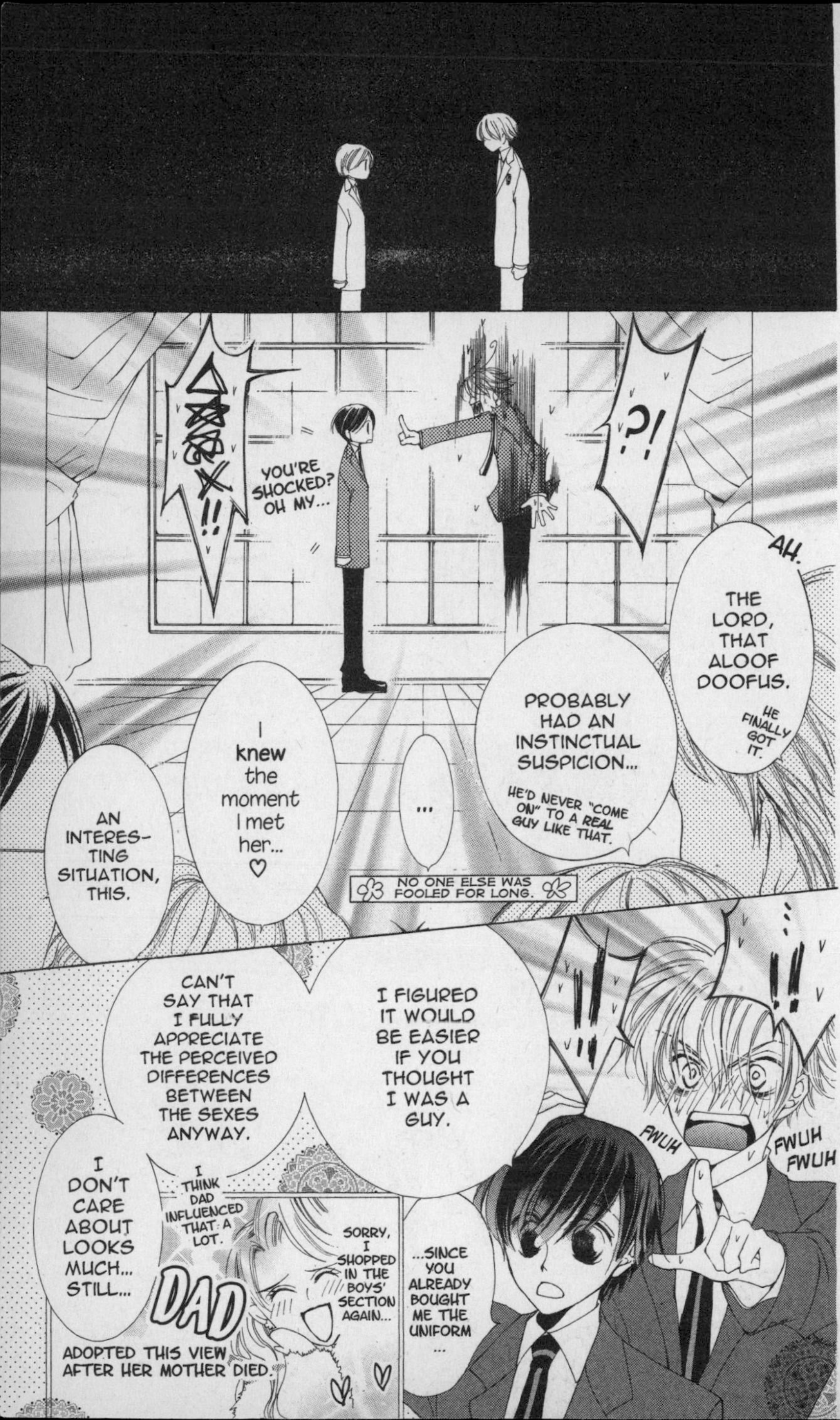
?!
YOU'RE SHOCKED? OH MY...
AH.
THE LORD, THAT ALOOF DOOFUS.
HE FINALLY GOT IT.
PROBABLY HAD AN INSTINCTUAL SUSPICION...
HE'D NEVER "COME ON" TO A REAL GUY LIKE THAT.
...
I knew the moment I met her... ♡
AN INTERESTING SITUATION, THIS.
NO ONE ELSE WAS FOOLED FOR LONG.
!!
FWUH FWUH FWUH
I FIGURED IT WOULD BE EASIER IF YOU THOUGHT I WAS A GUY.
CAN'T SAY THAT I FULLY APPRECIATE THE PERCEIVED DIFFERENCES BETWEEN THE SEXES ANYWAY.
...SINCE YOU ALREADY BOUGHT ME THE UNIFORM ...
SORRY, I SHOPPED IN THE BOYS' SECTION AGAIN...
I DON'T CARE ABOUT LOOKS MUCH... STILL...
I THINK DAD INFLUENCED THAT A LOT.
DAD
ADOPTED THIS VIEW AFTER HER MOTHER DIED.

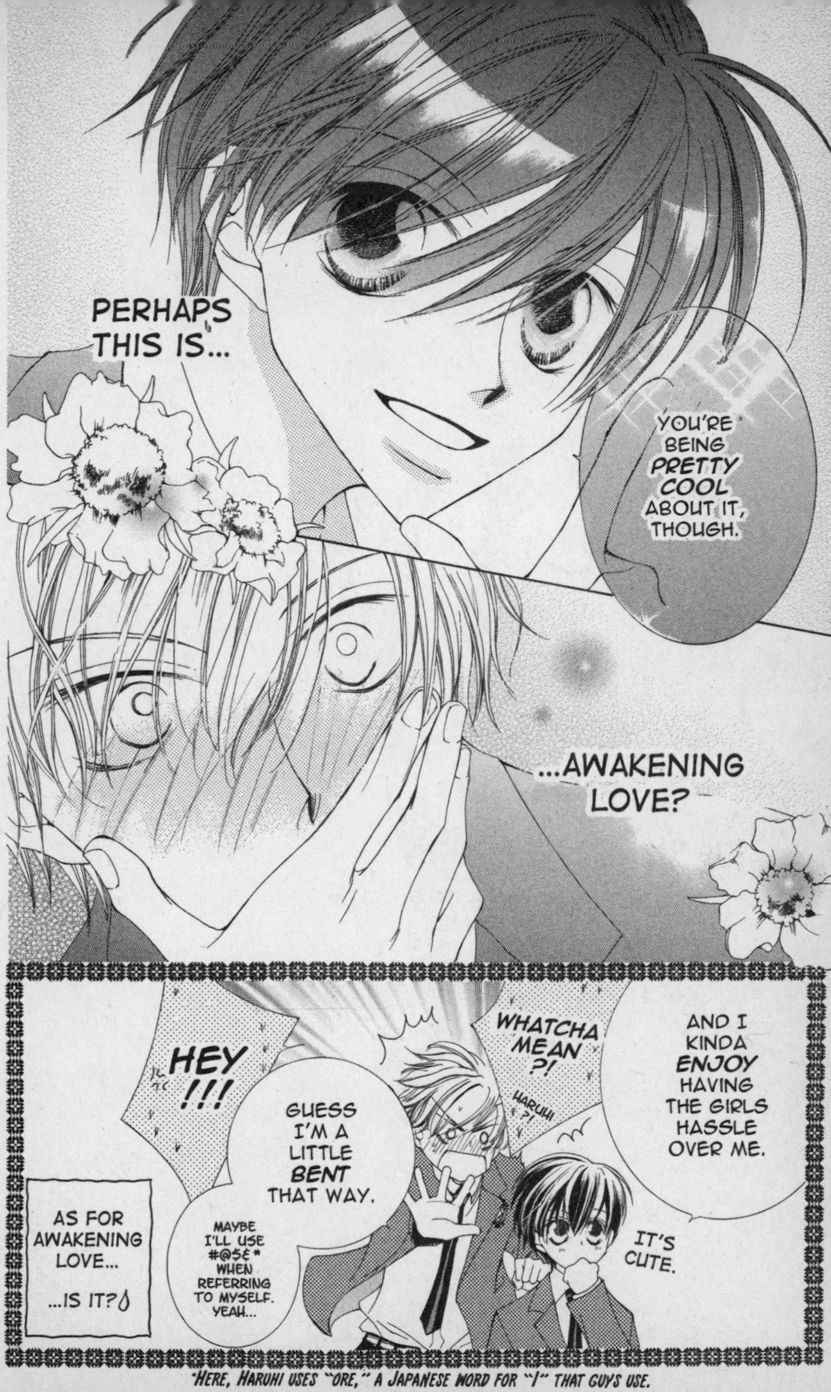
YOU'RE BEING PRETTY COOL ABOUT IT, THOUGH.
PERHAPS THIS IS...
...AWAKENING LOVE?
AND I KINDA ENJOY HAVING THE GIRLS HASSLE OVER ME.
IT'S CUTE.
WHATCHA MEAN ?!
HARUHI ?!
GUESS I'M A LITTLE BENT THAT WAY.
MAYBE I'LL USE #@$&* WHEN REFERRING TO MYSELF. YEAH...
HEY !!!
AS FOR AWAKENING LOVE...
...IS IT?

*Here, Haruhi uses "ore," a Japanese word for "I" that guys use.

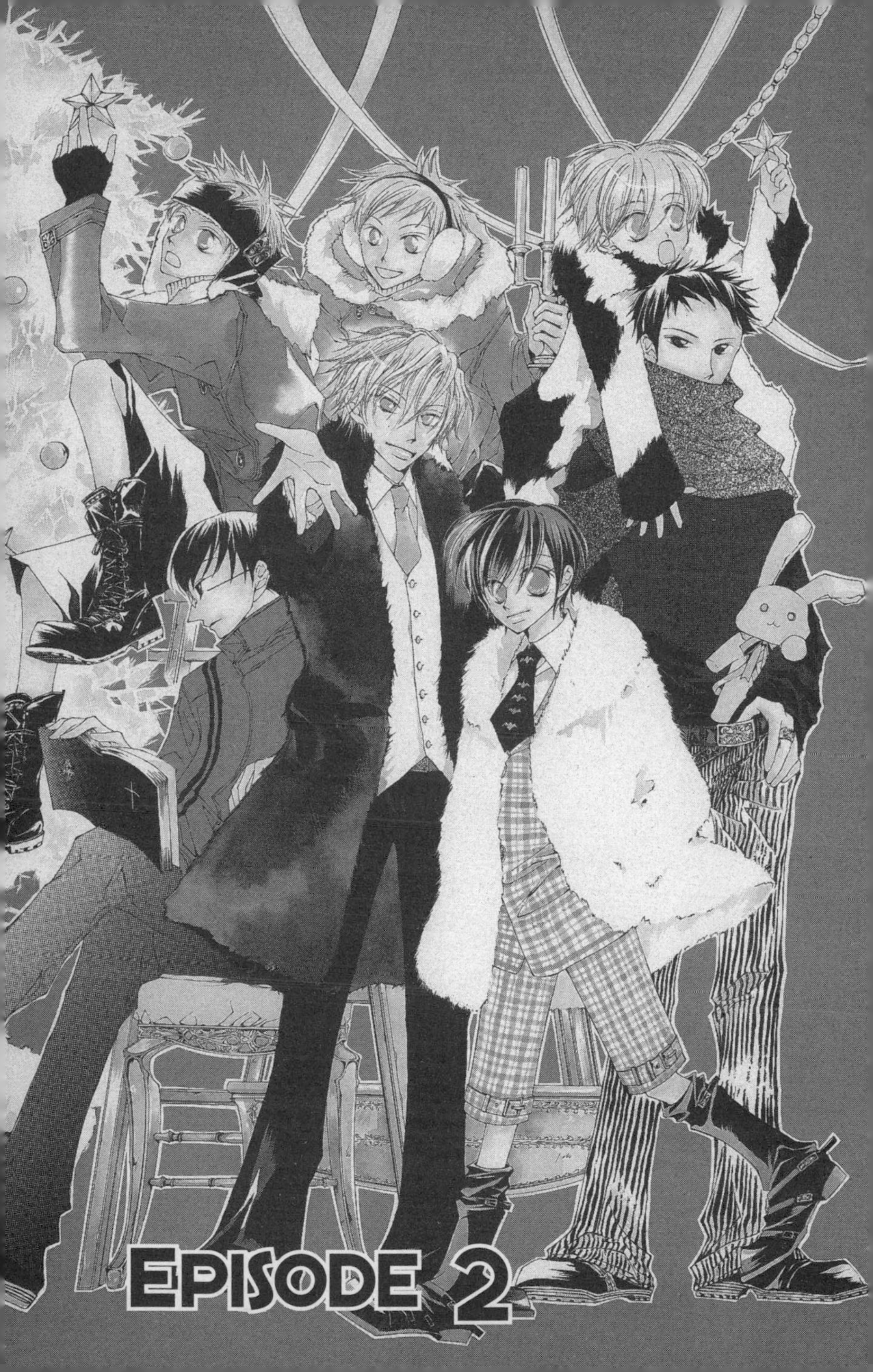
EPISODE 2

Preview Manga

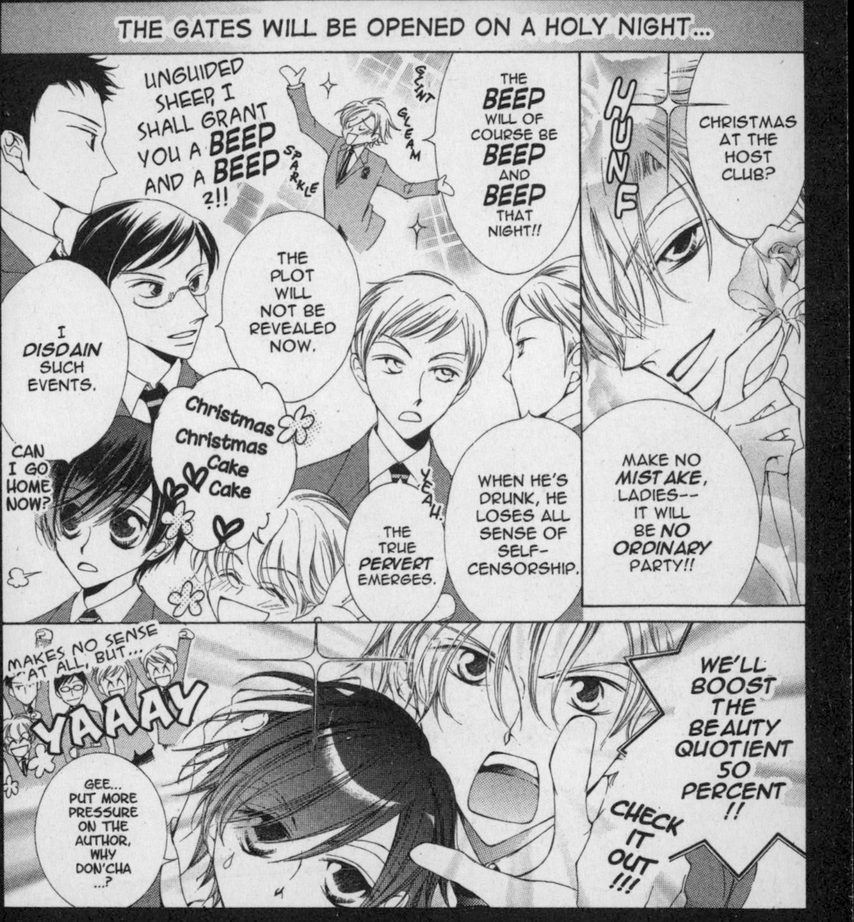
THE GATES WILL BE OPENED ON A HOLY NIGHT...
HUNF
CHRISTMAS AT THE HOST CLUB?
MAKE NO MISTAKE, LADIES-- IT WILL BE NO ORDINARY PARTY!!
GLINT
GLEAM
THE BEEP WILL OF COURSE BE BEEP AND BEEP THAT NIGHT!!
UNGUIDED SHEEP, I SHALL GRANT YOU A BEEP AND A BEEP ?!!
SPARKLE
THE PLOT WILL NOT BE REVEALED NOW.
WHEN HE'S DRUNK, HE LOSES ALL SENSE OF SELF-CENSORSHIP.
YEAH.
THE TRUE PERVERT EMERGES.
Christmas Christmas Cake Cake
I DISDAIN SUCH EVENTS.
CAN I GO HOME NOW?
WE'LL BOOST THE BEAUTY QUOTIENT 50 PERCENT !!
CHECK IT OUT !!!
MAKES NO SENSE AT ALL, BUT...
YAAAY
GEE... PUT MORE PRESSURE ON THE AUTHOR, WHY DON'CHA ...?

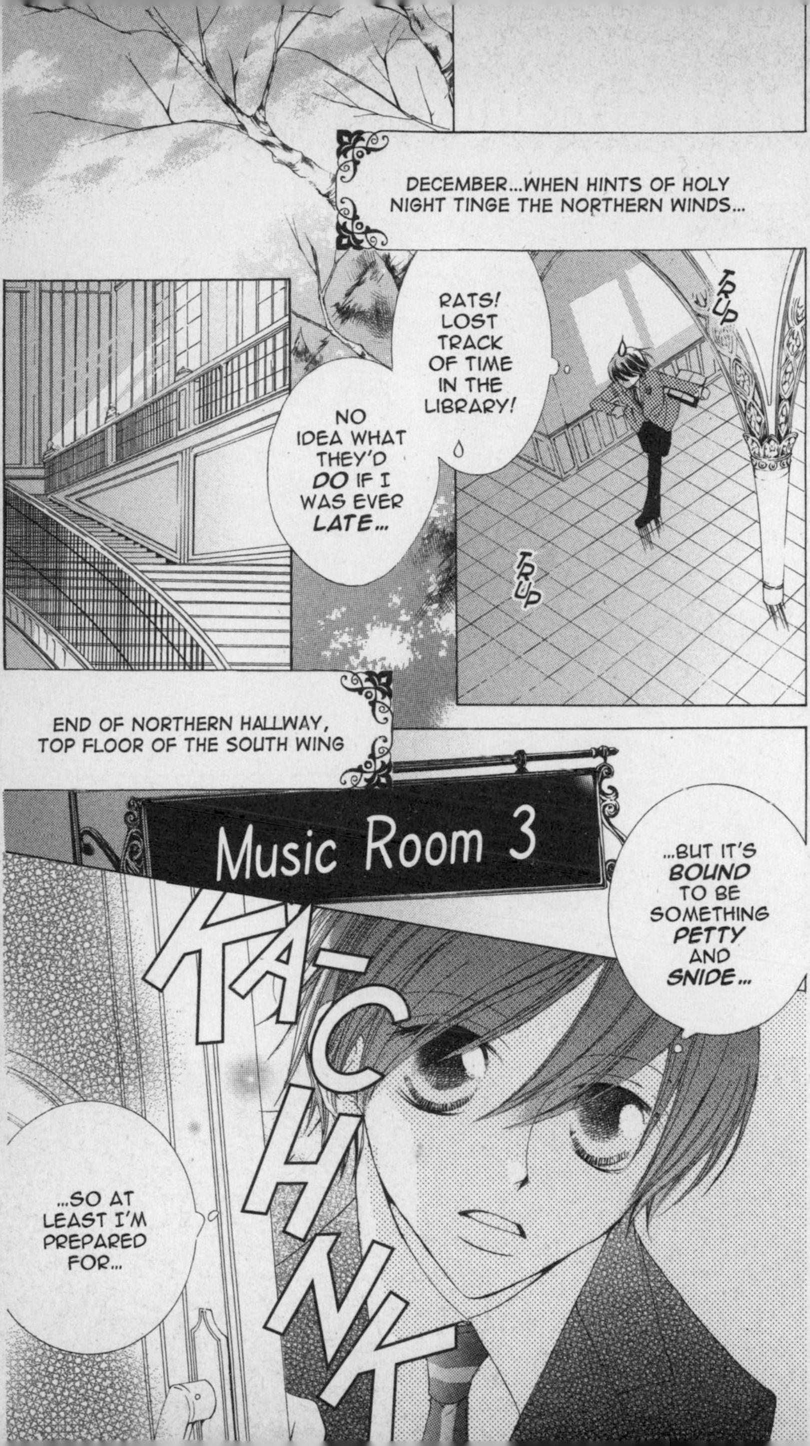
DECEMBER...WHEN HINTS OF HOLY NIGHT TINGE THE NORTHERN WINDS...
TRUP
RATS! LOST TRACK OF TIME IN THE LIBRARY!
NO IDEA WHAT THEY'D DO IF I WAS EVER LATE...
TRUP
END OF NORTHERN HALLWAY, TOP FLOOR OF THE SOUTH WING
Music Room 3
...BUT IT'S BOUND TO BE SOMETHING PETTY AND SNIDE...
KA-CHNK
...SO AT LEAST I'M PREPARED FOR...

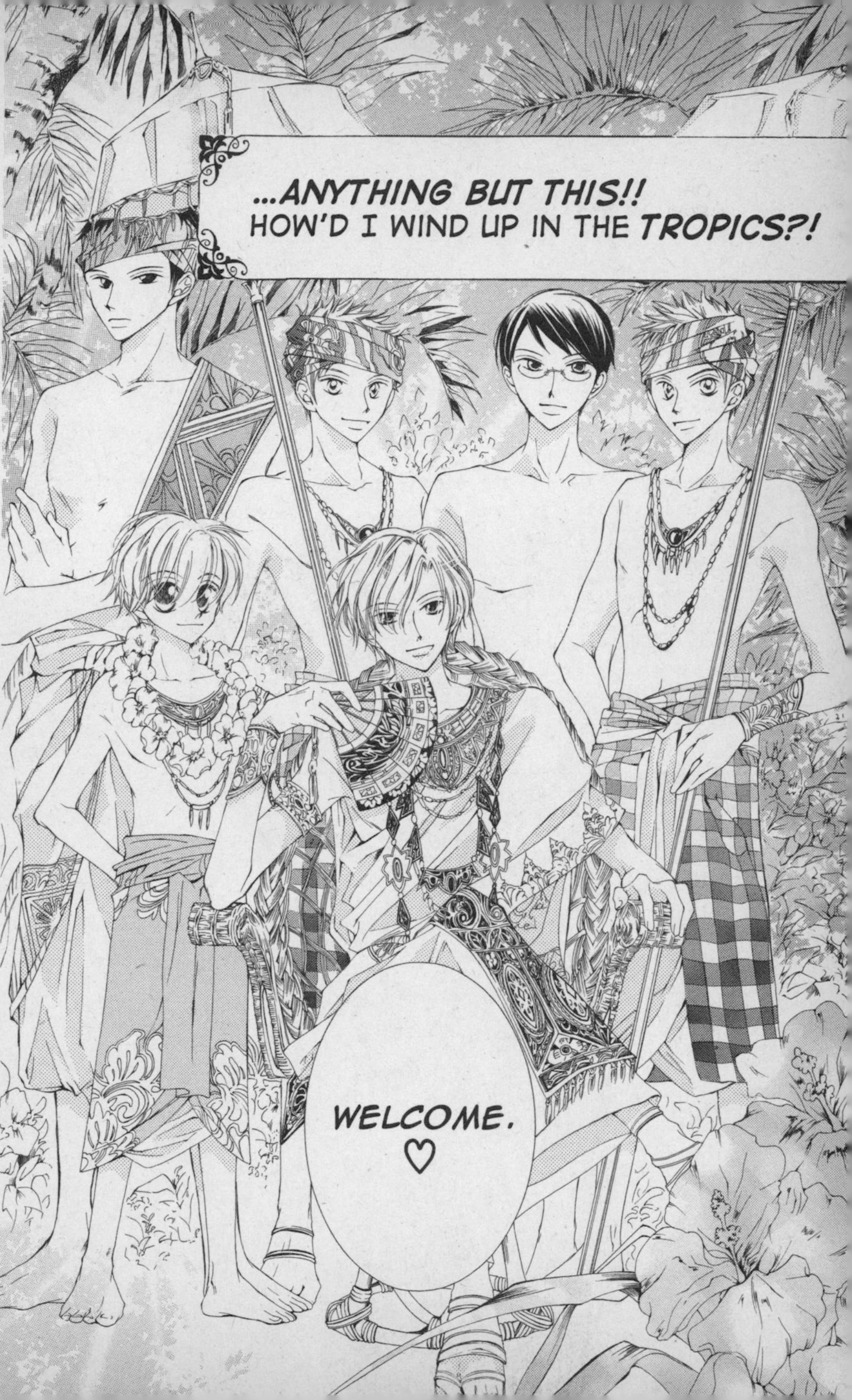
...ANYTHING BUT THIS!!
HOW'D I WIND UP IN THE TROPICS?!
WELCOME. ♡

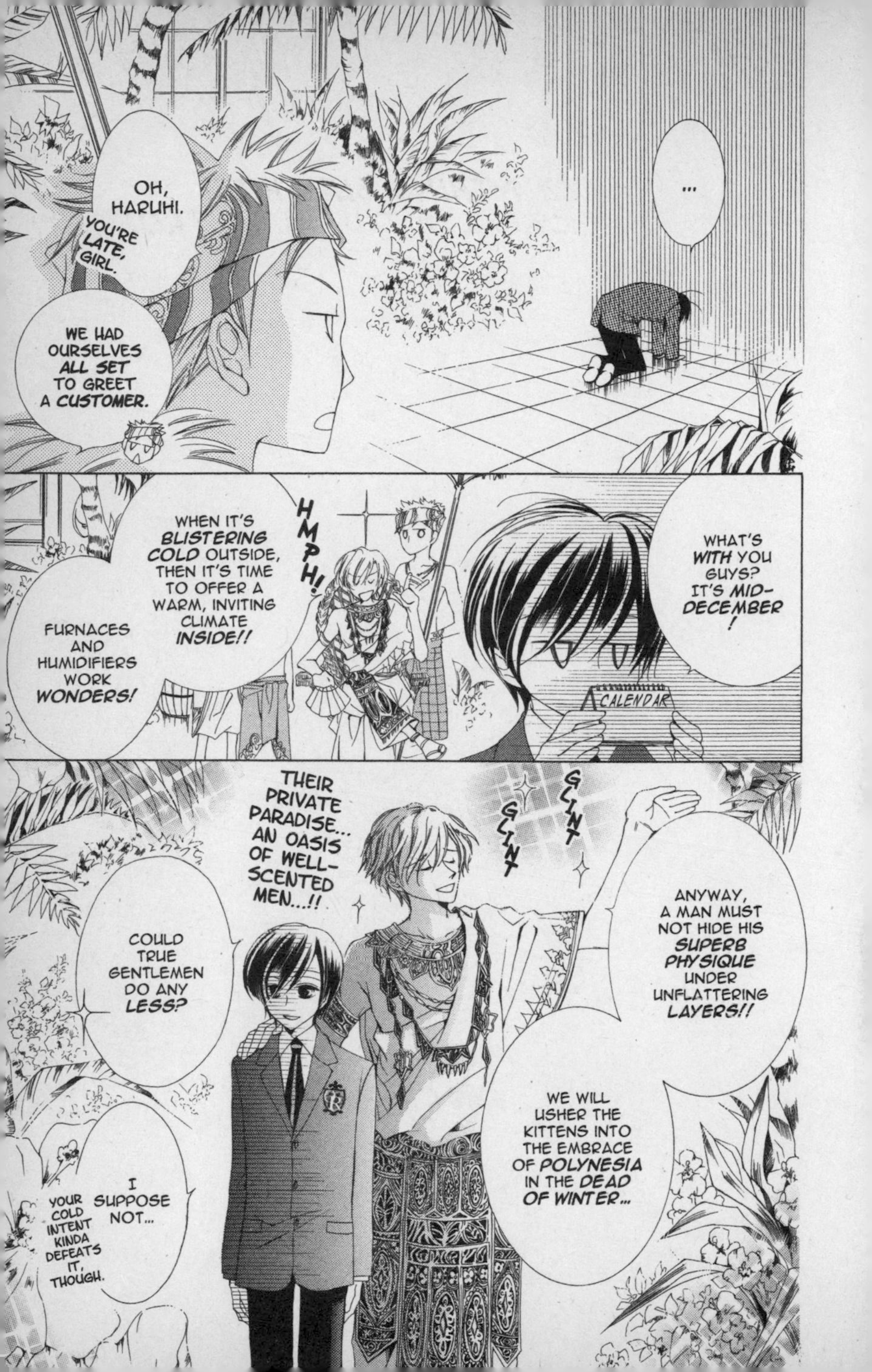
...
OH, HARUHI.
YOU'RE LATE, GIRL.
WE HAD OURSELVES ALL SET TO GREET A CUSTOMER.
WHAT'S WITH YOU GUYS? IT'S MID-DECEMBER!
CALENDAR
HMPH!
WHEN IT'S BLISTERING COLD OUTSIDE, THEN IT'S TIME TO OFFER A WARM, INVITING CLIMATE INSIDE!!
FURNACES AND HUMIDIFIERS WORK WONDERS!
ANYWAY, A MAN MUST NOT HIDE HIS SUPERB PHYSIQUE UNDER UNFLATTERING LAYERS!!
WE WILL USHER THE KITTENS INTO THE EMBRACE OF POLYNESIA IN THE DEAD OF WINTER...
GLINT
GLINT
THEIR PRIVATE PARADISE... AN OASIS OF WELL-SCENTED MEN...!!
COULD TRUE GENTLEMEN DO ANY LESS?
I SUPPOSE NOT...
YOUR COLD INTENT KINDA DEFEATS IT, THOUGH.

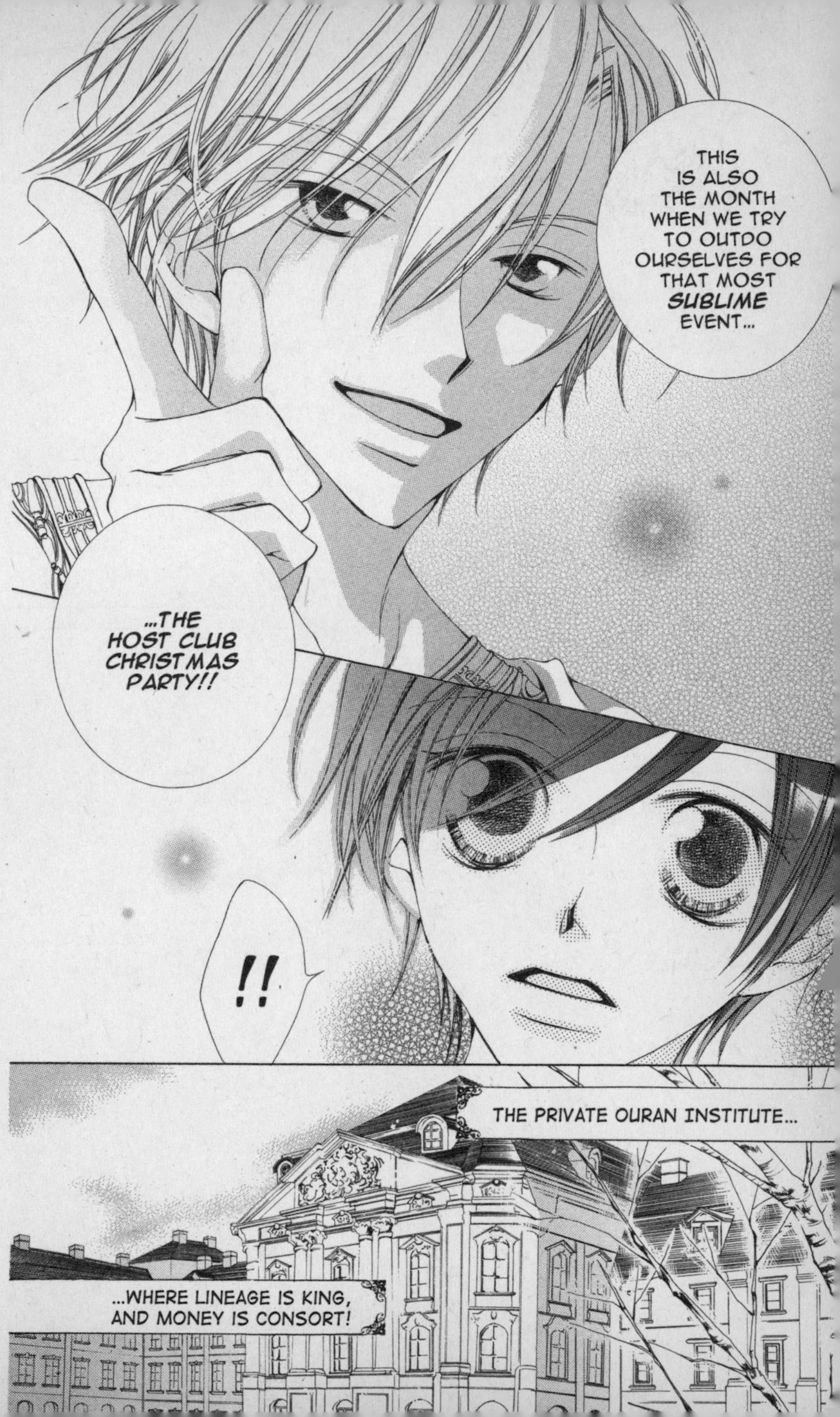
THIS IS ALSO THE MONTH WHEN WE TRY TO OUTDO OURSELVES FOR THAT MOST ***SUBLIME*** EVENT...
...THE HOST CLUB CHRISTMAS PARTY!!
!!
THE PRIVATE OURAN INSTITUTE...
...WHERE LINEAGE IS KING, AND MONEY IS CONSORT!

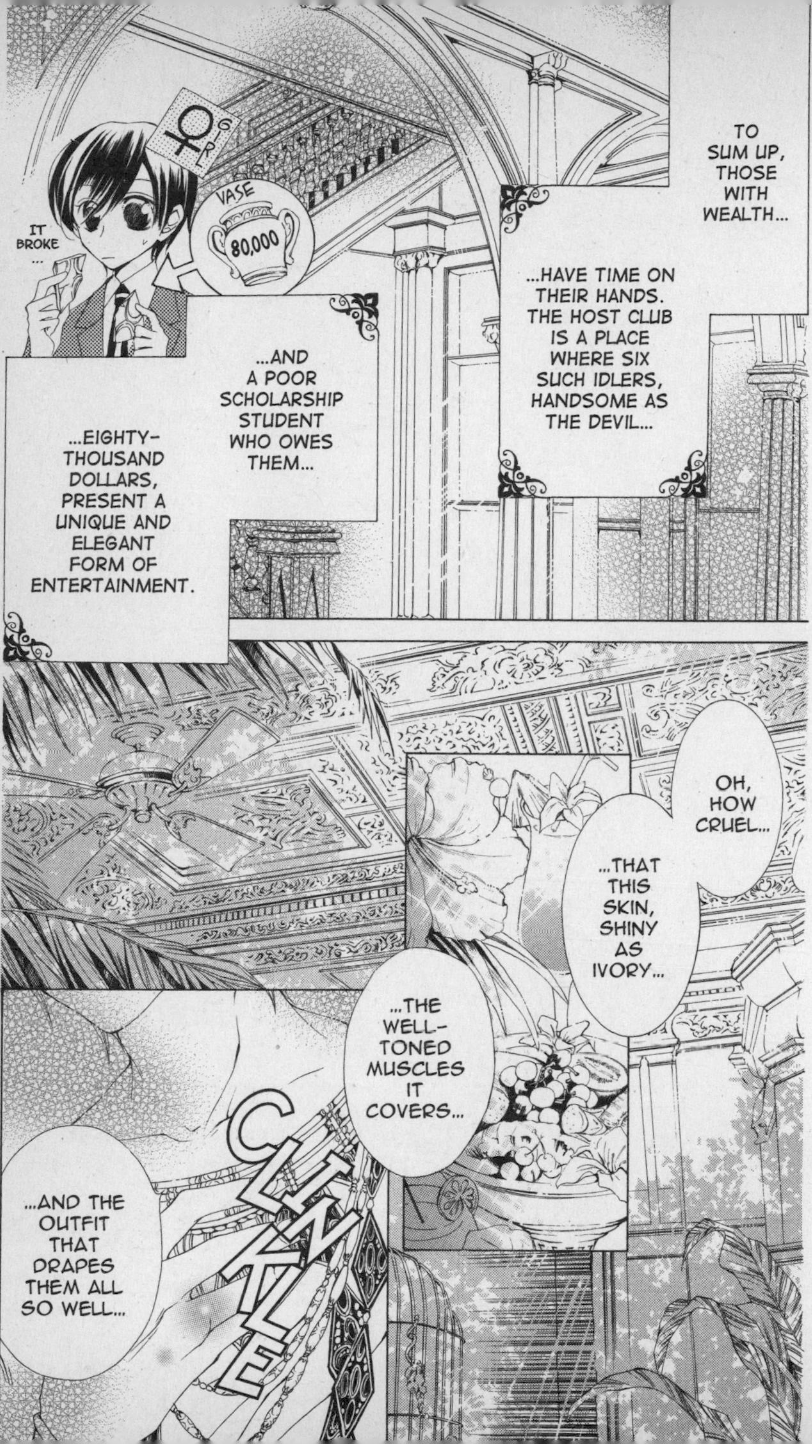
TO SUM UP, THOSE WITH WEALTH...
...HAVE TIME ON THEIR HANDS. THE HOST CLUB IS A PLACE WHERE SIX SUCH IDLERS, HANDSOME AS THE DEVIL...
...AND A POOR SCHOLARSHIP STUDENT WHO OWES THEM...
GIRL
VASE
80,000
IT BROKE...
...EIGHTY-THOUSAND DOLLARS, PRESENT A UNIQUE AND ELEGANT FORM OF ENTERTAINMENT.
OH, HOW CRUEL...
...THAT THIS SKIN, SHINY AS IVORY...
...THE WELL-TONED MUSCLES IT COVERS...
CLINKLE
...AND THE OUTFIT THAT DRAPES THEM ALL SO WELL...

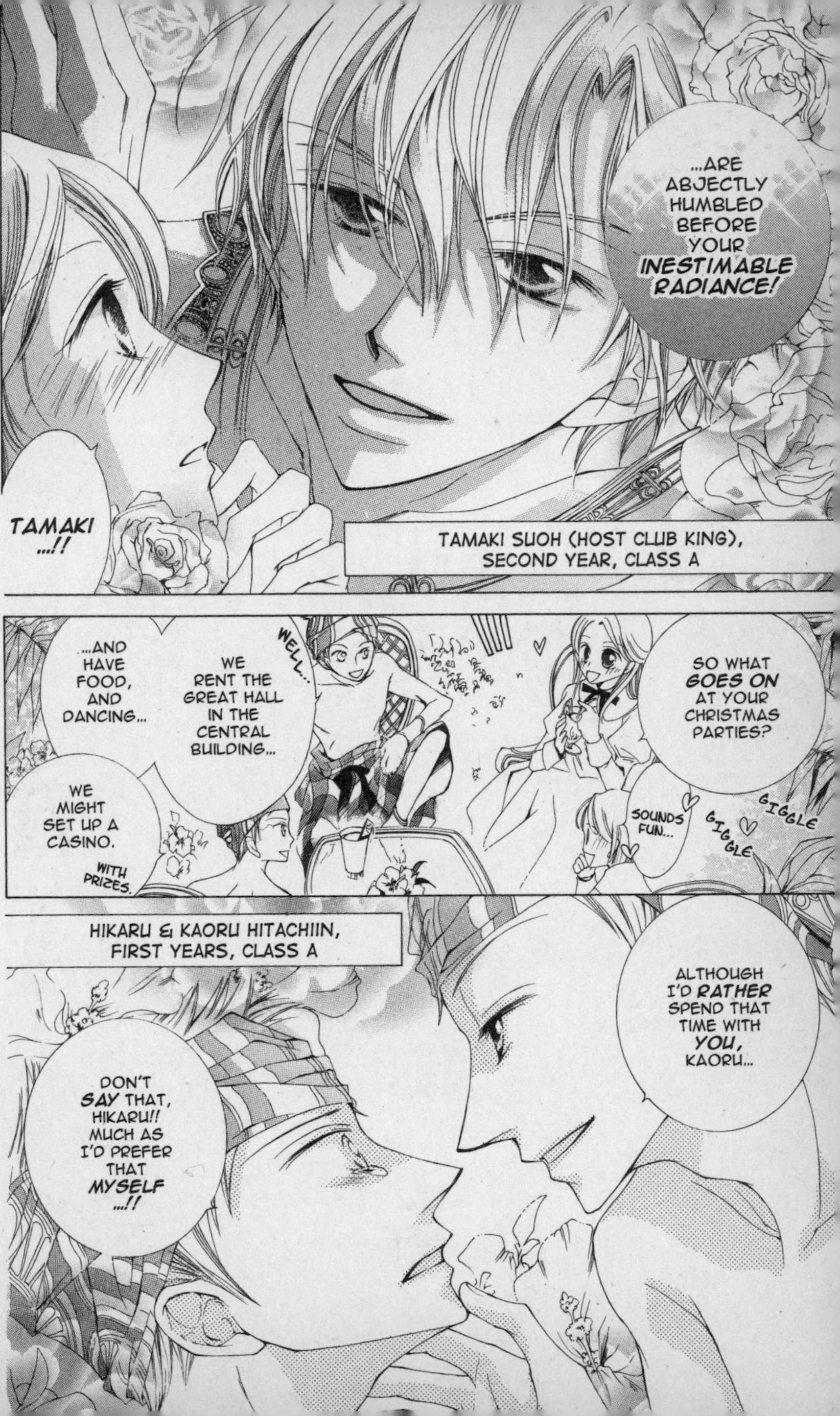
...ARE ABJECTLY HUMBLED BEFORE YOUR INESTIMABLE RADIANCE!
TAMAKI ...!!
TAMAKI SUOH (HOST CLUB KING), SECOND YEAR, CLASS A
SO WHAT GOES ON AT YOUR CHRISTMAS PARTIES?
SOUNDS FUN...
GIGGLE
GIGGLE
WELL...
WE RENT THE GREAT HALL IN THE CENTRAL BUILDING...
...AND HAVE FOOD, AND DANCING...
WE MIGHT SET UP A CASINO.
WITH PRIZES.
HIKARU & KAORU HITACHIIN, FIRST YEARS, CLASS A
ALTHOUGH I'D RATHER SPEND THAT TIME WITH YOU, KAORU...
DON'T SAY THAT, HIKARU!! MUCH AS I'D PREFER THAT MYSELF ...!!

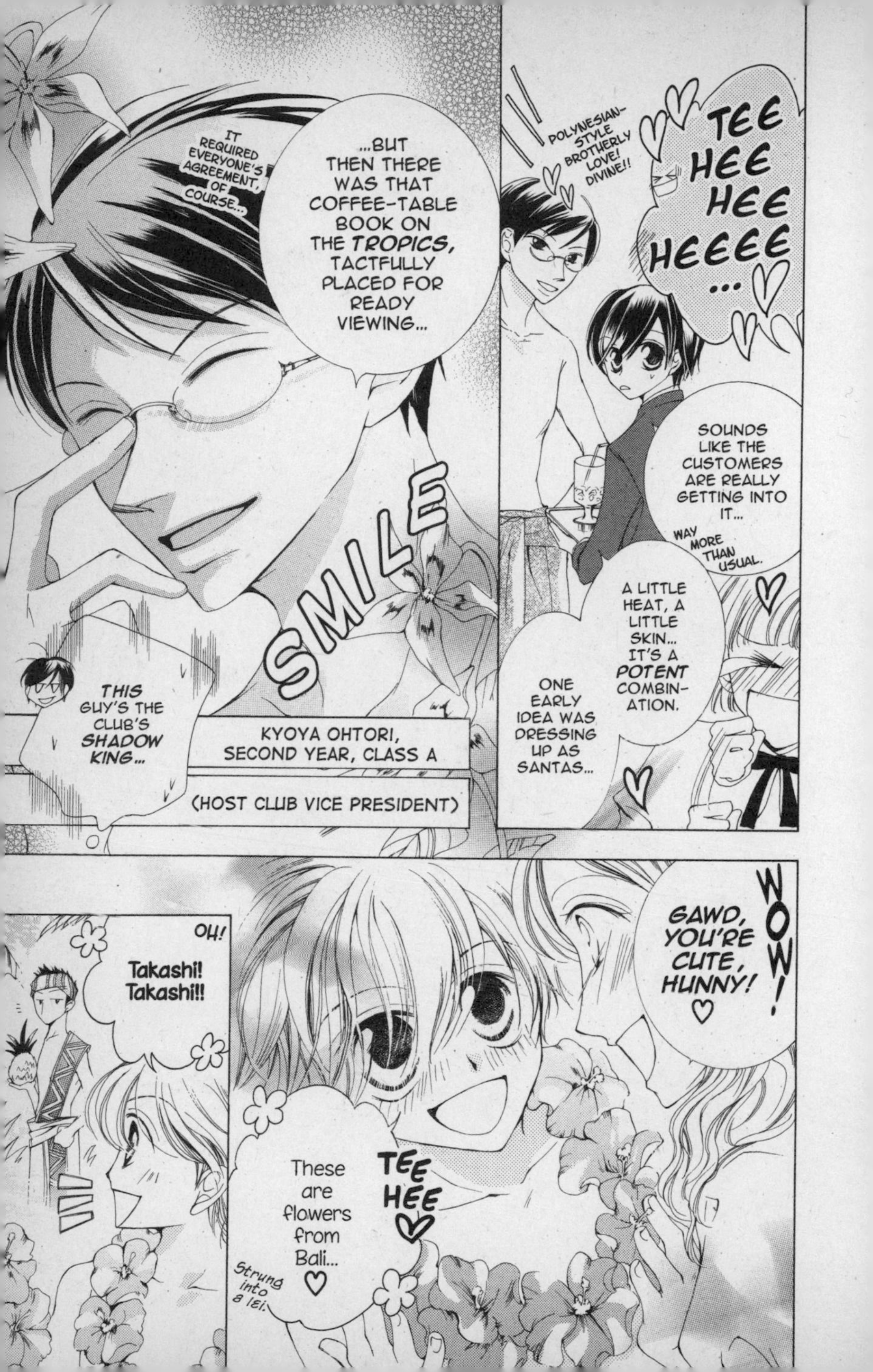
TEE HEE HEE HEEEE...
POLYNESIAN-STYLE BROTHERLY LOVE! DIVINE!!
SOUNDS LIKE THE CUSTOMERS ARE REALLY GETTING INTO IT...
WAY MORE THAN USUAL.
A LITTLE HEAT, A LITTLE SKIN... IT'S A POTENT COMBINATION.
ONE EARLY IDEA WAS DRESSING UP AS SANTAS...
...BUT THEN THERE WAS THAT COFFEE-TABLE BOOK ON THE TROPICS, TACTFULLY PLACED FOR READY VIEWING...
IT REQUIRED EVERYONE'S AGREEMENT, OF COURSE...
SMILE
KYOYA OHTORI, SECOND YEAR, CLASS A
(HOST CLUB VICE PRESIDENT)
THIS GUY'S THE CLUB'S SHADOW KING...
WOW!
GAWD, YOU'RE CUTE, HUNNY! ♡
TEE HEE ♡
These are flowers from Bali... ♡
Strung into a lei.
OH!
Takashi! Takashi!!

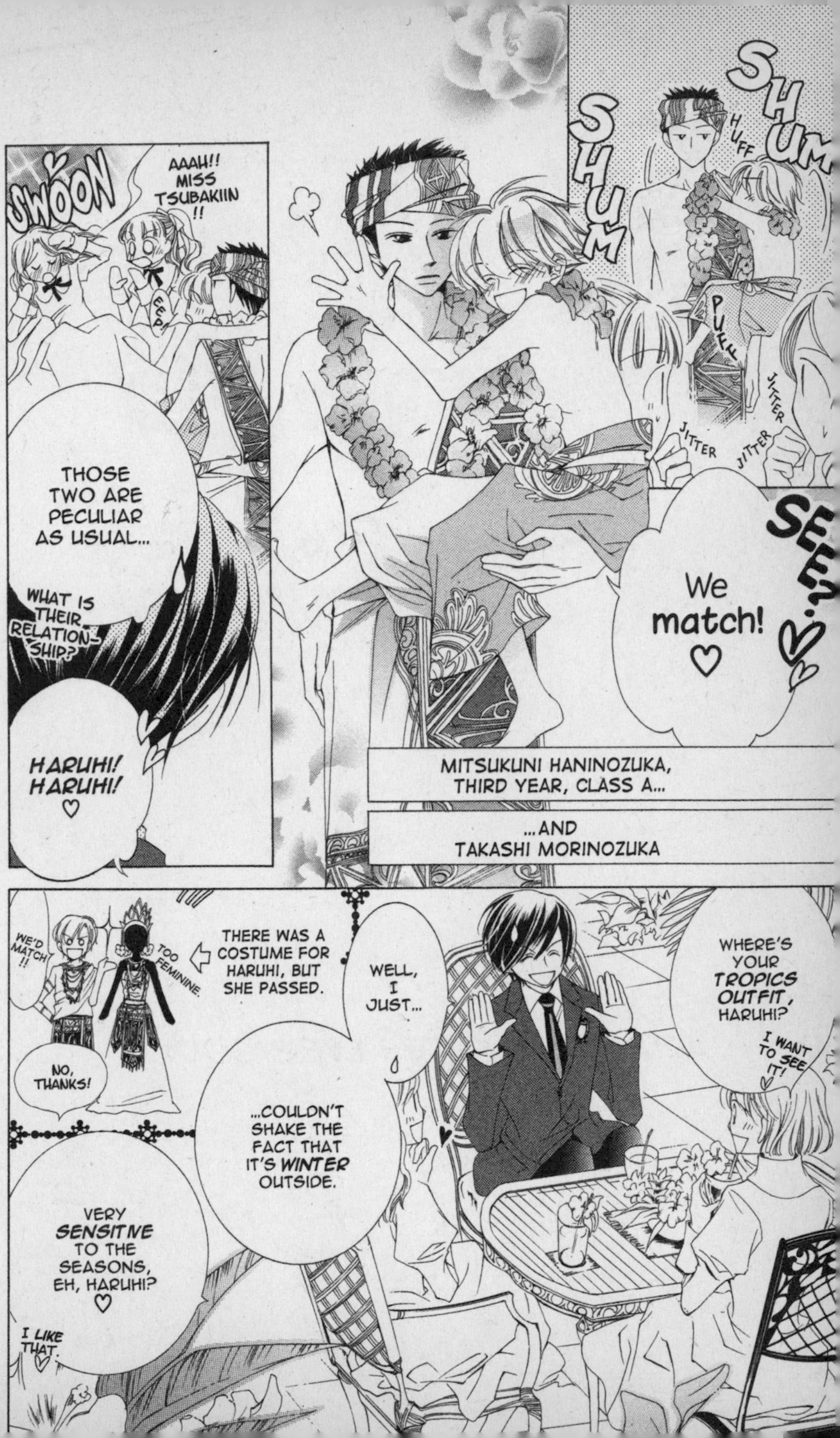
SHUM SHUM SHUM
HUFF
PUFF
JITTER JITTER JITTER
We match! ♡
SEE?♡
MITSUKUNI HANINOZUKA, THIRD YEAR, CLASS A...
...AND TAKASHI MORINOZUKA
SWOON
AAAH!! MISS TSUBAKIIN!!
EEP!
THOSE TWO ARE PECULIAR AS USUAL...
WHAT IS THEIR RELATIONSHIP?
HARUHI! HARUHI! ♡
WHERE'S YOUR *TROPICS OUTFIT*, HARUHI?
I WANT TO SEE IT! ♡
WELL, I JUST...
...COULDN'T SHAKE THE FACT THAT IT'S *WINTER* OUTSIDE.
THERE WAS A COSTUME FOR HARUHI, BUT SHE PASSED.
WE'D MATCH!!
TOO FEMININE.
NO, THANKS!
VERY *SENSITIVE* TO THE SEASONS, EH, HARUHI? ♡
I LIKE THAT. ♡

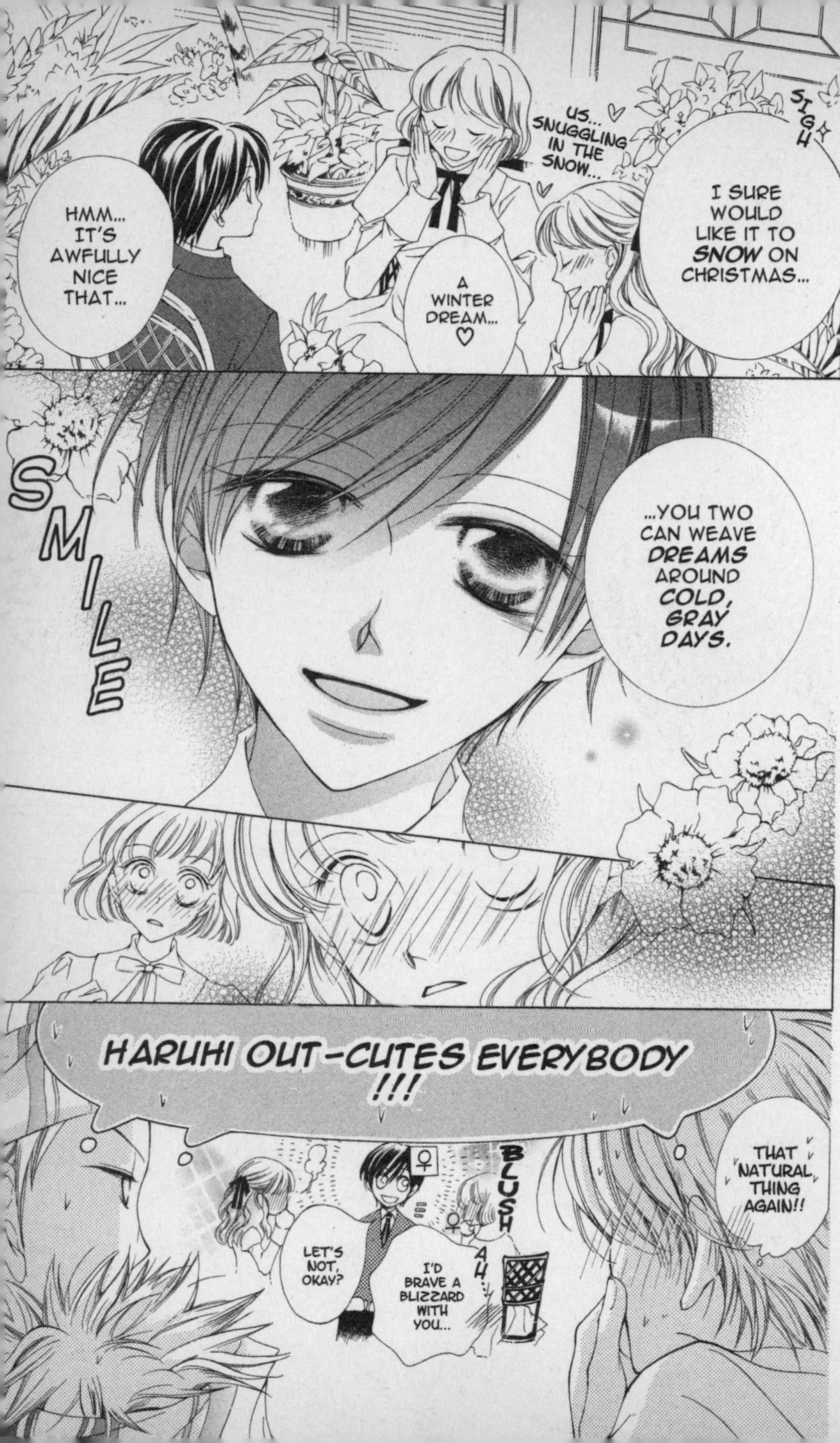
SIGH
I SURE WOULD LIKE IT TO SNOW ON CHRISTMAS...
US... SNUGGLING IN THE SNOW...
A WINTER DREAM...
HMM... IT'S AWFULLY NICE THAT...
...YOU TWO CAN WEAVE DREAMS AROUND COLD, GRAY DAYS.
SMILE
HARUHI OUT-CUTES EVERYBODY !!!
THAT NATURAL THING AGAIN!!
BLUSH
AH...
I'D BRAVE A BLIZZARD WITH YOU...
LET'S NOT, OKAY?

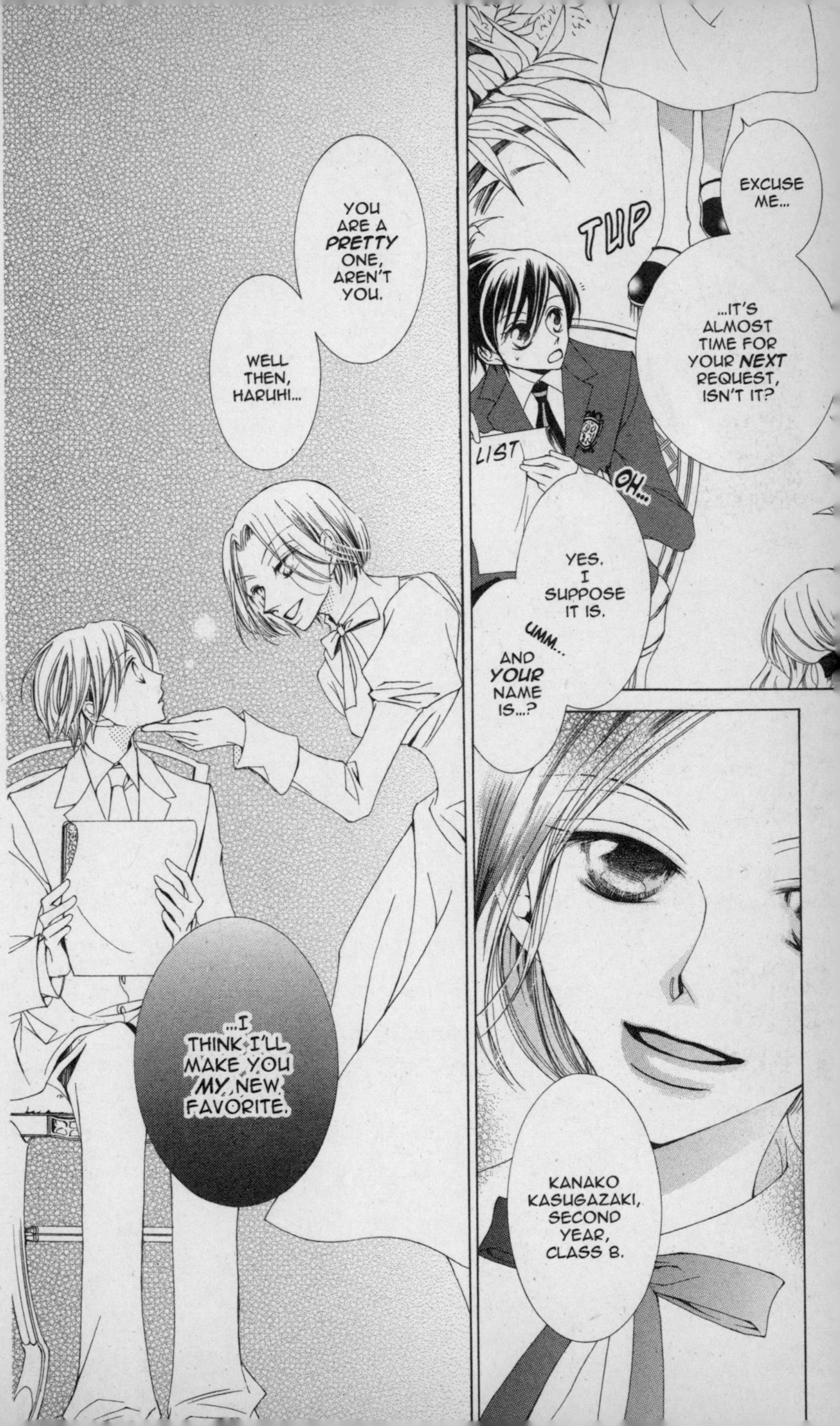
EXCUSE ME...
TUP
...IT'S ALMOST TIME FOR YOUR NEXT REQUEST, ISN'T IT?
LIST
OH...
YES. I SUPPOSE IT IS.
UMM...
AND YOUR NAME IS...?
KANAKO KASUGAZAKI, SECOND YEAR, CLASS B.
YOU ARE A PRETTY ONE, AREN'T YOU.
WELL THEN, HARUHI...
...I THINK I'LL MAKE YOU MY NEW FAVORITE.

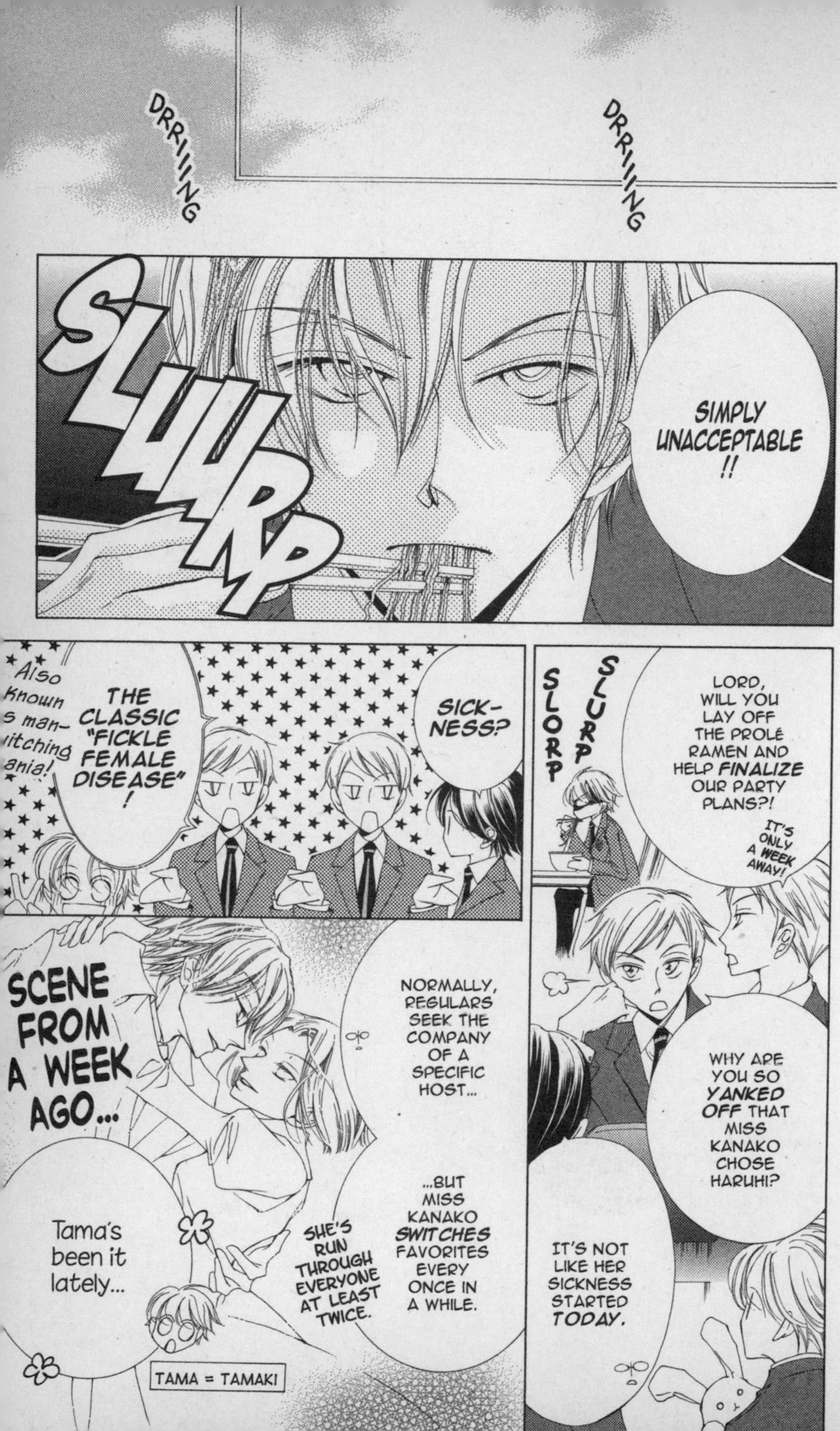
DRRIIING
DRRIIING
SIMPLY UNACCEPTABLE !!
SLURP
SLURP
SLORP
LORD, WILL YOU LAY OFF THE PROLE RAMEN AND HELP FINALIZE OUR PARTY PLANS?!
IT'S ONLY A WEEK AWAY!
WHY ARE YOU SO YANKED OFF THAT MISS KANAKO CHOSE HARUHI?
IT'S NOT LIKE HER SICKNESS STARTED TODAY.
SICK-NESS?
THE CLASSIC "FICKLE FEMALE DISEASE" !
Also known s man-itching ania!
SCENE FROM A WEEK AGO...
NORMALLY, REGULARS SEEK THE COMPANY OF A SPECIFIC HOST...
...BUT MISS KANAKO SWITCHES FAVORITES EVERY ONCE IN A WHILE.
SHE'S RUN THROUGH EVERYONE AT LEAST TWICE.
Tama's been it lately...
TAMA = TAMAKI

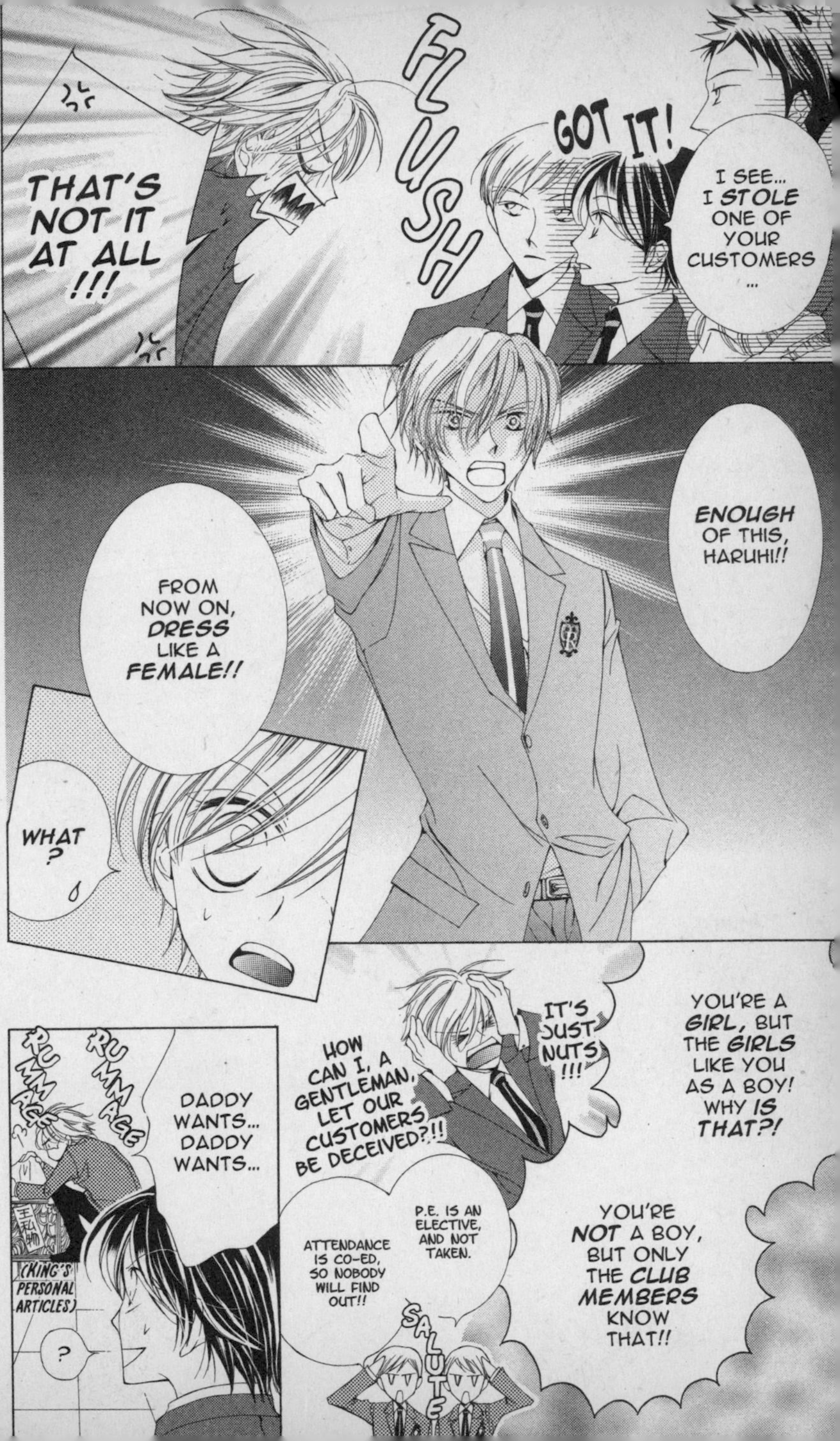
I SEE... I STOLE ONE OF YOUR CUSTOMERS ...
GOT IT!
FLUSH
THAT'S NOT IT AT ALL !!!
ENOUGH OF THIS, HARUHI!!
FROM NOW ON, DRESS LIKE A FEMALE!!
WHAT ?
YOU'RE A GIRL, BUT THE GIRLS LIKE YOU AS A BOY! WHY IS THAT?!
IT'S JUST NUTS !!!
HOW CAN I, A GENTLEMAN, LET OUR CUSTOMERS BE DECEIVED?!!
YOU'RE NOT A BOY, BUT ONLY THE CLUB MEMBERS KNOW THAT!!
P.E. IS AN ELECTIVE, AND NOT TAKEN.
ATTENDANCE IS CO-ED, SO NOBODY WILL FIND OUT!!
SALUTE
DADDY WANTS... DADDY WANTS...
RUMMAGE
RUMMAGE
(KING'S PERSONAL ARTICLES)
?

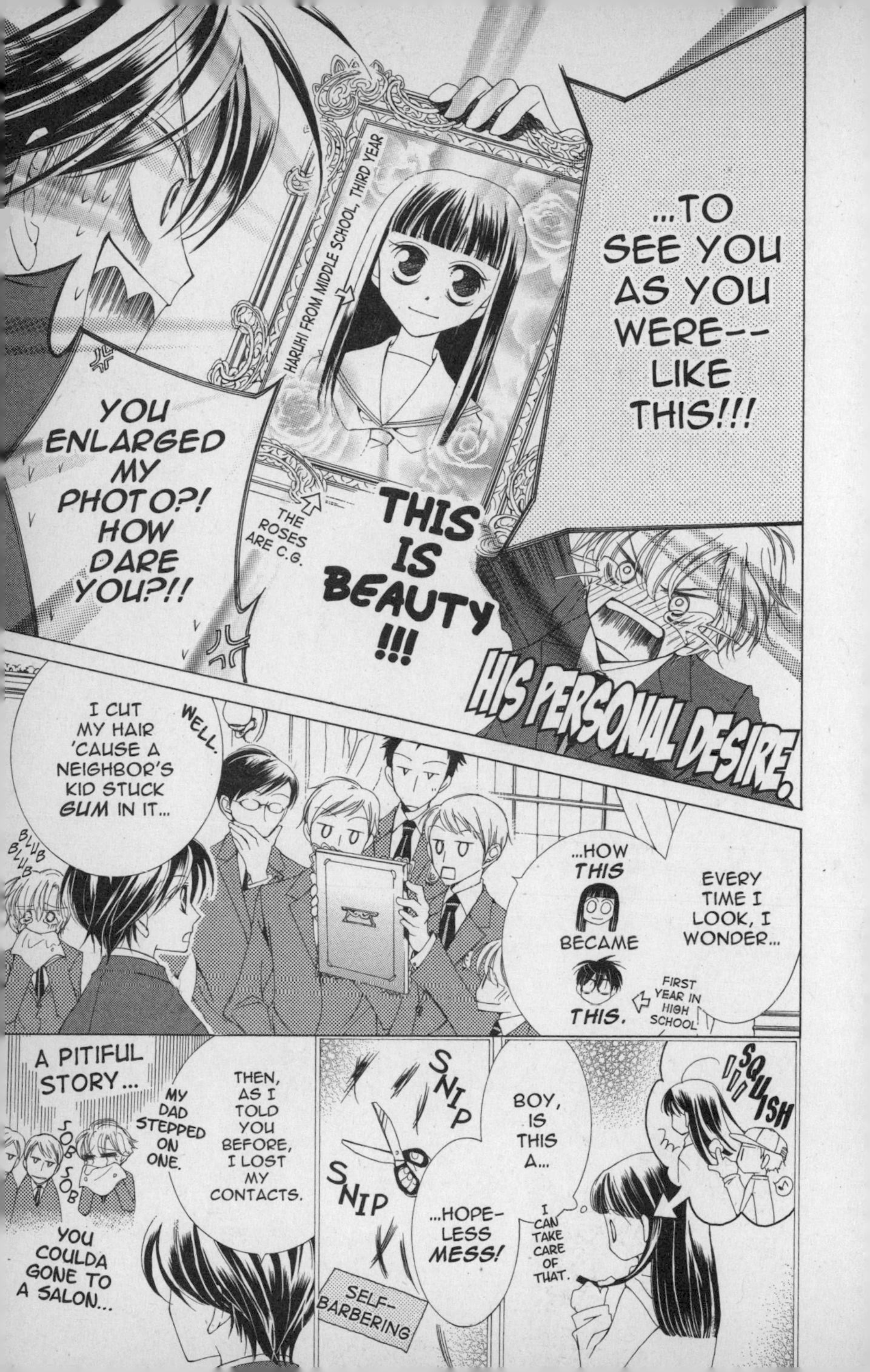
...TO SEE YOU AS YOU WERE--LIKE THIS!!!
THIS IS BEAUTY!!!
HIS PERSONAL DESIRE.
HARUHI FROM MIDDLE SCHOOL, THIRD YEAR
THE ROSES ARE C.G.
YOU ENLARGED MY PHOTO?! HOW DARE YOU?!!
EVERY TIME I LOOK, I WONDER...
...HOW THIS BECAME THIS.
FIRST YEAR IN HIGH SCHOOL
WELL.
I CUT MY HAIR 'CAUSE A NEIGHBOR'S KID STUCK GUM IN IT...
BLUB BLUB
SQUISH
BOY, IS THIS A...
I CAN TAKE CARE OF THAT.
SNIP
SNIP
...HOPE-LESS MESS!
SELF-BARBERING
THEN, AS I TOLD YOU BEFORE, I LOST MY CONTACTS.
MY DAD STEPPED ON ONE.
A PITIFUL STORY...
SOB SOB
YOU COULDA GONE TO A SALON...

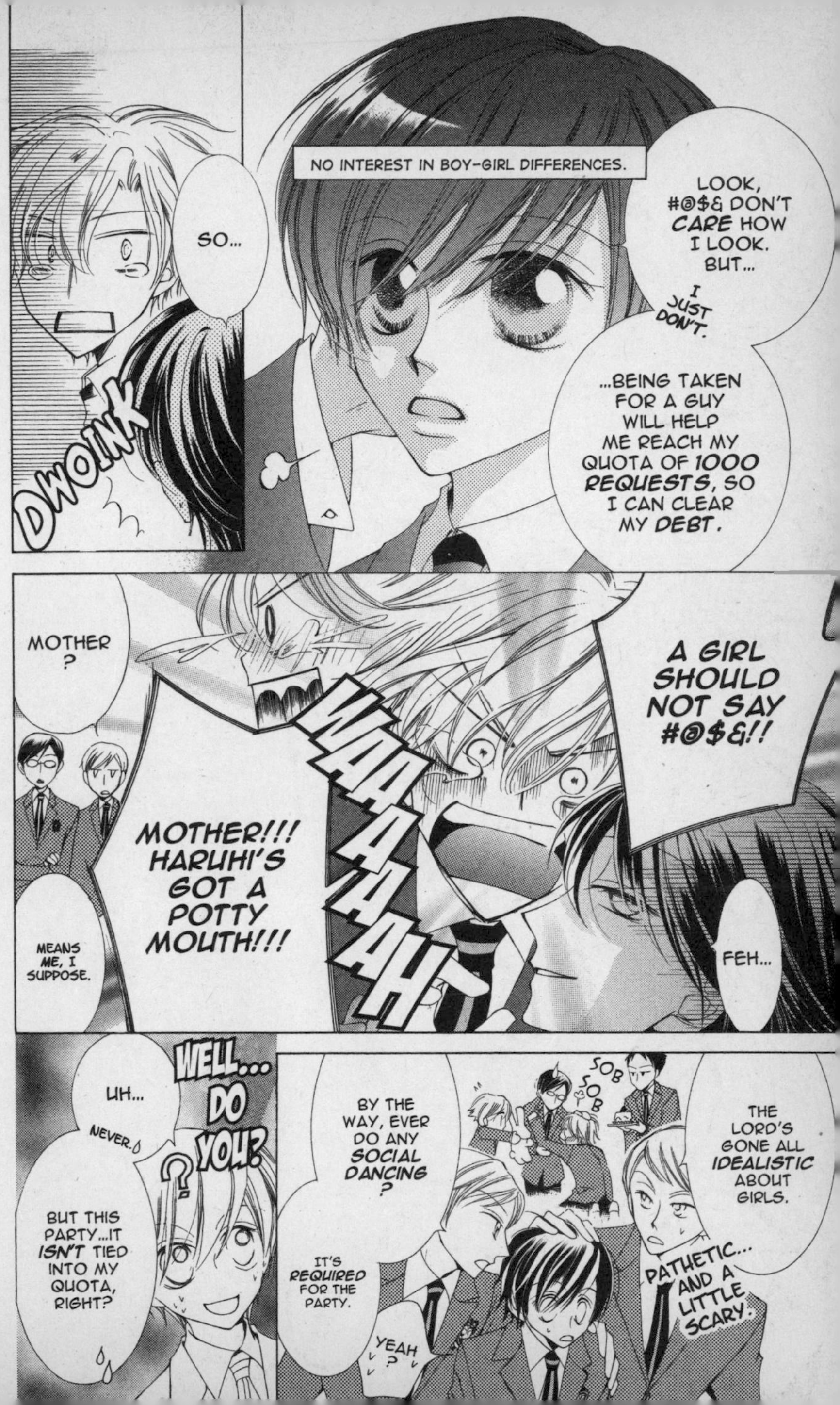

NO INTEREST IN BOY-GIRL DIFFERENCES.
LOOK, #@$& DON'T CARE HOW I LOOK. BUT...
I JUST DON'T.
...BEING TAKEN FOR A GUY WILL HELP ME REACH MY QUOTA OF 1000 REQUESTS, SO I CAN CLEAR MY DEBT.
SO...
DWOINK
A GIRL SHOULD NOT SAY #@$&!!
FEH...
WAAAAAH
MOTHER!!! HARUHI'S GOT A POTTY MOUTH!!!
MOTHER?
MEANS ME, I SUPPOSE.
THE LORD'S GONE ALL IDEALISTIC ABOUT GIRLS.
PATHETIC... AND A LITTLE SCARY.
SOB SOB
BY THE WAY, EVER DO ANY SOCIAL DANCING?
IT'S REQUIRED FOR THE PARTY.
YEAH?
WELL... DO YOU?
UH...
NEVER.
BUT THIS PARTY...IT ISN'T TIED INTO MY QUOTA, RIGHT?

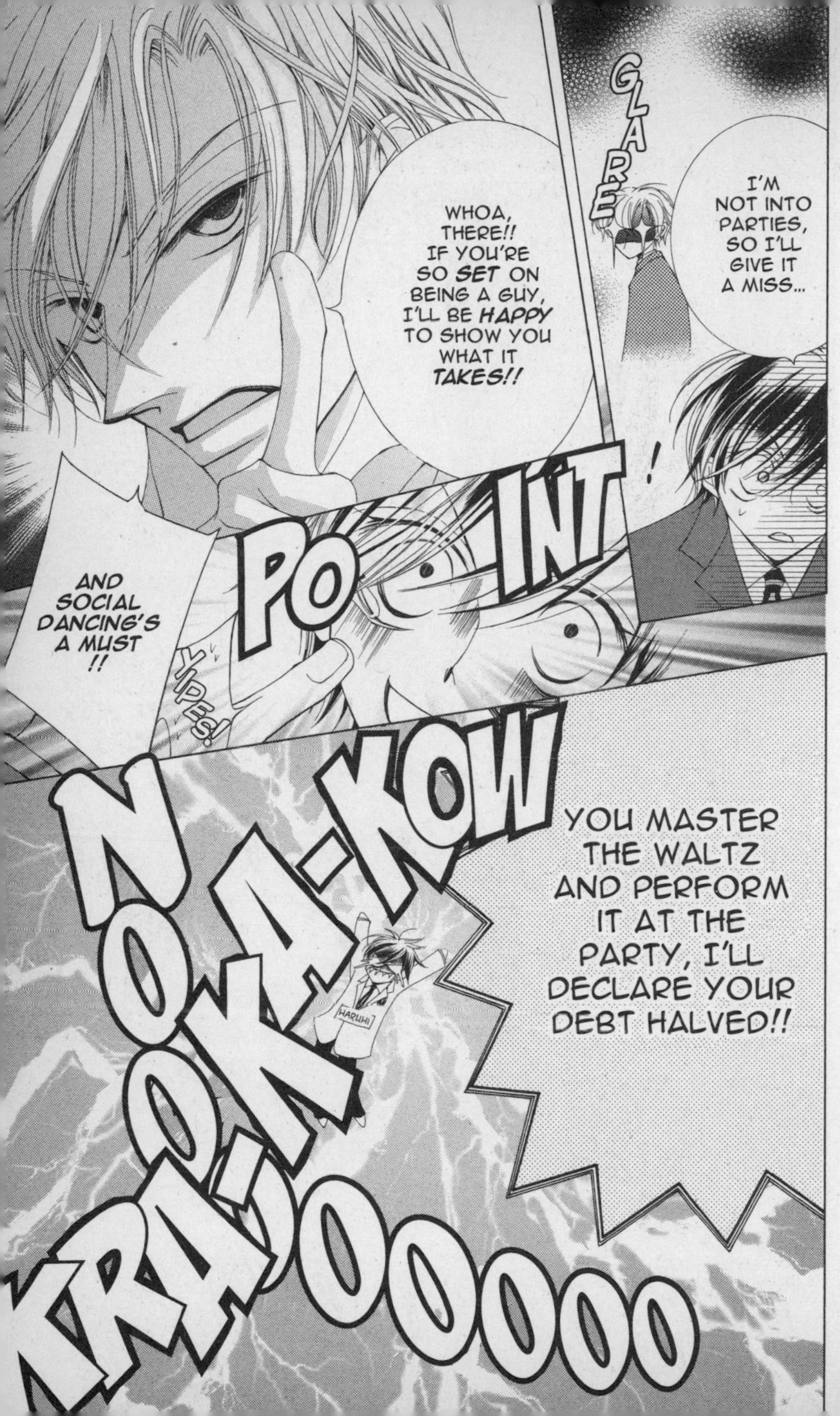
GLARE
I'M NOT INTO PARTIES, SO I'LL GIVE IT A MISS...
WHOA, THERE!! IF YOU'RE SO *SET* ON BEING A GUY, I'LL BE *HAPPY* TO SHOW YOU WHAT IT *TAKES!!*
!
AND SOCIAL DANCING'S A MUST!!
PO—INT
YIPES!
YOU MASTER THE WALTZ AND PERFORM IT AT THE PARTY, I'LL DECLARE YOUR DEBT HALVED!!
KRA-KOW
NOOOOOOOOO
HARUHI

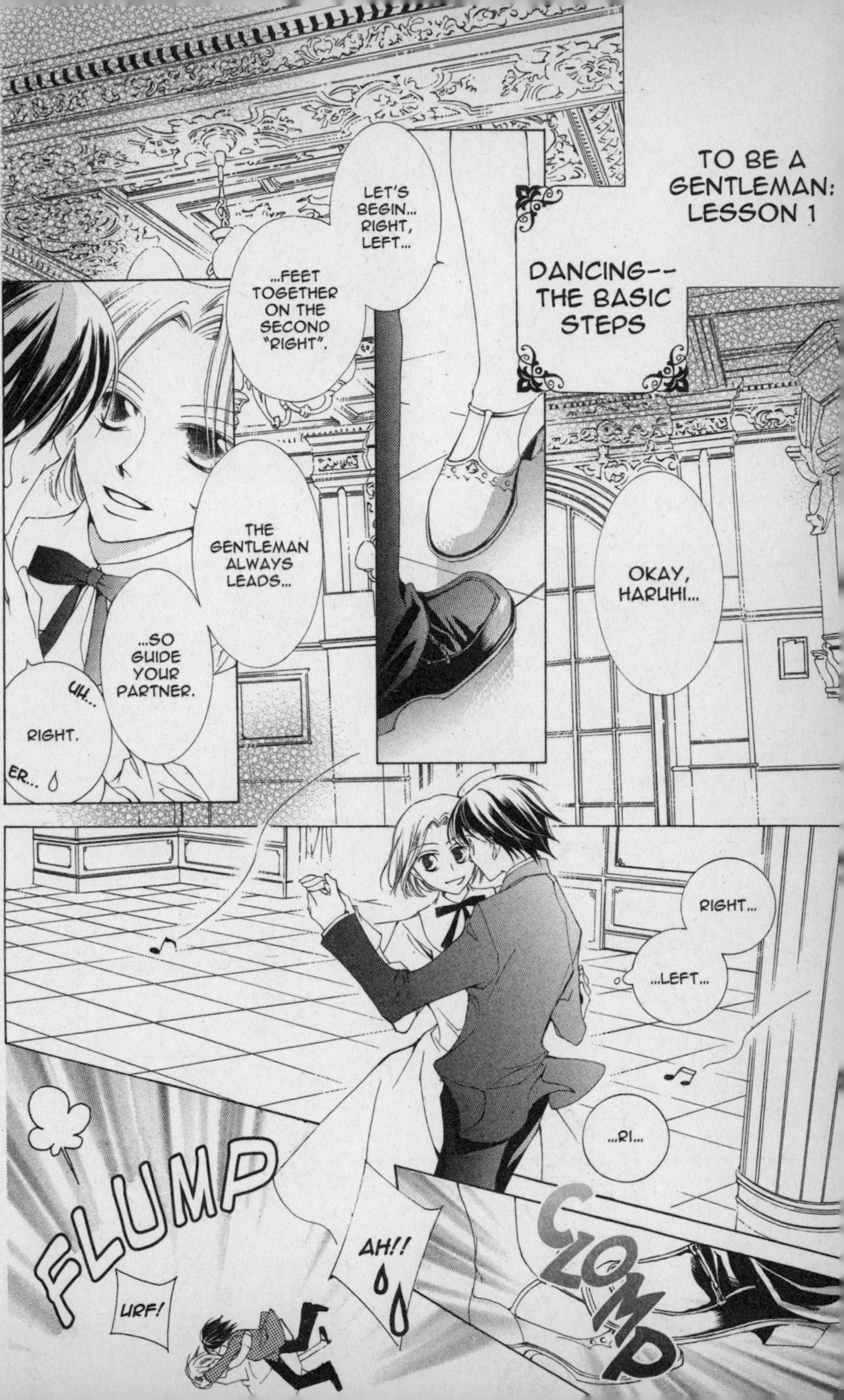
TO BE A GENTLEMAN: LESSON 1
DANCING-- THE BASIC STEPS
OKAY, HARUHI...
LET'S BEGIN... RIGHT, LEFT...
...FEET TOGETHER ON THE SECOND "RIGHT".
THE GENTLEMAN ALWAYS LEADS...
...SO GUIDE YOUR PARTNER.
UH... RIGHT.
ER...
RIGHT...
...LEFT...
...RI...
CLOMP
AH!!
FLUMP
URF!

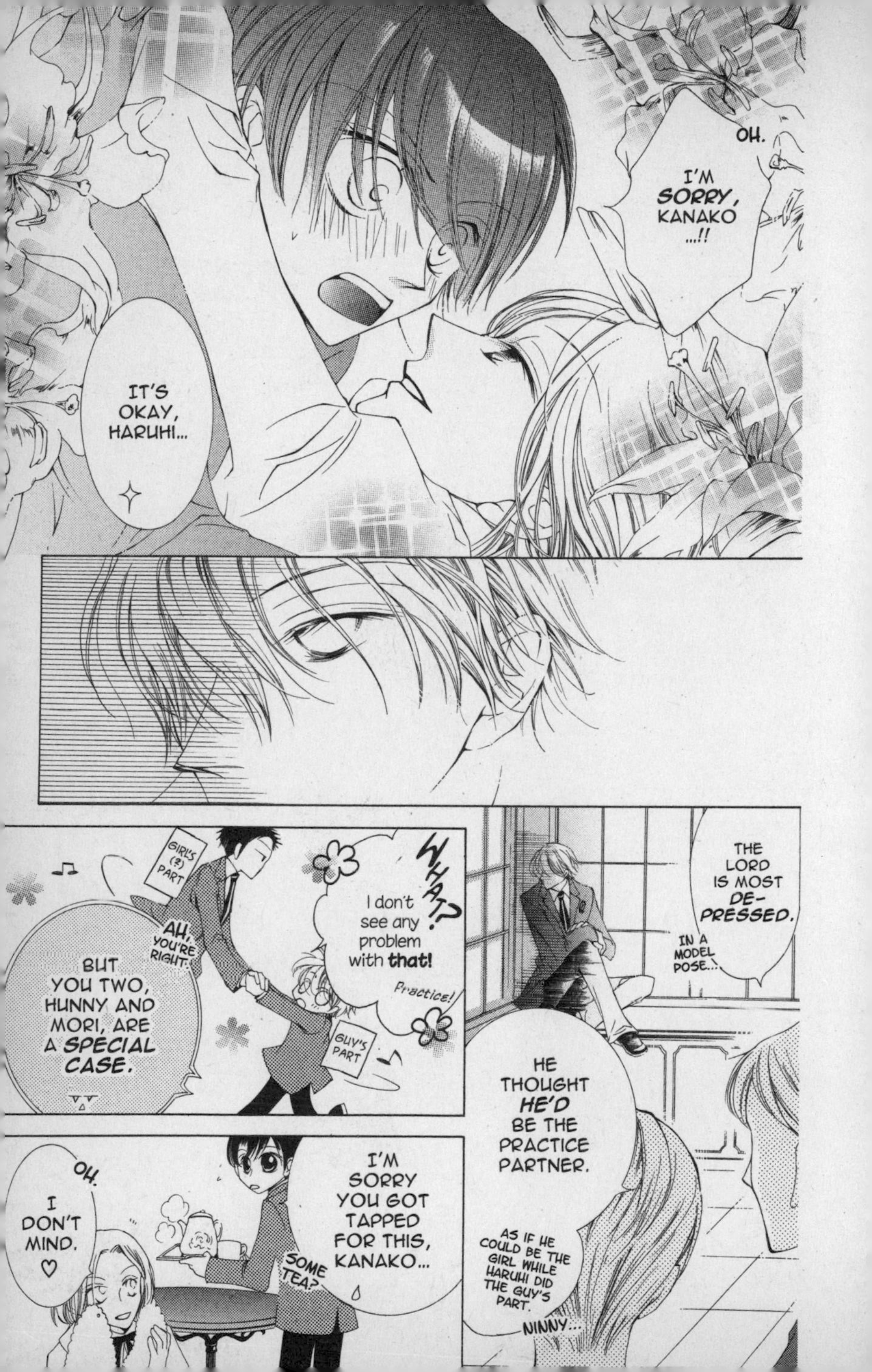
OH.
I'M SORRY, KANAKO ...!!
IT'S OKAY, HARUHI...
THE LORD IS MOST DE-PRESSED.
IN A MODEL POSE...
HE THOUGHT HE'D BE THE PRACTICE PARTNER.
AS IF HE COULD BE THE GIRL WHILE HARUHI DID THE GUY'S PART.
NINNY...
WHAT!?
I don't see any problem with that!
Practice!
GIRL'S (?) PART
GUY'S PART
AH, YOU'RE RIGHT.
BUT YOU TWO, HUNNY AND MORI, ARE A SPECIAL CASE.
I'M SORRY YOU GOT TAPPED FOR THIS, KANAKO...
SOME TEA?
OH. I DON'T MIND. ♡

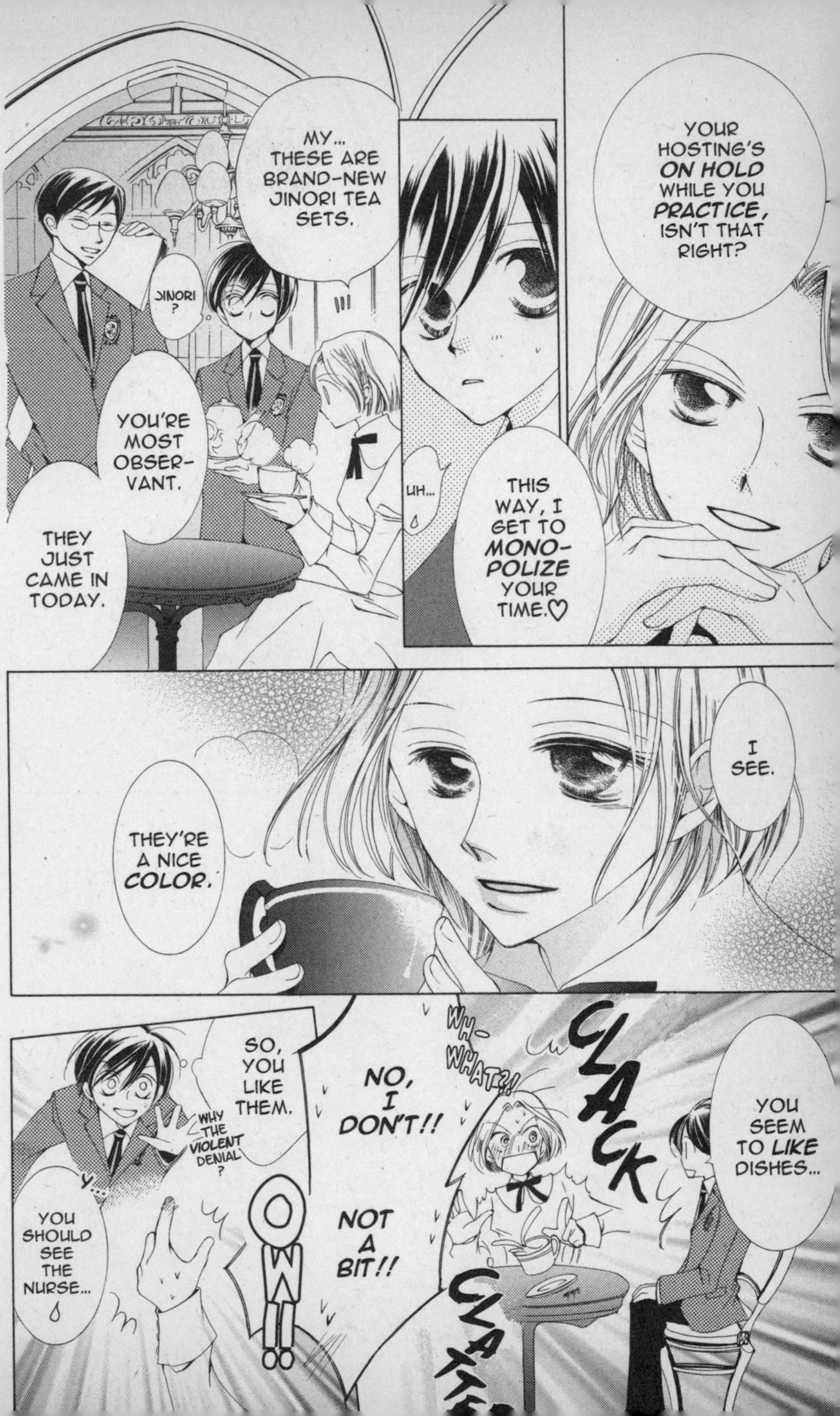
YOUR HOSTING'S ON HOLD WHILE YOU PRACTICE, ISN'T THAT RIGHT?
THIS WAY, I GET TO MONOPOLIZE YOUR TIME.♡
UH...
MY... THESE ARE BRAND-NEW JINORI TEA SETS.
JINORI?
YOU'RE MOST OBSERVANT.
THEY JUST CAME IN TODAY.
I SEE.
THEY'RE A NICE COLOR.
YOU SEEM TO LIKE DISHES...
CLACK
CLATTE
WH-WHAT?!
NO, I DON'T!!
NOT A BIT!!
SO, YOU LIKE THEM.
WHY THE VIOLENT DENIAL?
Y...
YOU SHOULD SEE THE NURSE...

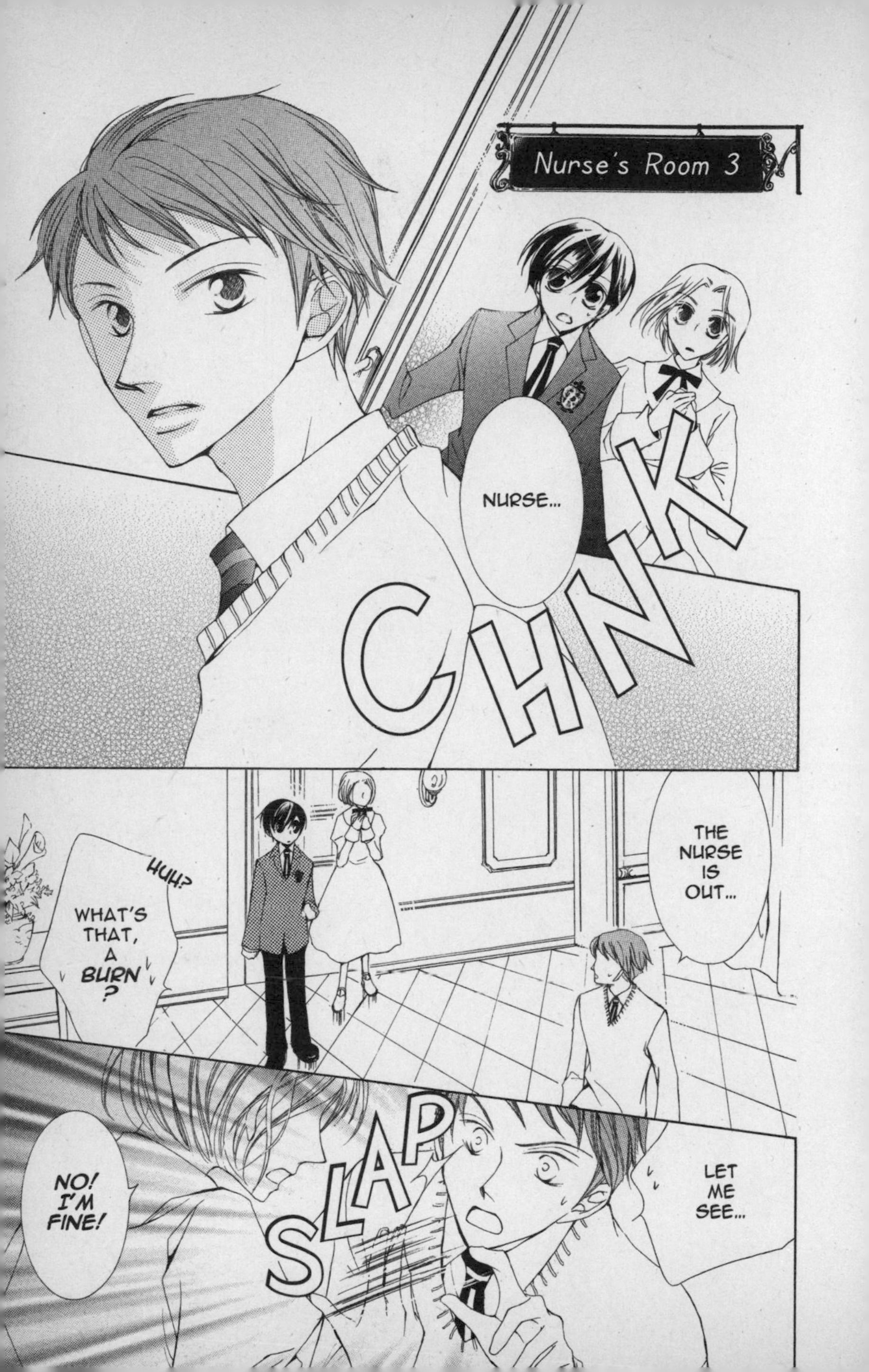

Nurse's Room 3
NURSE...
CHNK
THE NURSE IS OUT...
HUH? WHAT'S THAT, A BURN?
LET ME SEE...
SLAP
NO! I'M FINE!

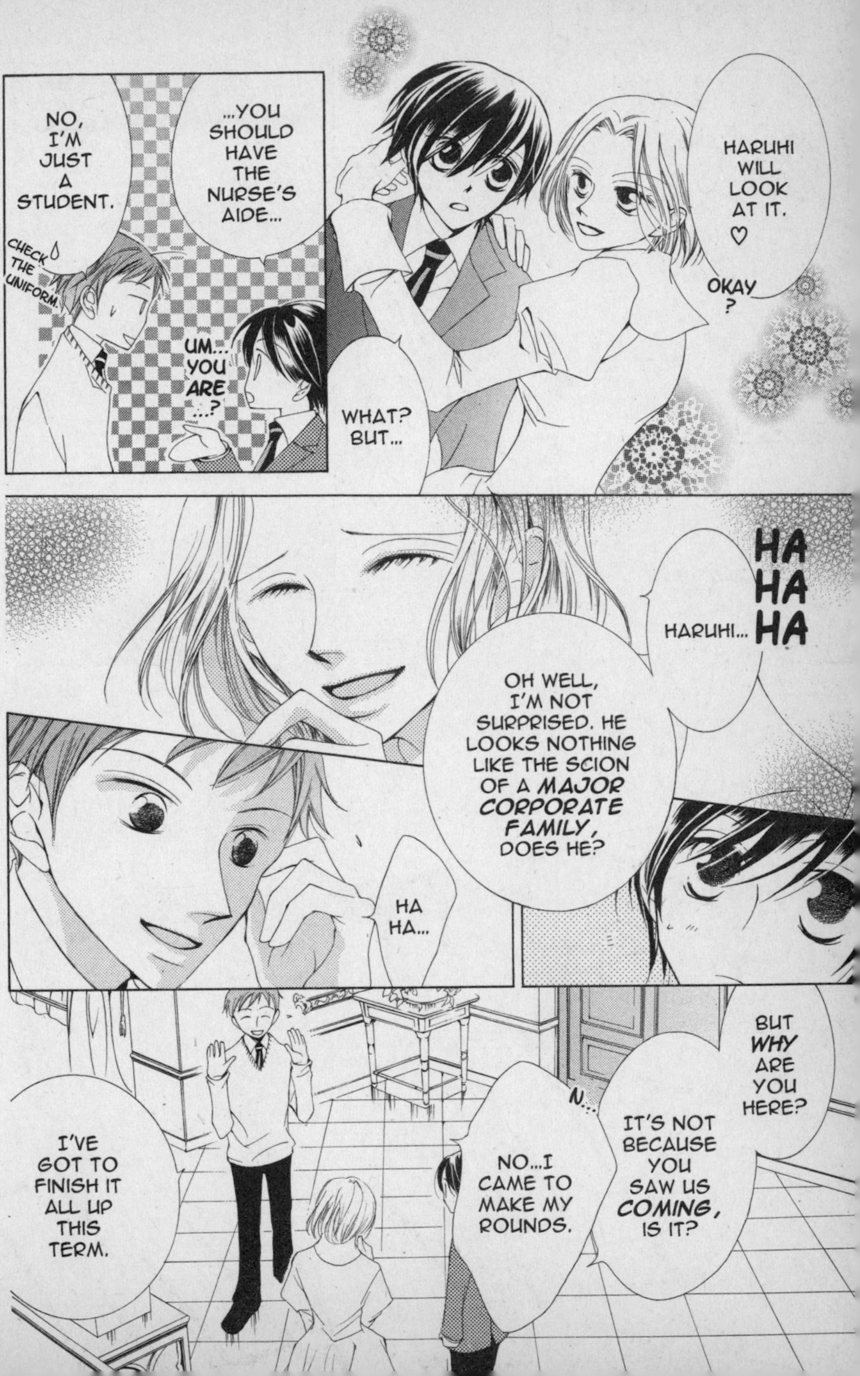
HARUHI WILL LOOK AT IT. ♡
OKAY ?
WHAT? BUT...
...YOU SHOULD HAVE THE NURSE'S AIDE...
UM... YOU ARE ...?
NO, I'M JUST A STUDENT.
CHECK THE UNIFORM.
HA HA HA
HARUHI...
OH WELL, I'M NOT SURPRISED. HE LOOKS NOTHING LIKE THE SCION OF A MAJOR CORPORATE FAMILY, DOES HE?
HA HA...
BUT WHY ARE YOU HERE?
IT'S NOT BECAUSE YOU SAW US COMING, IS IT?
N...
NO...I CAME TO MAKE MY ROUNDS.
I'VE GOT TO FINISH IT ALL UP THIS TERM.

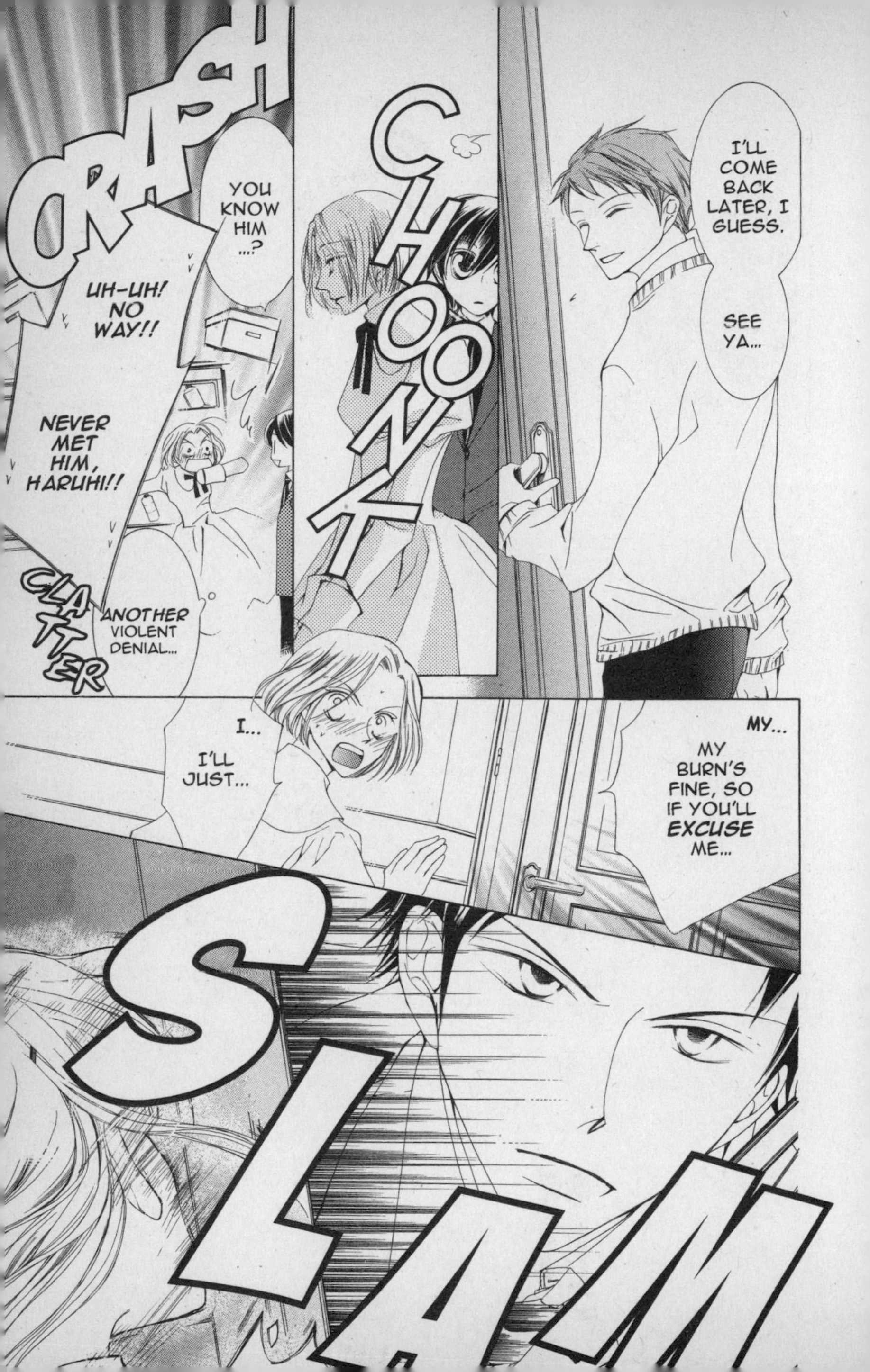
I'LL COME BACK LATER, I GUESS.
SEE YA...
CHOONK
CRASH
YOU KNOW HIM ...?
UH-UH! NO WAY!!
NEVER MET HIM, HARUHI!!
ANOTHER VIOLENT DENIAL...
CLATTER
MY...
MY BURN'S FINE, SO IF YOU'LL EXCUSE ME...
I...
I'LL JUST...
SLAM

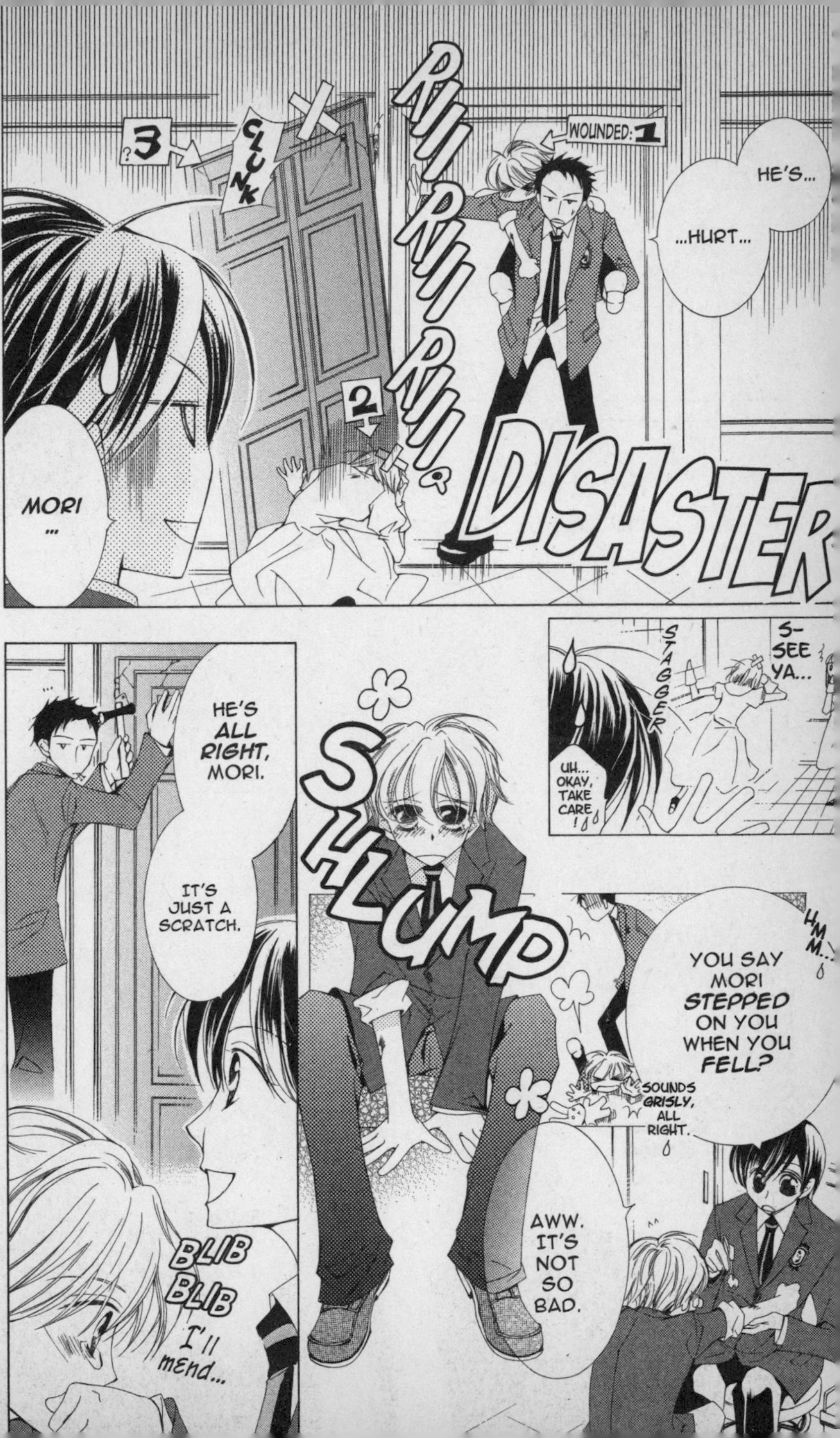
HE'S...
...HURT...
WOUNDED: 1
RIIIRIIIRIIIRIIIR
DISASTER
CLUNK
3
2
MORI...
S-SEE YA...
STAGGER
UH... OKAY, TAKE CARE!
HMM M...
YOU SAY MORI STEPPED ON YOU WHEN YOU FELL?
SOUNDS GRISLY, ALL RIGHT.
SHLUMP
AWW. IT'S NOT SO BAD.
HE'S ALL RIGHT, MORI.
IT'S JUST A SCRATCH.
BLIB BLIB
I'll mend...

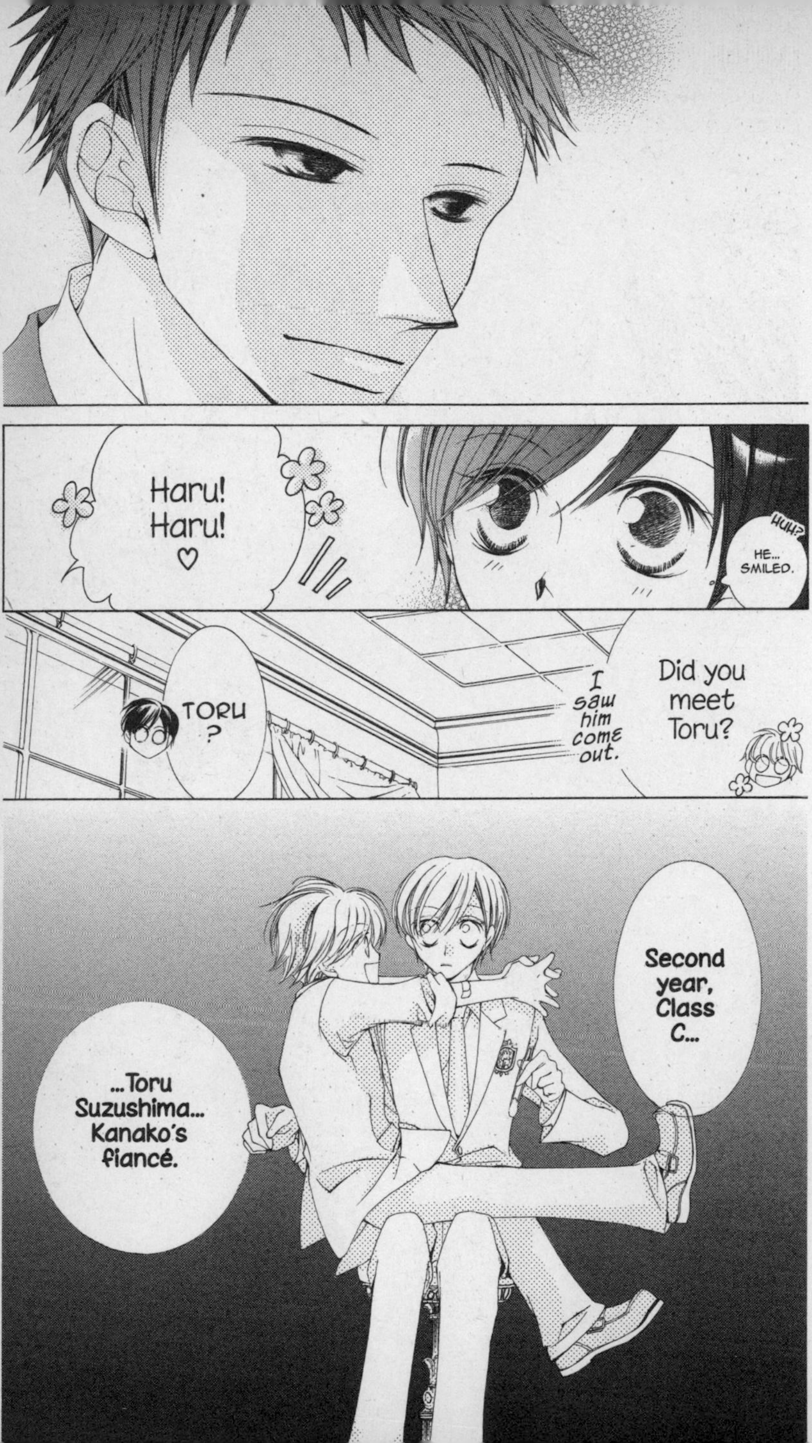
HUH?
HE... SMILED.
Haru! Haru! ♡
Did you meet Toru?
I saw him come out.
TORU?
Second year, Class C...
...Toru Suzushima... Kanako's fiancé.

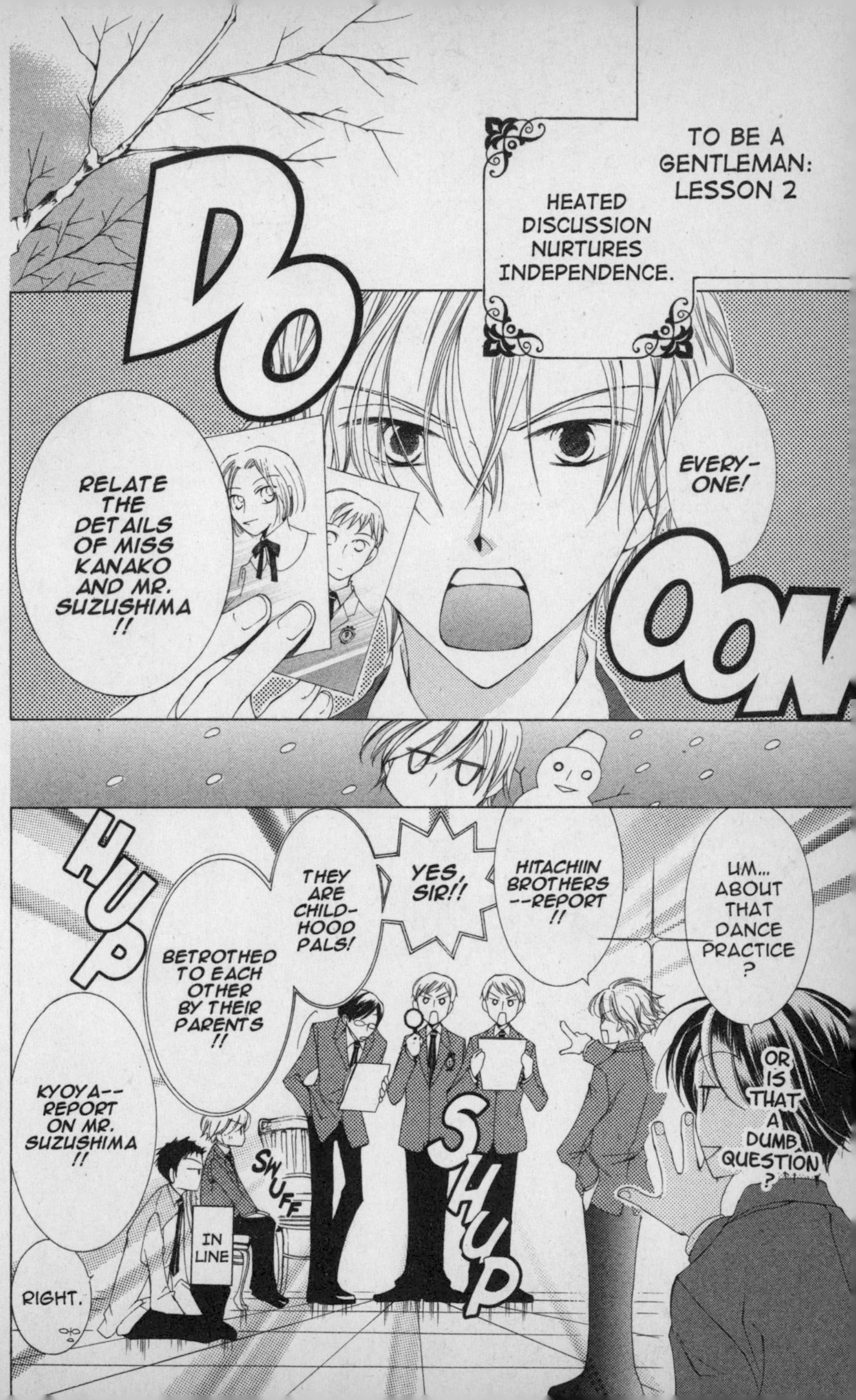
TO BE A GENTLEMAN: LESSON 2
HEATED DISCUSSION NURTURES INDEPENDENCE.
DO
OON
EVERY-ONE!
RELATE THE DETAILS OF MISS KANAKO AND MR. SUZUSHIMA !!
UM... ABOUT THAT DANCE PRACTICE ?
OR IS THAT A DUMB QUESTION ?
HITACHIIN BROTHERS --REPORT !!
YES, SIR!!
THEY ARE CHILD-HOOD PALS!
BETROTHED TO EACH OTHER BY THEIR PARENTS !!
HUP
SHUP
SWUFF
KYOYA--REPORT ON MR. SUZUSHIMA !!
IN LINE
RIGHT.

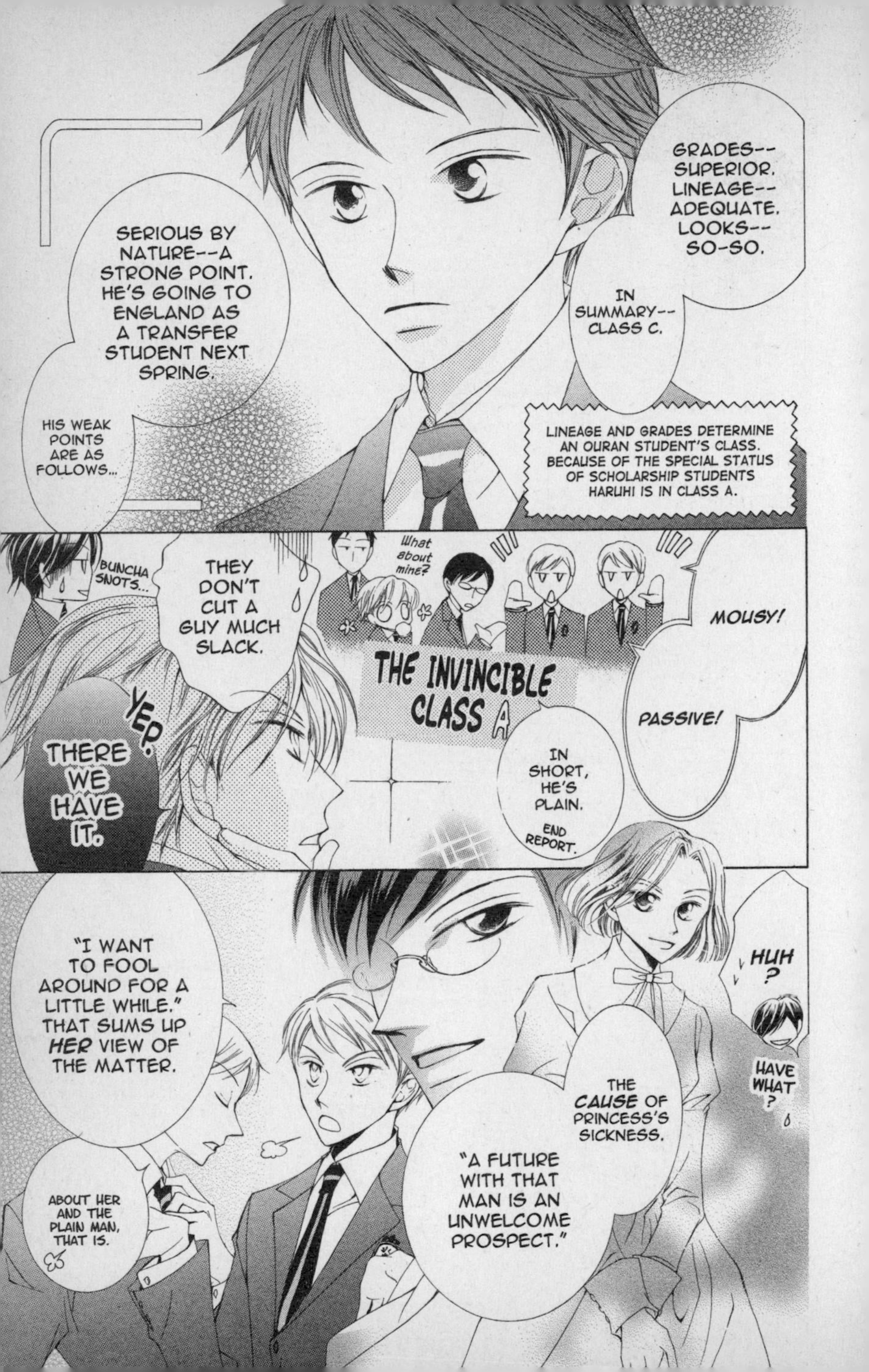
GRADES--SUPERIOR. LINEAGE--ADEQUATE. LOOKS--SO-SO.
IN SUMMARY--CLASS C.
LINEAGE AND GRADES DETERMINE AN OURAN STUDENT'S CLASS. BECAUSE OF THE SPECIAL STATUS OF SCHOLARSHIP STUDENTS HARUHI IS IN CLASS A.
SERIOUS BY NATURE--A STRONG POINT. HE'S GOING TO ENGLAND AS A TRANSFER STUDENT NEXT SPRING.
HIS WEAK POINTS ARE AS FOLLOWS...
MOUSY!
PASSIVE!
IN SHORT, HE'S PLAIN.
END REPORT.
THE INVINCIBLE CLASS A
What about mine?
THEY DON'T CUT A GUY MUCH SLACK.
BUNCHA SNOTS...
YEP.
THERE WE HAVE IT.
HUH?
HAVE WHAT?
THE CAUSE OF PRINCESS'S SICKNESS.
"A FUTURE WITH THAT MAN IS AN UNWELCOME PROSPECT."
"I WANT TO FOOL AROUND FOR A LITTLE WHILE." THAT SUMS UP HER VIEW OF THE MATTER.
ABOUT HER AND THE PLAIN MAN, THAT IS.

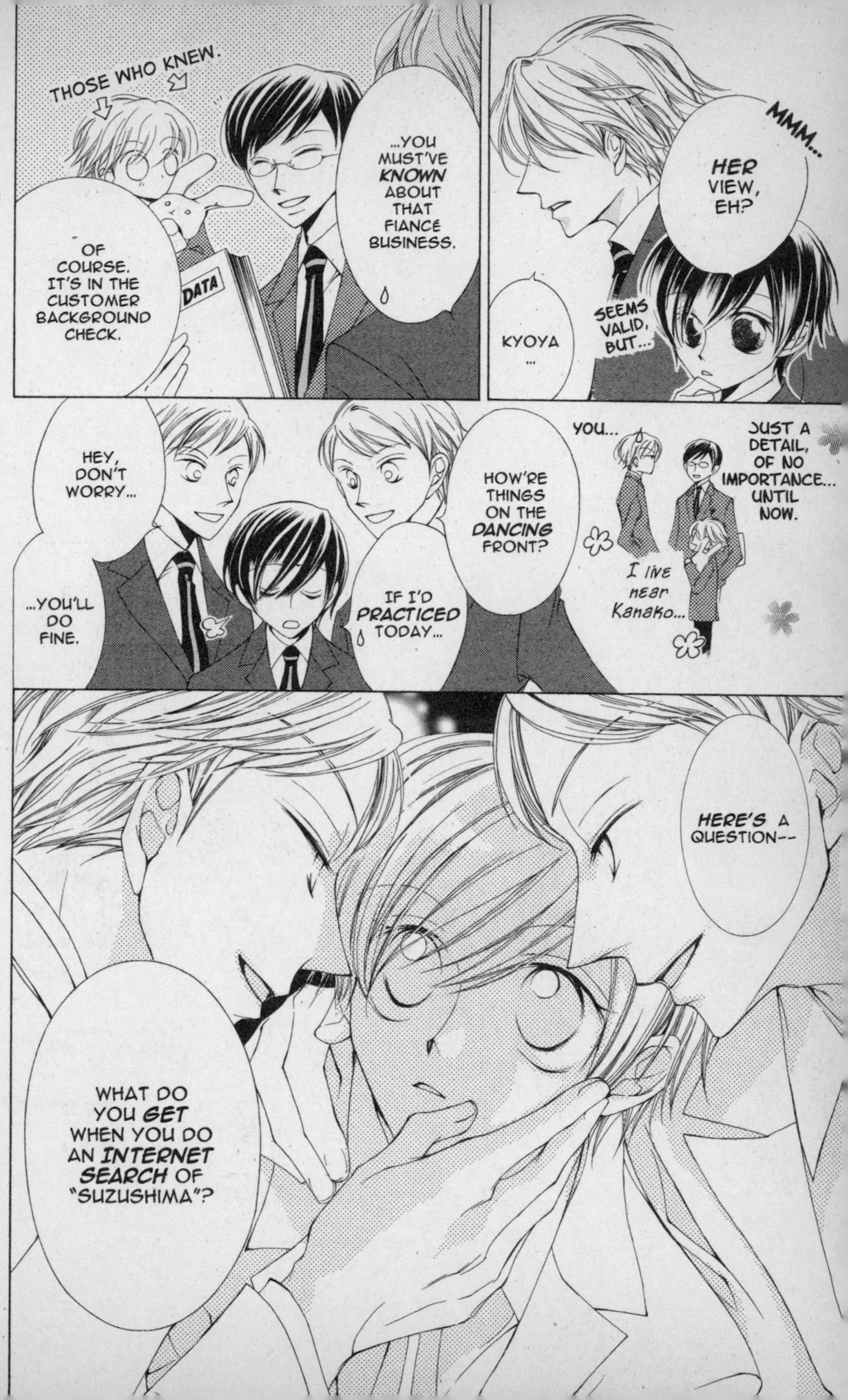
MMM...
HER VIEW, EH?
SEEMS VALID, BUT...
KYOYA ...
...YOU MUST'VE KNOWN ABOUT THAT FIANCÉ BUSINESS.
THOSE WHO KNEW.
OF COURSE. IT'S IN THE CUSTOMER BACKGROUND CHECK.
DATA
YOU...
JUST A DETAIL, OF NO IMPORTANCE... UNTIL NOW.
I live near Kanako...
HOW'RE THINGS ON THE DANCING FRONT?
IF I'D PRACTICED TODAY...
HEY, DON'T WORRY...
...YOU'LL DO FINE.
HERE'S A QUESTION--
WHAT DO YOU GET WHEN YOU DO AN INTERNET SEARCH OF "SUZUSHIMA"?

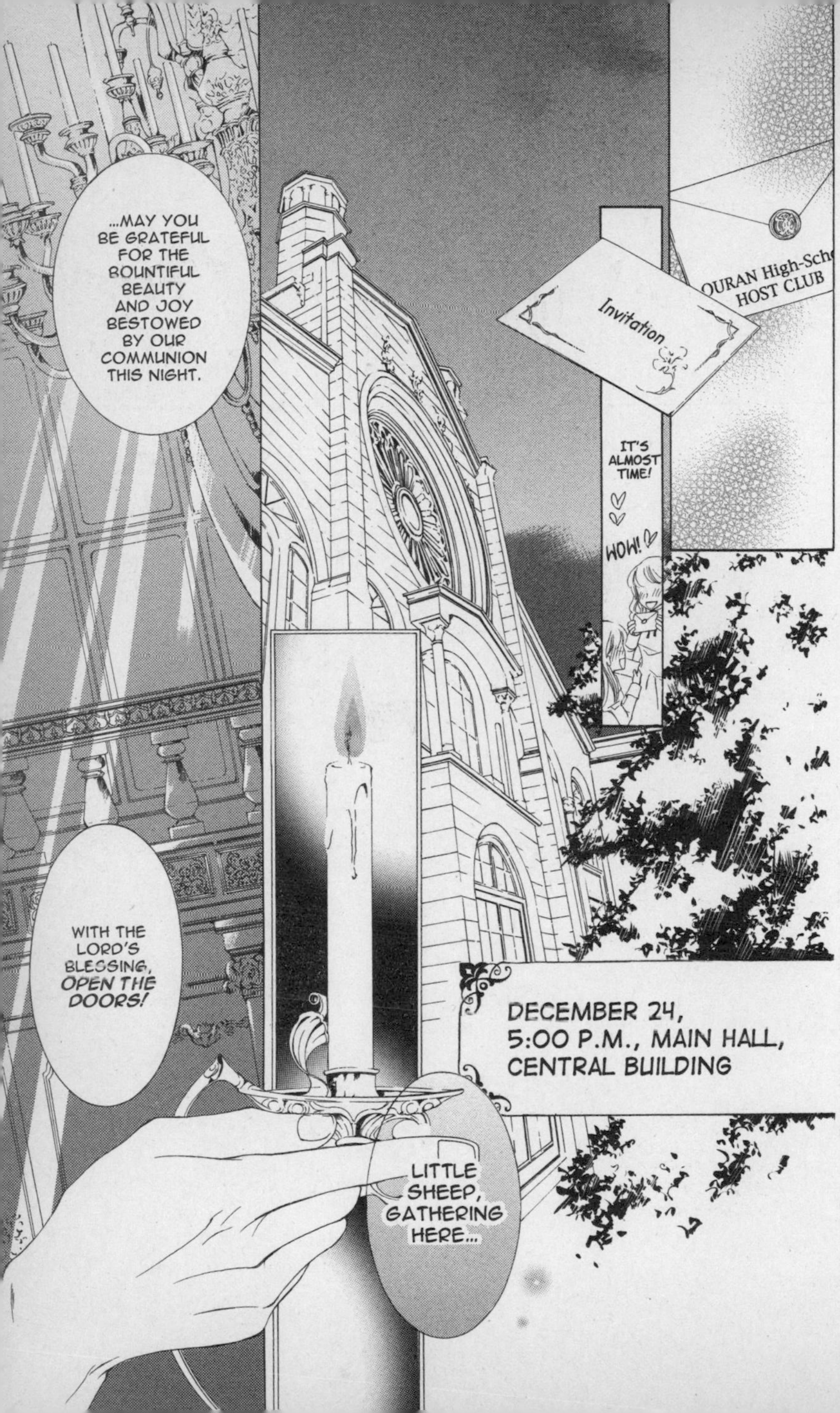
OURAN High-Sch
HOST CLUB
Invitation
IT'S ALMOST TIME!
WOW!
DECEMBER 24, 5:00 P.M., MAIN HALL, CENTRAL BUILDING
LITTLE SHEEP, GATHERING HERE...
...MAY YOU BE GRATEFUL FOR THE BOUNTIFUL BEAUTY AND JOY BESTOWED BY OUR COMMUNION THIS NIGHT.
WITH THE LORD'S BLESSING, *OPEN THE DOORS!*

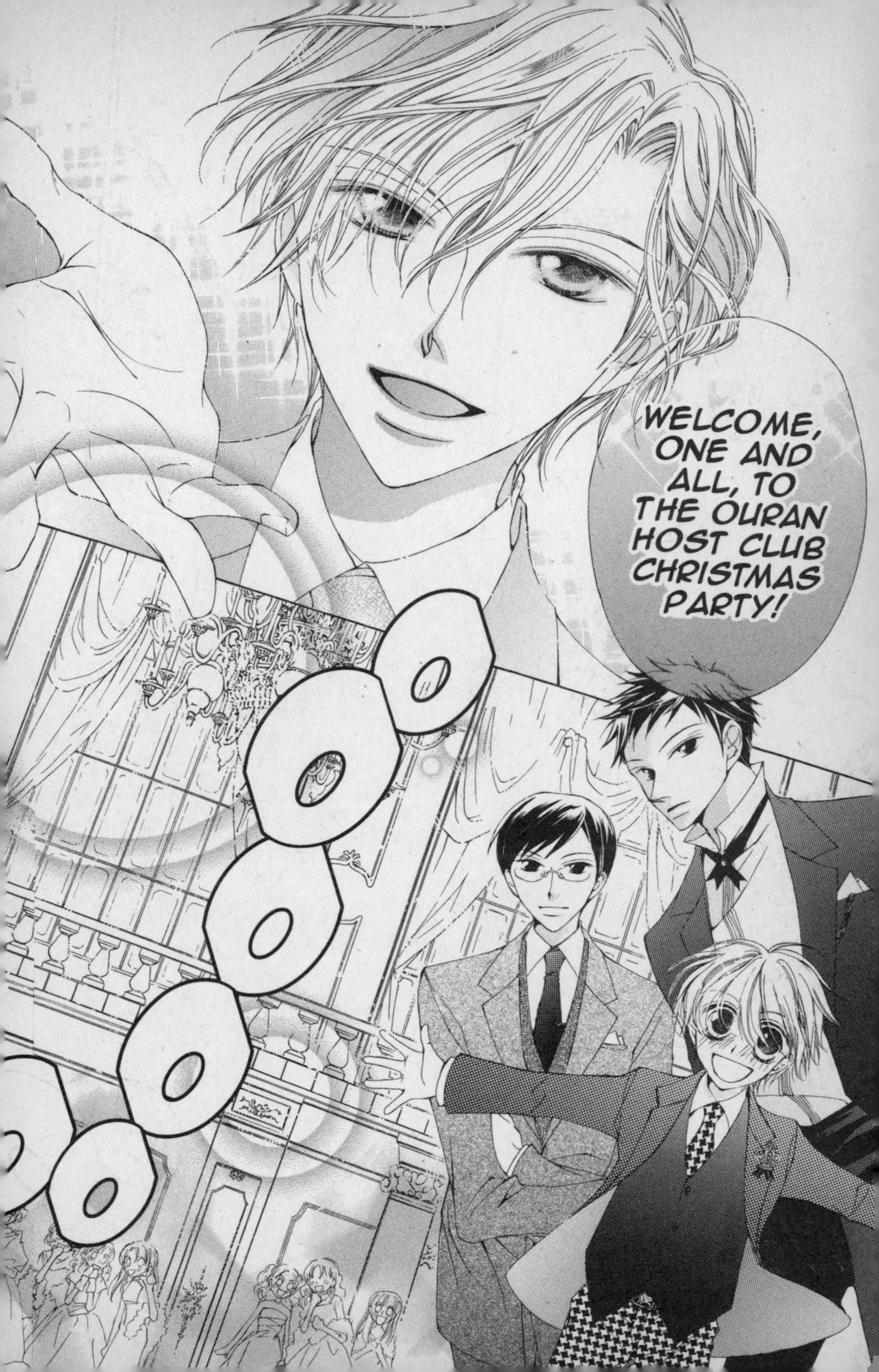
WELCOME, ONE AND ALL, TO THE OURAN HOST CLUB CHRISTMAS PARTY!

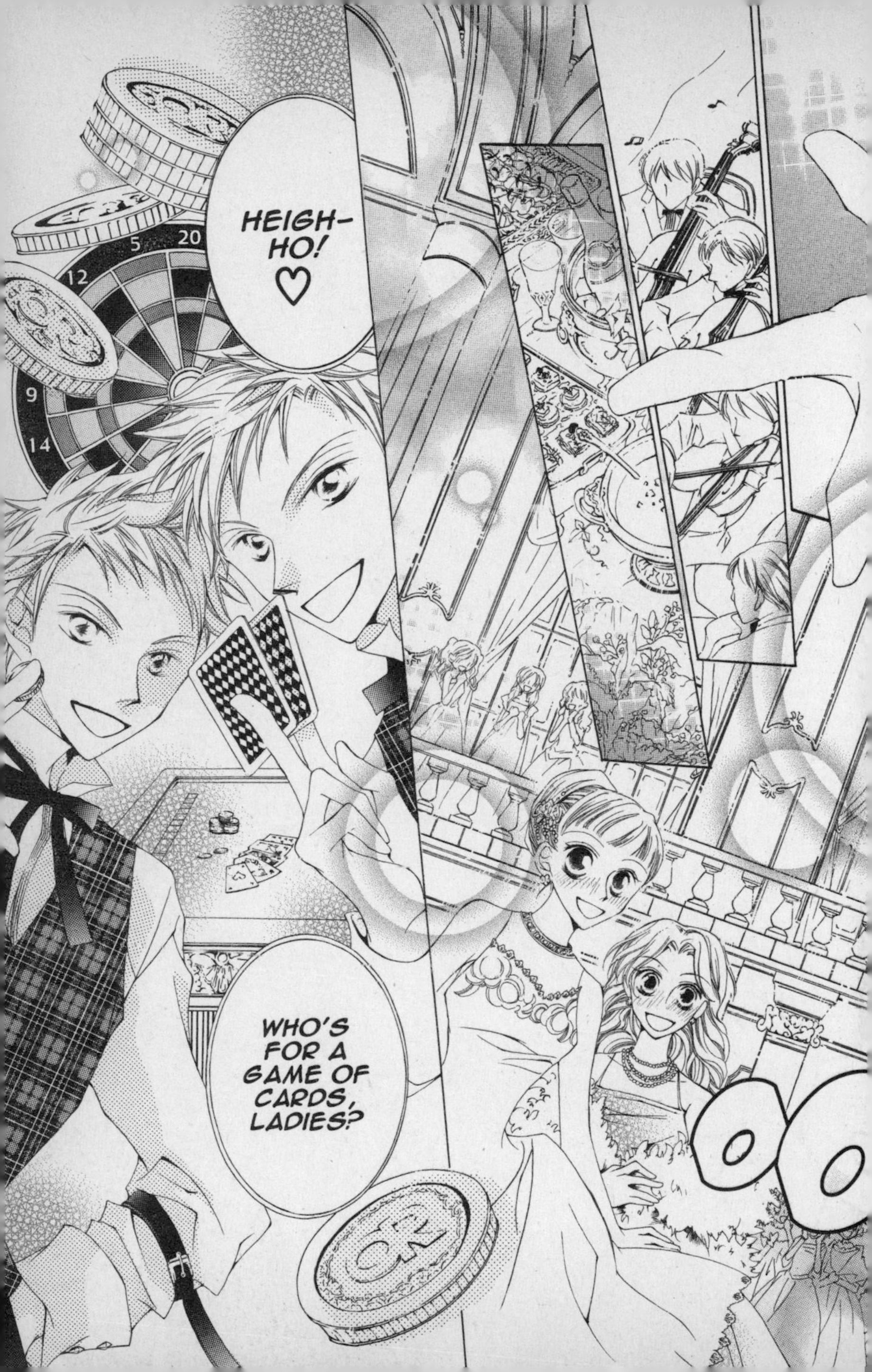
HEIGH-HO! ♡
WHO'S FOR A GAME OF CARDS, LADIES?

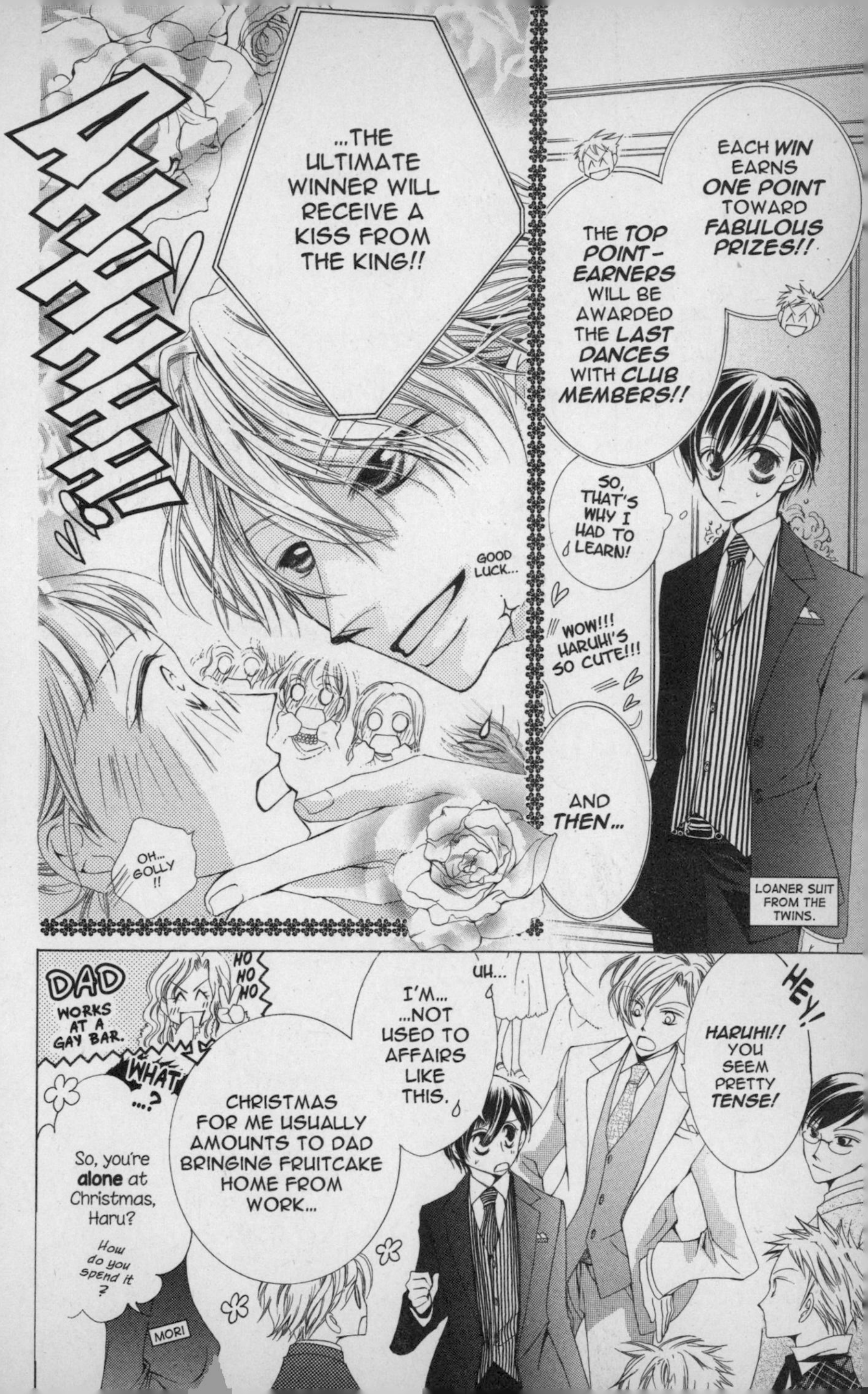
EACH WIN EARNS ONE POINT TOWARD FABULOUS PRIZES!!
THE TOP POINT-EARNERS WILL BE AWARDED THE LAST DANCES WITH CLUB MEMBERS!!
SO, THAT'S WHY I HAD TO LEARN!
WOW!!! HARUHI'S SO CUTE!!!
AND THEN...
LOANER SUIT FROM THE TWINS.
...THE ULTIMATE WINNER WILL RECEIVE A KISS FROM THE KING!!
GOOD LUCK...
OH... GOLLY!!
HEY!
HARUHI!! YOU SEEM PRETTY TENSE!
UH...
I'M... ...NOT USED TO AFFAIRS LIKE THIS.
CHRISTMAS FOR ME USUALLY AMOUNTS TO DAD BRINGING FRUITCAKE HOME FROM WORK...
HO HO HO
DAD WORKS AT A GAY BAR.
WHAT ...?
So, you're alone at Christmas, Haru?
How do you spend it?
MORI

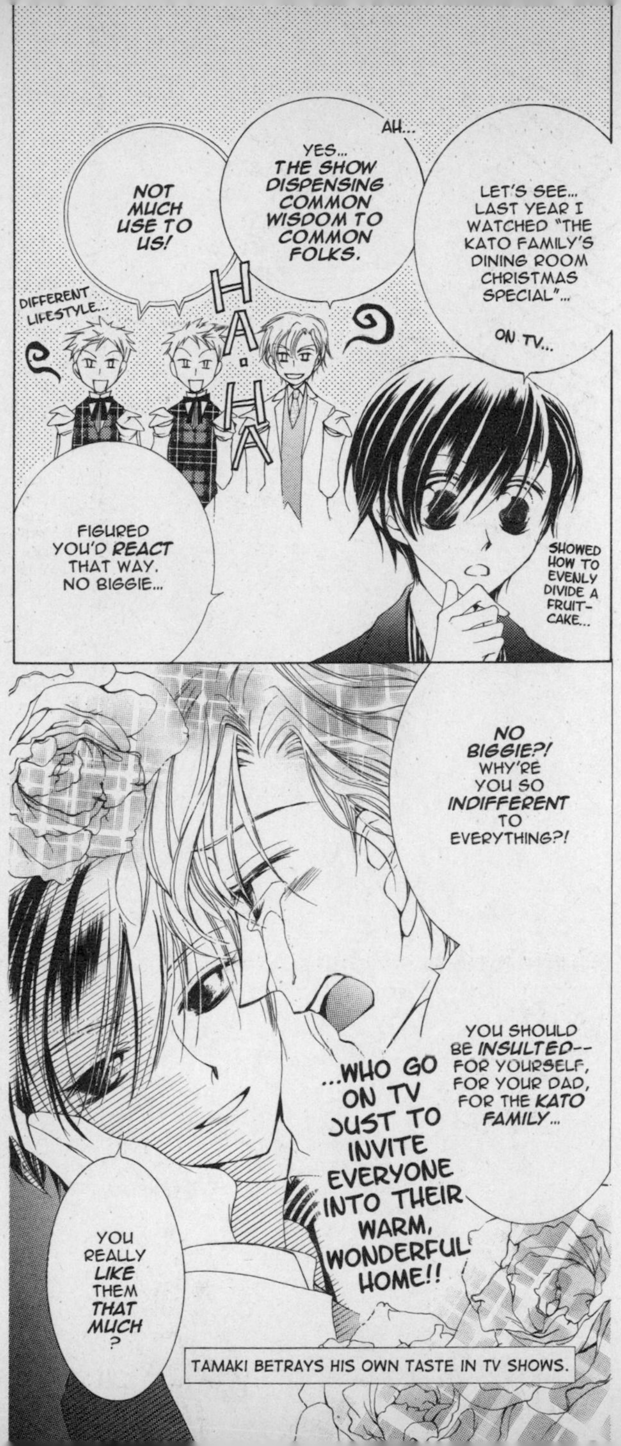
LET'S SEE... LAST YEAR I WATCHED "THE KATO FAMILY'S DINING ROOM CHRISTMAS SPECIAL"...
ON TV...
SHOWED HOW TO EVENLY DIVIDE A FRUIT-CAKE...
AH...
YES... *THE SHOW DISPENSING COMMON WISDOM TO COMMON FOLKS.*
NOT MUCH USE TO US!
HA HA HA
DIFFERENT LIFESTYLE...
FIGURED YOU'D *REACT* THAT WAY. NO BIGGIE...
NO BIGGIE?! WHY'RE YOU SO *INDIFFERENT* TO EVERYTHING?!
YOU SHOULD BE *INSULTED*-- FOR YOURSELF, FOR YOUR DAD, FOR THE *KATO FAMILY*...
...WHO GO ON TV JUST TO INVITE EVERYONE INTO THEIR WARM, WONDERFUL HOME!!
YOU REALLY *LIKE* THEM *THAT MUCH*?
TAMAKI BETRAYS HIS OWN TASTE IN TV SHOWS.

2

IN MY AREA, "HOST CLUB" IS HOW FOLKS USUALLY REFER TO THIS SERIES, BUT I SOMETIMES HEAR "OURAN" OR "OU HOS." I WOULD BE HAPPY TO HAVE PEOPLE CALL IT WHATEVER THEY LIKE, BUT JUST IN CASE, IF YOU TALK ABOUT IT ON THE TRAIN OR AT SCHOOL, SAYING "HOST CLUB" ALOUD MAY NOT BE THE SMARTEST THING... (LAUGH). TEACHERS AND OLDER MEN WOULD BE STARTLED!! (LAUGH). SO BE CAREFUL!!

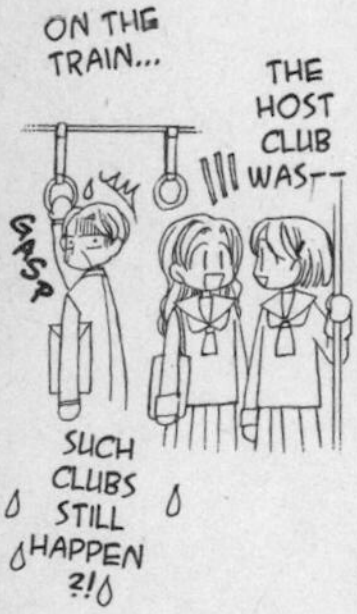
ON THE TRAIN...
THE HOST CLUB WAS--
GASP
SUCH CLUBS STILL HAPPEN?!

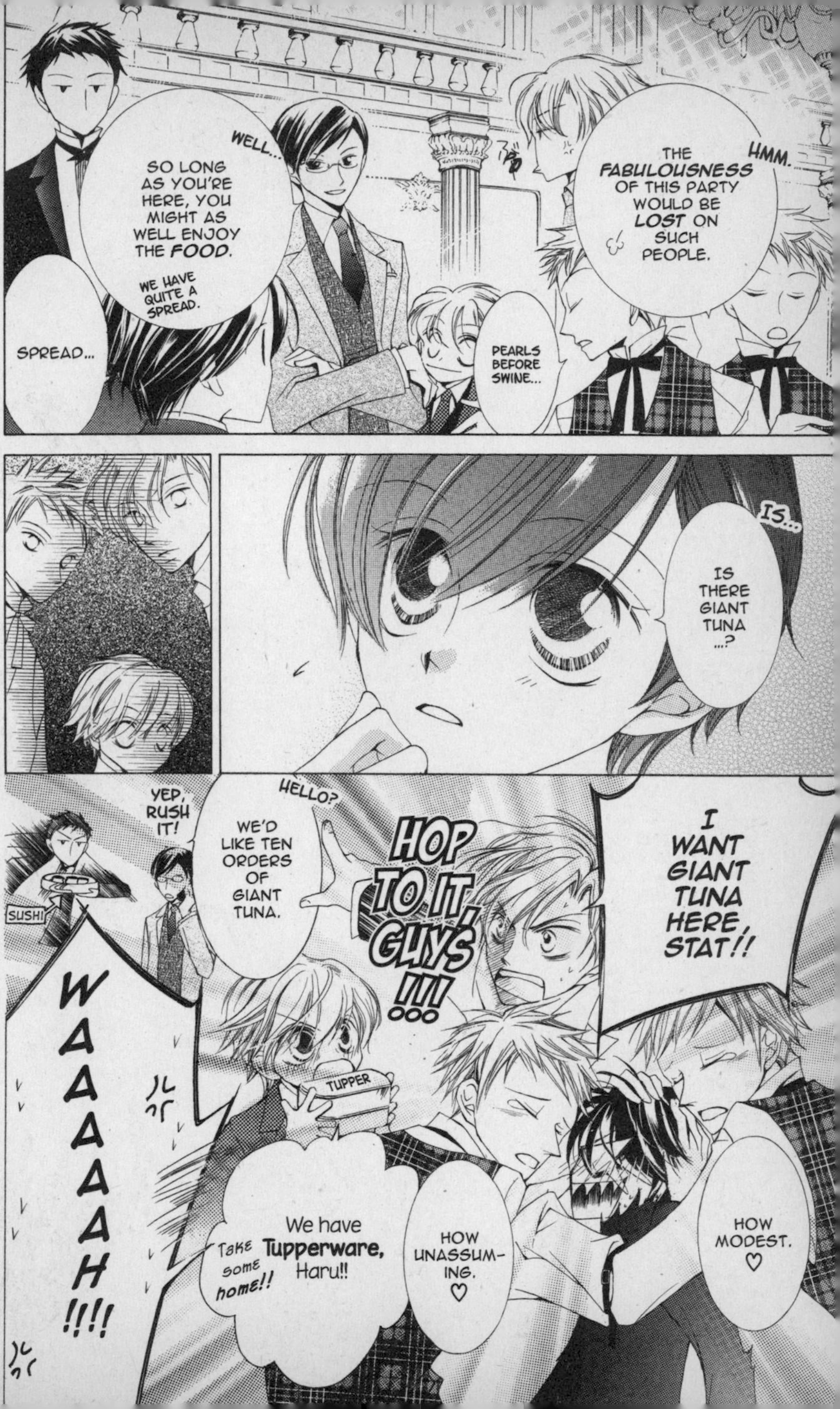
HMM.
THE **FABULOUSNESS** OF THIS PARTY WOULD BE **LOST** ON SUCH PEOPLE.
PEARLS BEFORE SWINE...
WELL...
SO LONG AS YOU'RE HERE, YOU MIGHT AS WELL ENJOY THE **FOOD**.
WE HAVE QUITE A SPREAD.
SPREAD...
IS...
IS THERE GIANT TUNA ...?
I WANT GIANT TUNA HERE, STAT!!
HOP TO IT, GUYS!!!
HELLO?
WE'D LIKE TEN ORDERS OF GIANT TUNA.
YEP, RUSH IT!
SUSHI
HOW MODEST. ♡
HOW UNASSUM-ING. ♡
We have **Tupperware,** Haru!!
Take some **home!!**
TUPPER
WAAAAAAH!!!!

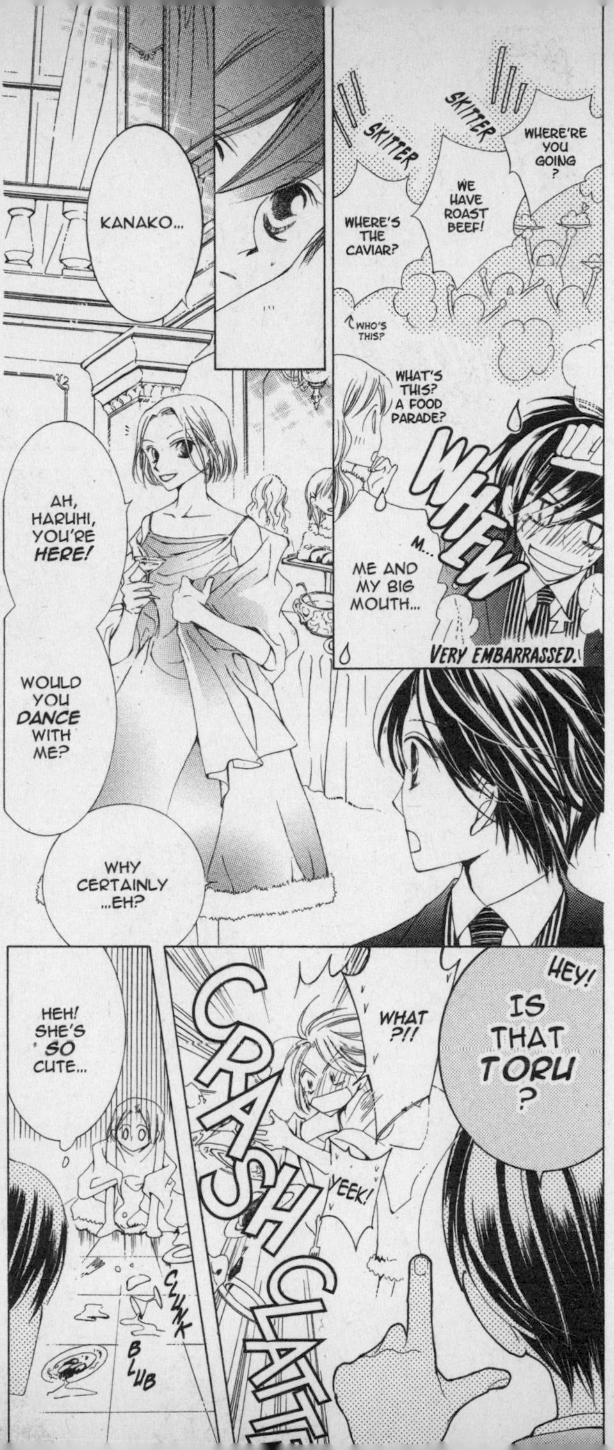
WHERE'RE YOU GOING?
SKITTER
SKITTER
WE HAVE ROAST BEEF!
WHERE'S THE CAVIAR?
WHO'S THIS?
WHAT'S THIS? A FOOD PARADE?
WHEW
M... ME AND MY BIG MOUTH...
VERY EMBARRASSED.
KANAKO...
AH, HARUHI, YOU'RE HERE!
WOULD YOU DANCE WITH ME?
WHY CERTAINLY ...EH?
HEY!
IS THAT TORU?
WHAT ?!!
YEEK!
CRASH
CLATTER
CLUNK
BLUB
HEH! SHE'S SO CUTE...

3

THOSE OF YOU WHO LIKED MY LAST WORK, "THOUSAND YEARS OF SNOW," MUST FIND "HOST CLUB" QUITE SURPRISING. I'M SURPRISED MYSELF (LAUGH). "COMEDY" AND WRITING THAT'S "CENTERED ON CHARACTERS" IS A NEW CHALLENGE FOR ME, SO I'VE BEEN RATHER WORRIED...

IN TERMS OF THE WORK ITSELF, THE TONE IS DIFFERENT FROM "THOUSAND YEARS." (GLAMOUR GONE OVERBOARD AS THE THEME! HA!)

I'VE CHANGED MY INK AND PAPER TO KEEP UP WITH THE PACE OF THE DRAWING, AND I'VE RECRUITED QUITE A STAFF TO HELP ME OUT WITH BACKGROUNDS AND WHATNOT. THIS IS A FIRST FOR ME IN MANY RESPECTS, BUT I HOPE TO ENJOY DOING IT, EVEN WITH THE CONSTANT STRUGGLES. I HOPE YOU'LL ALL FIND IT FUNNY. I'LL KEEP WORKING HARD TO MAKE IT SO, AND THEREFORE YOUR SUPPORT IS IMPORTANT.

ACTUALLY, "THOUSAND YEARS OF SNOW" ISN'T OVER YET (WHISPER). STAY TUNED...

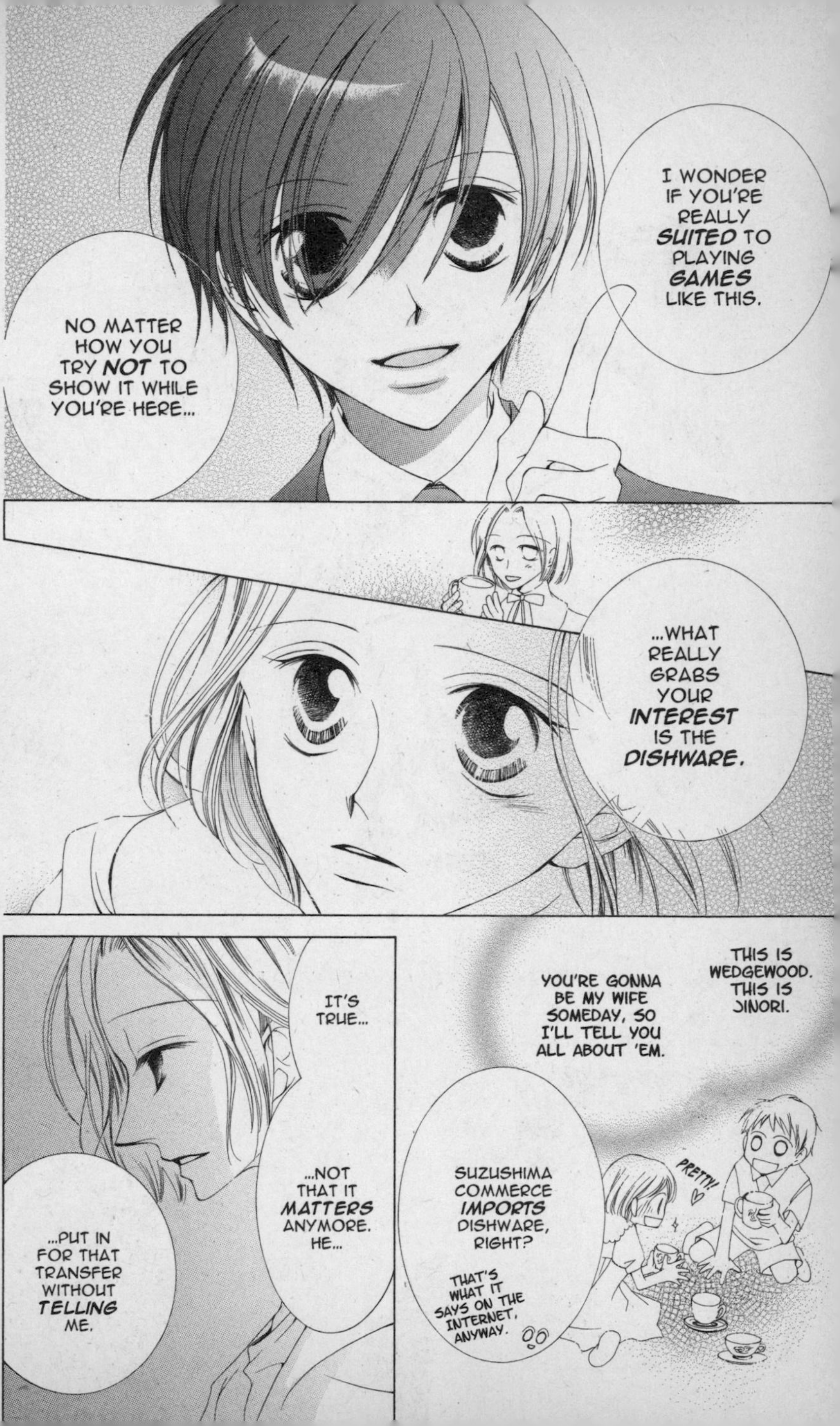
I WONDER IF YOU'RE REALLY SUITED TO PLAYING GAMES LIKE THIS.
NO MATTER HOW YOU TRY NOT TO SHOW IT WHILE YOU'RE HERE...
...WHAT REALLY GRABS YOUR INTEREST IS THE DISHWARE.
THIS IS WEDGEWOOD. THIS IS JINORI.
YOU'RE GONNA BE MY WIFE SOMEDAY, SO I'LL TELL YOU ALL ABOUT 'EM.
PRETTY!
SUZUSHIMA COMMERCE IMPORTS DISHWARE, RIGHT?
THAT'S WHAT IT SAYS ON THE INTERNET, ANYWAY.
IT'S TRUE...
...NOT THAT IT MATTERS ANYMORE. HE...
...PUT IN FOR THAT TRANSFER WITHOUT TELLING ME.

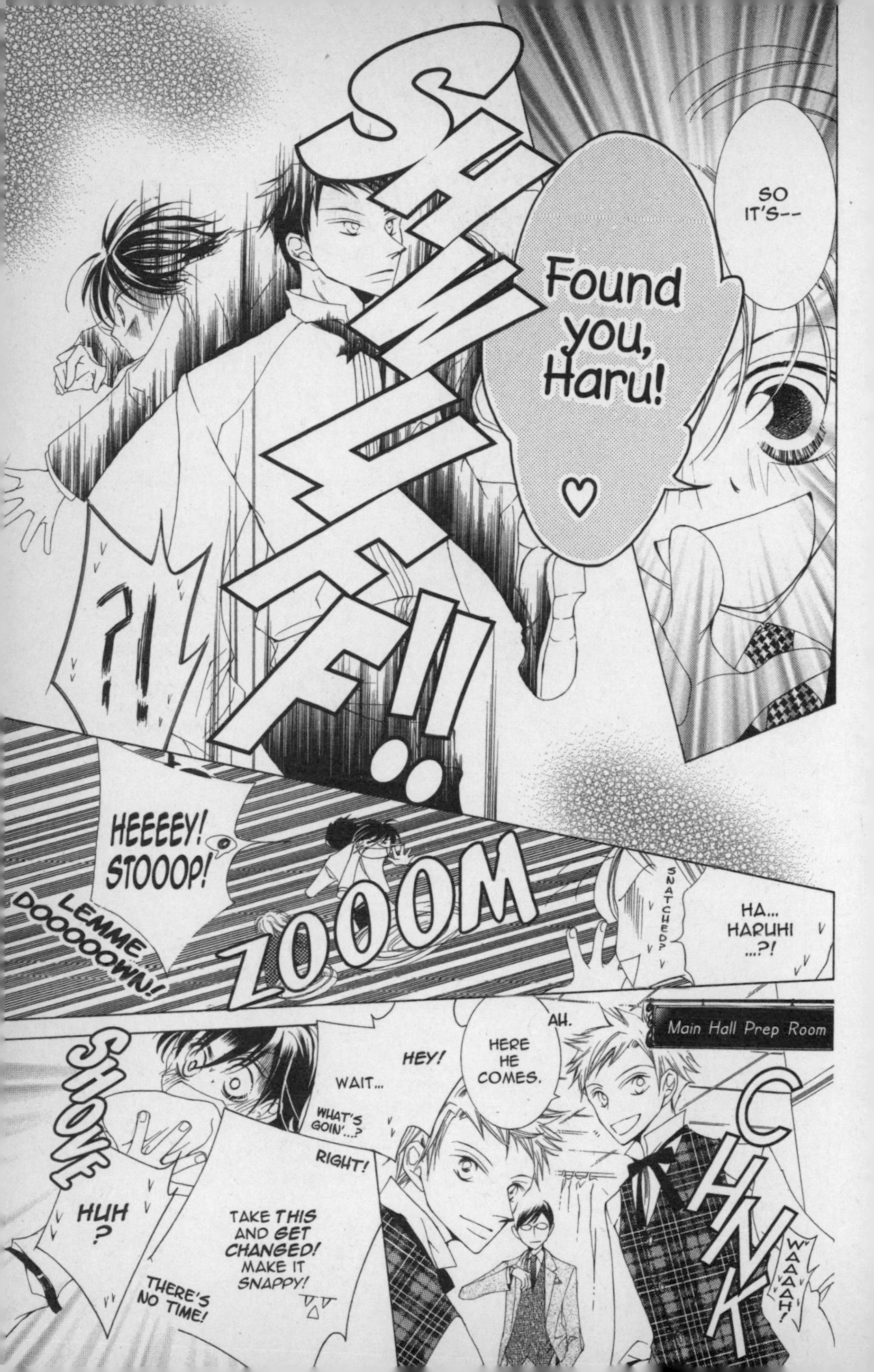
SO IT'S--
Found you, Haru! ♡
SHWUMP!!
?!
HA... HARUHI ...?!
SNATCHED?
ZOOOM
HEEEEY! STOOOP!
LEMME DOOOOOOWN!
Main Hall Prep Room
AH.
HERE HE COMES.
HEY!
WAIT...
WHAT'S GOIN'...?
RIGHT!
CHNK
W'WAAAAH!
TAKE THIS AND GET CHANGED! MAKE IT SNAPPY!
THERE'S NO TIME!
HUH?
SHOVE

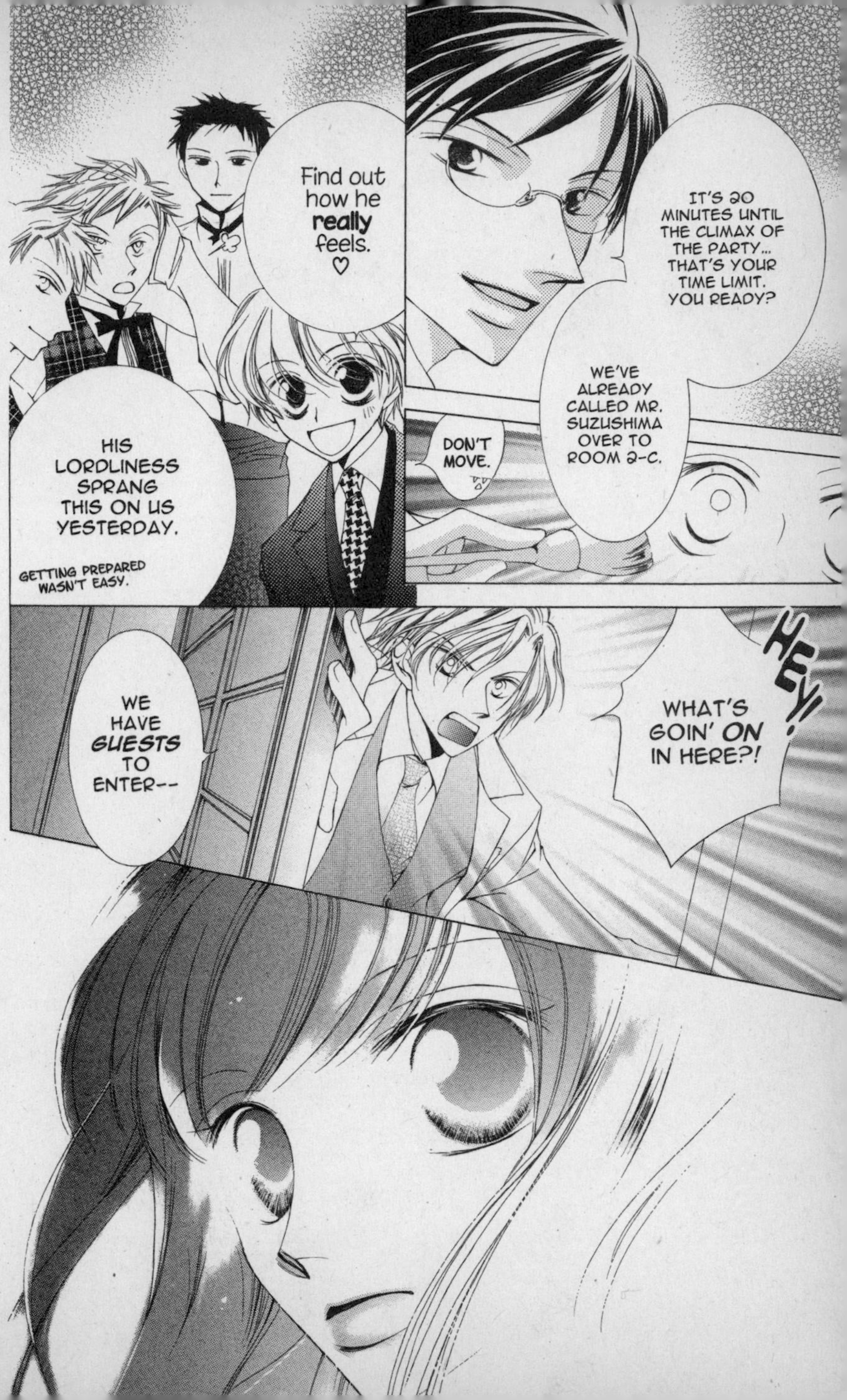
IT'S 20 MINUTES UNTIL THE CLIMAX OF THE PARTY... THAT'S YOUR TIME LIMIT. YOU READY?
WE'VE ALREADY CALLED MR. SUZUSHIMA OVER TO ROOM 2-C.
DON'T MOVE.
Find out how he **really** feels. ♡
HIS LORDLINESS SPRANG THIS ON US YESTERDAY.
GETTING PREPARED WASN'T EASY.
HEY!!
WHAT'S GOIN' ON IN HERE?!
WE HAVE *GUESTS* TO ENTER--

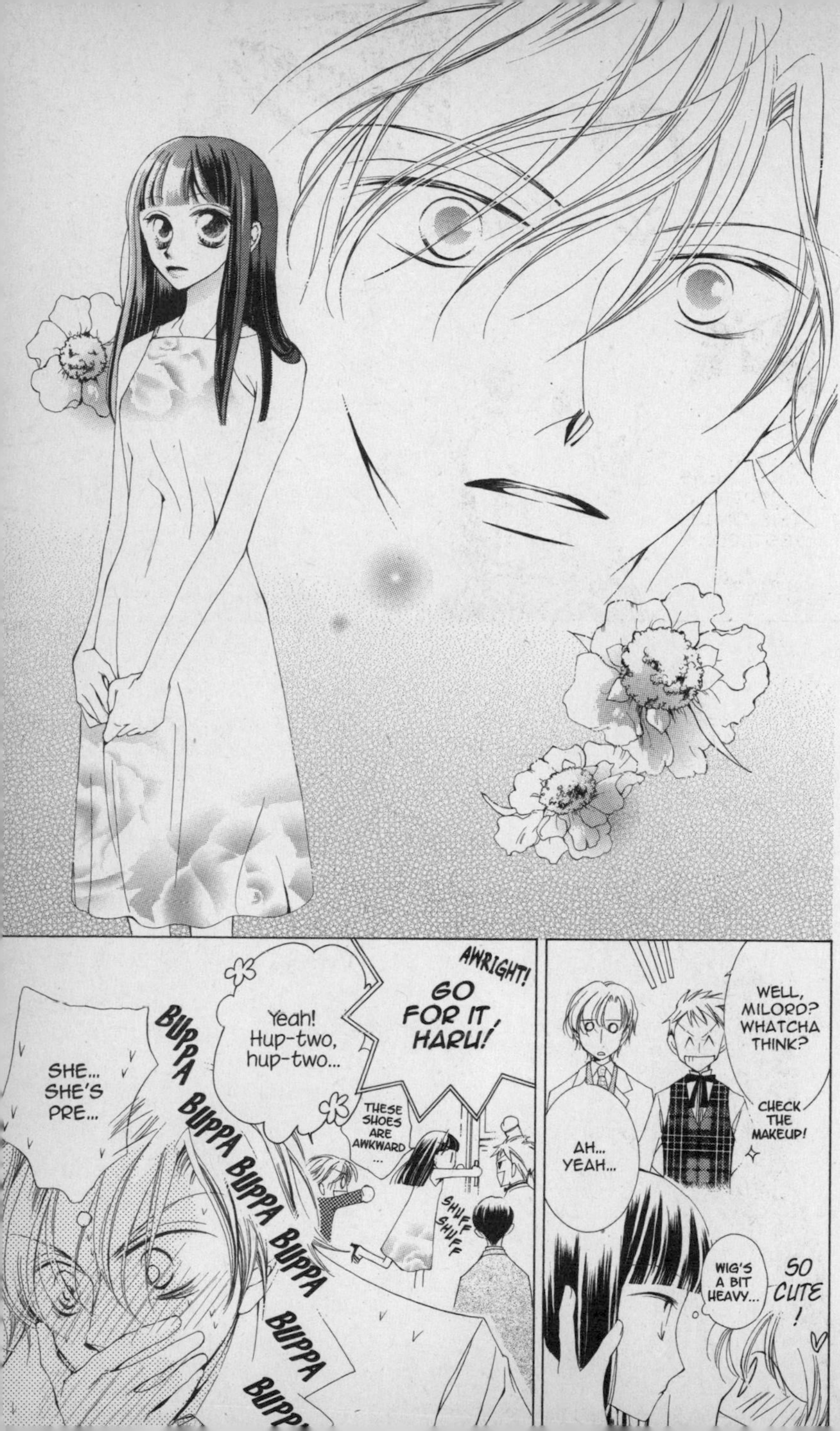
WELL, MILORD? WHATCHA THINK?
CHECK THE MAKEUP!
AH... YEAH...
WIG'S A BIT HEAVY...
SO CUTE!
AWRIGHT!
GO FOR IT, HARU!
Yeah! Hup-two, hup-two...
THESE SHOES ARE AWKWARD...
SHUFF SHUFF
SHE... SHE'S PRE...
BUPPA BUPPA BUPPA BUPPA BUPPA BUPPA

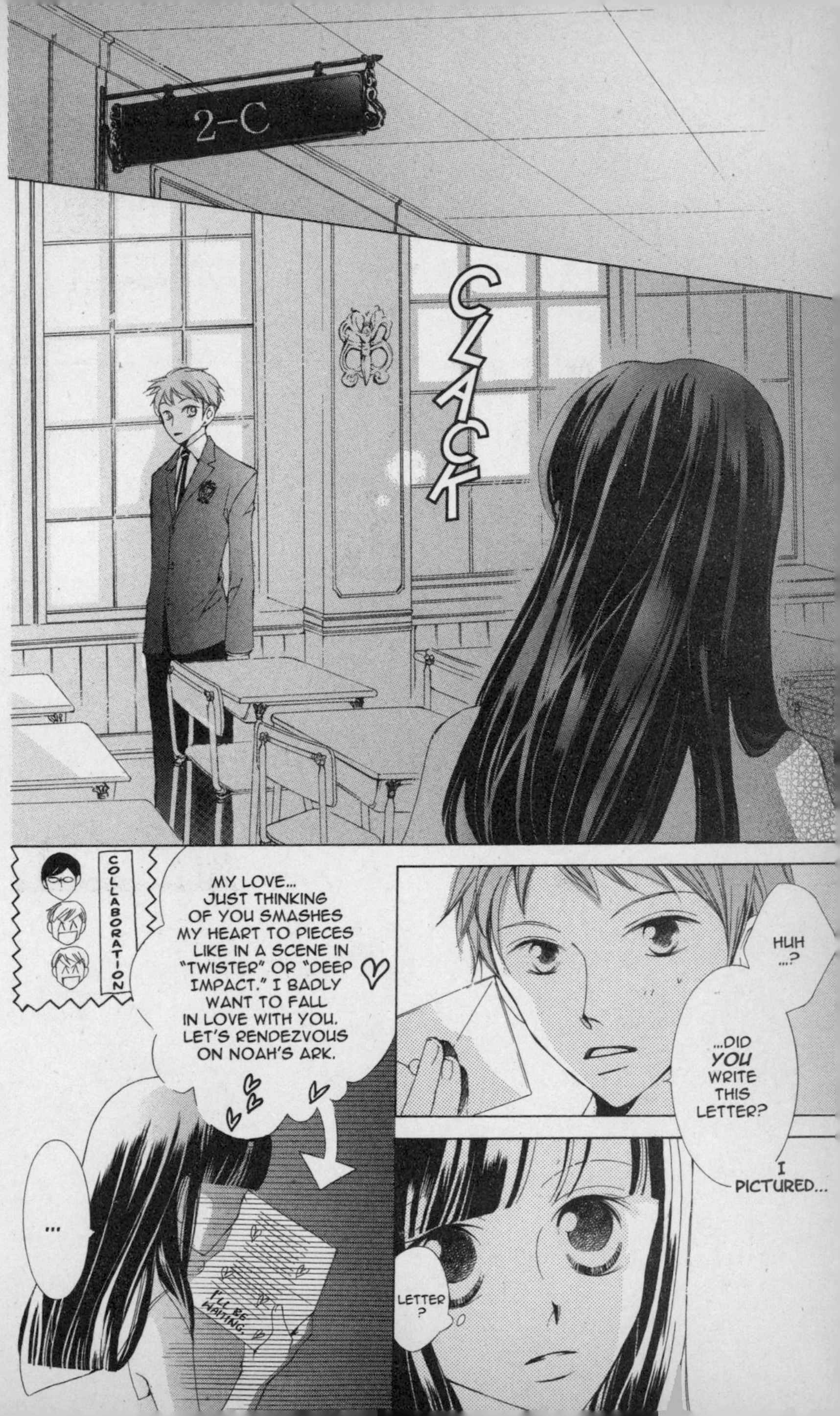
2-C
CLACK
HUH ...?
...DID YOU WRITE THIS LETTER?
I PICTURED...
LETTER ?
COLLABORATION
MY LOVE... JUST THINKING OF YOU SMASHES MY HEART TO PIECES LIKE IN A SCENE IN "TWISTER" OR "DEEP IMPACT." I BADLY WANT TO FALL IN LOVE WITH YOU. LET'S RENDEZVOUS ON NOAH'S ARK.
...
I'LL BE WAITING.

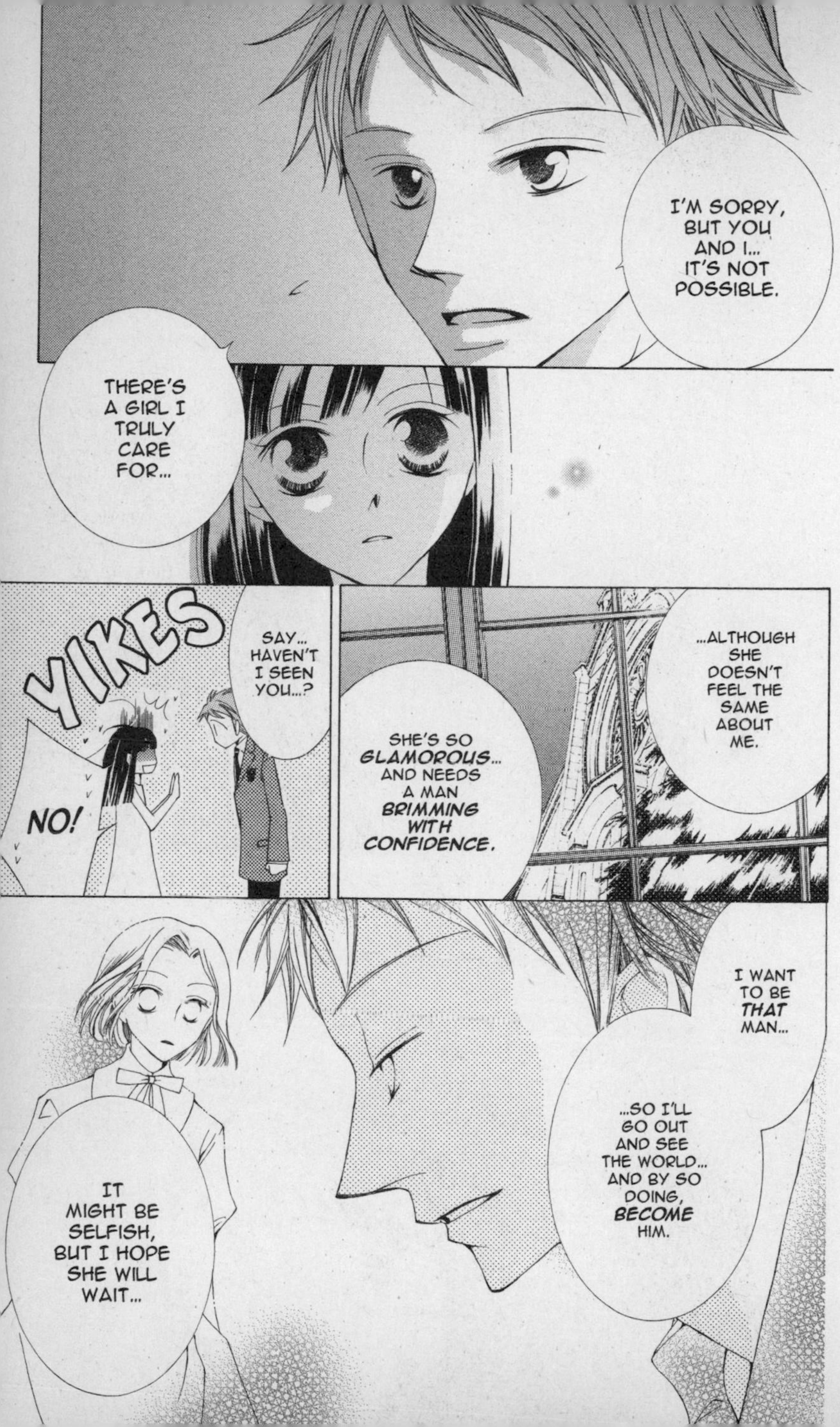
I'M SORRY, BUT YOU AND I... IT'S NOT POSSIBLE.
THERE'S A GIRL I TRULY CARE FOR...
...ALTHOUGH SHE DOESN'T FEEL THE SAME ABOUT ME.
SHE'S SO GLAMOROUS... AND NEEDS A MAN BRIMMING WITH CONFIDENCE.
SAY... HAVEN'T I SEEN YOU...?
YIKES
NO!
I WANT TO BE THAT MAN...
...SO I'LL GO OUT AND SEE THE WORLD... AND BY SO DOING, BECOME HIM.
IT MIGHT BE SELFISH, BUT I HOPE SHE WILL WAIT...

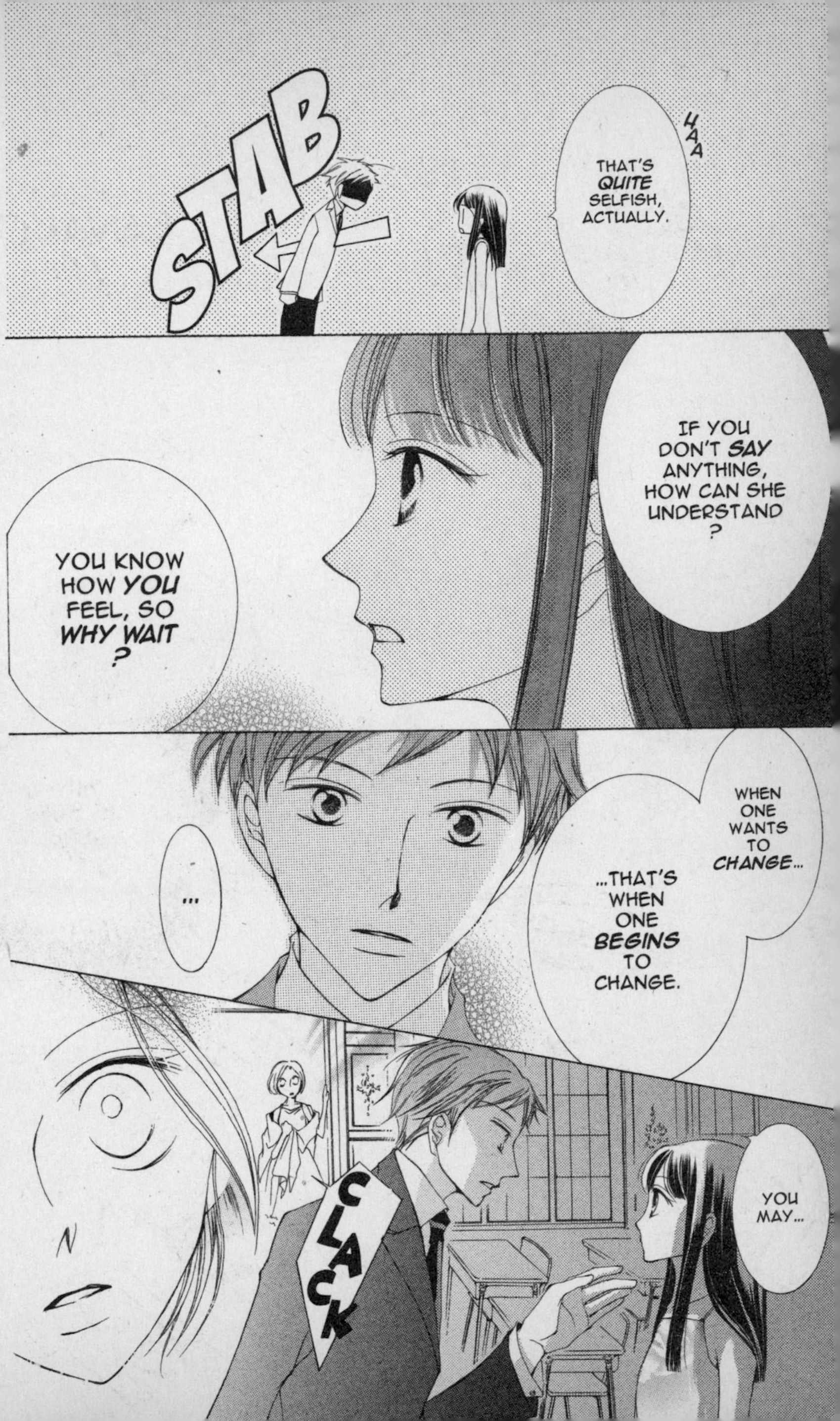
HAAA
THAT'S QUITE SELFISH, ACTUALLY.
STAB
IF YOU DON'T SAY ANYTHING, HOW CAN SHE UNDERSTAND?
YOU KNOW HOW YOU FEEL, SO WHY WAIT?
WHEN ONE WANTS TO CHANGE...
...THAT'S WHEN ONE BEGINS TO CHANGE.
...
YOU MAY...
CLACK

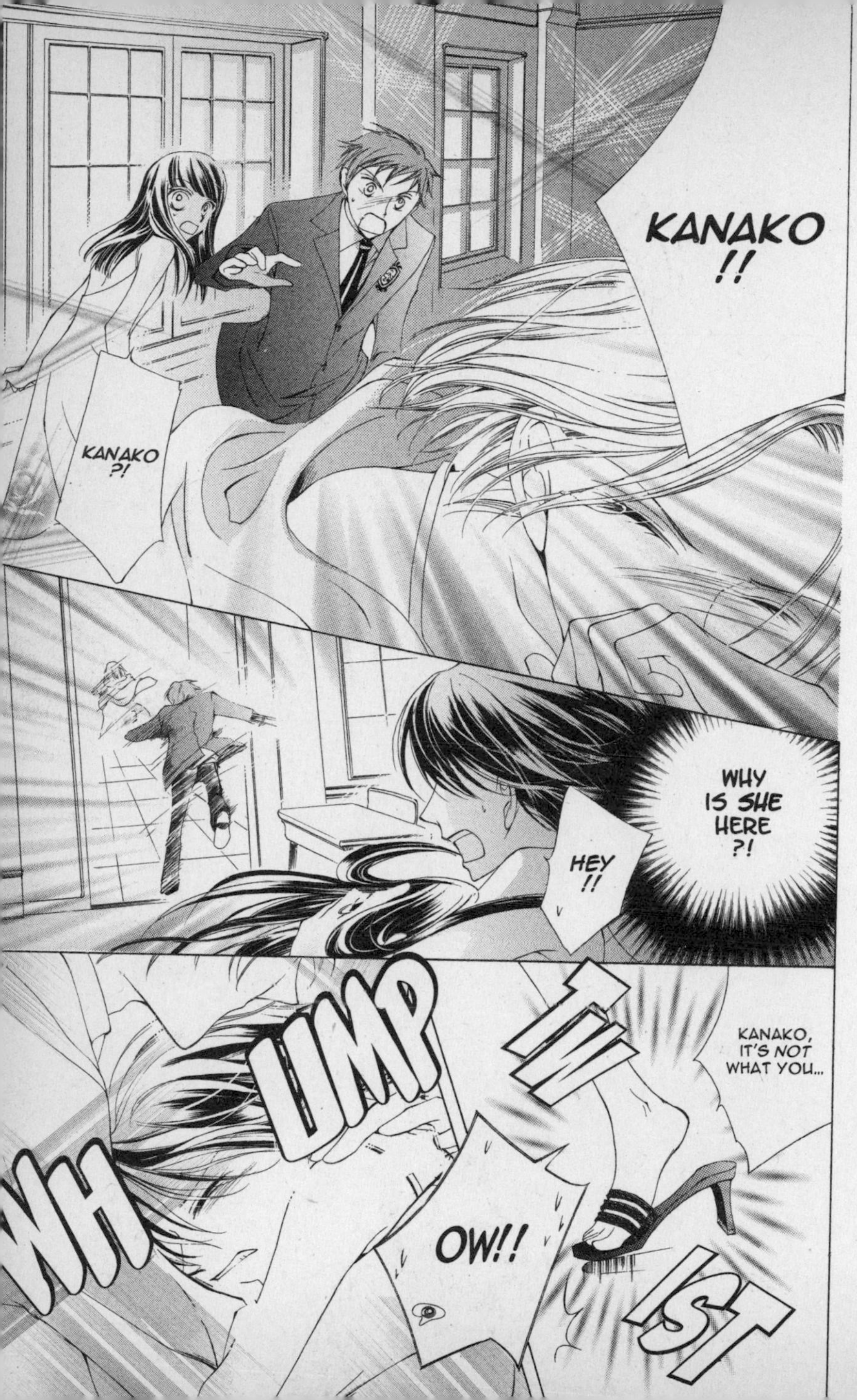
KANAKO!!
KANAKO?!
WHY IS SHE HERE?!
HEY!!
KANAKO, IT'S NOT WHAT YOU...
TWIST
OW!!
WHUMP

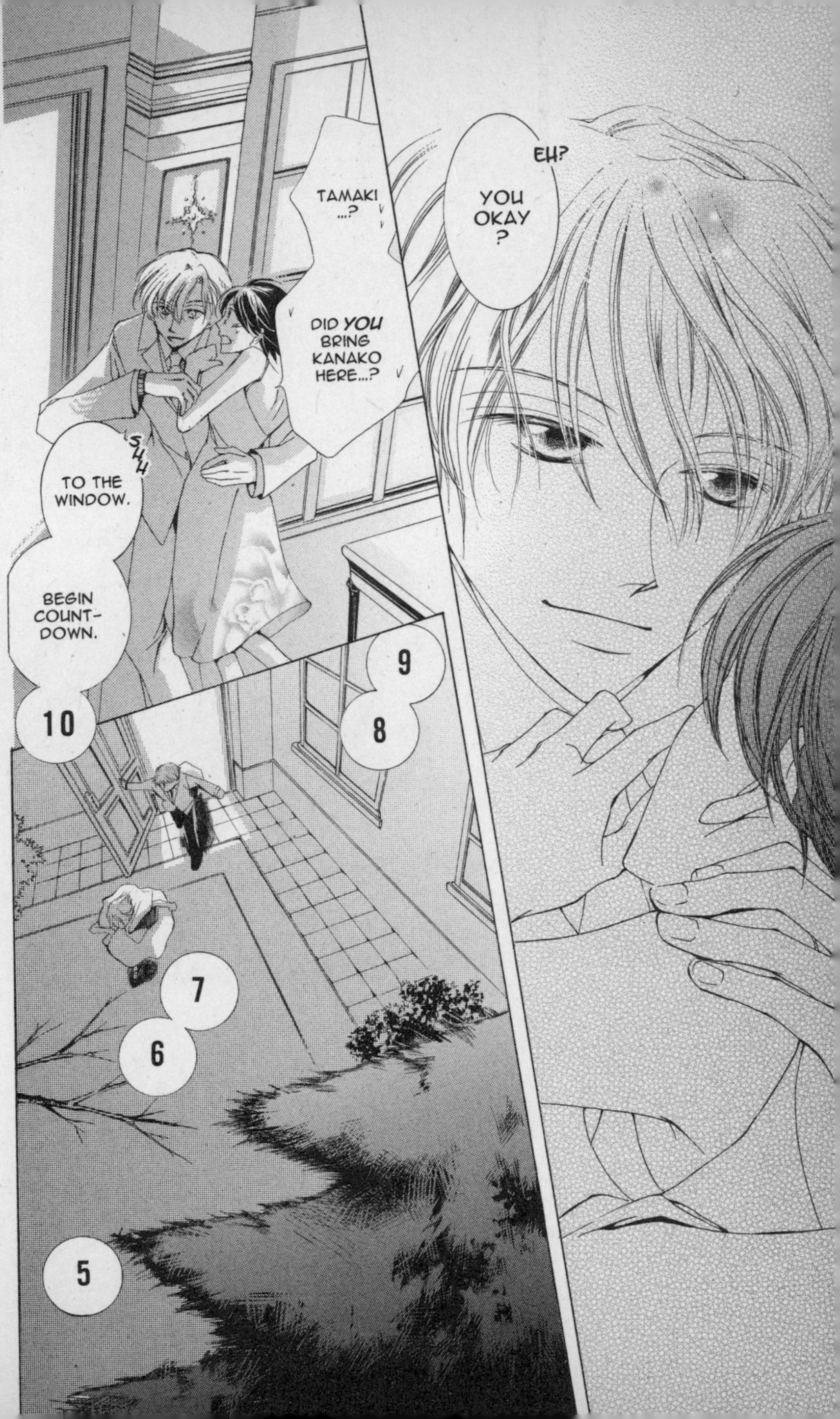
EH?
YOU OKAY ?
TAMAKI ...?
DID YOU BRING KANAKO HERE...?
SHH
TO THE WINDOW.
BEGIN COUNT-DOWN.
10
9
8
7
6
5

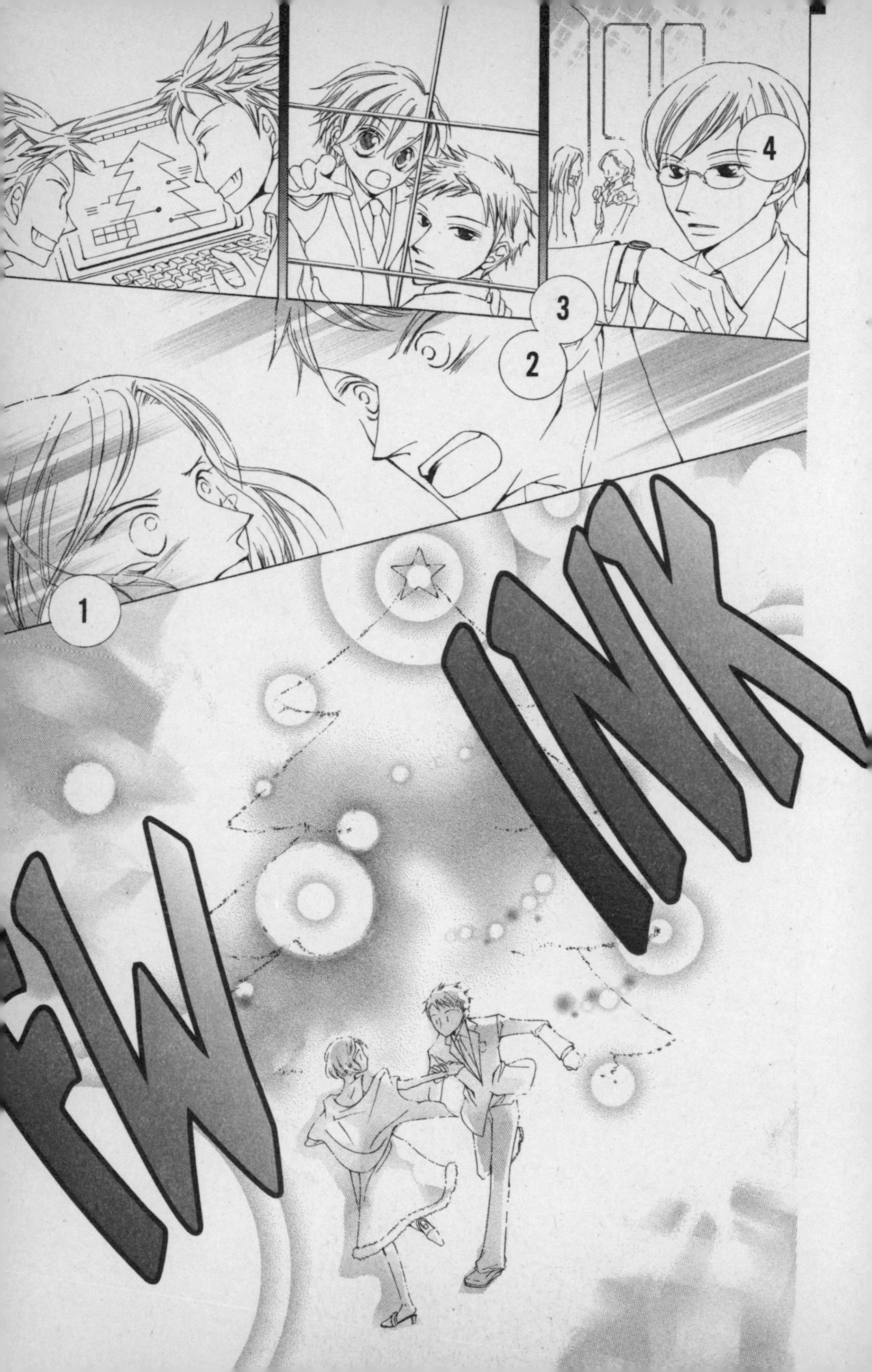
4
3
2
1
W
INK

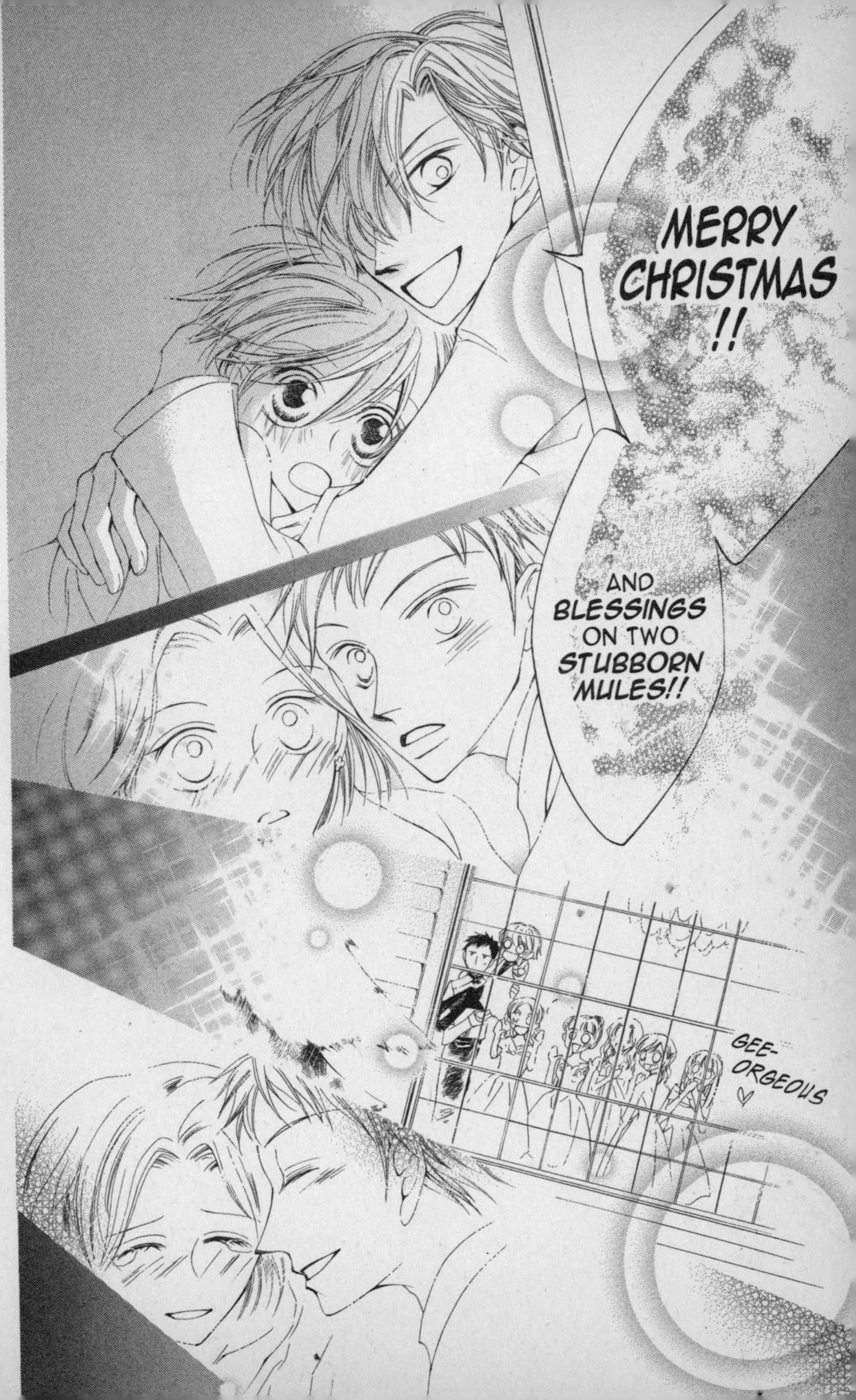
MERRY CHRISTMAS!!
AND BLESSINGS ON TWO STUBBORN MULES!!
GEE-ORGEOUS ♡

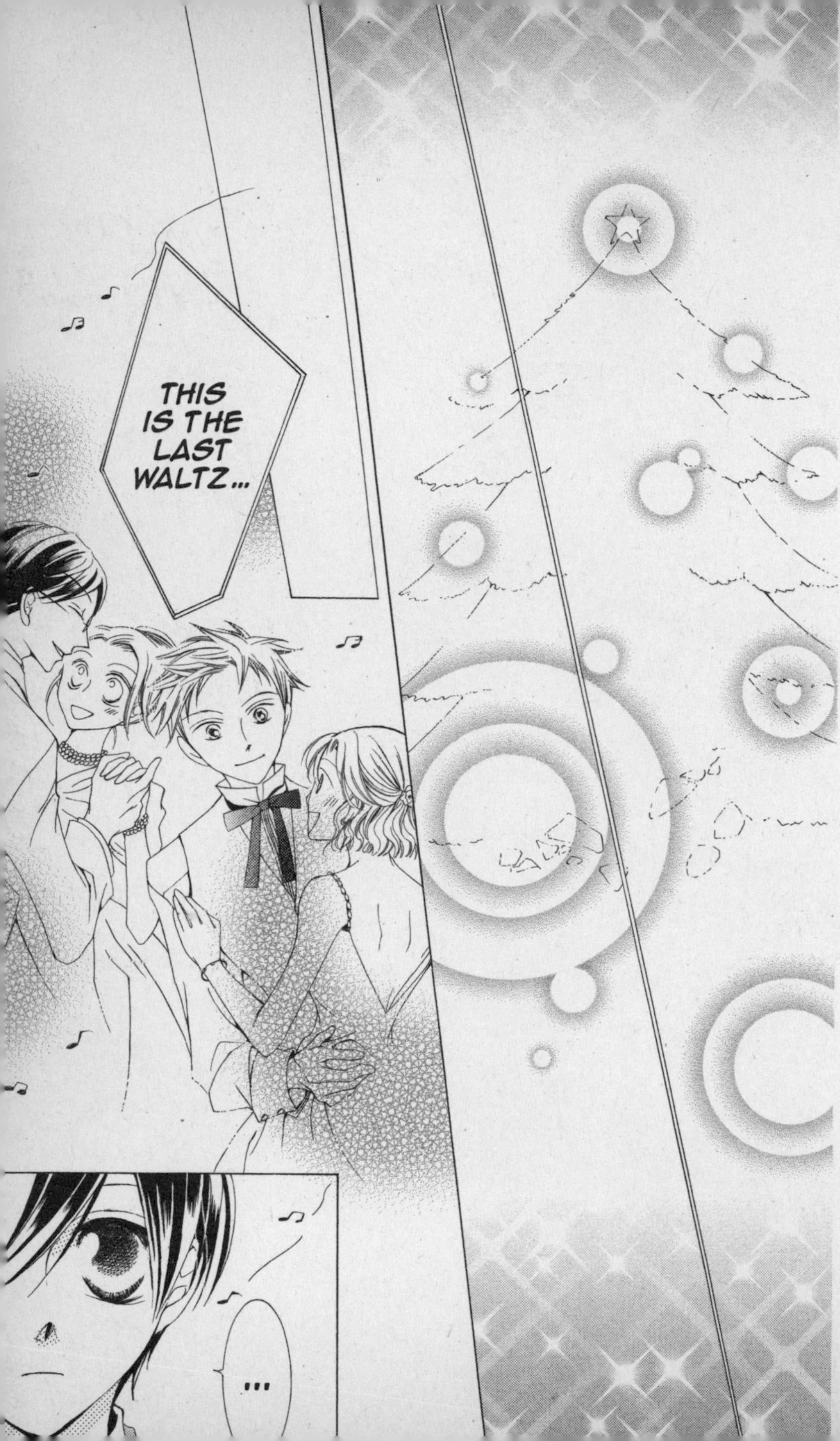
THIS IS THE LAST WALTZ...
...

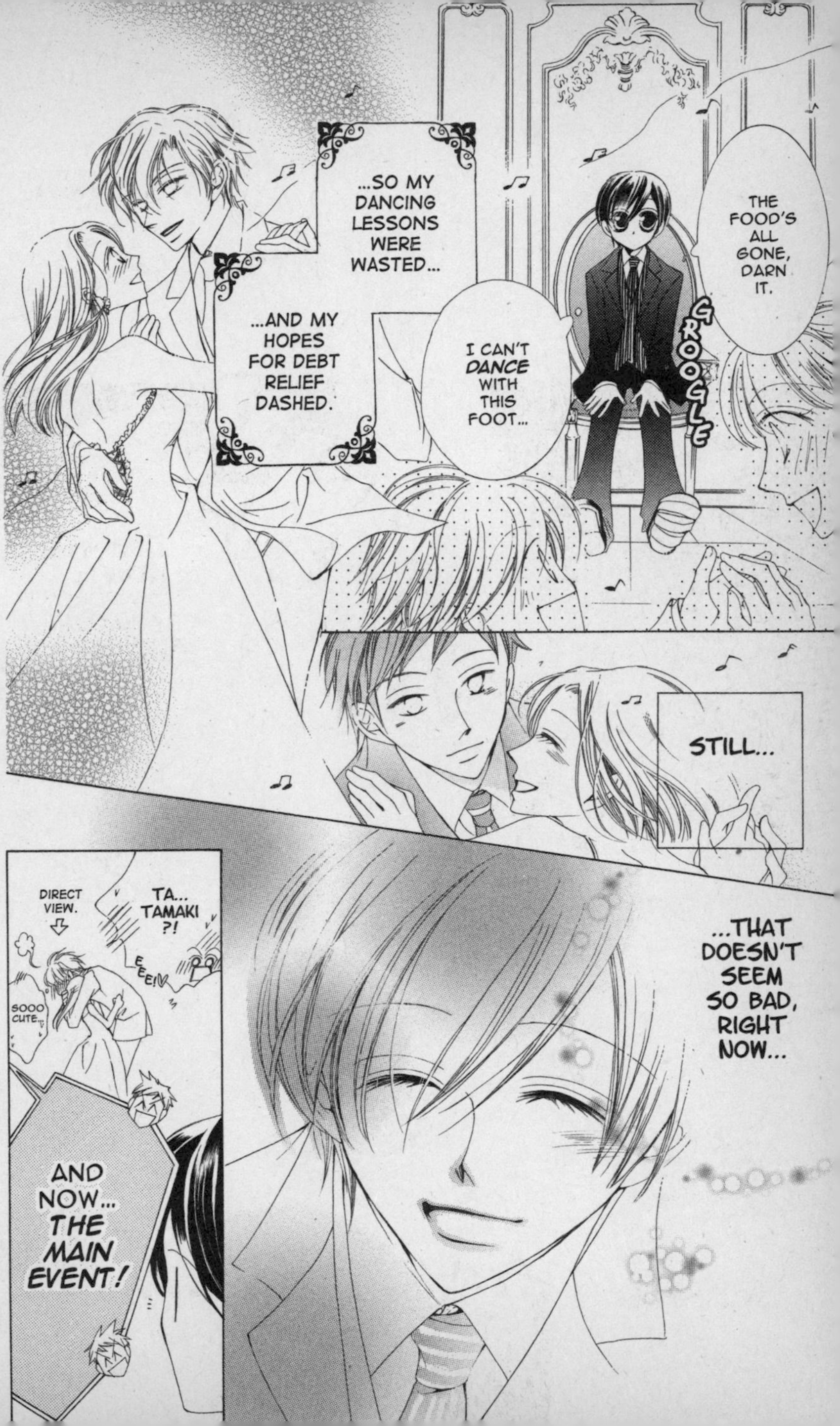
THE FOOD'S ALL GONE, DARN IT.
GROOGLE
I CAN'T DANCE WITH THIS FOOT...
...SO MY DANCING LESSONS WERE WASTED...
...AND MY HOPES FOR DEBT RELIEF DASHED.
STILL...
...THAT DOESN'T SEEM SO BAD, RIGHT NOW...
TA... TAMAKI ?!
DIRECT VIEW.
EEE!♥
SOOO CUTE...
AND NOW... THE MAIN EVENT!

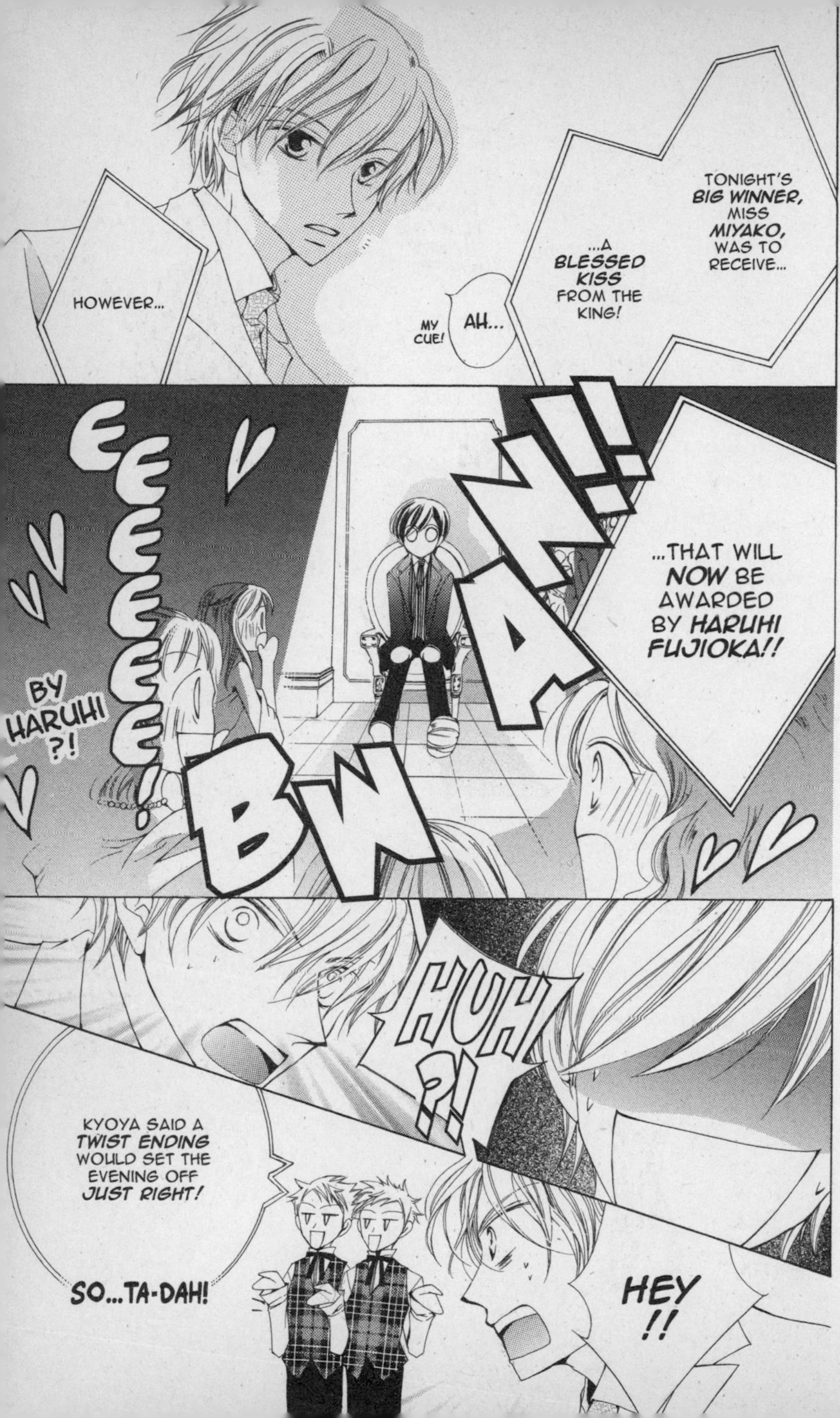
TONIGHT'S BIG WINNER, MISS MIYAKO, WAS TO RECEIVE...
...A BLESSED KISS FROM THE KING!
AH...
MY CUE!
HOWEVER...
...THAT WILL NOW BE AWARDED BY HARUHI FUJIOKA!!
BWAAH!!
EEEEEEEE!
BY HARUHI ?!
HUH ?!
KYOYA SAID A TWIST ENDING WOULD SET THE EVENING OFF JUST RIGHT!
SO...TA-DAH!
HEY !!

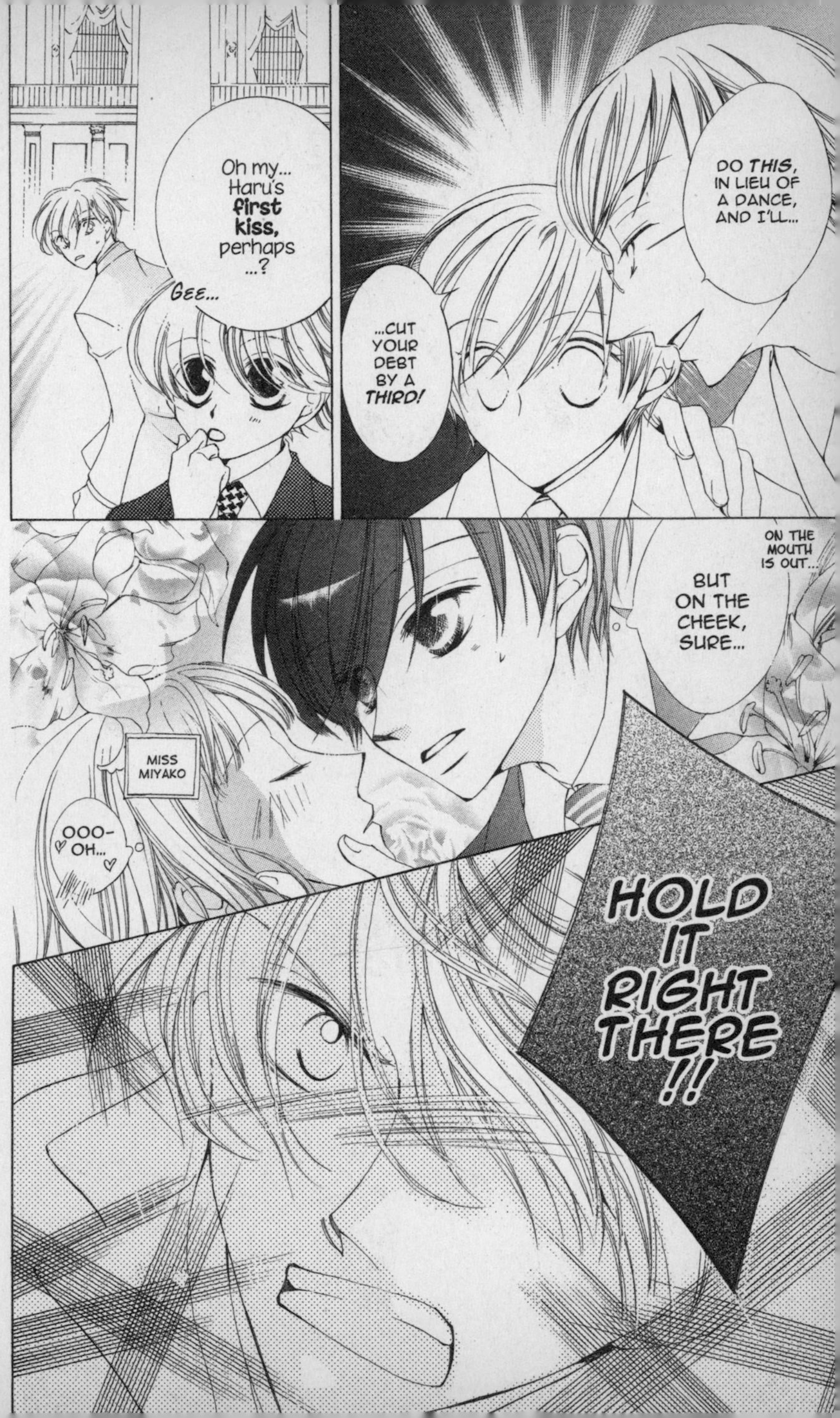
DO THIS, IN LIEU OF A DANCE, AND I'LL...
...CUT YOUR DEBT BY A THIRD!
Oh my... Haru's first kiss, perhaps ...?
GEE...
ON THE MOUTH IS OUT...
BUT ON THE CHEEK, SURE...
MISS MIYAKO
OOO-OH...
HOLD IT RIGHT THERE !!

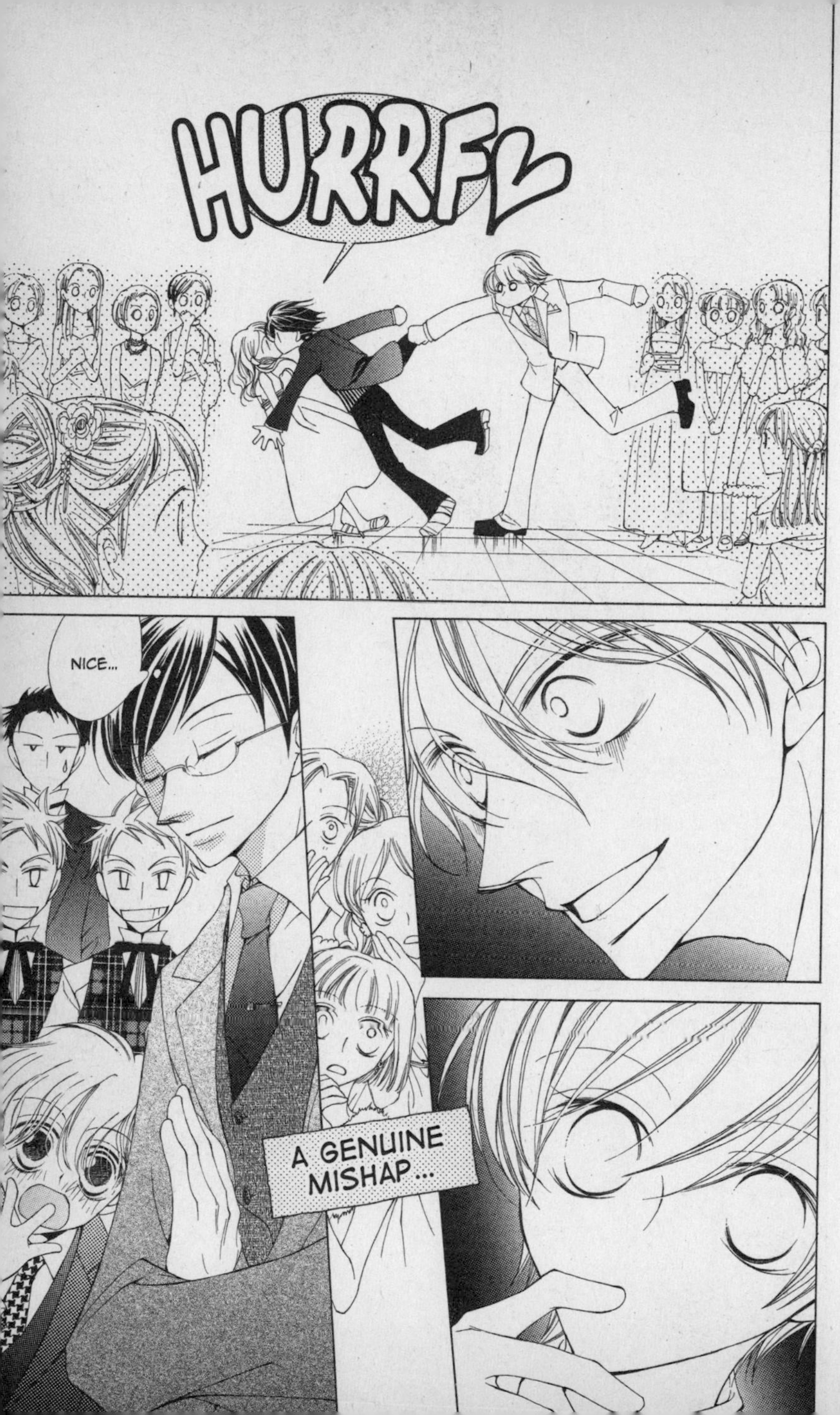
HURRF♥
NICE...
A GENUINE MISHAP...

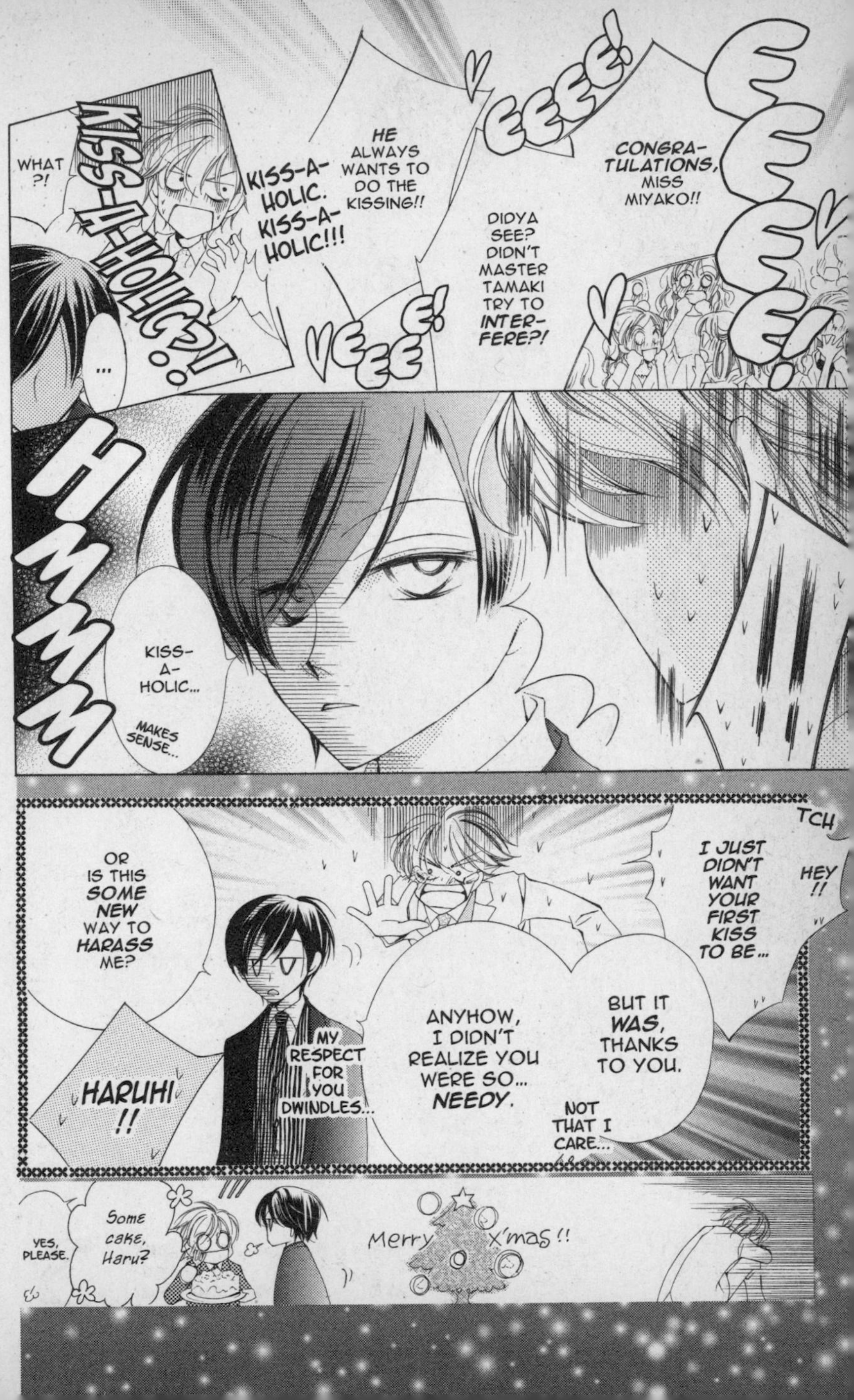
EEEEEE!
CONGRATULATIONS, MISS MIYAKO!!
DIDYA SEE? DIDN'T MASTER TAMAKI TRY TO INTERFERE?!
EEEE!
HE ALWAYS WANTS TO DO THE KISSING!!
EEEE!
KISS-A-HOLIC. KISS-A-HOLIC!!!
KISS-A-HOLIC?!!
WHAT?!
...
HMMMM
KISS-A-HOLIC...
MAKES SENSE...
TCH
HEY!!
I JUST DIDN'T WANT YOUR FIRST KISS TO BE...
BUT IT WAS, THANKS TO YOU.
NOT THAT I CARE...
ANYHOW, I DIDN'T REALIZE YOU WERE SO... NEEDY.
MY RESPECT FOR YOU DWINDLES...
OR IS THIS SOME NEW WAY TO HARASS ME?
HARUHI!!
Merry X'mas!!
Some cake, Haru?
YES, PLEASE.

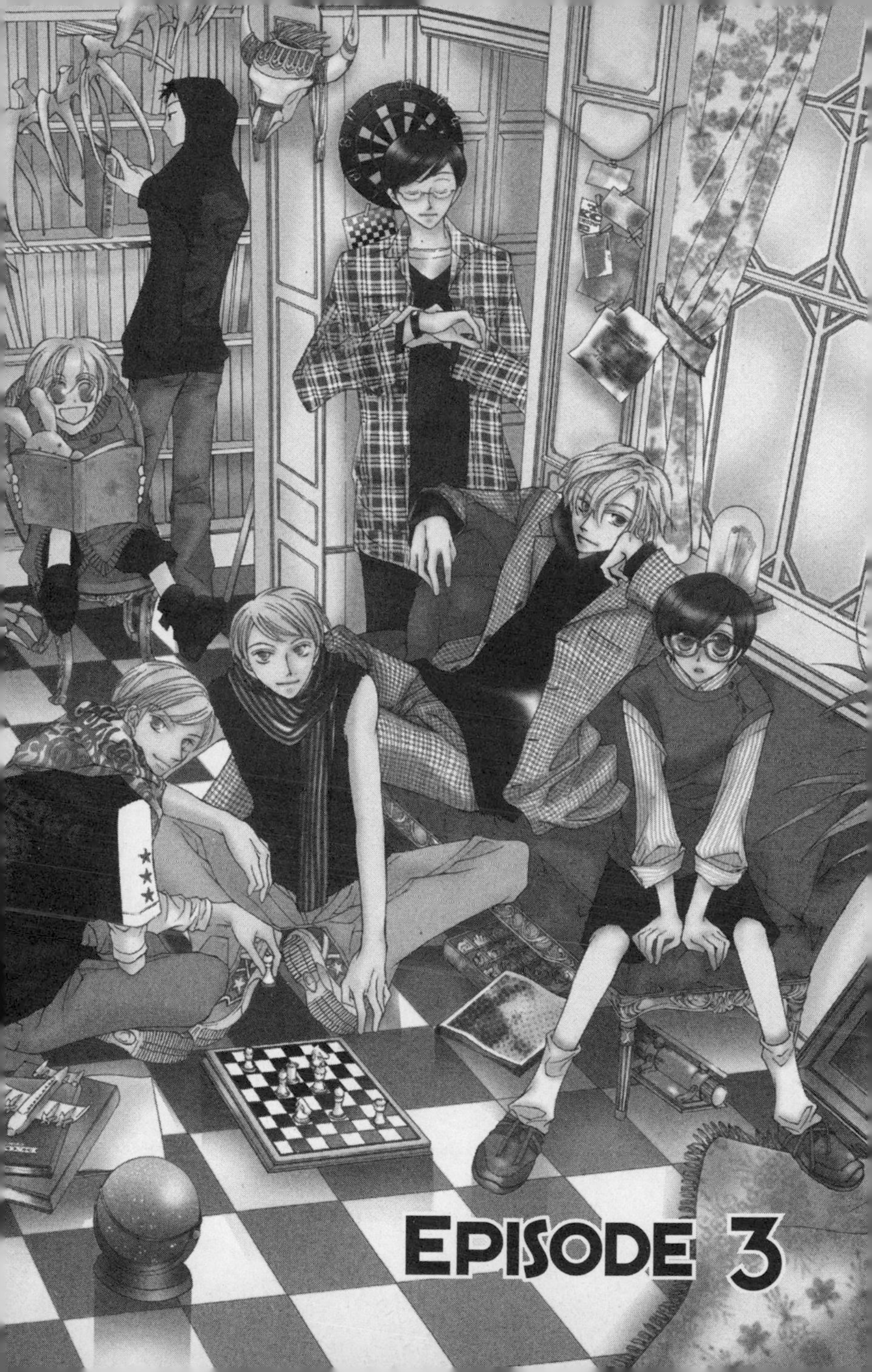
EPISODE 3

Preview Manga

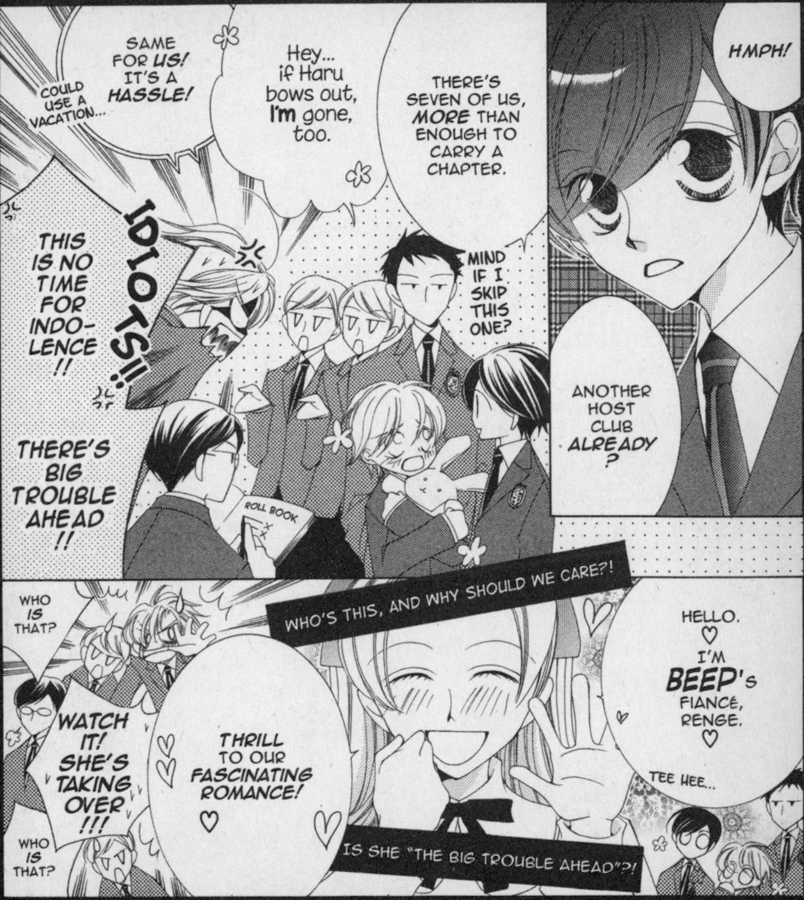

HMPH!
ANOTHER HOST CLUB ALREADY?
THERE'S SEVEN OF US, MORE THAN ENOUGH TO CARRY A CHAPTER.
MIND IF I SKIP THIS ONE?
Hey... if Haru bows out, I'm gone, too.
SAME FOR US! IT'S A HASSLE!
COULD USE A VACATION...
IDIOTS!!!
THIS IS NO TIME FOR INDO-LENCE!!
THERE'S BIG TROUBLE AHEAD!!
ROLL BOOK
HELLO. ♡ I'M BEEP's FIANCÉ, RENGE. ♡
TEE HEE...
WHO'S THIS, AND WHY SHOULD WE CARE?!
THRILL TO OUR FASCINATING ROMANCE! ♡
IS SHE "THE BIG TROUBLE AHEAD"?!
WATCH IT! SHE'S TAKING OVER!!!
WHO IS THAT?
WHO IS THAT?

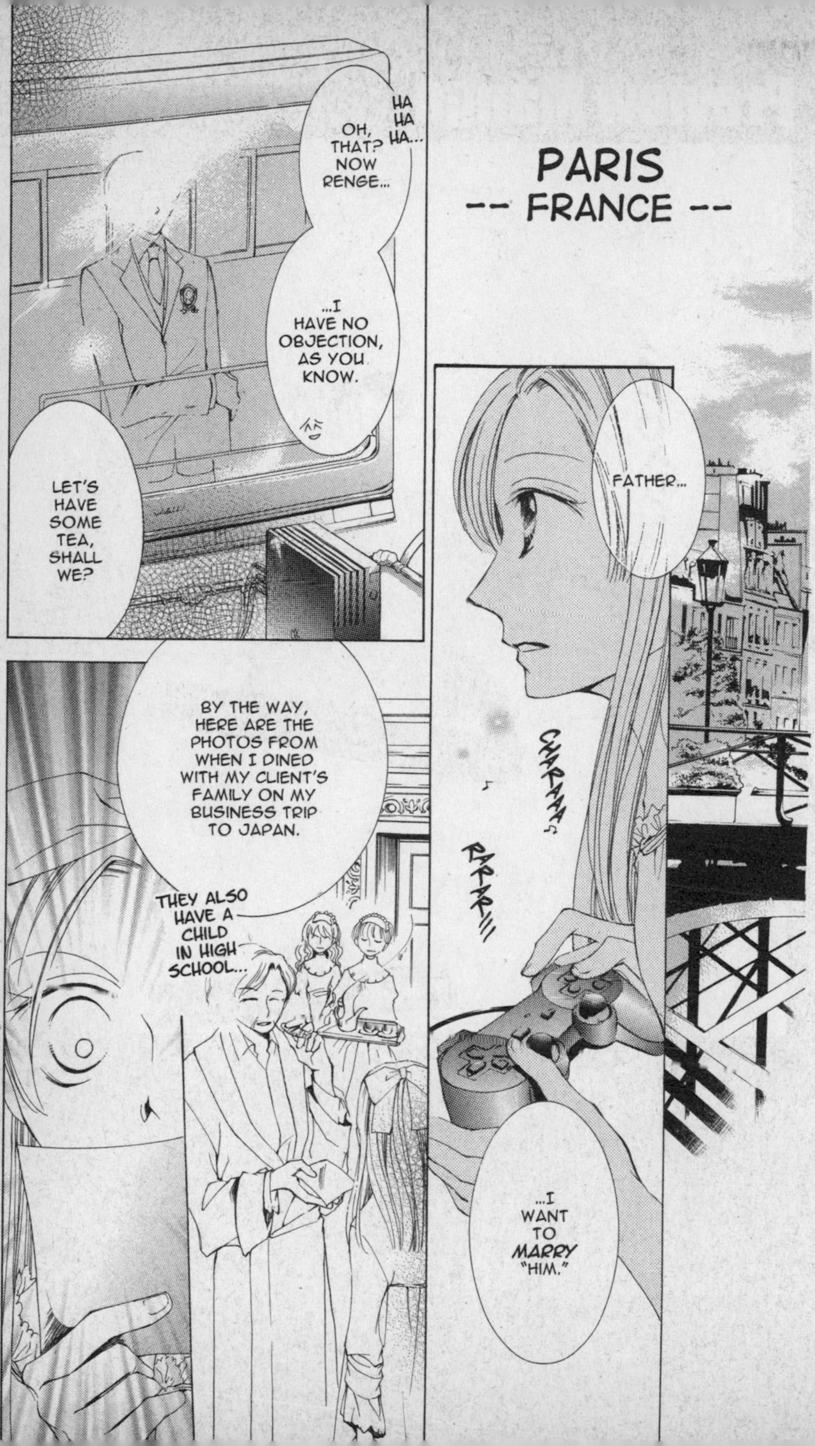
PARIS
-- FRANCE --
FATHER...
CHARAAA♪
RARAR!!!
...I WANT TO MARRY "HIM."
HA HA HA...
OH, THAT? NOW RENGE...
...I HAVE NO OBJECTION, AS YOU KNOW.
LET'S HAVE SOME TEA, SHALL WE?
BY THE WAY, HERE ARE THE PHOTOS FROM WHEN I DINED WITH MY CLIENT'S FAMILY ON MY BUSINESS TRIP TO JAPAN.
THEY ALSO HAVE A CHILD IN HIGH SCHOOL...

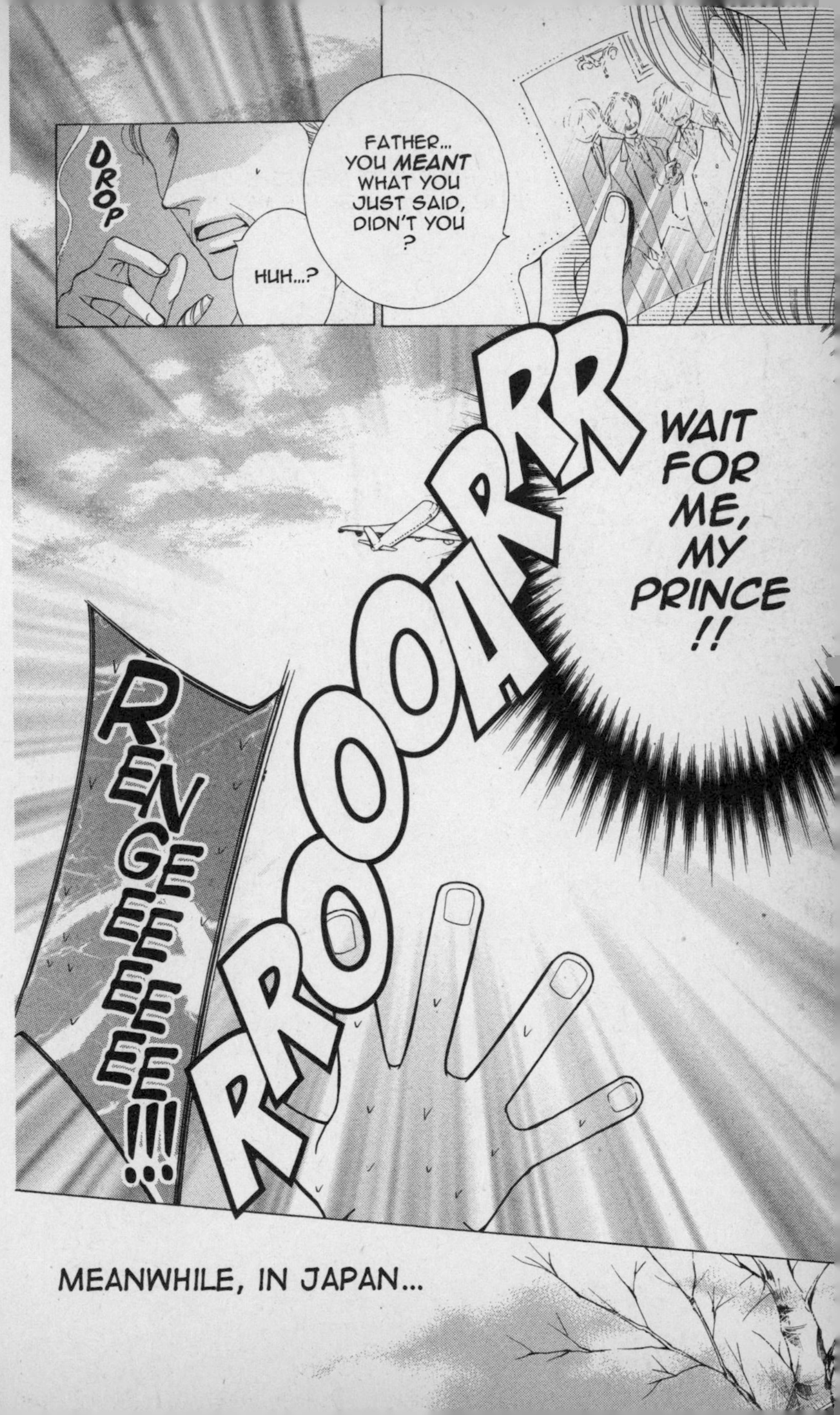
FATHER... YOU *MEANT* WHAT YOU JUST SAID, DIDN'T YOU?
HUH...?
DROP
WAIT FOR ME, MY PRINCE!!
RROOARRR
RENGEEEEEEEE!!!
MEANWHILE, IN JAPAN...

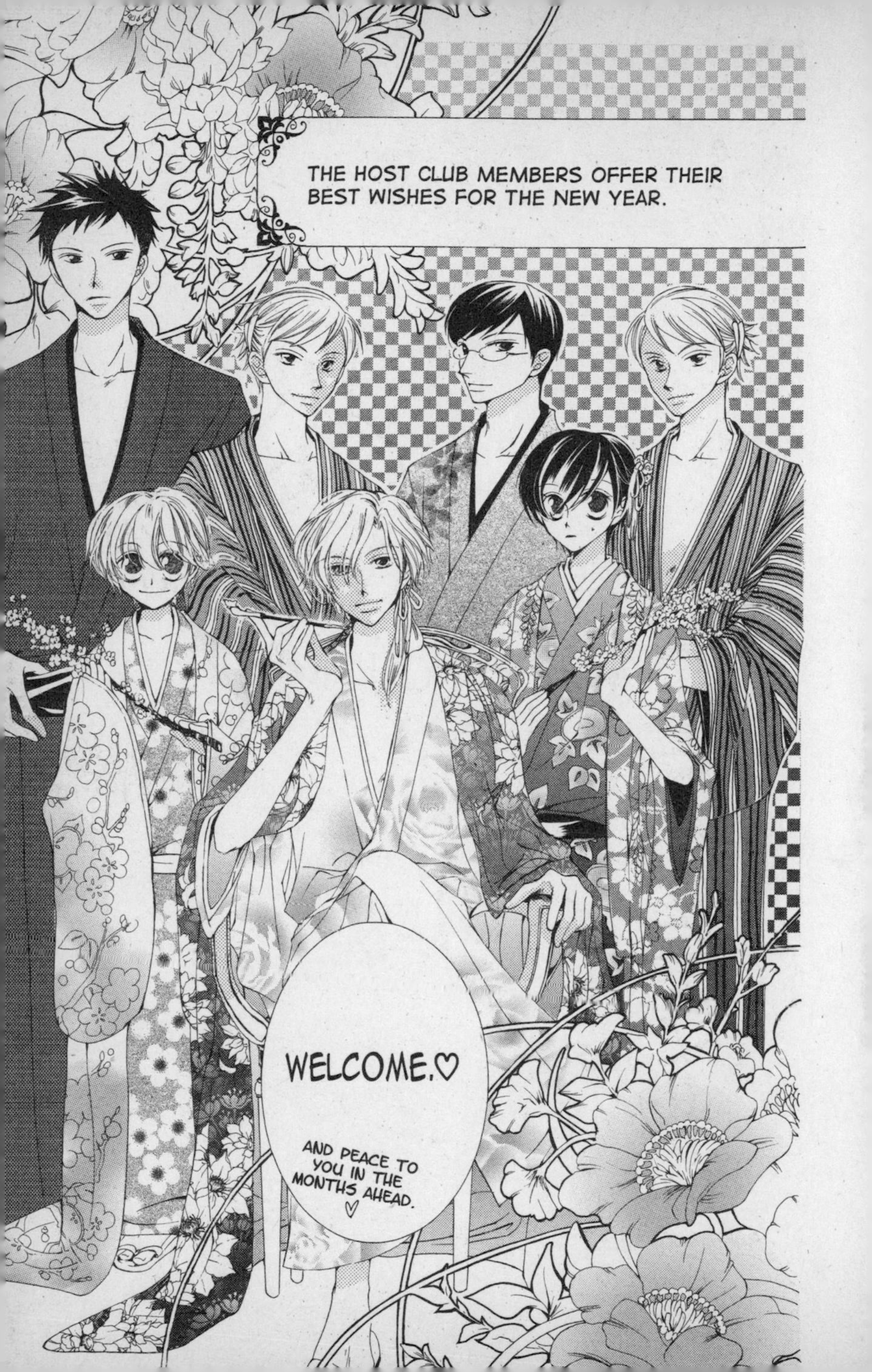
THE HOST CLUB MEMBERS OFFER THEIR BEST WISHES FOR THE NEW YEAR.
WELCOME.♡
AND PEACE TO YOU IN THE MONTHS AHEAD. ♡

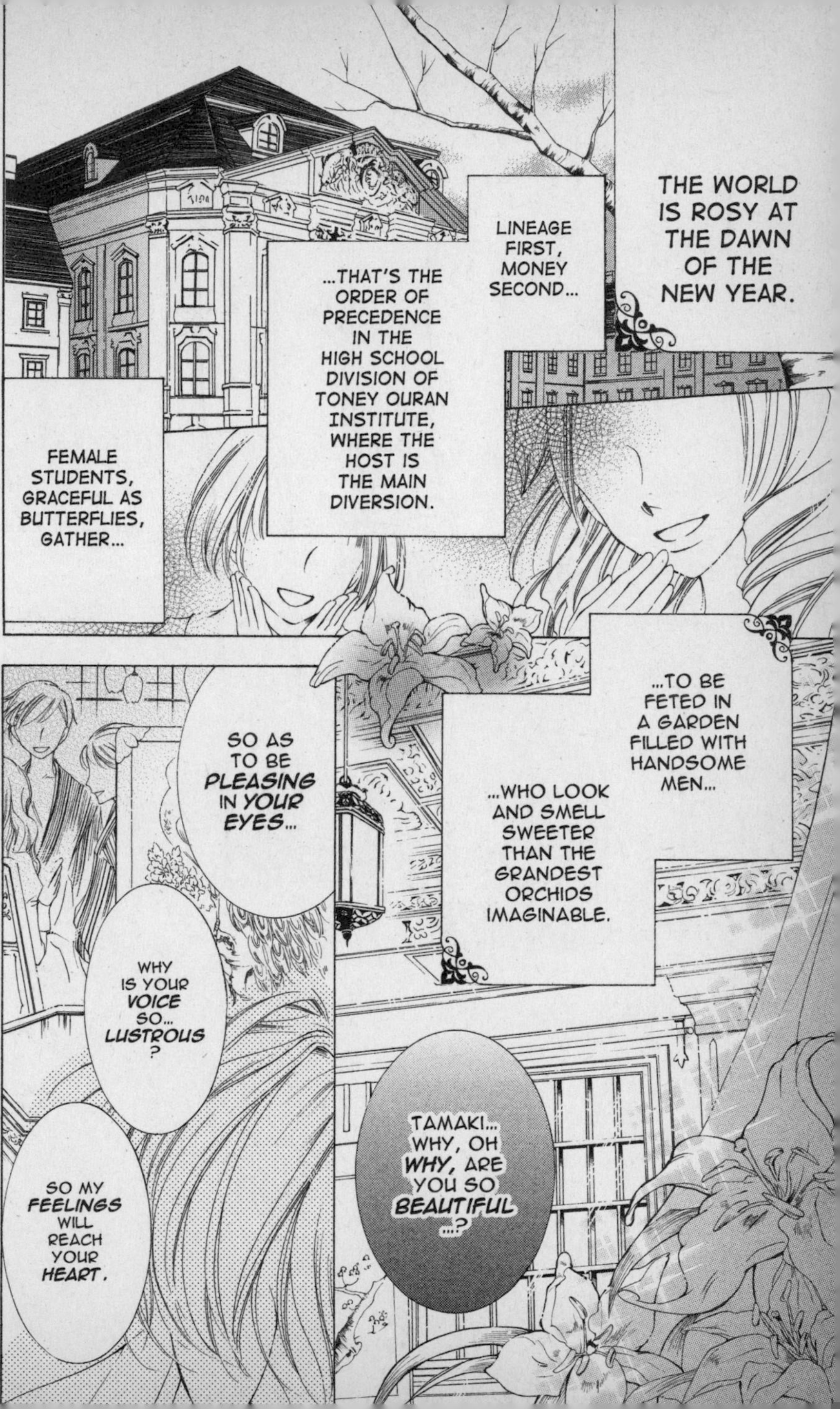
THE WORLD IS ROSY AT THE DAWN OF THE NEW YEAR.
LINEAGE FIRST, MONEY SECOND...
...THAT'S THE ORDER OF PRECEDENCE IN THE HIGH SCHOOL DIVISION OF TONEY OURAN INSTITUTE, WHERE THE HOST IS THE MAIN DIVERSION.
FEMALE STUDENTS, GRACEFUL AS BUTTERFLIES, GATHER...
...TO BE FETED IN A GARDEN FILLED WITH HANDSOME MEN...
...WHO LOOK AND SMELL SWEETER THAN THE GRANDEST ORCHIDS IMAGINABLE.
TAMAKI... WHY, OH WHY, ARE YOU SO BEAUTIFUL ...?
SO AS TO BE PLEASING IN YOUR EYES...
WHY IS YOUR VOICE SO... LUSTROUS ?
SO MY FEELINGS WILL REACH YOUR HEART.

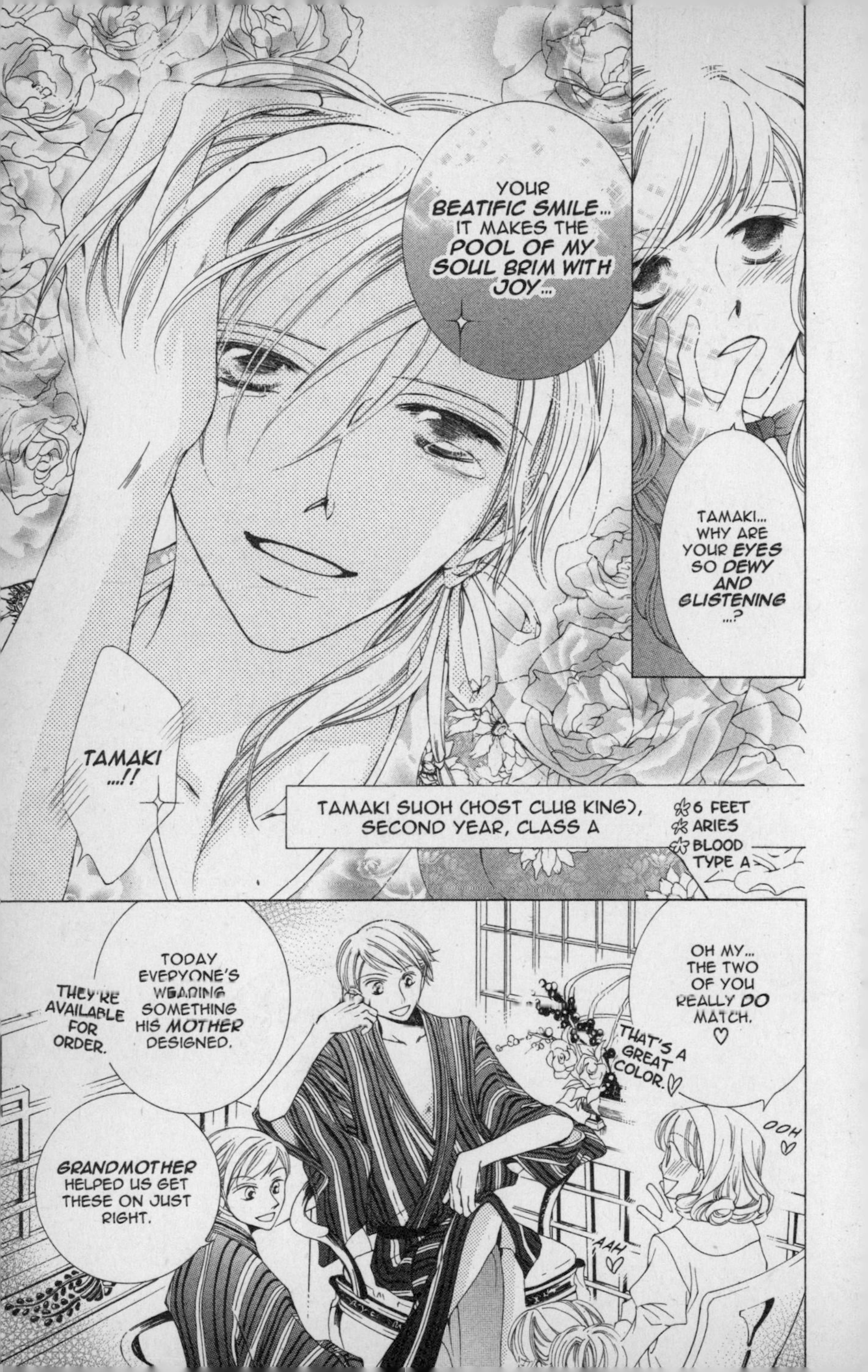

TAMAKI... WHY ARE YOUR EYES SO DEWY AND GLISTENING ...?
YOUR BEATIFIC SMILE... IT MAKES THE POOL OF MY SOUL BRIM WITH JOY...
TAMAKI ...!!
TAMAKI SUOH (HOST CLUB KING), SECOND YEAR, CLASS A
6 FEET
ARIES
BLOOD TYPE A
OH MY... THE TWO OF YOU REALLY DO MATCH. ♡
THAT'S A GREAT COLOR. ♡
OOH ♡
AAH ♡
TODAY EVERYONE'S WEARING SOMETHING HIS MOTHER DESIGNED.
THEY'RE AVAILABLE FOR ORDER.
GRANDMOTHER HELPED US GET THESE ON JUST RIGHT.

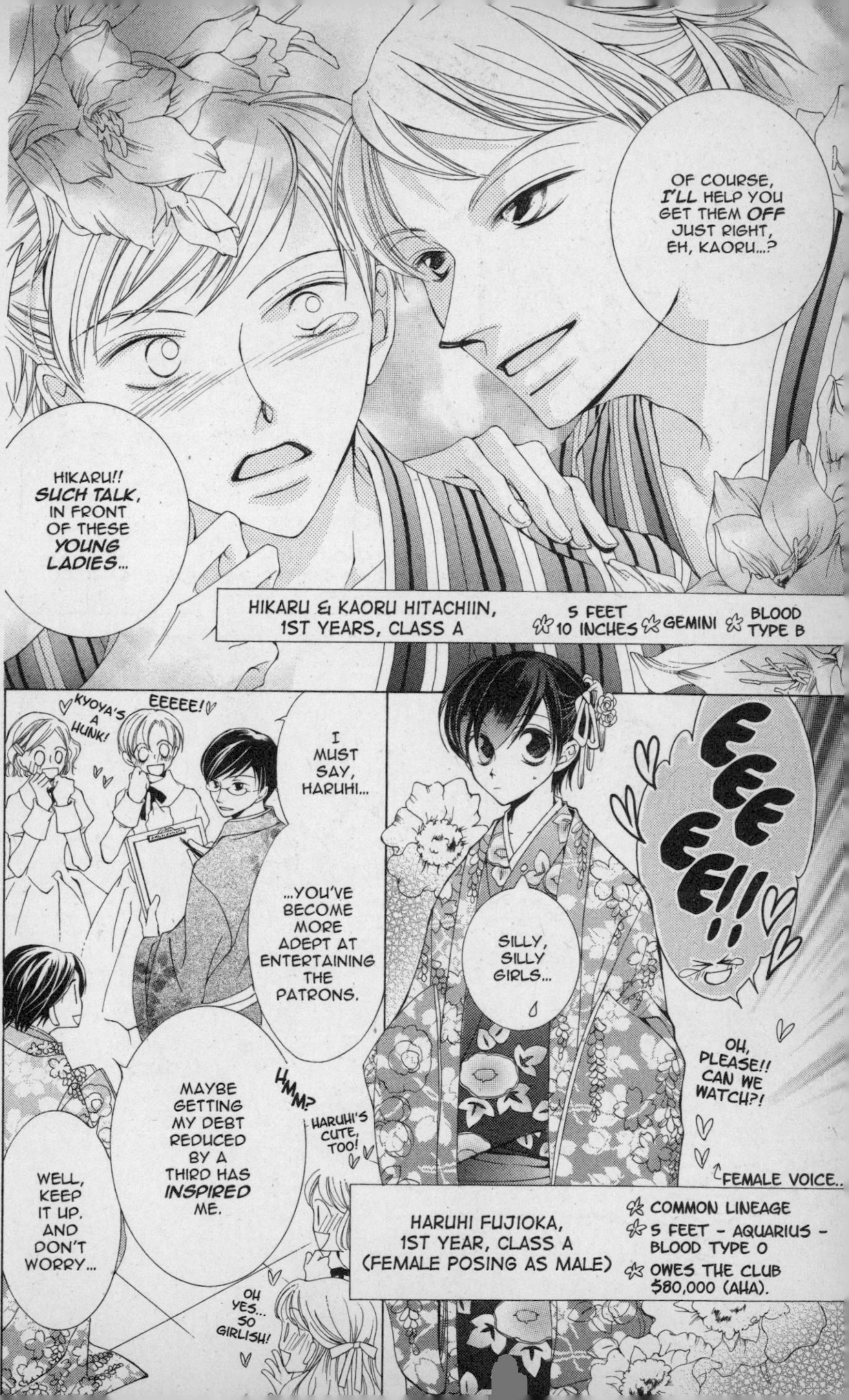

OF COURSE, I'LL HELP YOU GET THEM OFF JUST RIGHT, EH, KAORU...?
HIKARU!! SUCH TALK, IN FRONT OF THESE YOUNG LADIES...
HIKARU & KAORU HITACHIIN, 1ST YEARS, CLASS A
5 FEET 10 INCHES
GEMINI
BLOOD TYPE B
EEEEEE!!
SILLY, SILLY GIRLS...
OH, PLEASE!! CAN WE WATCH?!
FEMALE VOICE..
HARUHI FUJIOKA, 1ST YEAR, CLASS A (FEMALE POSING AS MALE)
COMMON LINEAGE
5 FEET - AQUARIUS - BLOOD TYPE O
OWES THE CLUB $80,000 (AHA).
EEEEE!
KYOYA'S A HUNK!
I MUST SAY, HARUHI...
...YOU'VE BECOME MORE ADEPT AT ENTERTAINING THE PATRONS.
HMM?
HARUHI'S CUTE, TOO!
MAYBE GETTING MY DEBT REDUCED BY A THIRD HAS INSPIRED ME.
WELL, KEEP IT UP. AND DON'T WORRY...
OH YES... SO GIRLISH!

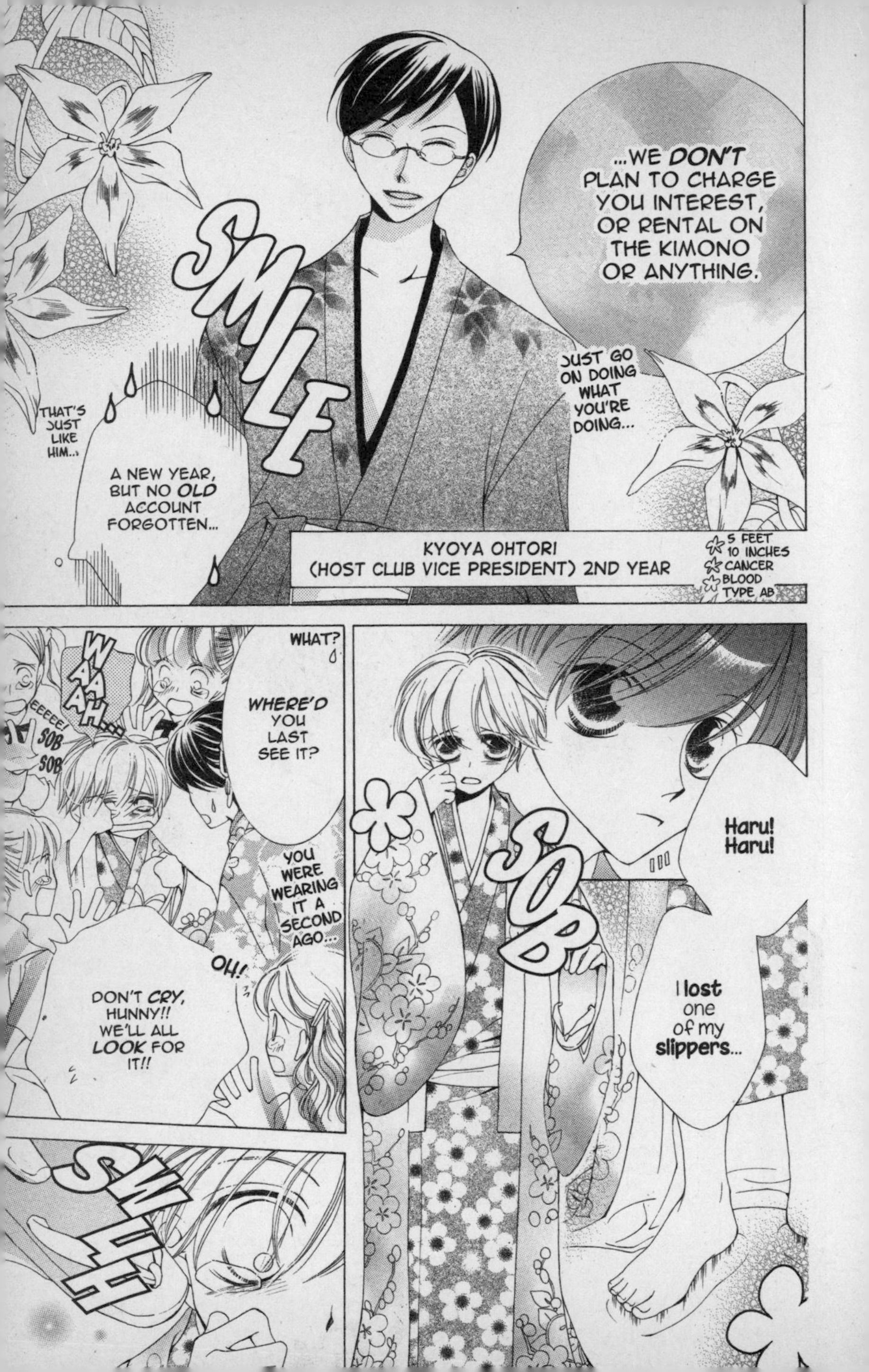
...WE DON'T PLAN TO CHARGE YOU INTEREST, OR RENTAL ON THE KIMONO OR ANYTHING.
JUST GO ON DOING WHAT YOU'RE DOING...
SMILE
THAT'S JUST LIKE HIM...
A NEW YEAR, BUT NO OLD ACCOUNT FORGOTTEN...
KYOYA OHTORI (HOST CLUB VICE PRESIDENT) 2ND YEAR
5 FEET 10 INCHES
CANCER
BLOOD TYPE AB
Haru! Haru!
SOB
I lost one of my slippers...
WHAT?
WHERE'D YOU LAST SEE IT?
WAAAH...
EEEEE! SOB SOB
YOU WERE WEARING IT A SECOND AGO...
OH!
DON'T CRY, HUNNY!! WE'LL ALL LOOK FOR IT!!
SWISH

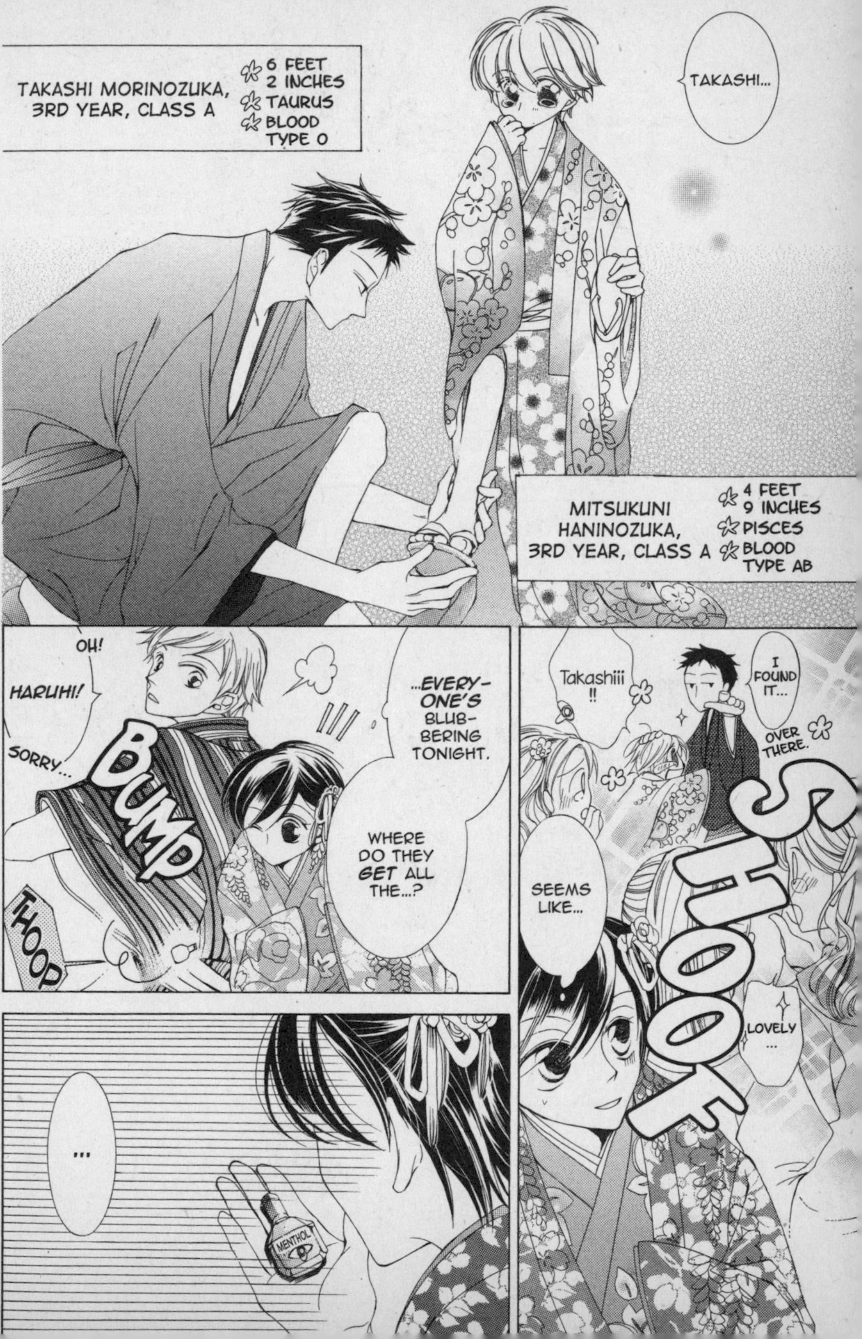
TAKASHI...
TAKASHI MORINOZUKA, 3RD YEAR, CLASS A
6 FEET 2 INCHES
TAURUS
BLOOD TYPE O
MITSUKUNI HANINOZUKA, 3RD YEAR, CLASS A
4 FEET 9 INCHES
PISCES
BLOOD TYPE AB
I FOUND IT... OVER THERE.
Takashiii!!
SHOOF
SEEMS LIKE...
LOVELY...
...EVERYONE'S BLUBBERING TONIGHT.
WHERE DO THEY GET ALL THE...?
OH! HARUHI! SORRY...
BUMP
THOOP
...
MENTHOL

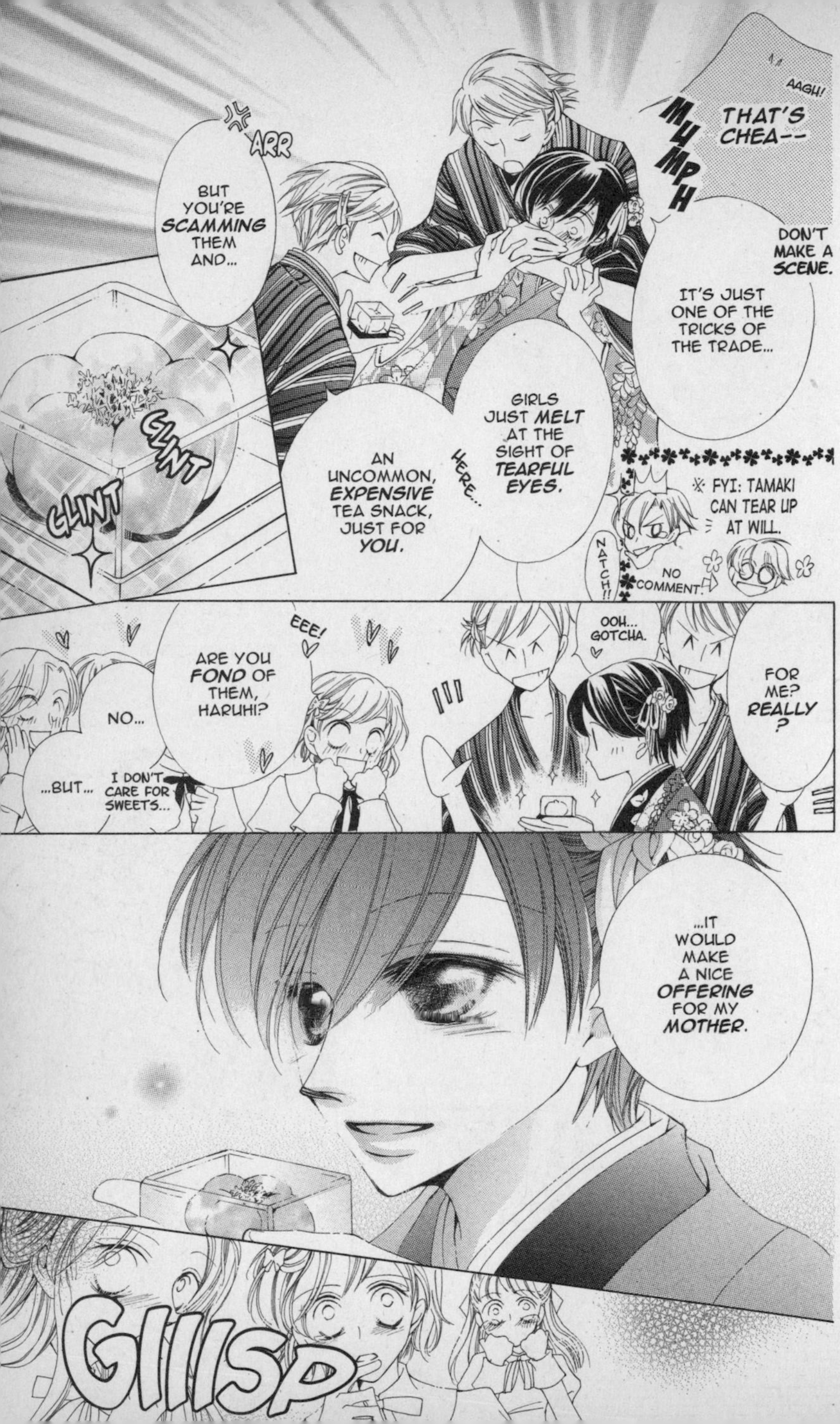
AAGH!
THAT'S CHEA--
MUMPH
BUT YOU'RE SCAMMING THEM AND...
ARR
DON'T MAKE A SCENE.
IT'S JUST ONE OF THE TRICKS OF THE TRADE...
GIRLS JUST MELT AT THE SIGHT OF TEARFUL EYES.
※ FYI: TAMAKI CAN TEAR UP AT WILL.
NATCH!!
NO COMMENT.
HERE...
AN UNCOMMON, EXPENSIVE TEA SNACK, JUST FOR YOU.
GLINT
GLINT
FOR ME? REALLY?
OOH... GOTCHA.
EEE!
ARE YOU FOND OF THEM, HARUHI?
NO...
...BUT...
I DON'T CARE FOR SWEETS...
...IT WOULD MAKE A NICE OFFERING FOR MY MOTHER.
GIIISP

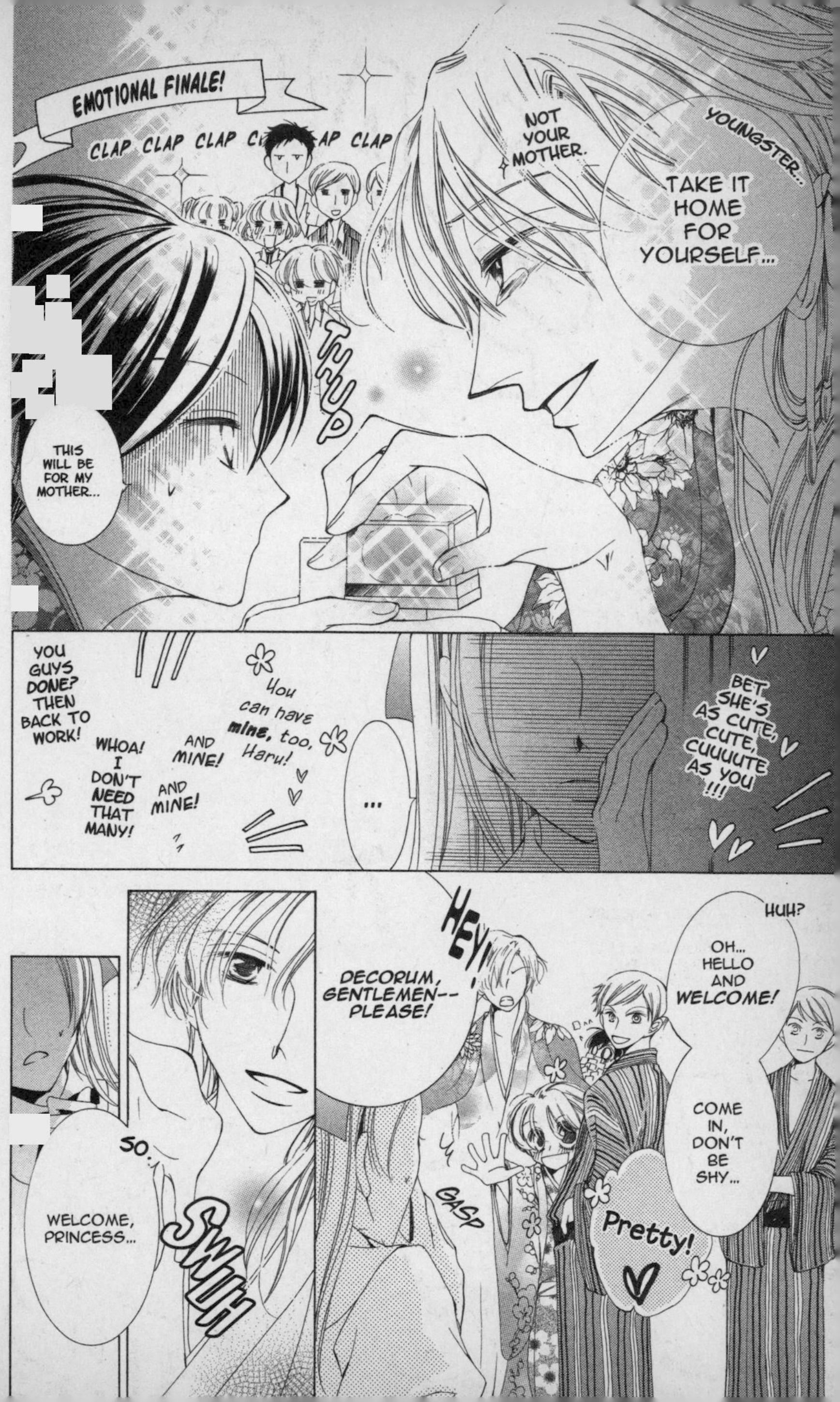
YOUNGSTER...
TAKE IT HOME FOR YOURSELF...
NOT YOUR MOTHER.
EMOTIONAL FINALE!
CLAP CLAP CLAP C- -AP CLAP
THUP
THIS WILL BE FOR MY MOTHER...
BET SHE'S AS CUTE, CUTE, CUUUUTE AS YOU!!!
...
You can have mine, too, Haru!
AND MINE!
AND MINE!
WHOA! I DON'T NEED THAT MANY!
YOU GUYS DONE? THEN BACK TO WORK!
HUH?
OH... HELLO AND WELCOME!
COME IN, DON'T BE SHY...
Pretty!
HEY!
DECORUM, GENTLEMEN-- PLEASE!
GASP
SO..
WELCOME, PRINCESS...

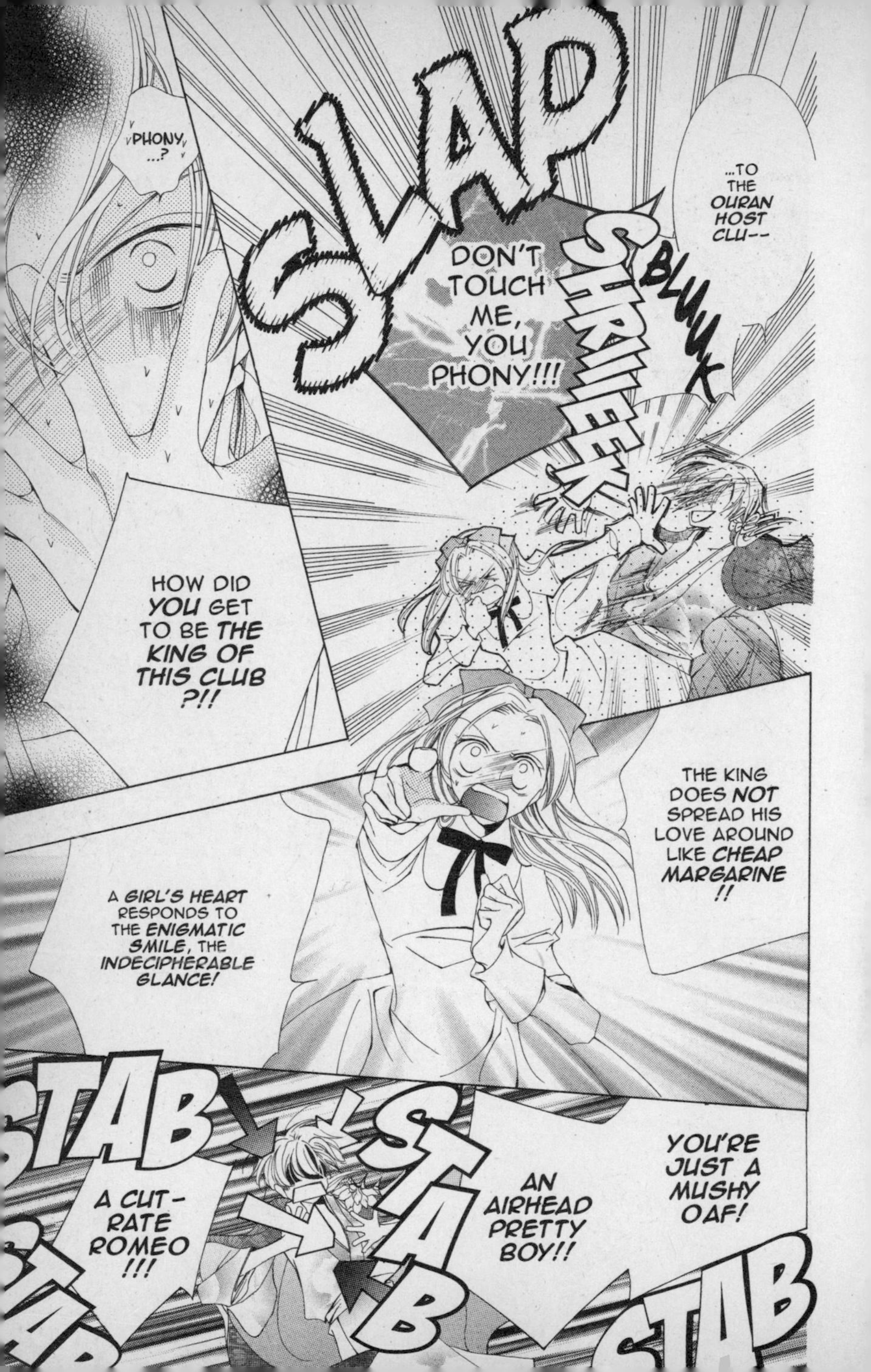

...TO THE OURAN HOST CLU--
SLAP
SHRIIIEEK
BLUUUK
DON'T TOUCH ME, YOU PHONY!!!
PHONY ...?
THE KING DOES NOT SPREAD HIS LOVE AROUND LIKE CHEAP MARGARINE !!
HOW DID YOU GET TO BE THE KING OF THIS CLUB ?!!
A GIRL'S HEART RESPONDS TO THE ENIGMATIC SMILE, THE INDECIPHERABLE GLANCE!
YOU'RE JUST A MUSHY OAF!
STAB
AN AIRHEAD PRETTY BOY!!
STAB
A CUT-RATE ROMEO !!!
STAB
STAB

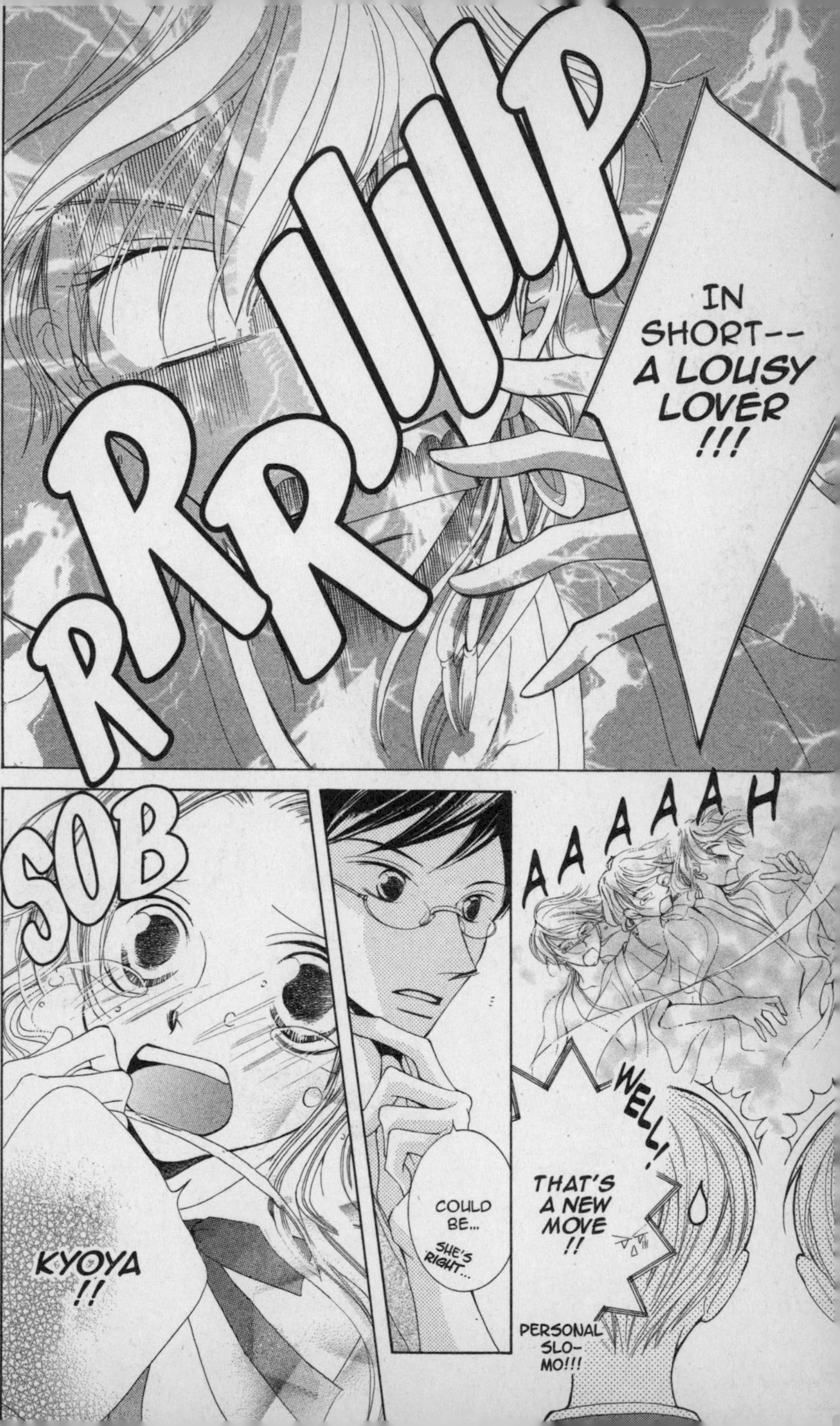
IN SHORT-- A LOUSY LOVER !!!
RRRIIIIP
AAAAAH
WELL!
THAT'S A NEW MOVE !!
PERSONAL SLO-MO!!!
COULD BE...
SHE'S RIGHT...
SOB
KYOYA !!

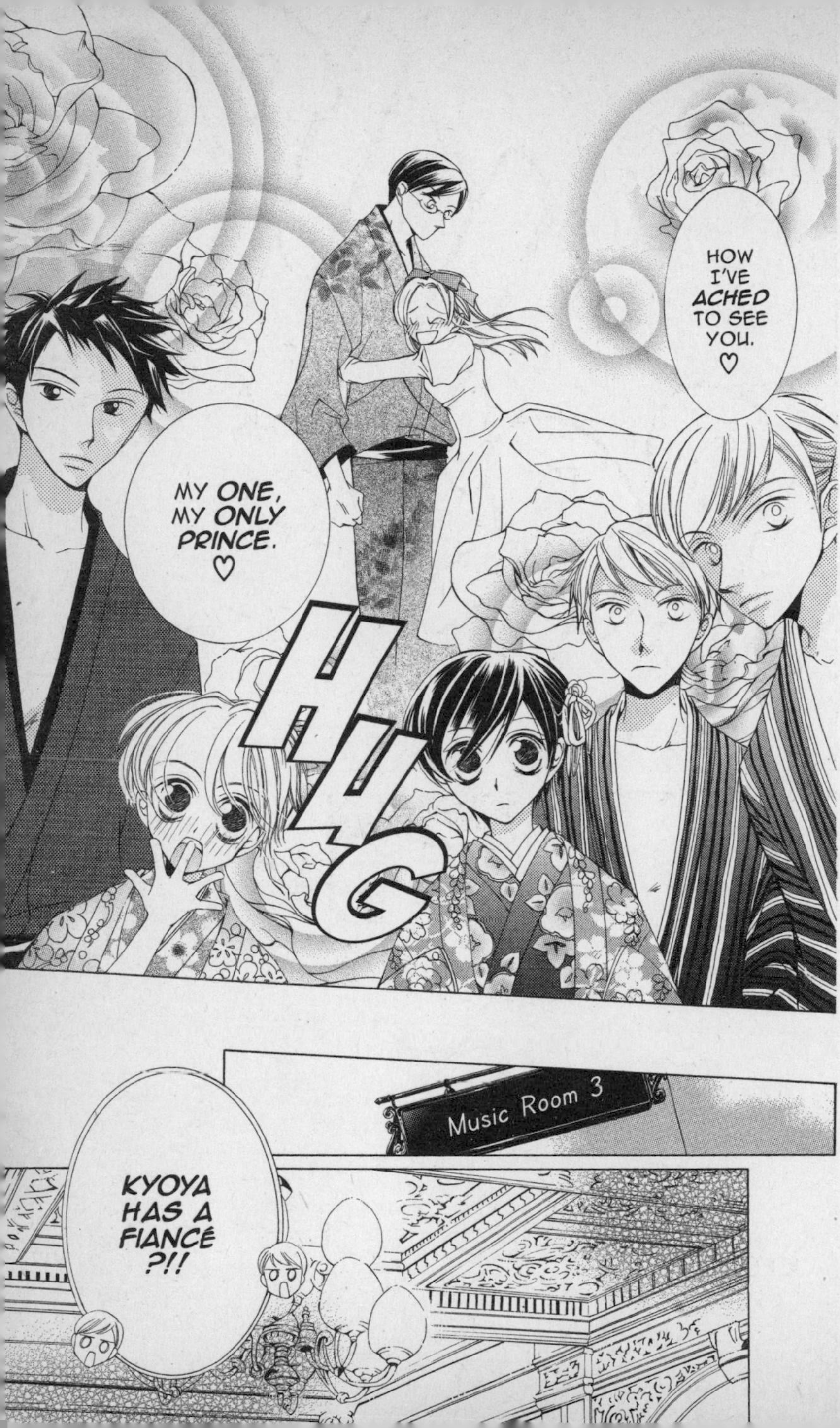
HOW I'VE ACHED TO SEE YOU. ♡
MY ONE, MY ONLY PRINCE. ♡
HUG
Music Room 3
KYOYA HAS A FIANCÉ ?!!

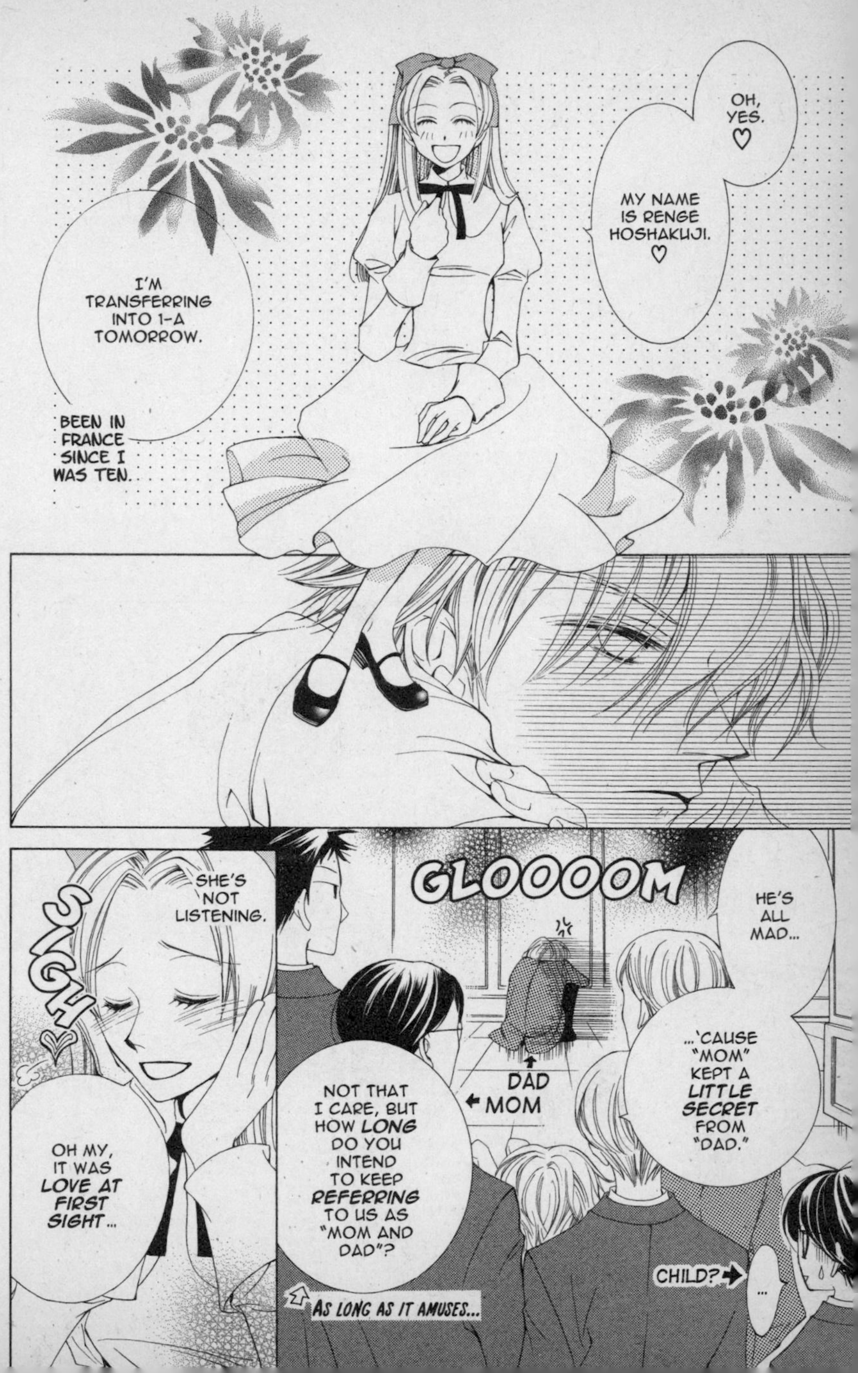
OH, YES. ♡
MY NAME IS RENGE HOSHAKUJI. ♡
I'M TRANSFERRING INTO 1-A TOMORROW.
BEEN IN FRANCE SINCE I WAS TEN.
HE'S ALL MAD...
GLOOOOM
...'CAUSE "MOM" KEPT A LITTLE SECRET FROM "DAD."
DAD
MOM
NOT THAT I CARE, BUT HOW LONG DO YOU INTEND TO KEEP REFERRING TO US AS "MOM AND DAD"?
CHILD?
...
AS LONG AS IT AMUSES...
SHE'S NOT LISTENING.
SIGH
OH MY, IT WAS LOVE AT FIRST SIGHT...

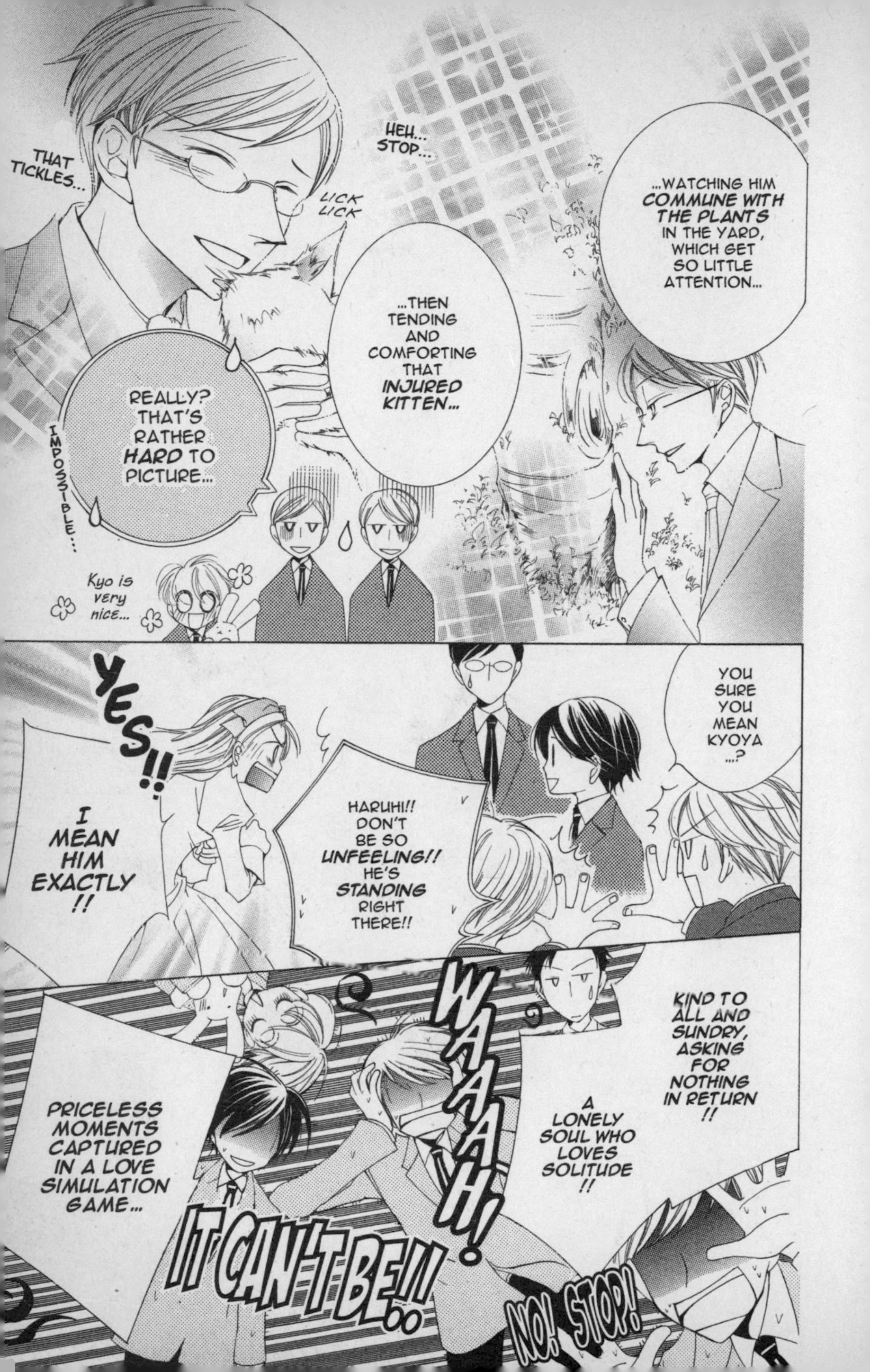
...WATCHING HIM COMMUNE WITH THE PLANTS IN THE YARD, WHICH GET SO LITTLE ATTENTION...
...THEN TENDING AND COMFORTING THAT INJURED KITTEN...
HEH... STOP...
LICK LICK
THAT TICKLES...
REALLY? THAT'S RATHER HARD TO PICTURE...
IMPOSSIBLE...
Kyo is very nice...
YOU SURE YOU MEAN KYOYA ...?
HARUHI!! DON'T BE SO UNFEELING!! HE'S STANDING RIGHT THERE!!
YES!!
I MEAN HIM EXACTLY !!
KIND TO ALL AND SUNDRY, ASKING FOR NOTHING IN RETURN !!
A LONELY SOUL WHO LOVES SOLITUDE !!
WAAAAH!
NO! STOP!
IT CAN'T BE!!..
PRICELESS MOMENTS CAPTURED IN A LOVE SIMULATION GAME...

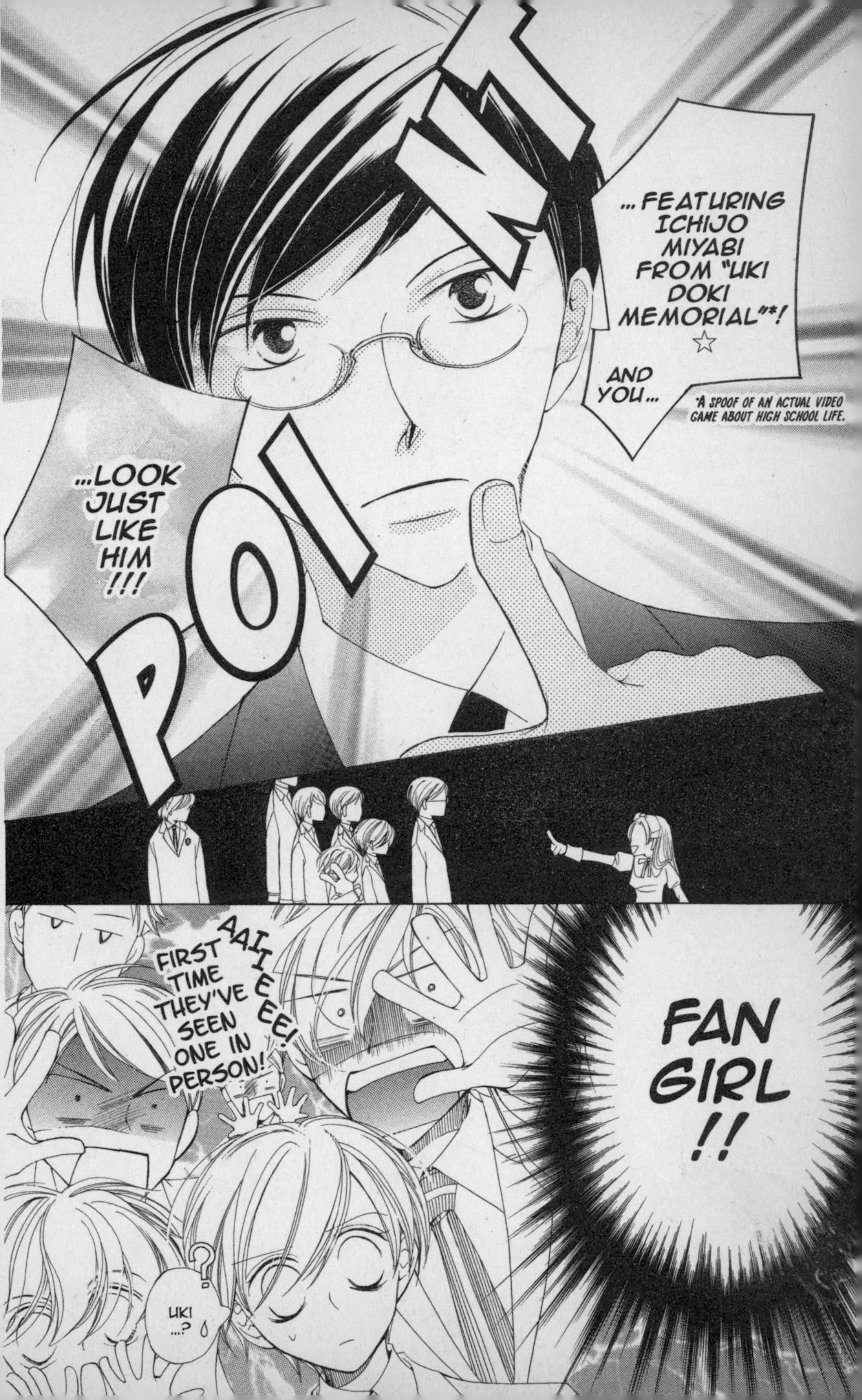
...FEATURING ICHIJO MIYABI FROM "UKI DOKI MEMORIAL"*! ☆
AND YOU...
*A SPOOF OF AN ACTUAL VIDEO GAME ABOUT HIGH SCHOOL LIFE.
...LOOK JUST LIKE HIM!!!
POI
FAN GIRL!!
AAIIEEEE!
FIRST TIME THEY'VE SEEN ONE IN PERSON!
UKI ...?

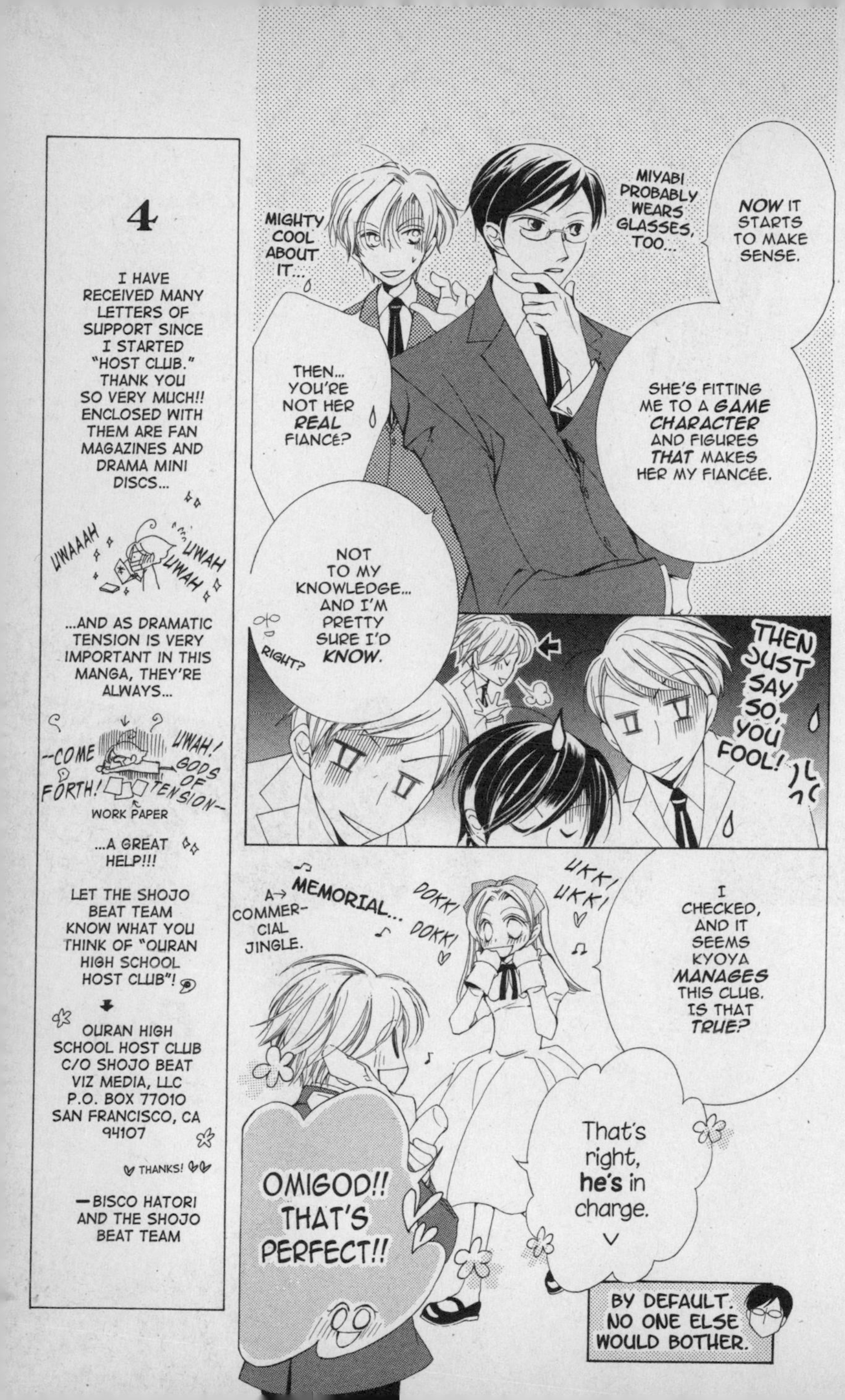
NOW IT STARTS TO MAKE SENSE.
MIYABI PROBABLY WEARS GLASSES, TOO...
MIGHTY COOL ABOUT IT...
SHE'S FITTING ME TO A GAME CHARACTER AND FIGURES THAT MAKES HER MY FIANCÉE.
THEN... YOU'RE NOT HER REAL FIANCÉ?
NOT TO MY KNOWLEDGE... AND I'M PRETTY SURE I'D KNOW.
THEN JUST SAY SO, YOU FOOL!
RIGHT?
I CHECKED, AND IT SEEMS KYOYA MANAGES THIS CLUB. IS THAT TRUE?
UKKI UKKI
DOKKI DOKKI
MEMORIAL...
A→ COMMERCIAL JINGLE.
That's right, he's in charge.
OMIGOD!! THAT'S PERFECT!!
BY DEFAULT. NO ONE ELSE WOULD BOTHER.

4

I HAVE RECEIVED MANY LETTERS OF SUPPORT SINCE I STARTED "HOST CLUB." THANK YOU SO VERY MUCH!! ENCLOSED WITH THEM ARE FAN MAGAZINES AND DRAMA MINI DISCS...

UWAAAH UWAH UWAH

...AND AS DRAMATIC TENSION IS VERY IMPORTANT IN THIS MANGA, THEY'RE ALWAYS...

--COME FORTH! UWAH! GODS OF TENSION--

WORK PAPER

...A GREAT HELP!!!

LET THE SHOJO BEAT TEAM KNOW WHAT YOU THINK OF "OURAN HIGH SCHOOL HOST CLUB"!

OURAN HIGH SCHOOL HOST CLUB
C/O SHOJO BEAT
VIZ MEDIA, LLC
P.O. BOX 77010
SAN FRANCISCO, CA
94107

THANKS!

—BISCO HATORI AND THE SHOJO BEAT TEAM

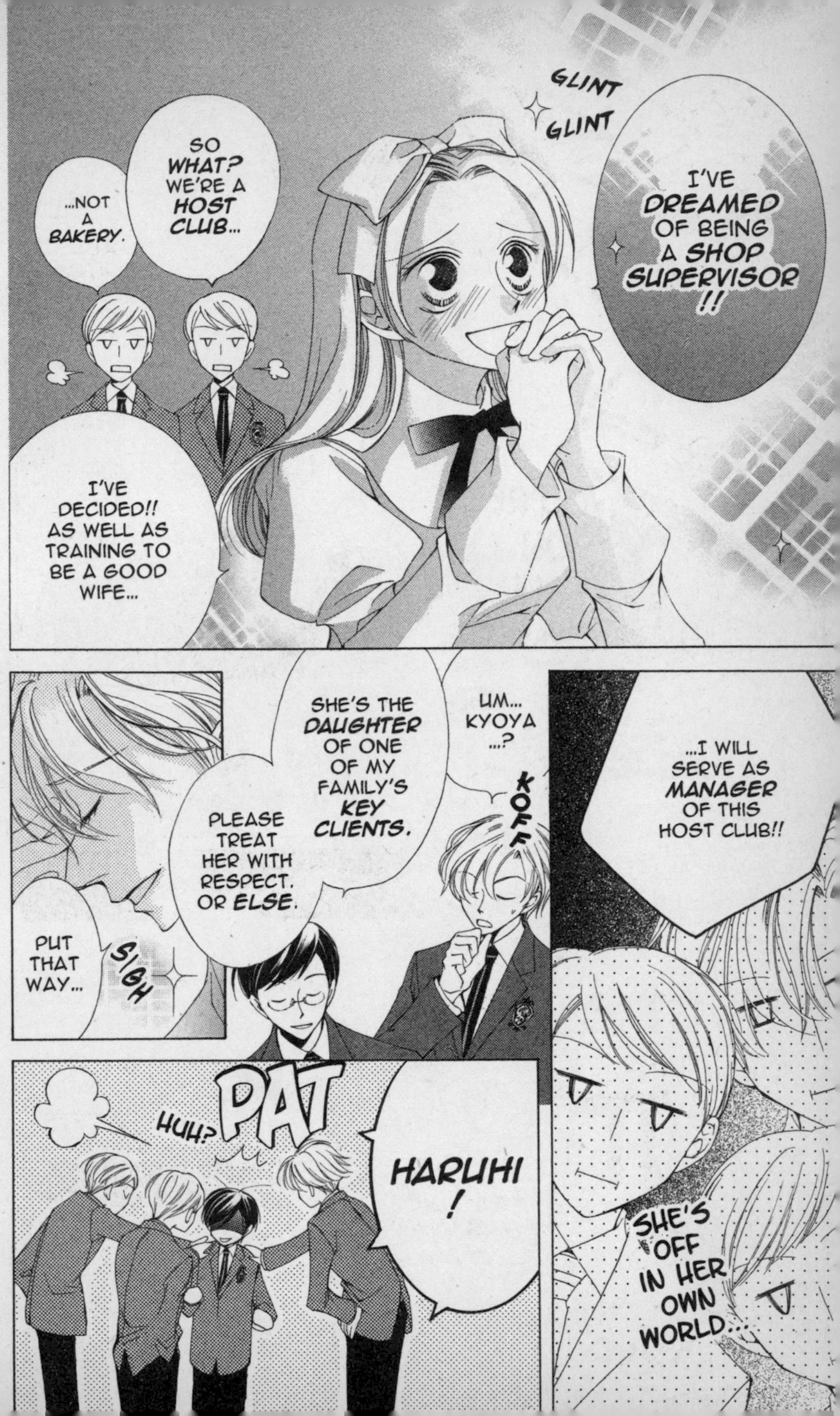
GLINT
GLINT
I'VE DREAMED OF BEING A SHOP SUPERVISOR!!
SO WHAT? WE'RE A HOST CLUB...
...NOT A BAKERY.
I'VE DECIDED!! AS WELL AS TRAINING TO BE A GOOD WIFE...
...I WILL SERVE AS MANAGER OF THIS HOST CLUB!!
SHE'S OFF IN HER OWN WORLD...
UM... KYOYA ...?
KOFF
SHE'S THE DAUGHTER OF ONE OF MY FAMILY'S KEY CLIENTS.
PLEASE TREAT HER WITH RESPECT. OR ELSE.
PUT THAT WAY...
SIGH
HARUHI!
PAT
HUH?

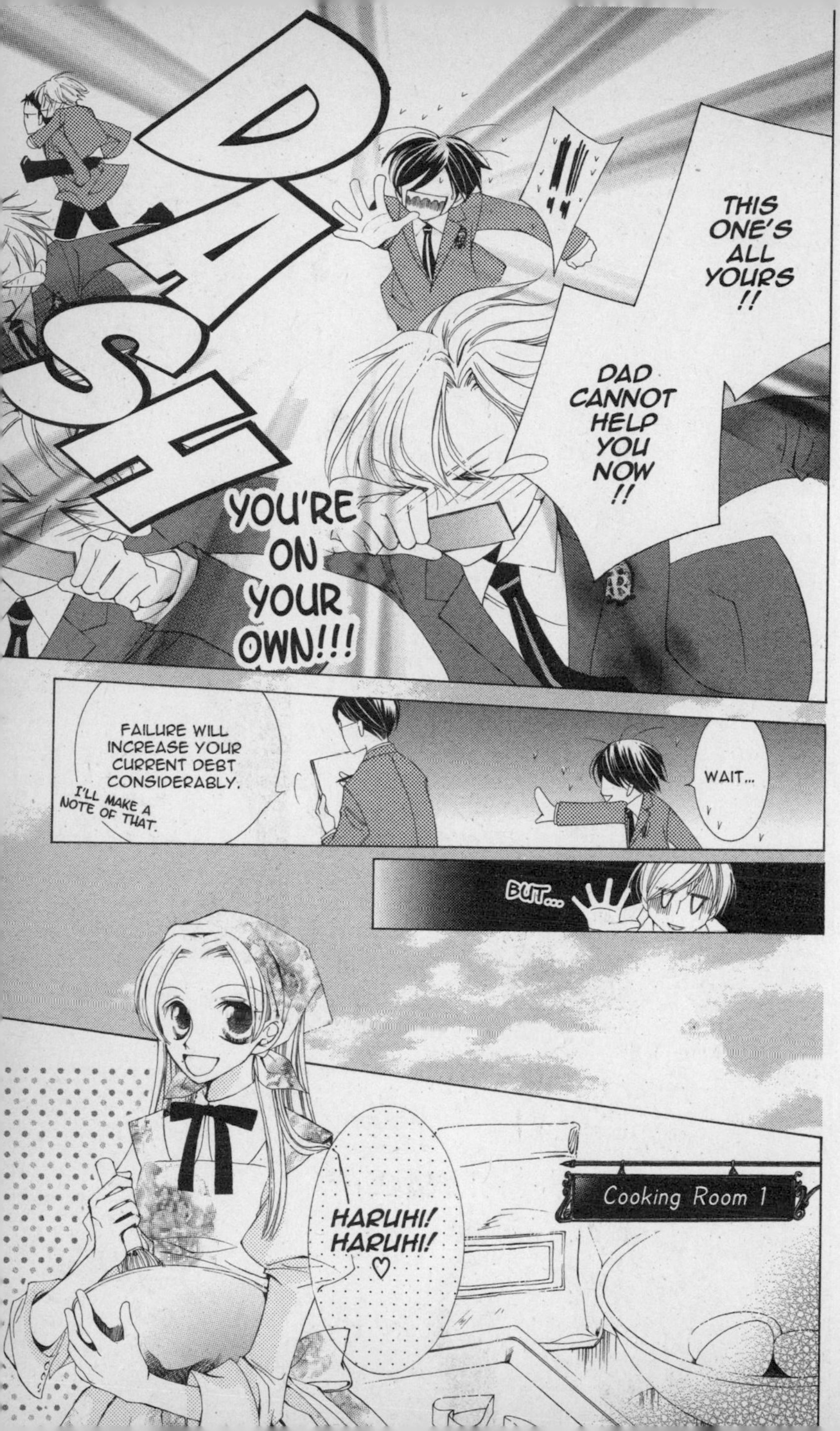
THIS ONE'S ALL YOURS!!
DAD CANNOT HELP YOU NOW!!
DASH
YOU'RE ON YOUR OWN!!!
WAIT...
FAILURE WILL INCREASE YOUR CURRENT DEBT CONSIDERABLY.
I'LL MAKE A NOTE OF THAT.
BUT...
Cooking Room 1
HARUHI! HARUHI! ♡

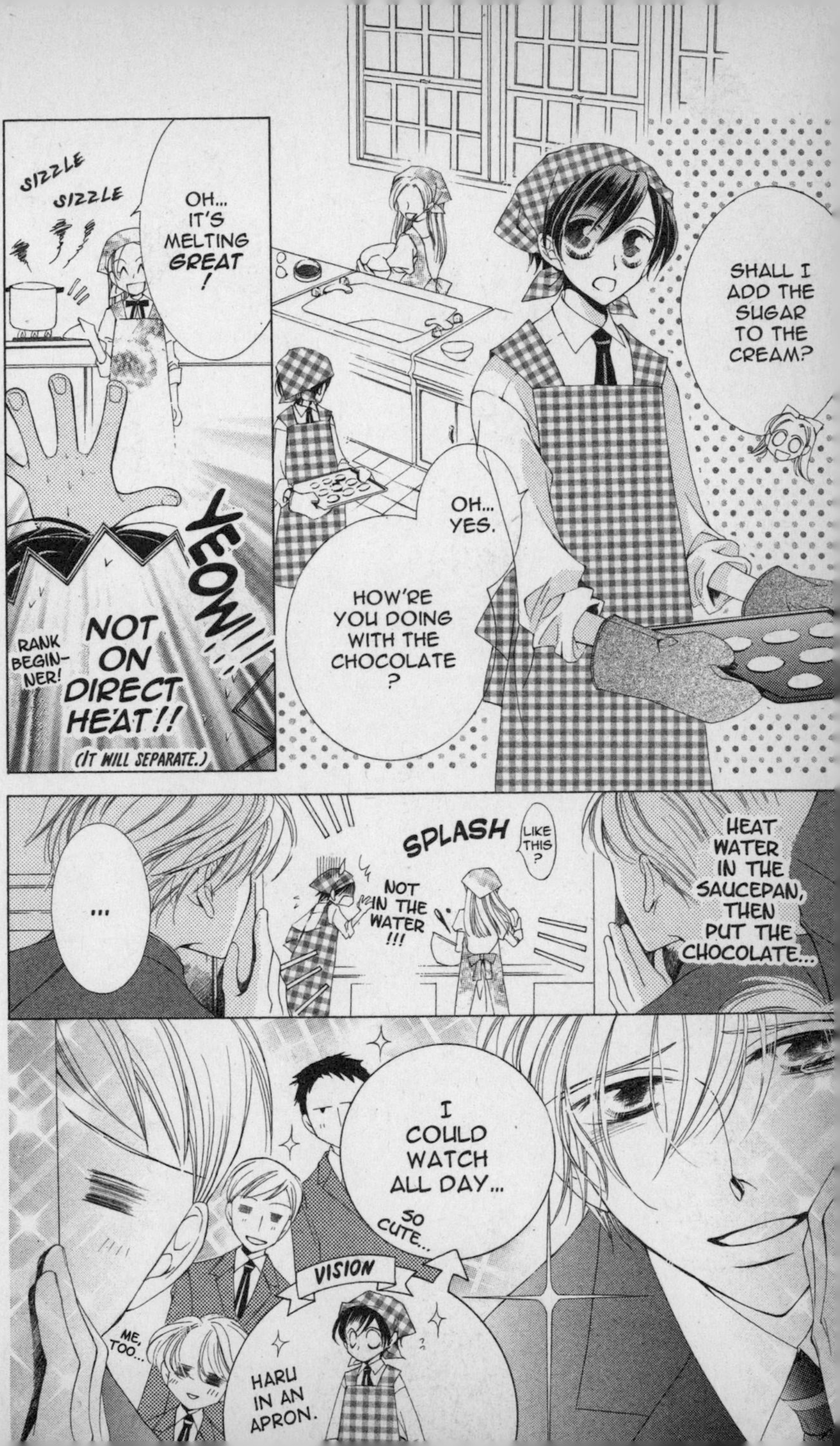
SHALL I ADD THE SUGAR TO THE CREAM?
OH... YES.
HOW'RE YOU DOING WITH THE CHOCOLATE?
SIZZLE
SIZZLE
OH... IT'S MELTING GREAT!
YEOW!!!
NOT ON DIRECT HEAT!!
RANK BEGIN-NER!
(IT WILL SEPARATE.)
HEAT WATER IN THE SAUCEPAN, THEN PUT THE CHOCOLATE...
LIKE THIS?
SPLASH
NOT IN THE WATER!!!
...
I COULD WATCH ALL DAY...
SO CUTE...
VISION
HARU IN AN APRON.
ME, TOO...

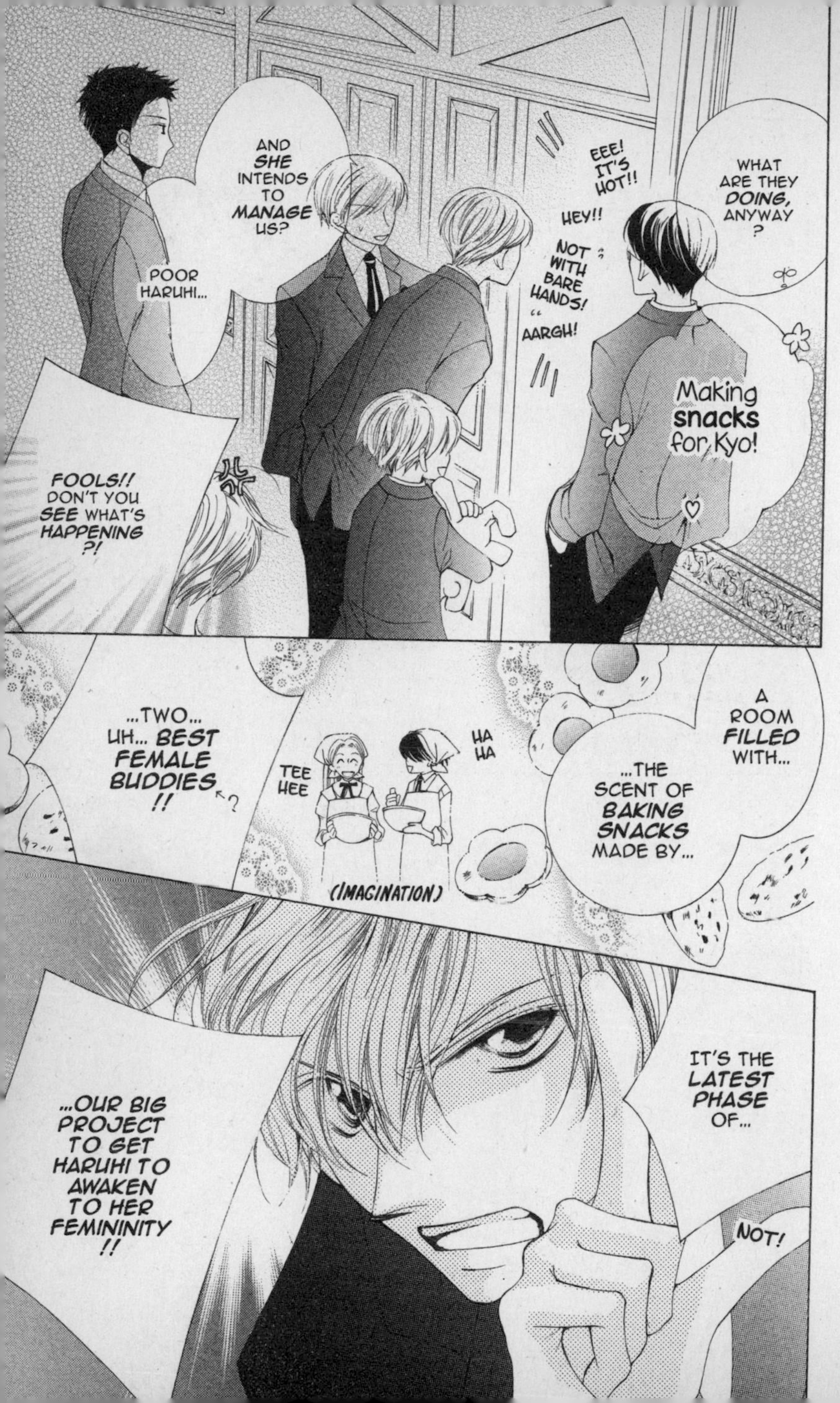
WHAT ARE THEY DOING, ANYWAY?
Making snacks for Kyo!
EEE! IT'S HOT!!
HEY!!
NOT WITH BARE HANDS!
AARGH!
AND SHE INTENDS TO MANAGE US?
POOR HARUHI...
FOOLS!! DON'T YOU SEE WHAT'S HAPPENING?!
A ROOM FILLED WITH...
...THE SCENT OF BAKING SNACKS MADE BY...
HA HA
TEE HEE
(IMAGINATION)
...TWO... UH... BEST FEMALE BUDDIES!!
?
IT'S THE LATEST PHASE OF...
...OUR BIG PROJECT TO GET HARUHI TO AWAKEN TO HER FEMININITY!!
NOT!

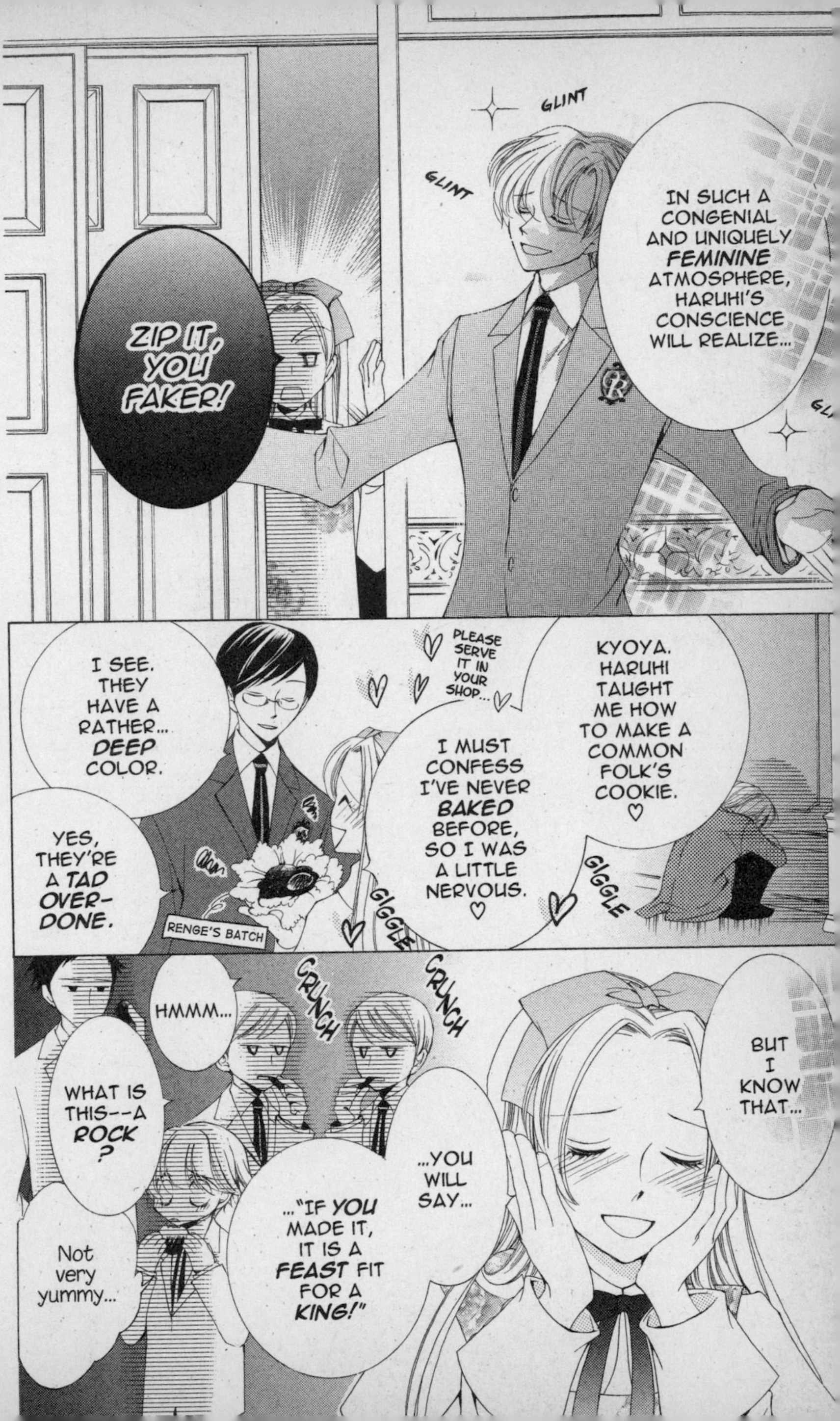
GLINT
GLINT
IN SUCH A CONGENIAL AND UNIQUELY FEMININE ATMOSPHERE, HARUHI'S CONSCIENCE WILL REALIZE...
ZIP IT, YOU FAKER!
KYOYA. HARUHI TAUGHT ME HOW TO MAKE A COMMON FOLK'S COOKIE. ♡
PLEASE SERVE IT IN YOUR SHOP... ♡
I MUST CONFESS I'VE NEVER BAKED BEFORE, SO I WAS A LITTLE NERVOUS. ♡
GIGGLE
GIGGLE
I SEE. THEY HAVE A RATHER... DEEP COLOR.
YES, THEY'RE A TAD OVER-DONE.
RENGE'S BATCH
BUT I KNOW THAT...
...YOU WILL SAY...
..."IF YOU MADE IT, IT IS A FEAST FIT FOR A KING!"
CRUNCH
CRUNCH
HMMM...
WHAT IS THIS--A ROCK?
Not very yummy...

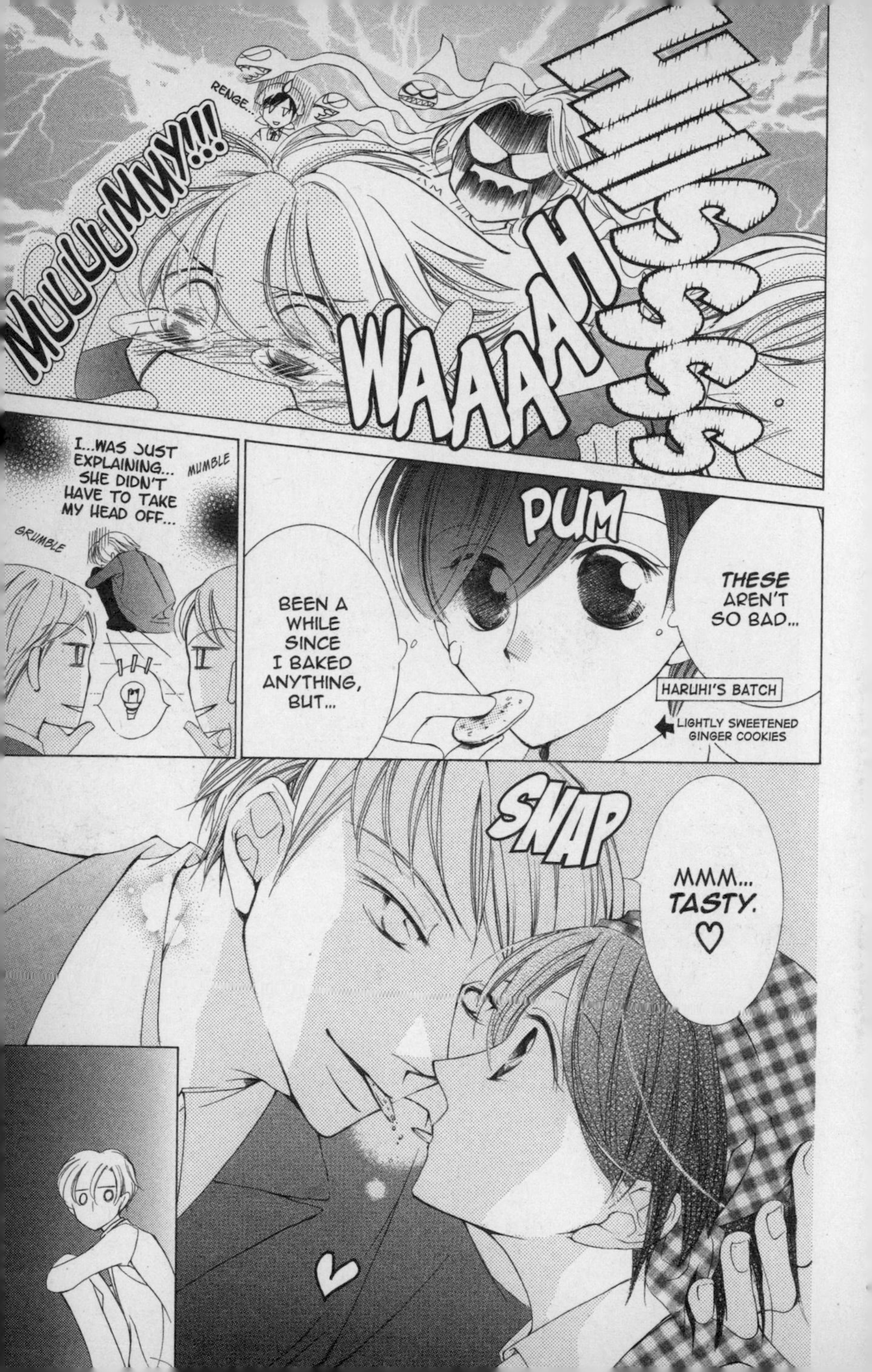
HISSSS
RENGE...
WAAAAH
MUUUUMMY!!!
THESE AREN'T SO BAD...
PUM
BEEN A WHILE SINCE I BAKED ANYTHING, BUT...
HARUHI'S BATCH
LIGHTLY SWEETENED GINGER COOKIES
MUMBLE
I...WAS JUST EXPLAINING... SHE DIDN'T HAVE TO TAKE MY HEAD OFF...
GRUMBLE
SNAP
MMM... TASTY. ♡

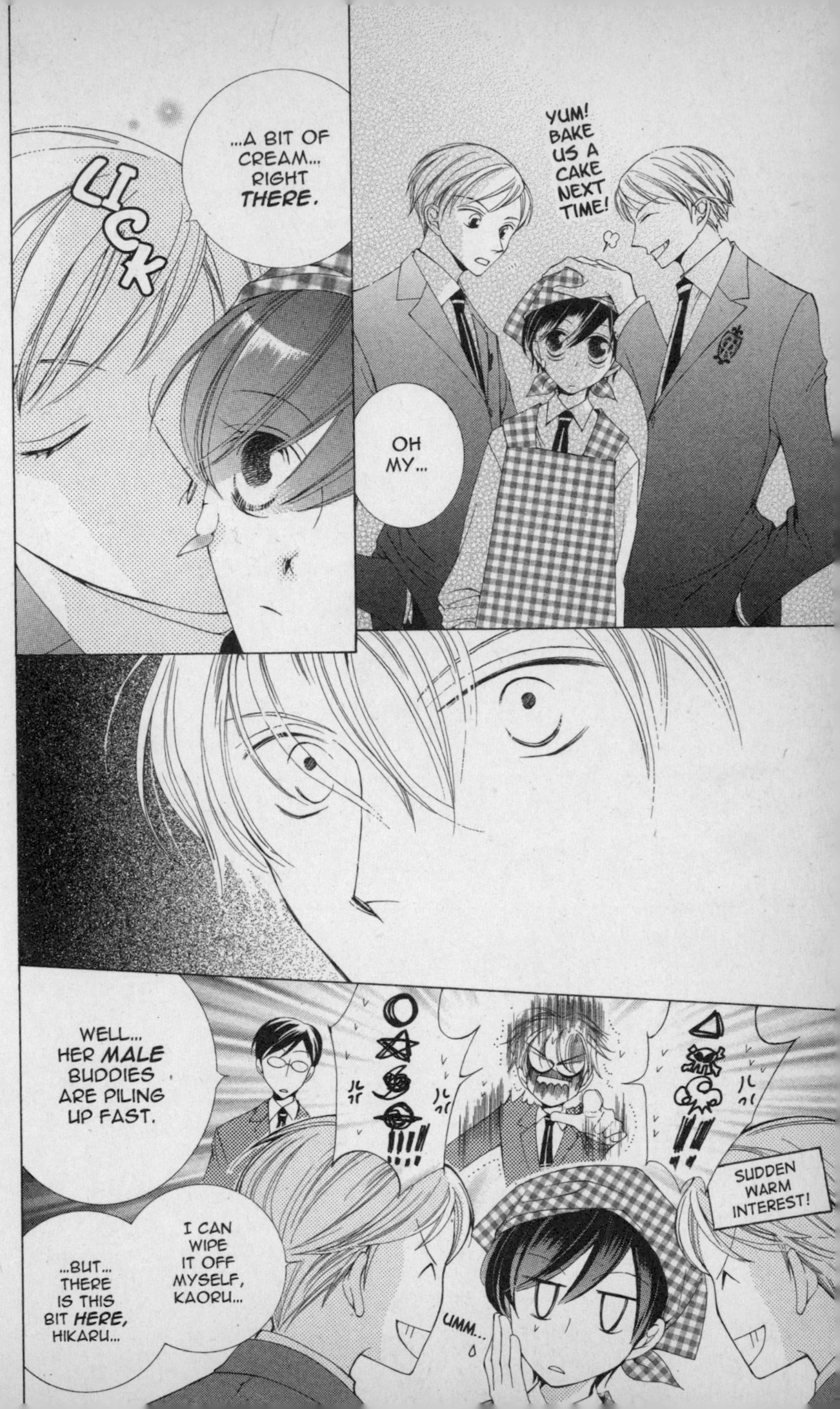
YUM! BAKE US A CAKE NEXT TIME!
OH MY...
...A BIT OF CREAM... RIGHT THERE.
LICK
SUDDEN WARM INTEREST!
WELL... HER MALE BUDDIES ARE PILING UP FAST.
UMM...
I CAN WIPE IT OFF MYSELF, KAORU...
...BUT... THERE IS THIS BIT HERE, HIKARU...

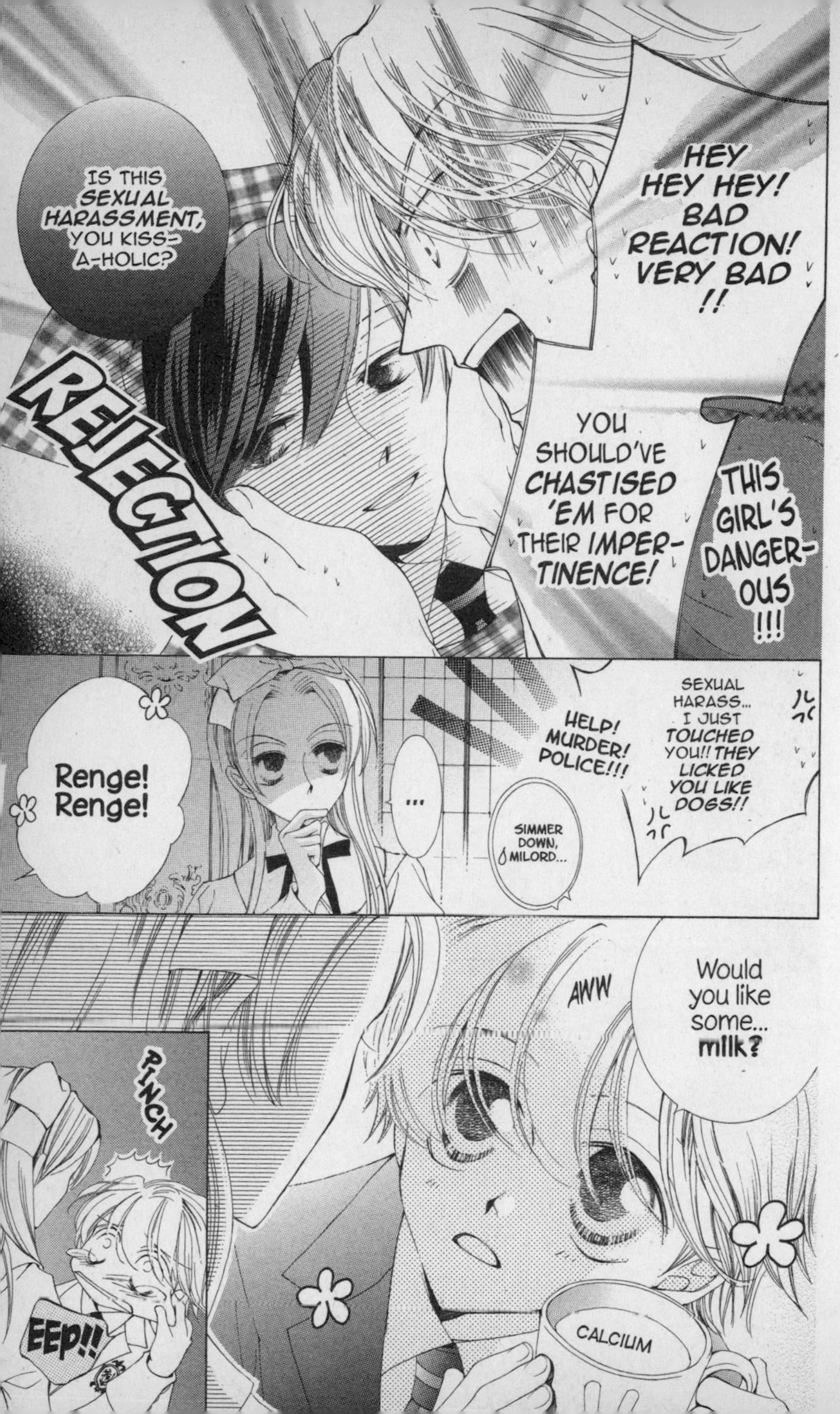
HEY HEY HEY! BAD REACTION! VERY BAD !!
THIS GIRL'S DANGER-OUS !!!
YOU SHOULD'VE CHASTISED 'EM FOR THEIR IMPER-TINENCE!
IS THIS SEXUAL HARASSMENT, YOU KISS-A-HOLIC?
REJECTION
SEXUAL HARASS... I JUST TOUCHED YOU!! THEY LICKED YOU LIKE DOGS!!
HELP! MURDER! POLICE!!!
SIMMER DOWN, MILORD...
...
Renge! Renge!
Would you like some... milk?
AWW
CALCIUM
PINCH
EEP!!

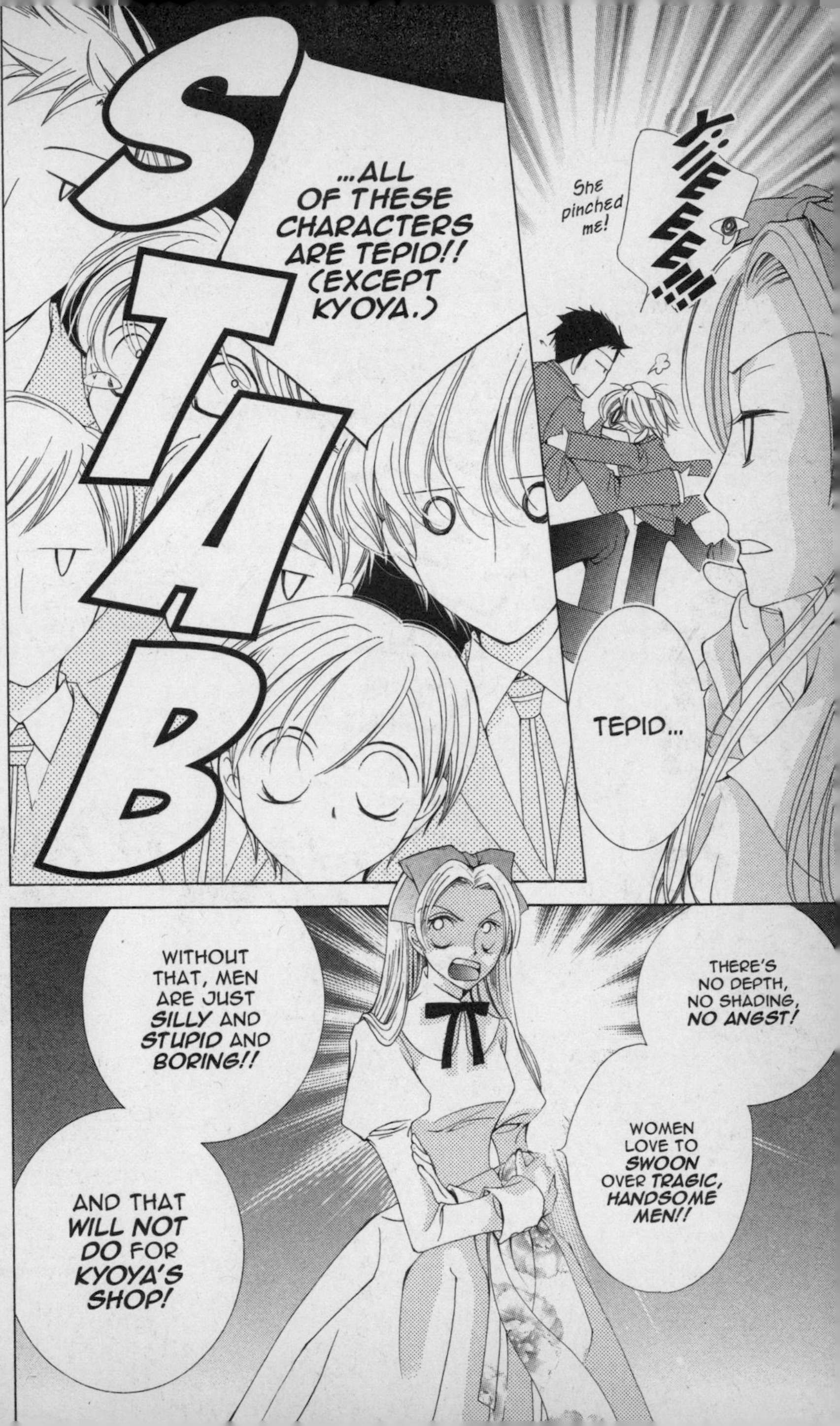
YIIIEEEE!!!
She pinched me!
TEPID...
...ALL OF THESE CHARACTERS ARE TEPID!! (EXCEPT KYOYA.)
STAB
THERE'S NO DEPTH, NO SHADING, NO ANGST!
WOMEN LOVE TO SWOON OVER TRAGIC, HANDSOME MEN!!
WITHOUT THAT, MEN ARE JUST SILLY AND STUPID AND BORING!!
AND THAT WILL NOT DO FOR KYOYA'S SHOP!

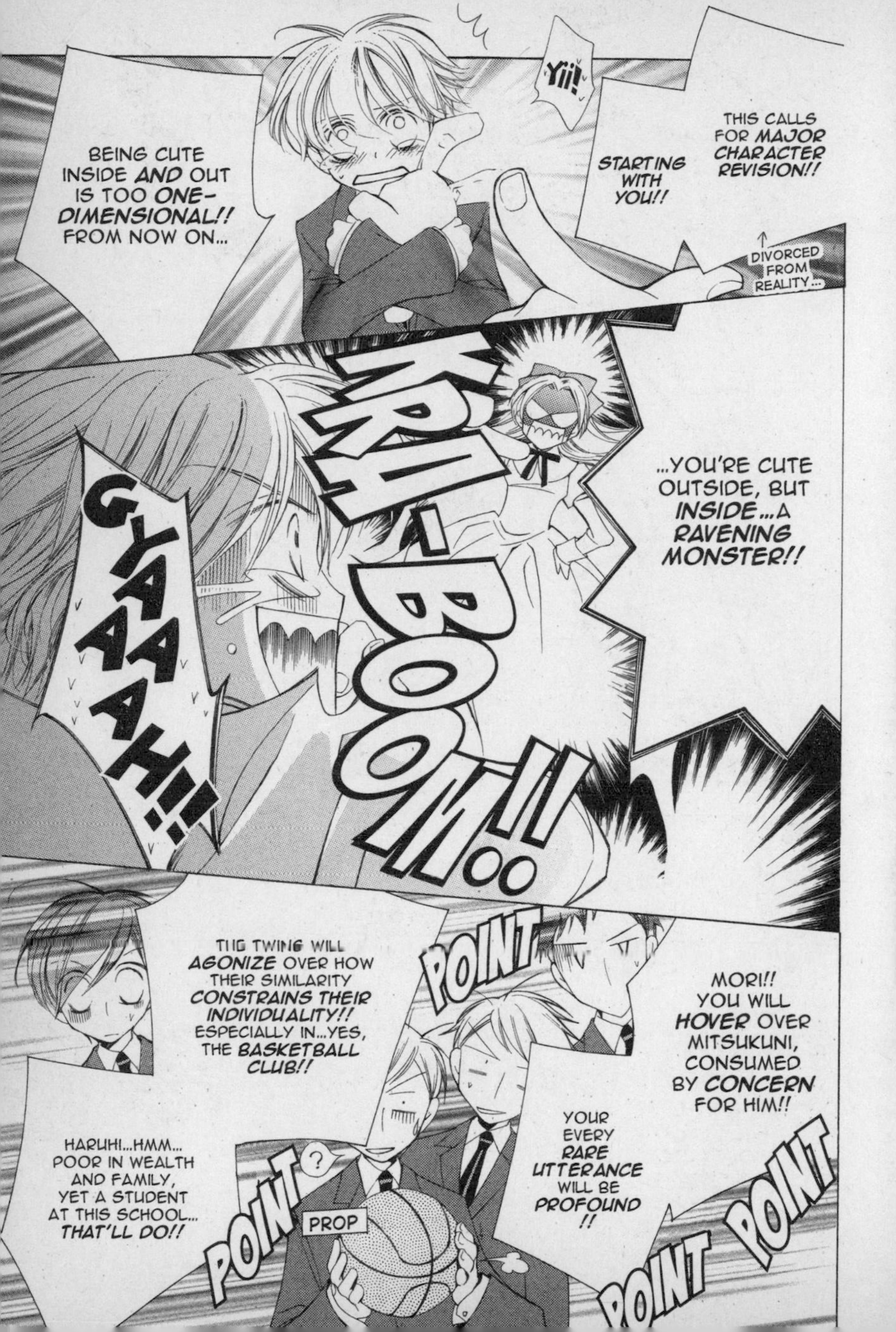
THIS CALLS FOR MAJOR CHARACTER REVISION!!
STARTING WITH YOU!!
Yii!
BEING CUTE INSIDE AND OUT IS TOO ONE-DIMENSIONAL!! FROM NOW ON...
DIVORCED FROM REALITY...
...YOU'RE CUTE OUTSIDE, BUT INSIDE...A RAVENING MONSTER!!
KRA-BOOM!!
GYAAAAH!!
MORI!! YOU WILL HOVER OVER MITSUKUNI, CONSUMED BY CONCERN FOR HIM!!
POINT
THE TWINS WILL AGONIZE OVER HOW THEIR SIMILARITY CONSTRAINS THEIR INDIVIDUALITY!! ESPECIALLY IN...YES, THE BASKETBALL CLUB!!
YOUR EVERY RARE UTTERANCE WILL BE PROFOUND!!
POINT POINT
POINT
?
PROP
POINT
HARUHI...HMM... POOR IN WEALTH AND FAMILY, YET A STUDENT AT THIS SCHOOL... THAT'LL DO!!

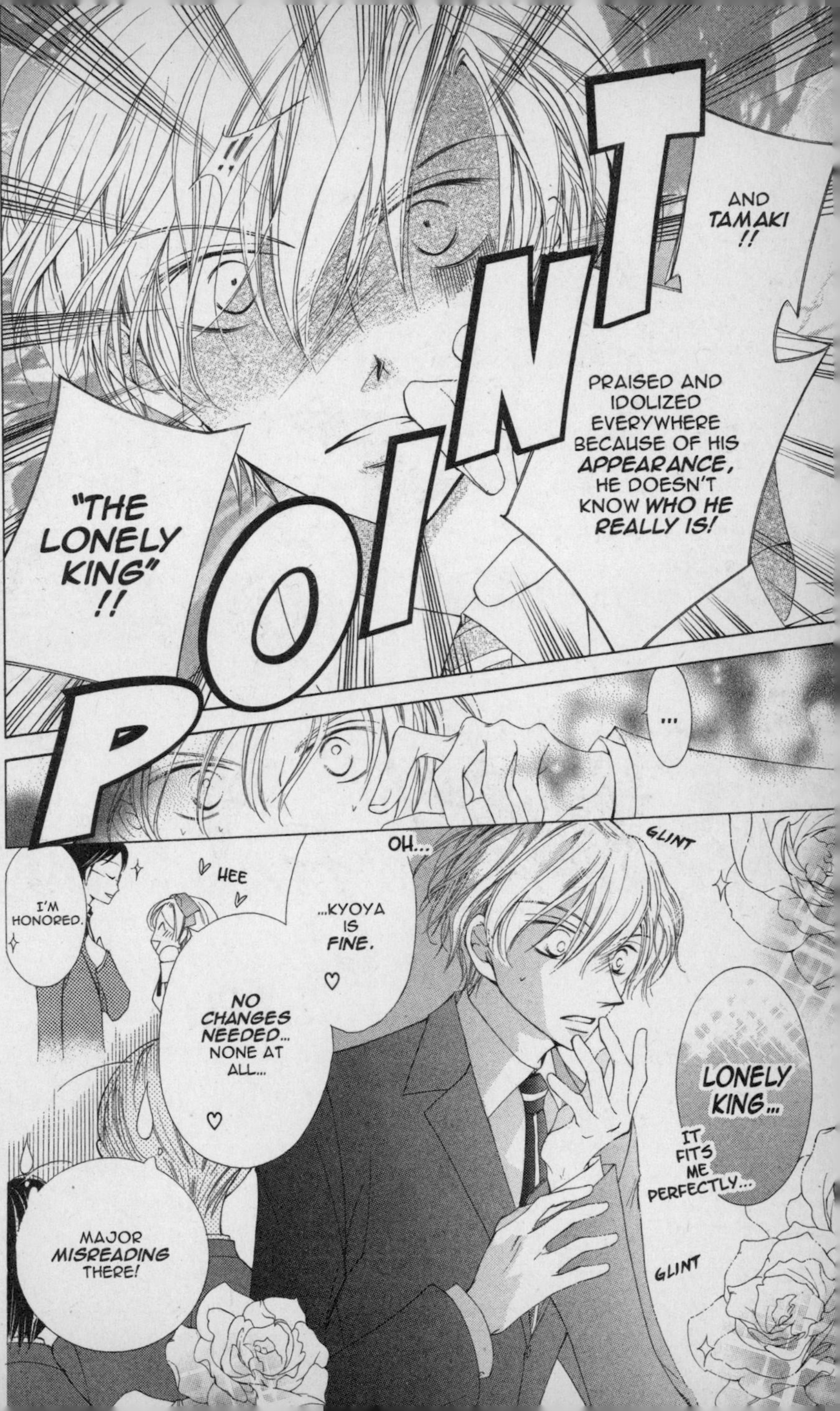
AND TAMAKI!!
PRAISED AND IDOLIZED EVERYWHERE BECAUSE OF HIS APPEARANCE, HE DOESN'T KNOW WHO HE REALLY IS!
POINT
"THE LONELY KING"!!
...
GLINT
LONELY KING...
IT FITS ME PERFECTLY...
GLINT
OH...
...KYOYA IS FINE.
NO CHANGES NEEDED... NONE AT ALL...
HEE
I'M HONORED.
MAJOR MISREADING THERE!

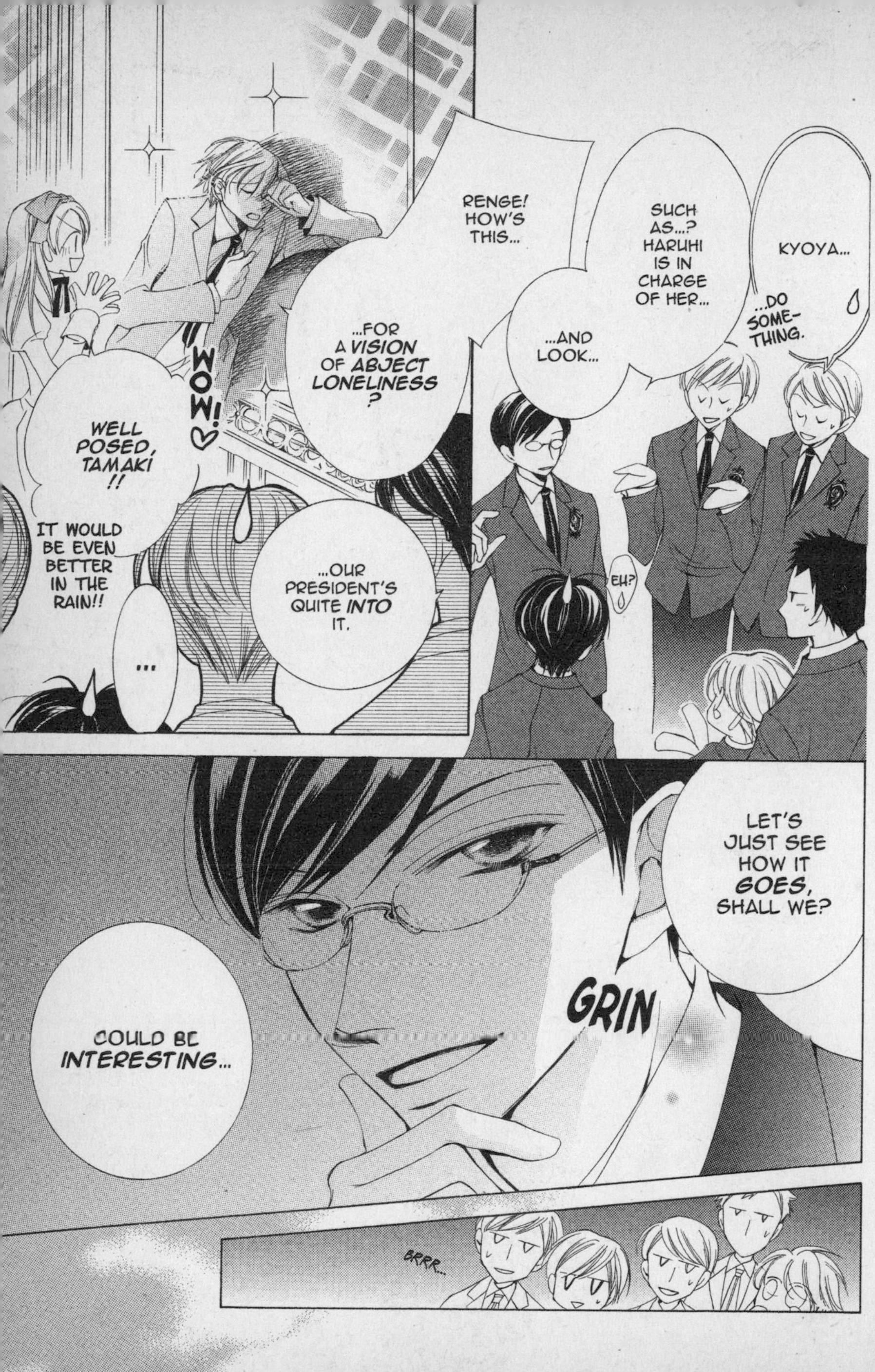
KYOYA...
...DO SOMETHING.
SUCH AS...? HARUHI IS IN CHARGE OF HER...
...AND LOOK...
EH?
RENGE! HOW'S THIS...
...FOR A VISION OF ABJECT LONELINESS?
WOW!
WELL POSED, TAMAKI!!
IT WOULD BE EVEN BETTER IN THE RAIN!!
...OUR PRESIDENT'S QUITE INTO IT.
...
LET'S JUST SEE HOW IT GOES, SHALL WE?
GRIN
COULD BE INTERESTING...
BRRR...

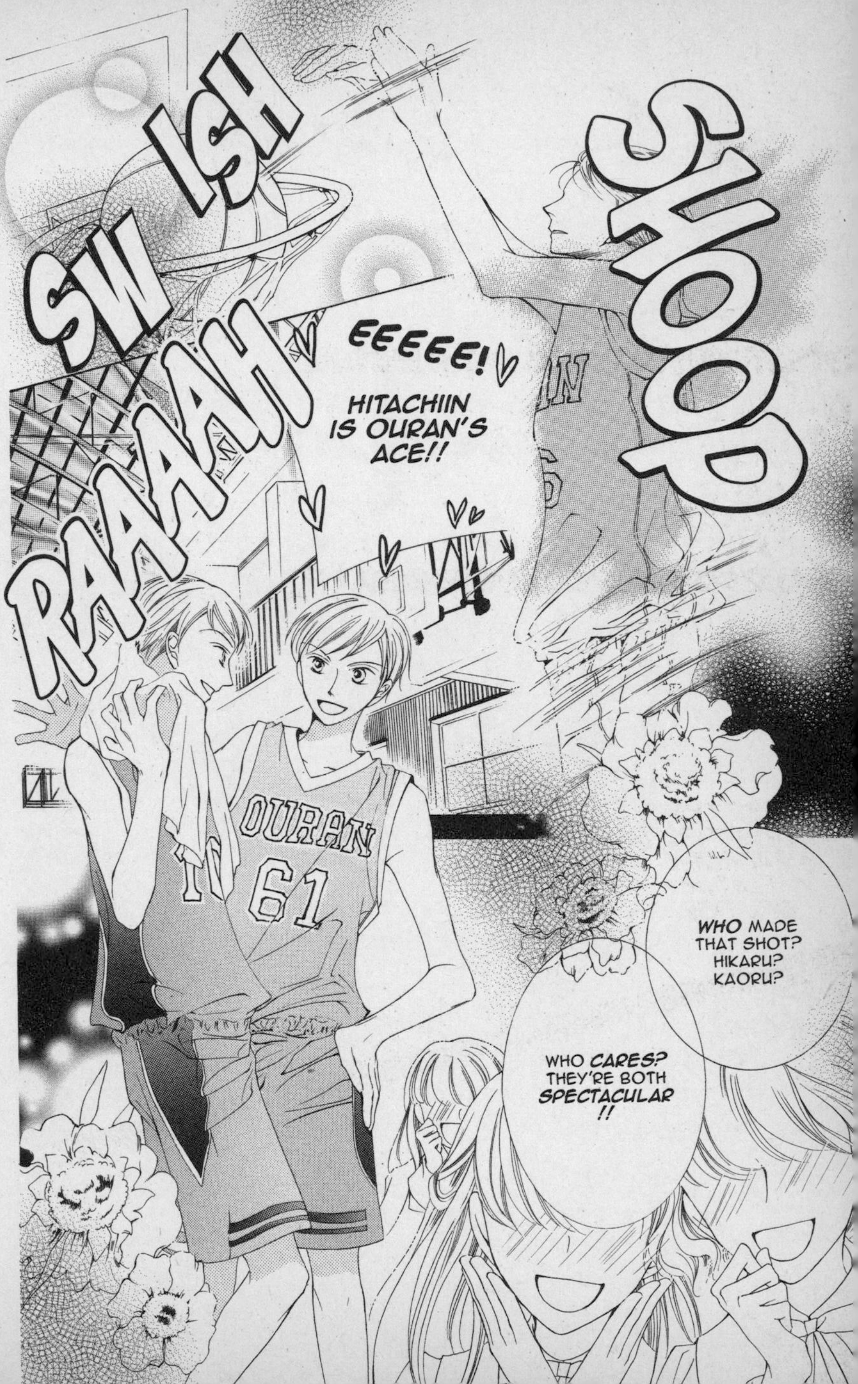
SHOOP
SW ISH
RAAAAH
EEEEE!
HITACHIIN IS OURAN'S ACE!!
OURAN 61
WHO MADE THAT SHOT? HIKARU? KAORU?
WHO CARES? THEY'RE BOTH SPECTACULAR!!

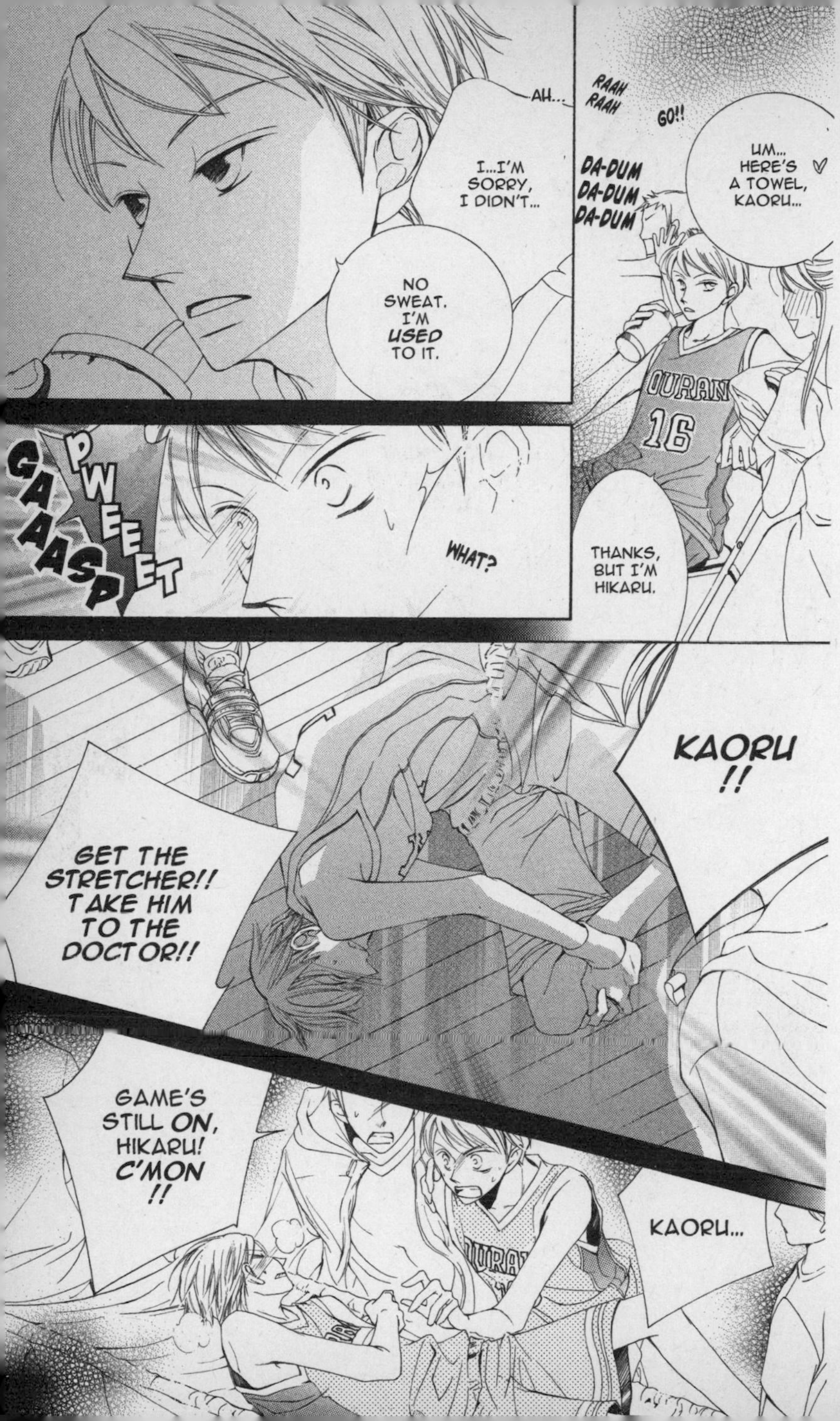
RAAH RAAH
GO!!
DA-DUM DA-DUM DA-DUM
UM... HERE'S A TOWEL, KAORU... ♡
THANKS, BUT I'M HIKARU.
AH...
I...I'M SORRY, I DIDN'T...
NO SWEAT. I'M USED TO IT.
PWEEEET
GAAASP
WHAT?
KAORU !!
GET THE STRETCHER!! TAKE HIM TO THE DOCTOR!!
KAORU...
GAME'S STILL ON, HIKARU! C'MON !!

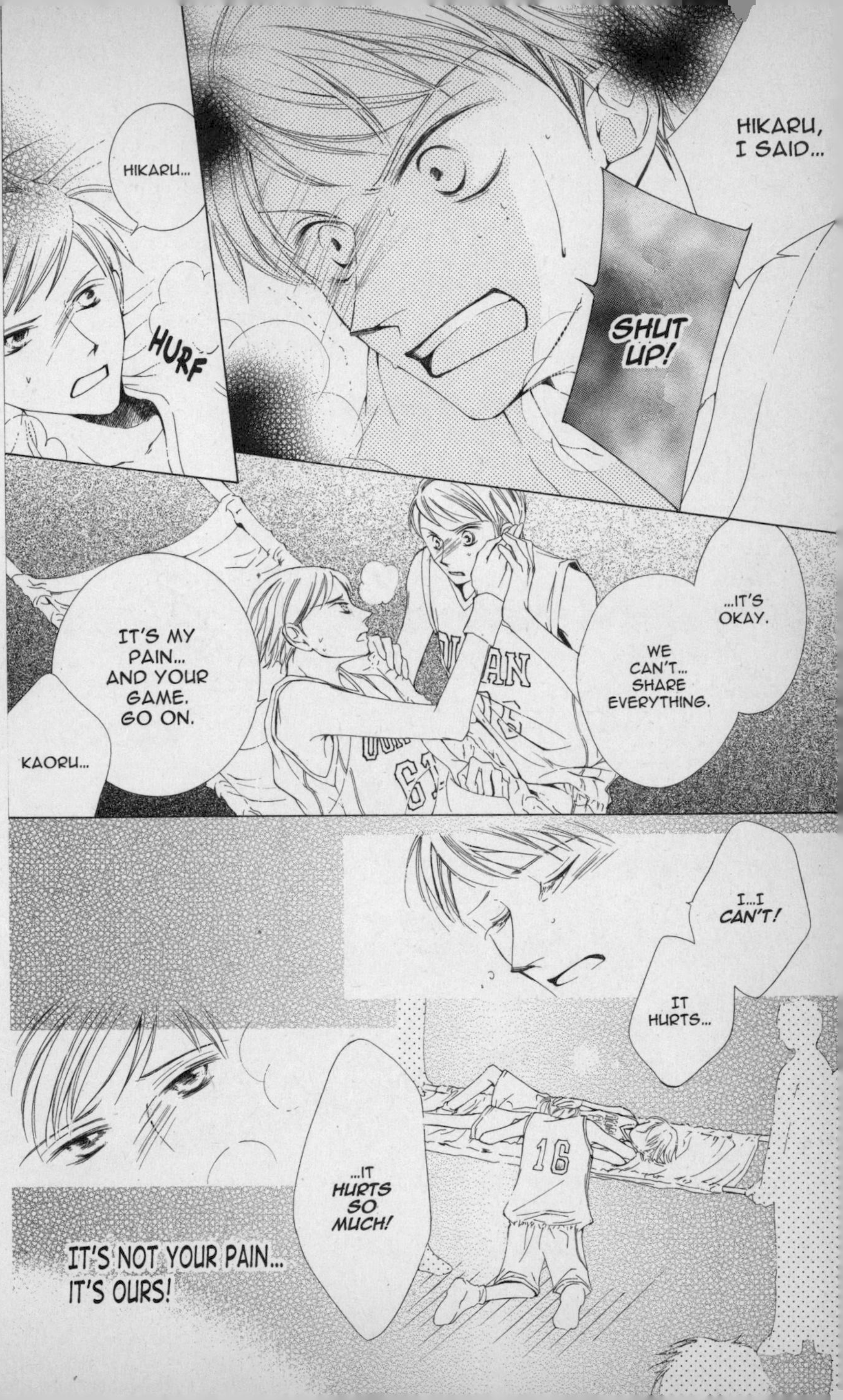
HIKARU, I SAID...
SHUT UP!
HIKARU...
HURF
...IT'S OKAY.
WE CAN'T... SHARE EVERYTHING.
IT'S MY PAIN... AND YOUR GAME. GO ON.
KAORU...
I...I CAN'T!
IT HURTS...
...IT HURTS SO MUCH!
IT'S NOT YOUR PAIN... IT'S OURS!

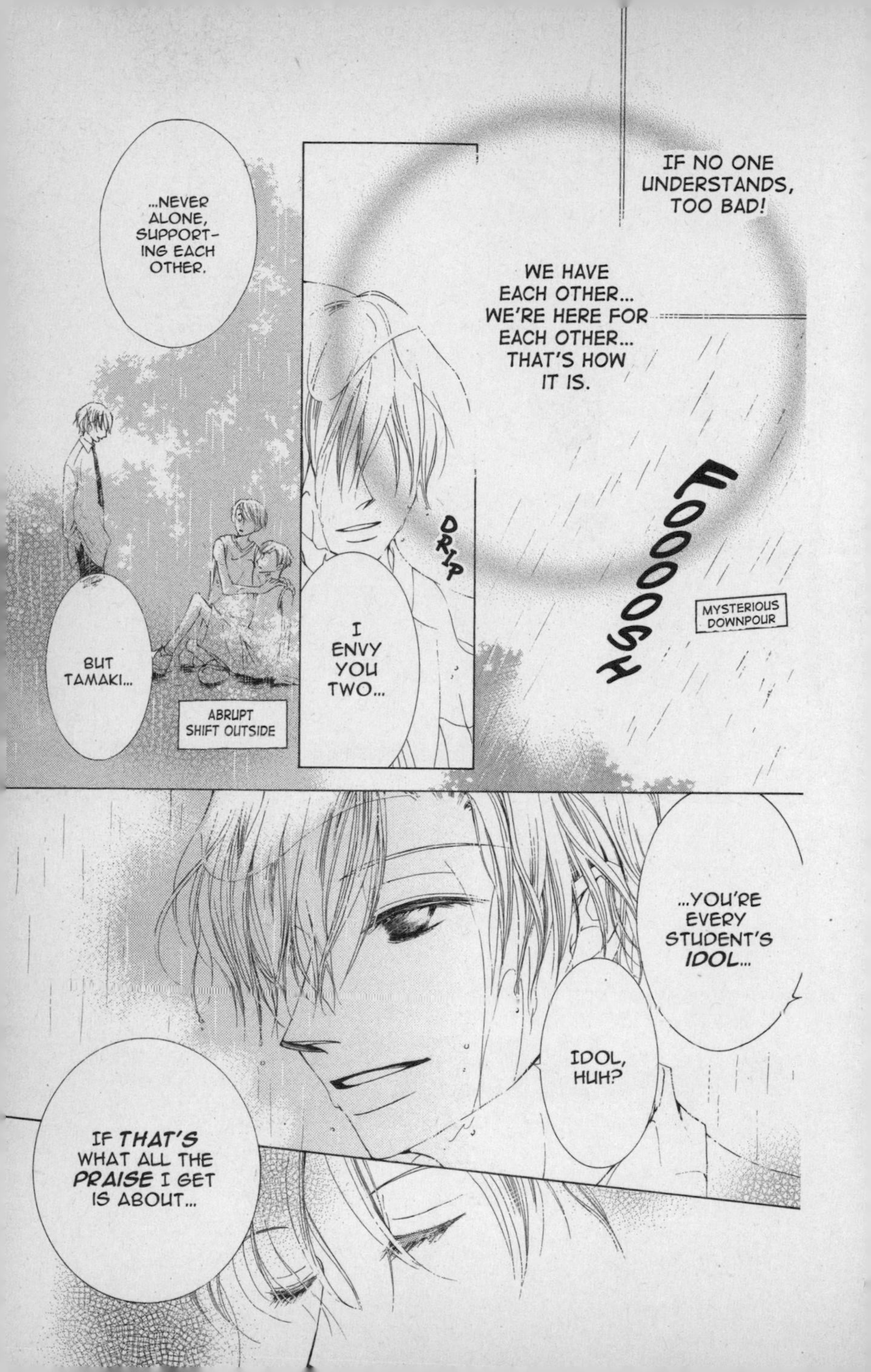
IF NO ONE UNDERSTANDS, TOO BAD!
WE HAVE EACH OTHER... WE'RE HERE FOR EACH OTHER... THAT'S HOW IT IS.
FOOOOOSH
MYSTERIOUS DOWNPOUR
DRIP
I ENVY YOU TWO...
...NEVER ALONE, SUPPORT-ING EACH OTHER.
BUT TAMAKI...
ABRUPT SHIFT OUTSIDE
...YOU'RE EVERY STUDENT'S *IDOL*...
IDOL, HUH?
IF *THAT'S* WHAT ALL THE *PRAISE* I GET IS ABOUT...

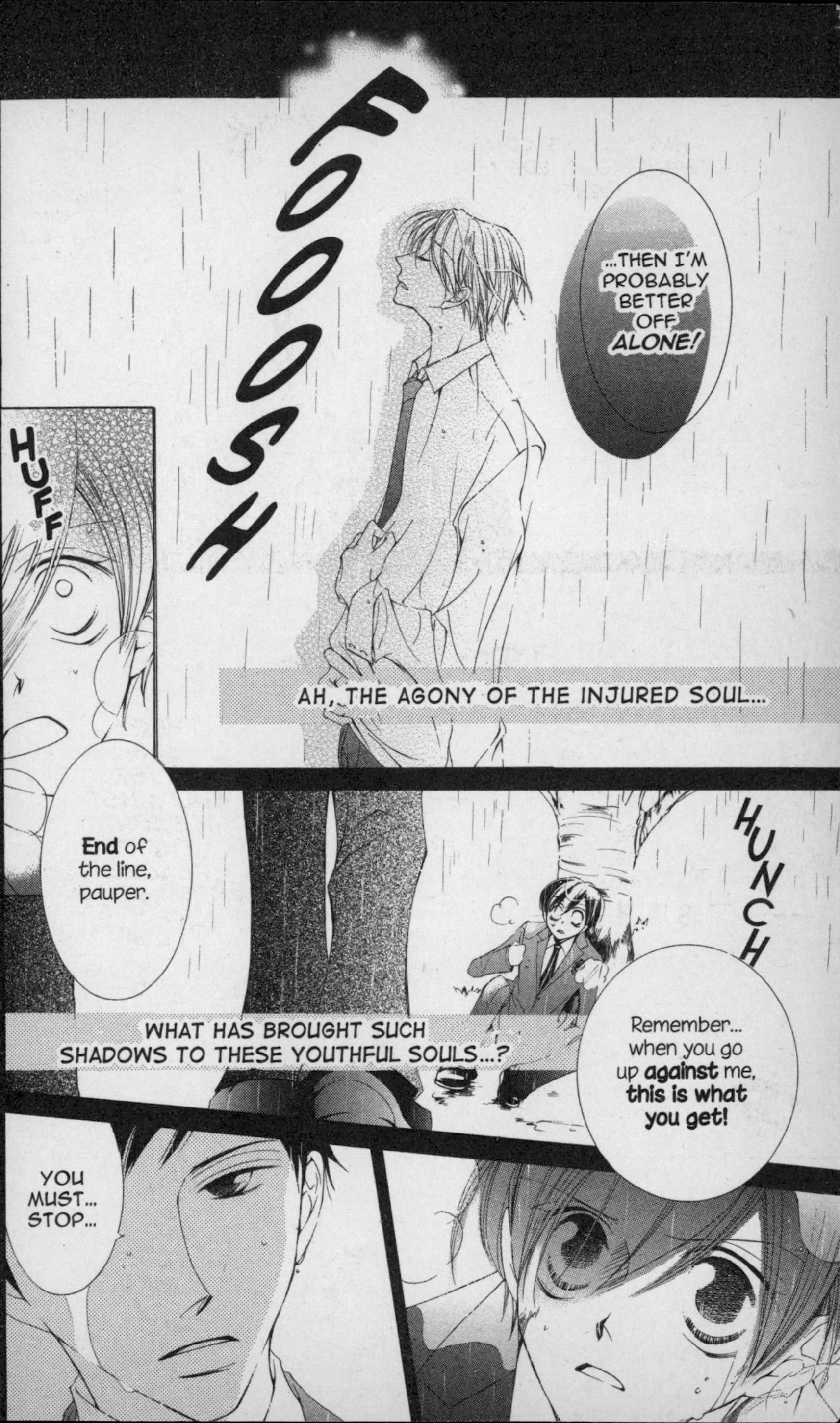
FOOOOSH
...THEN I'M PROBABLY BETTER OFF ALONE!
HUFF
AH, THE AGONY OF THE INJURED SOUL...
HUNCH
End of the line, pauper.
Remember... when you go up against me, this is what you get!
WHAT HAS BROUGHT SUCH SHADOWS TO THESE YOUTHFUL SOULS...?
YOU MUST... STOP...

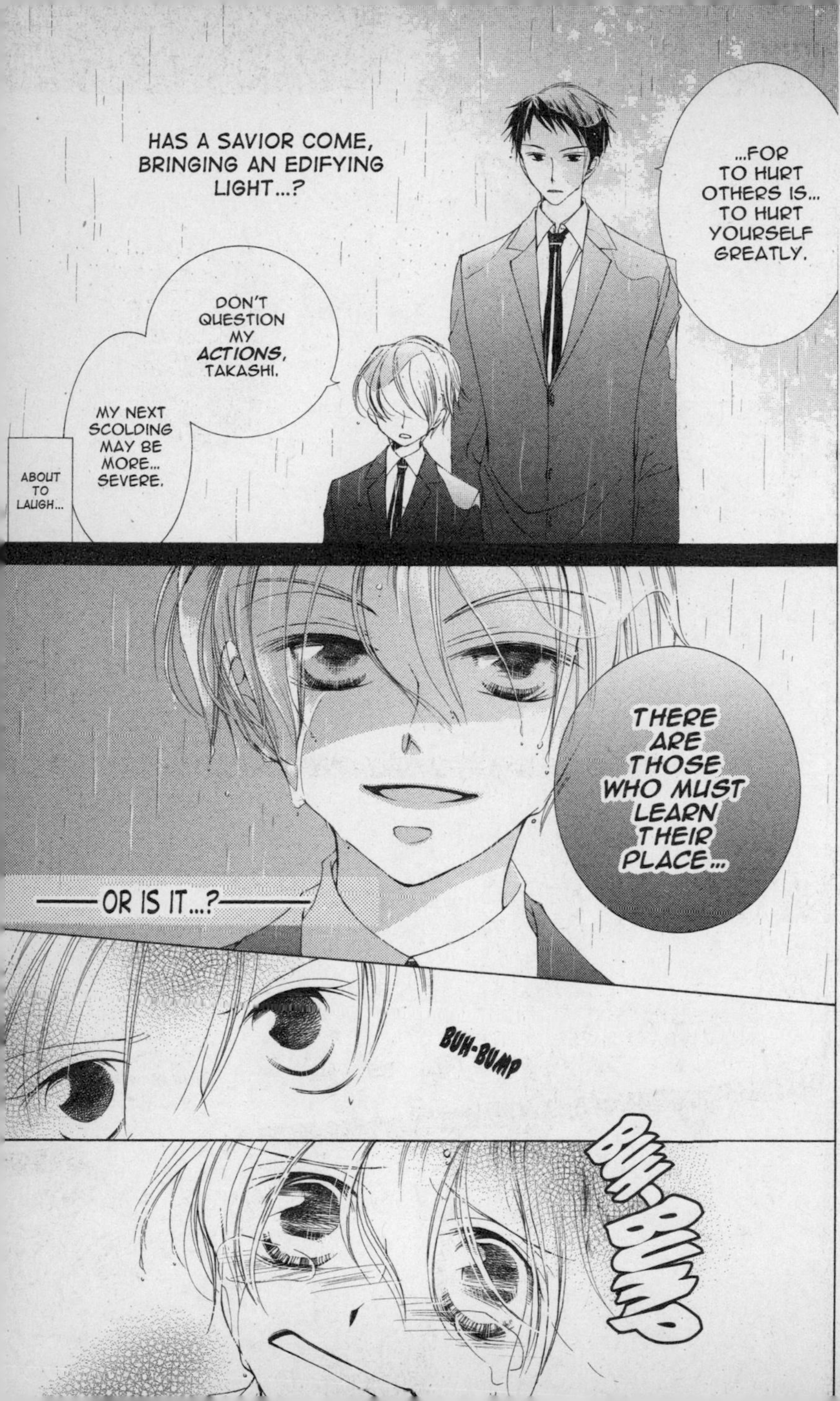
...FOR TO HURT OTHERS IS... TO HURT YOURSELF GREATLY.
HAS A SAVIOR COME, BRINGING AN EDIFYING LIGHT...?
DON'T QUESTION MY *ACTIONS*, TAKASHI.
MY NEXT SCOLDING MAY BE MORE... SEVERE.
ABOUT TO LAUGH...
THERE ARE THOSE WHO MUST LEARN THEIR PLACE...
——OR IS IT...?——
BUH-BUMP
BUH-BUMP

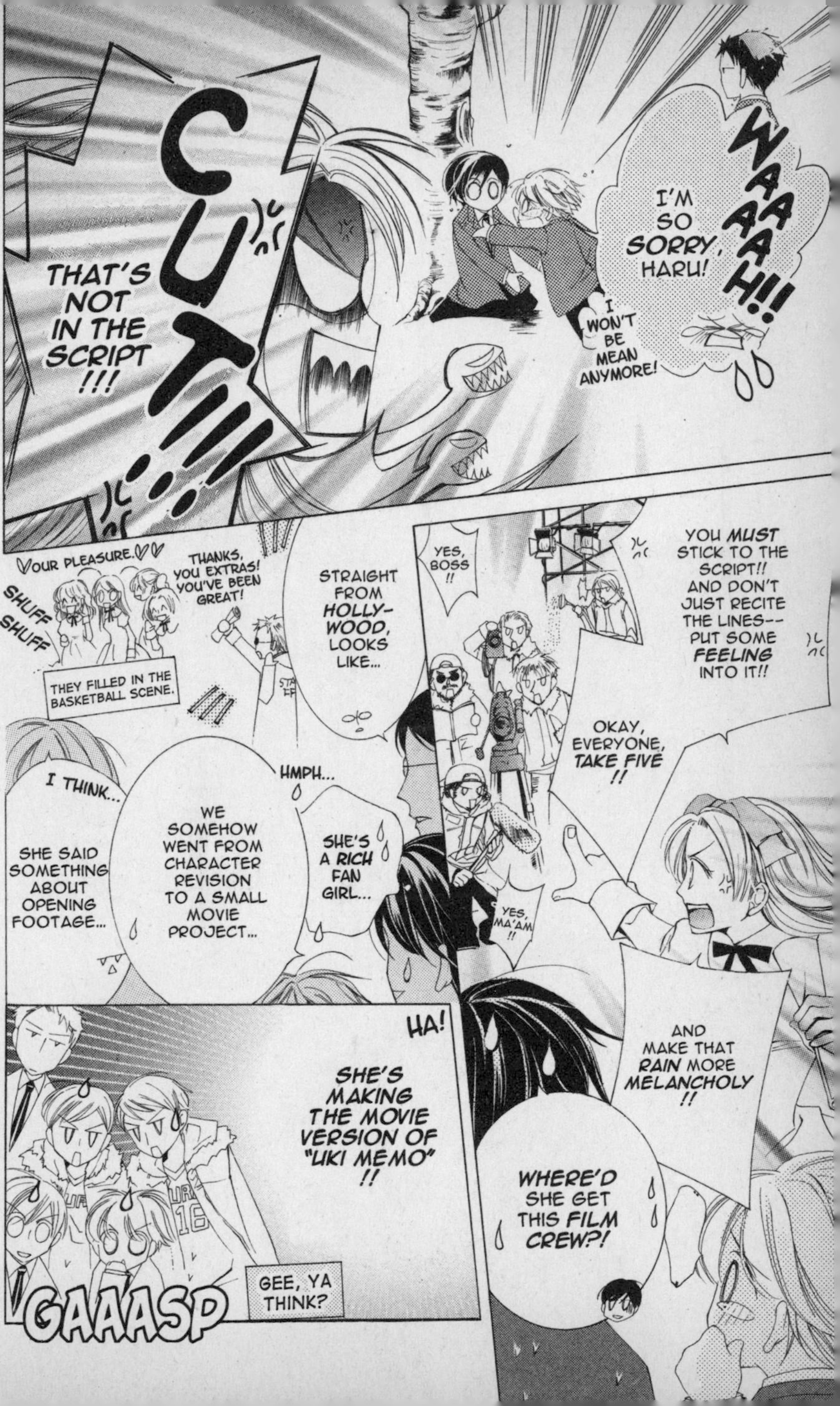
WAAAAH!!
I'M SO SORRY, HARU!
I WON'T BE MEAN ANYMORE!
CUT!!...!!
THAT'S NOT IN THE SCRIPT!!!
YOU MUST STICK TO THE SCRIPT!! AND DON'T JUST RECITE THE LINES-- PUT SOME FEELING INTO IT!!
YES, BOSS!!
OKAY, EVERYONE, TAKE FIVE!!
YES, MA'AM!!
AND MAKE THAT RAIN MORE MELANCHOLY!!
STRAIGHT FROM HOLLYWOOD, LOOKS LIKE...
THANKS, YOU EXTRAS! YOU'VE BEEN GREAT!
YOUR PLEASURE.
SHUFF SHUFF
THEY FILLED IN THE BASKETBALL SCENE.
HMPH...
SHE'S A RICH FAN GIRL...
WE SOMEHOW WENT FROM CHARACTER REVISION TO A SMALL MOVIE PROJECT...
I THINK...
SHE SAID SOMETHING ABOUT OPENING FOOTAGE...
WHERE'D SHE GET THIS FILM CREW?!
HA!
SHE'S MAKING THE MOVIE VERSION OF "UKI MEMO"!!
GEE, YA THINK?
GAAASP

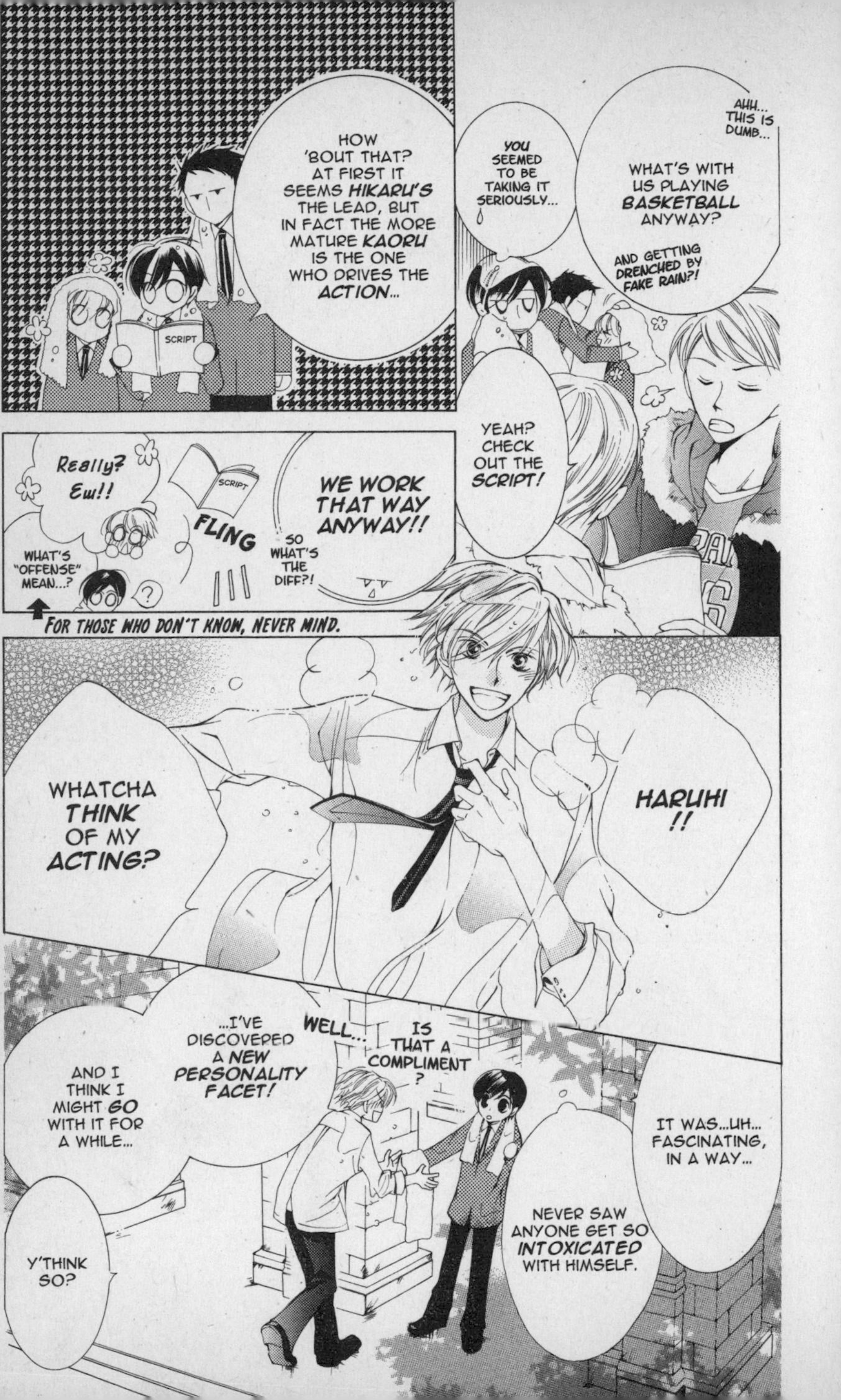
AHH... THIS IS DUMB...
WHAT'S WITH US PLAYING BASKETBALL ANYWAY?
AND GETTING DRENCHED BY FAKE RAIN?!
YOU SEEMED TO BE TAKING IT SERIOUSLY...
YEAH? CHECK OUT THE SCRIPT!
HOW 'BOUT THAT? AT FIRST IT SEEMS HIKARU'S THE LEAD, BUT IN FACT THE MORE MATURE KAORU IS THE ONE WHO DRIVES THE ACTION...
SCRIPT
WE WORK THAT WAY ANYWAY!!
SO WHAT'S THE DIFF?!
FLING
SCRIPT
Really? Ew!!
WHAT'S "OFFENSE" MEAN...?
FOR THOSE WHO DON'T KNOW, NEVER MIND.
HARUHI!!
WHATCHA THINK OF MY ACTING?
IT WAS...UH... FASCINATING, IN A WAY...
NEVER SAW ANYONE GET SO INTOXICATED WITH HIMSELF.
IS THAT A COMPLIMENT?
WELL...
...I'VE DISCOVERED A NEW PERSONALITY FACET!
AND I THINK I MIGHT GO WITH IT FOR A WHILE...
Y'THINK SO?

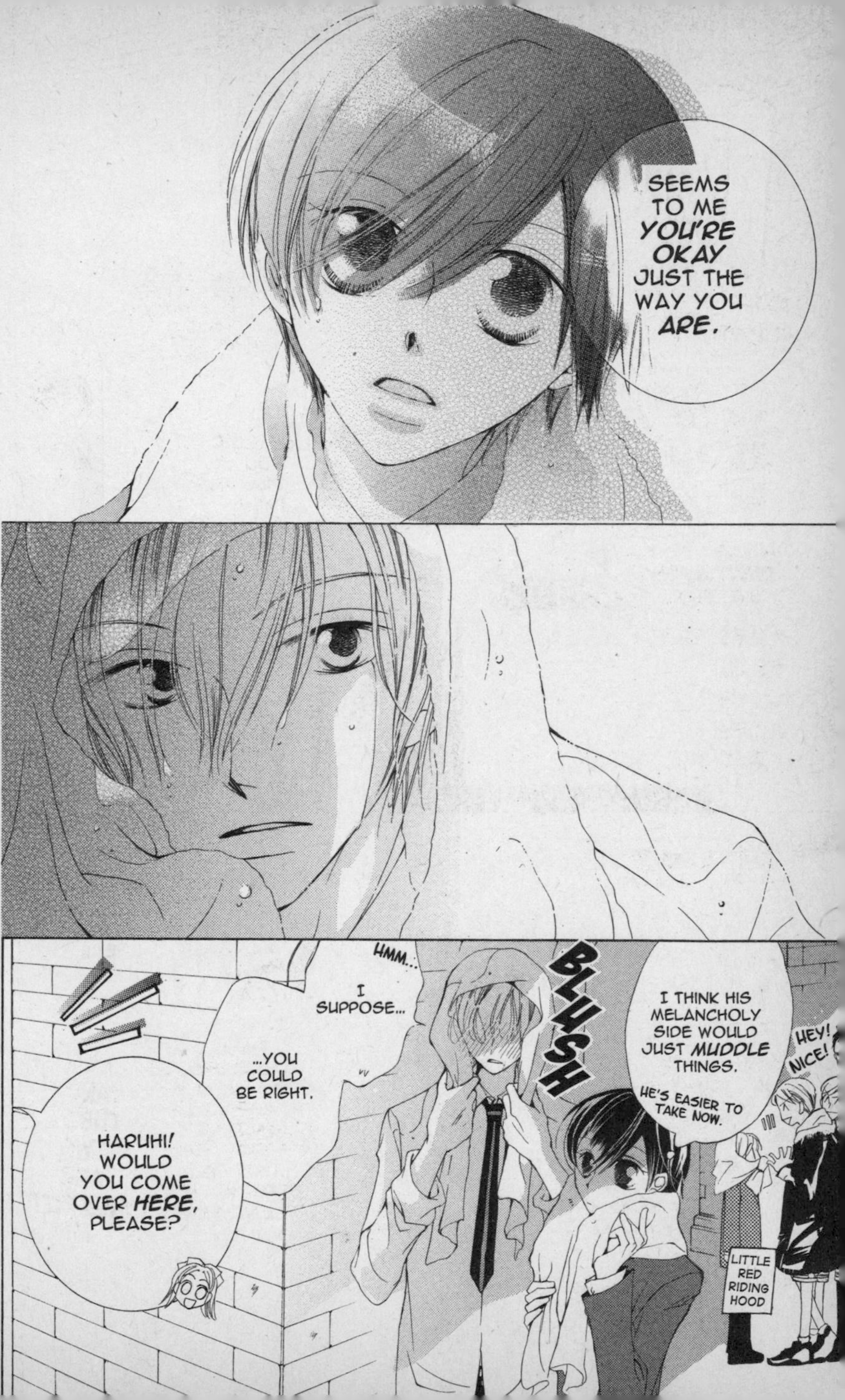
SEEMS TO ME *YOU'RE OKAY* JUST THE WAY YOU *ARE.*
HEY! NICE!
I THINK HIS MELANCHOLY SIDE WOULD JUST *MUDDLE* THINGS.
HE'S EASIER TO TAKE NOW.
BLUSH
HMM...
I SUPPOSE...
...YOU COULD BE RIGHT.
LITTLE RED RIDING HOOD
HARUHI! WOULD YOU COME OVER *HERE,* PLEASE?

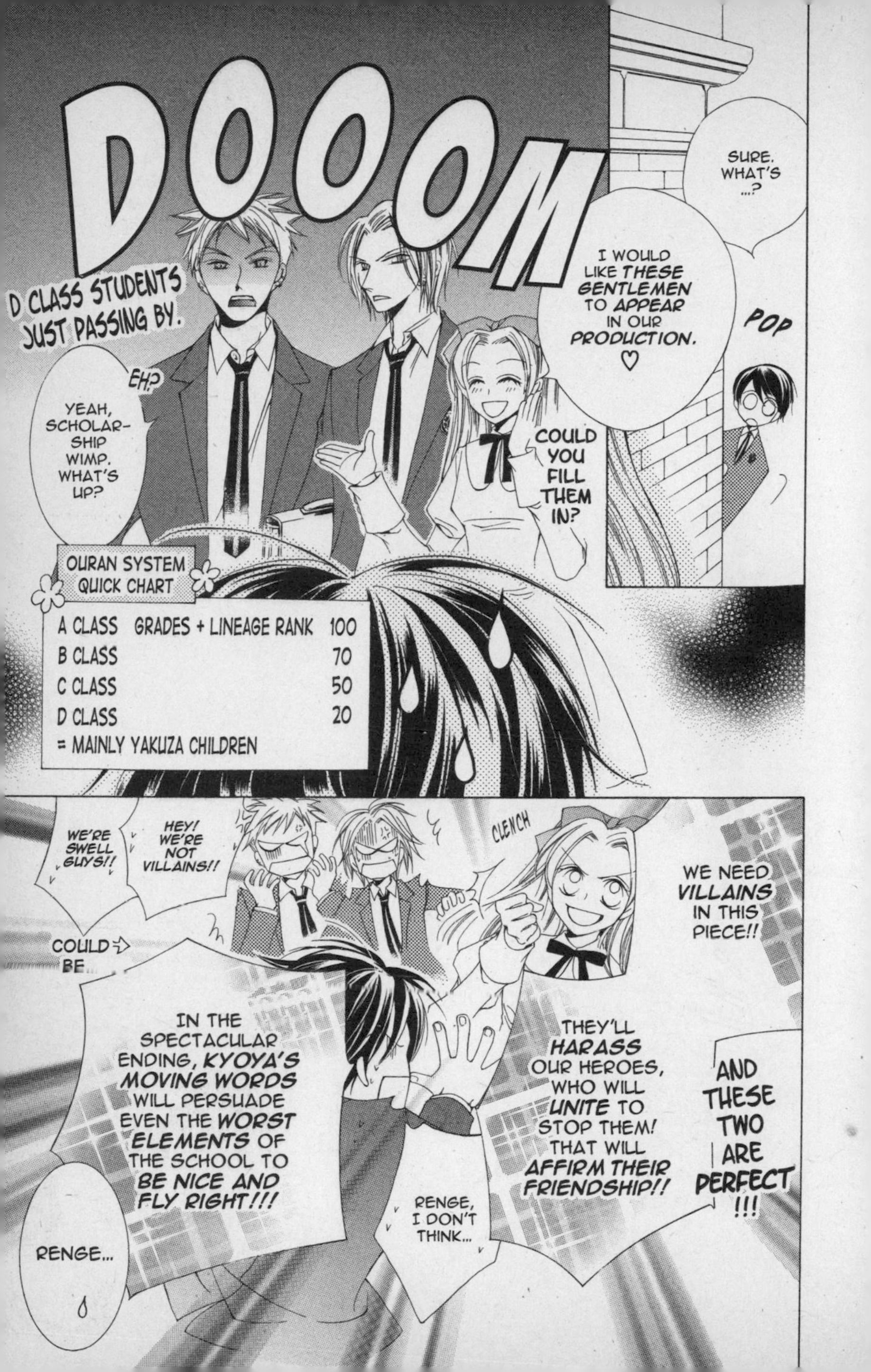
SURE. WHAT'S ...?
POP
I WOULD LIKE THESE GENTLEMEN TO APPEAR IN OUR PRODUCTION. ♡
COULD YOU FILL THEM IN?
EH?
YEAH, SCHOLARSHIP WIMP. WHAT'S UP?
DOOOM
D CLASS STUDENTS JUST PASSING BY.
OURAN SYSTEM QUICK CHART
A CLASS GRADES + LINEAGE RANK 100
B CLASS 70
C CLASS 50
D CLASS 20
= MAINLY YAKUZA CHILDREN
WE NEED VILLAINS IN THIS PIECE!!
CLENCH
HEY! WE'RE NOT VILLAINS!!
WE'RE SWELL GUYS!!
COULD BE...
AND THESE TWO ARE PERFECT!!!
THEY'LL HARASS OUR HEROES, WHO WILL UNITE TO STOP THEM! THAT WILL AFFIRM THEIR FRIENDSHIP!!
IN THE SPECTACULAR ENDING, KYOYA'S MOVING WORDS WILL PERSUADE EVEN THE WORST ELEMENTS OF THE SCHOOL TO BE NICE AND FLY RIGHT!!!
RENGE, I DON'T THINK...
RENGE...

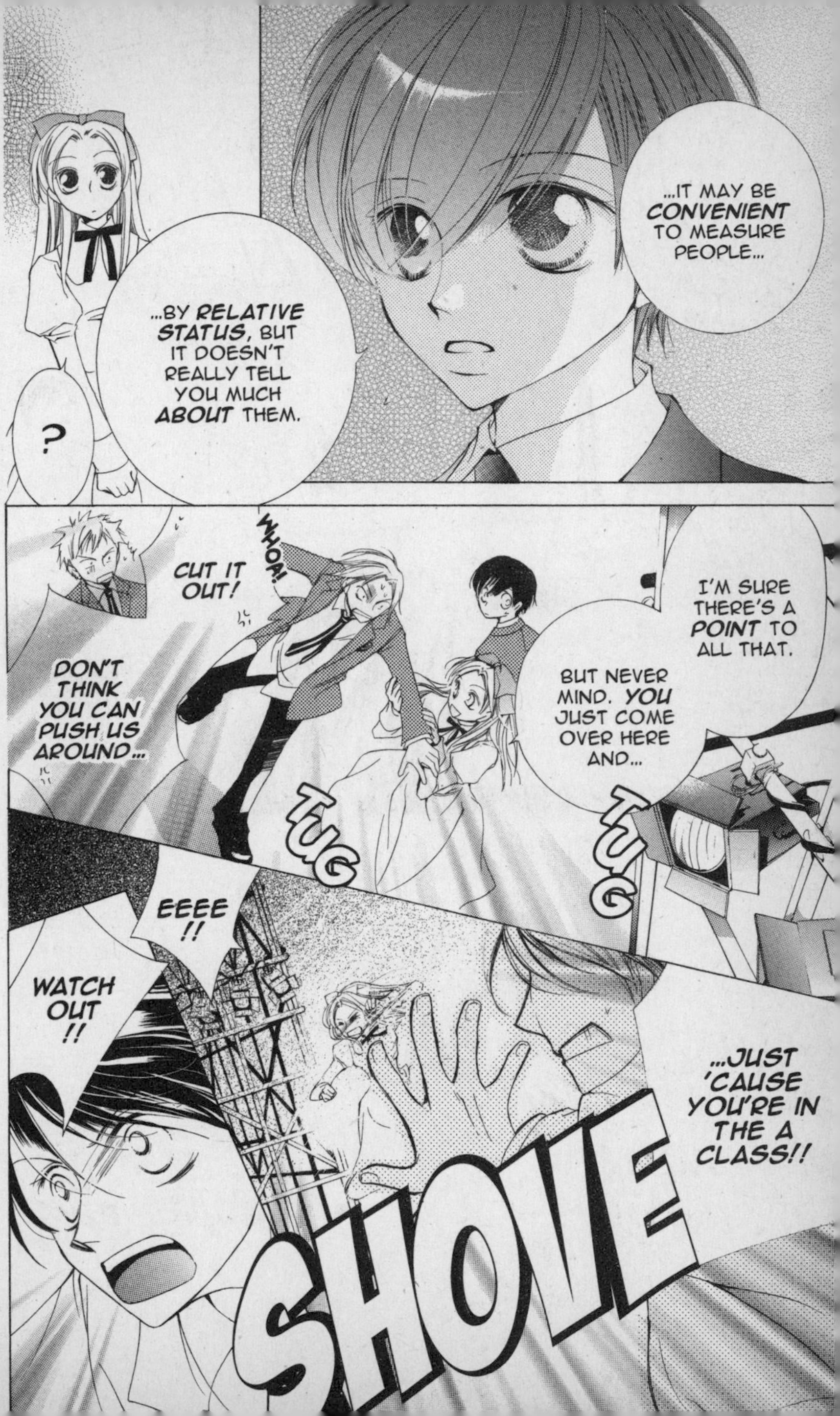
...IT MAY BE CONVENIENT TO MEASURE PEOPLE...
...BY RELATIVE STATUS, BUT IT DOESN'T REALLY TELL YOU MUCH ABOUT THEM.
?
I'M SURE THERE'S A POINT TO ALL THAT.
BUT NEVER MIND. YOU JUST COME OVER HERE AND...
TUG
TUG
WHOA!
CUT IT OUT!
DON'T THINK YOU CAN PUSH US AROUND...
...JUST 'CAUSE YOU'RE IN THE A CLASS!!
SHOVE
EEEE!!
WATCH OUT!!

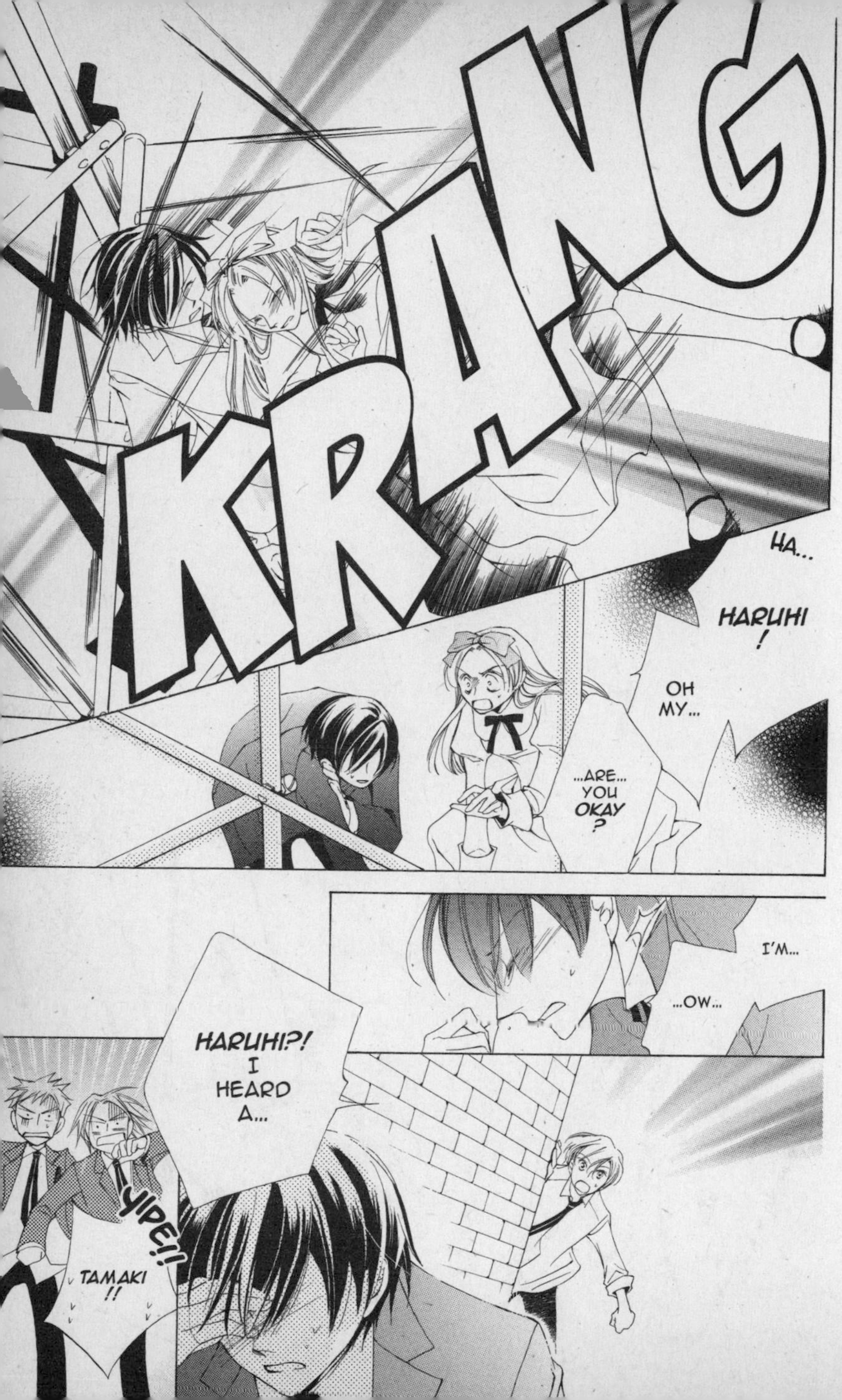
KRANG.
HA...
HARUHI!
OH MY...
...ARE... YOU OKAY?
I'M...
...OW...
HARUHI?! I HEARD A...
YIPE!!
TAMAKI!!

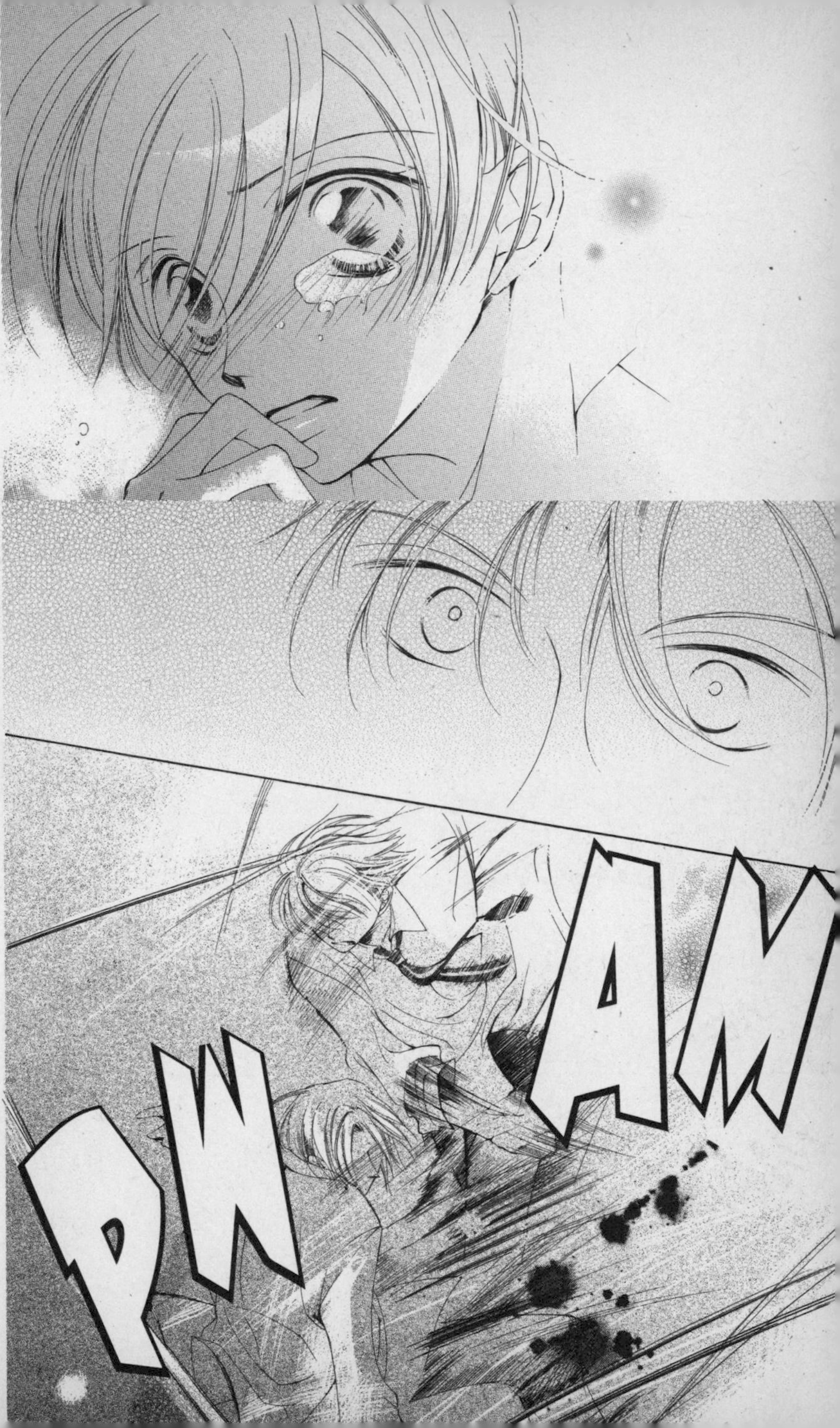
PWAM

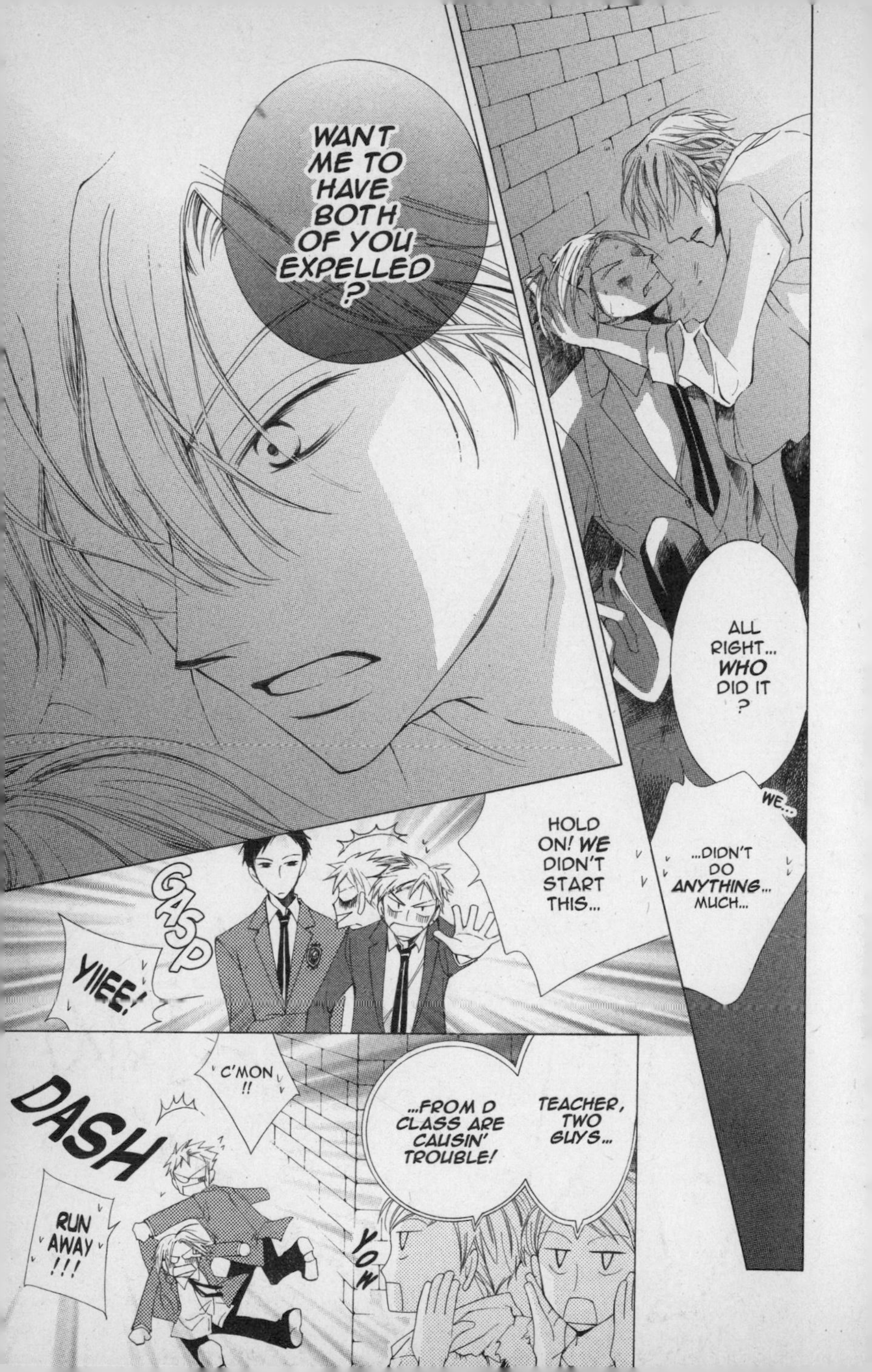
ALL RIGHT... WHO DID IT?
WANT ME TO HAVE BOTH OF YOU EXPELLED?
WE...
...DIDN'T DO ANYTHING... MUCH...
HOLD ON! WE DIDN'T START THIS...
GASP
YIIEE!
TEACHER, TWO GUYS...
...FROM D CLASS ARE CAUSIN' TROUBLE!
YOW
C'MON!!
DASH
RUN AWAY!!!

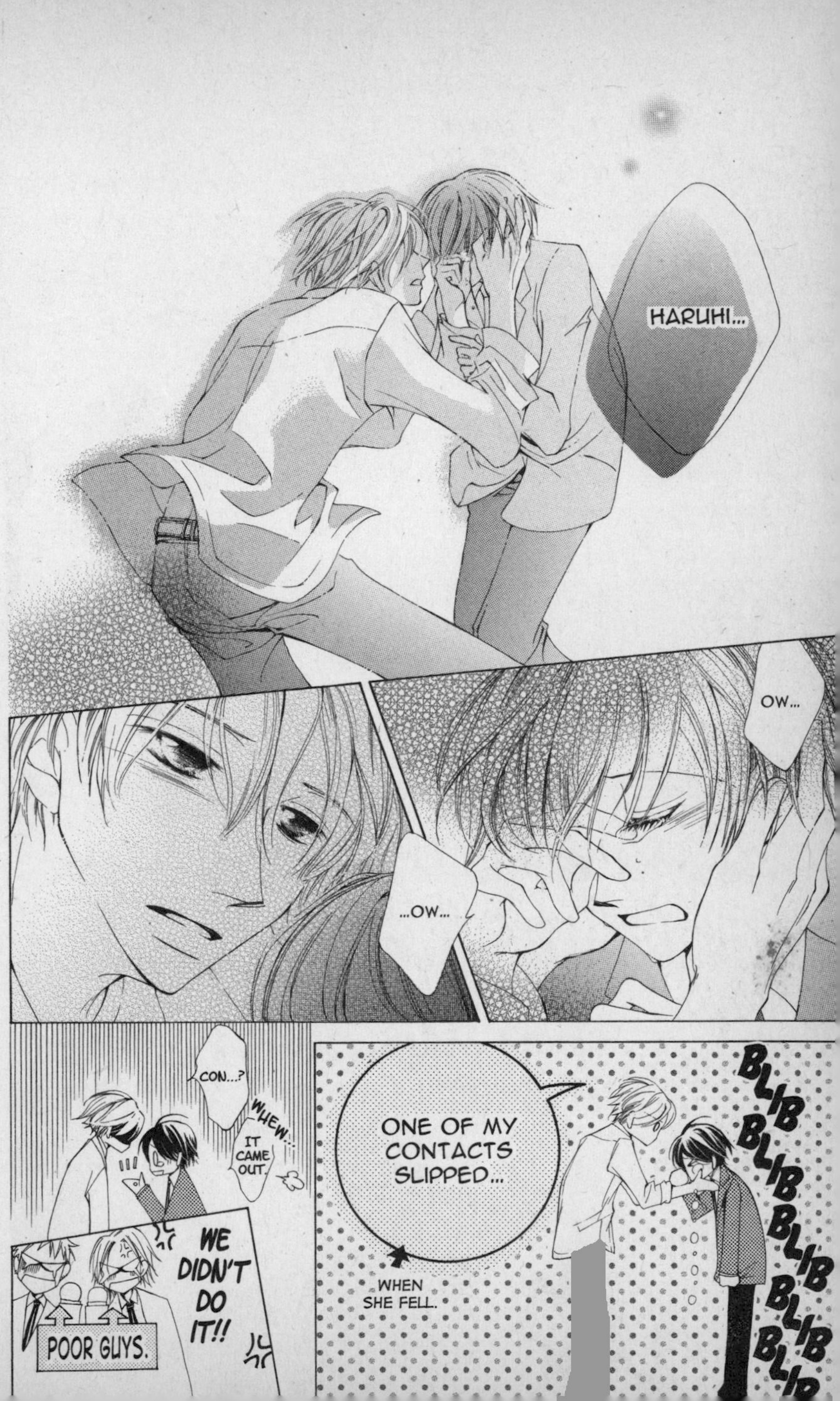
HARUHI...
OW...
...OW...
ONE OF MY CONTACTS SLIPPED...
WHEN SHE FELL.
BLIB BLIB BLIB BLIB BLIB BLIB BLIB
CON...?
WHEW...
IT CAME OUT.
WE DIDN'T DO IT!!
POOR GUYS.

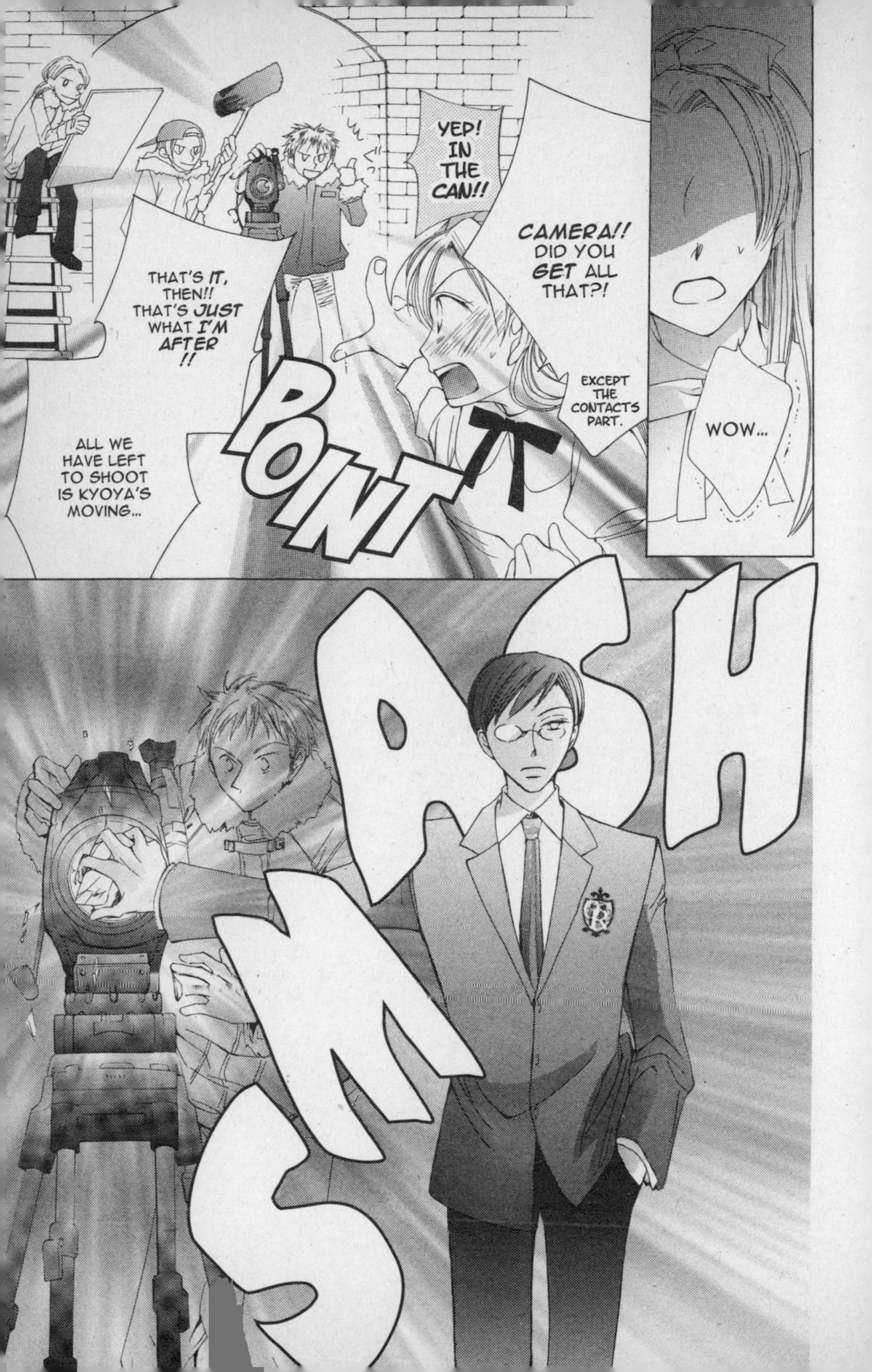
WOW...
CAMERA!! DID YOU GET ALL THAT?!
YEP! IN THE CAN!!
EXCEPT THE CONTACTS PART.
POINT
THAT'S IT, THEN!! THAT'S JUST WHAT I'M AFTER!!
ALL WE HAVE LEFT TO SHOOT IS KYOYA'S MOVING...
SMASH

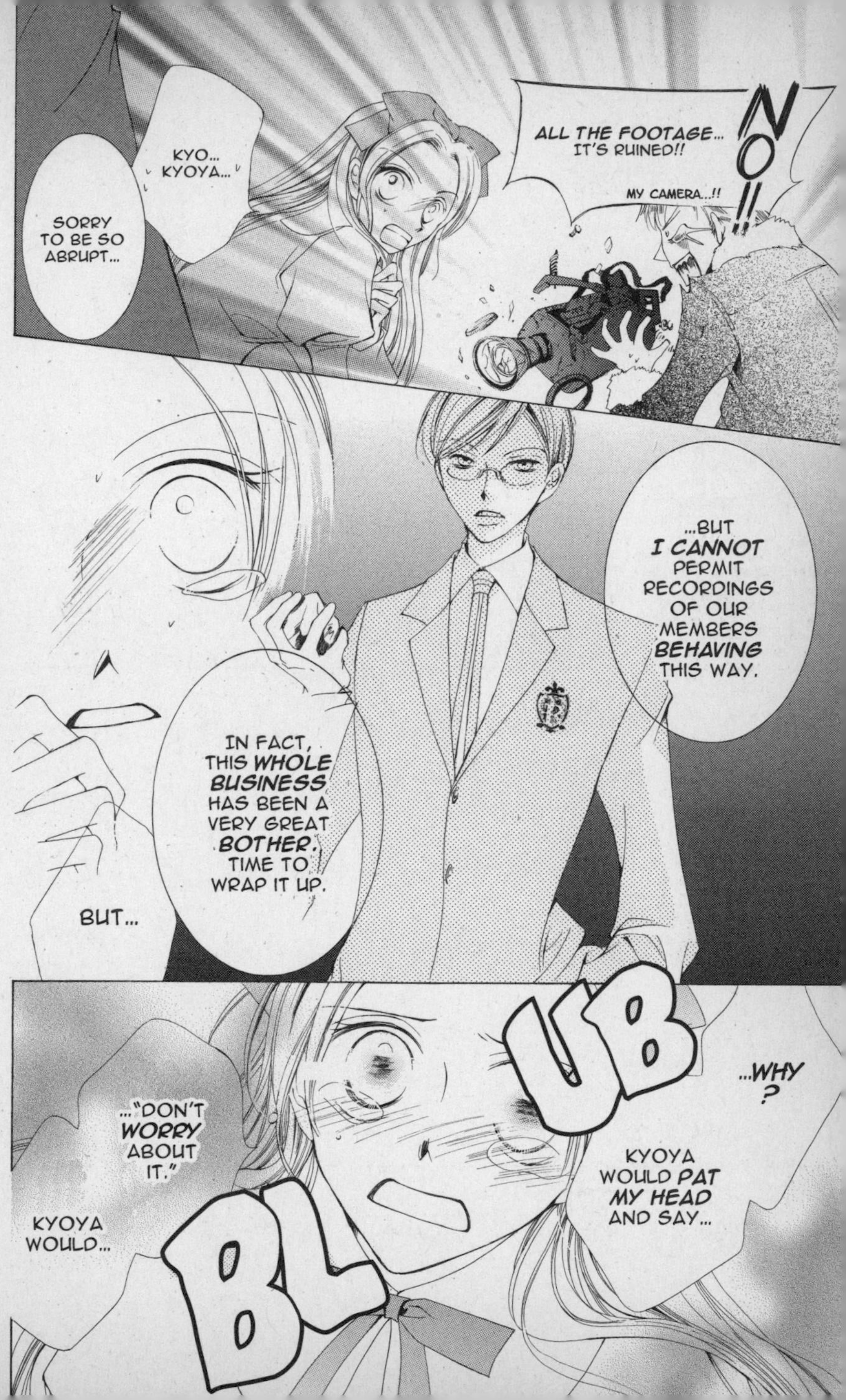
NO!!
ALL THE FOOTAGE... IT'S RUINED!!
MY CAMERA...!!
KYO... KYOYA...
SORRY TO BE SO ABRUPT...
...BUT I CANNOT PERMIT RECORDINGS OF OUR MEMBERS BEHAVING THIS WAY.
IN FACT, THIS WHOLE BUSINESS HAS BEEN A VERY GREAT BOTHER. TIME TO WRAP IT UP.
BUT...
...WHY?
KYOYA WOULD PAT MY HEAD AND SAY...
BLUB
..."DON'T WORRY ABOUT IT."
KYOYA WOULD...

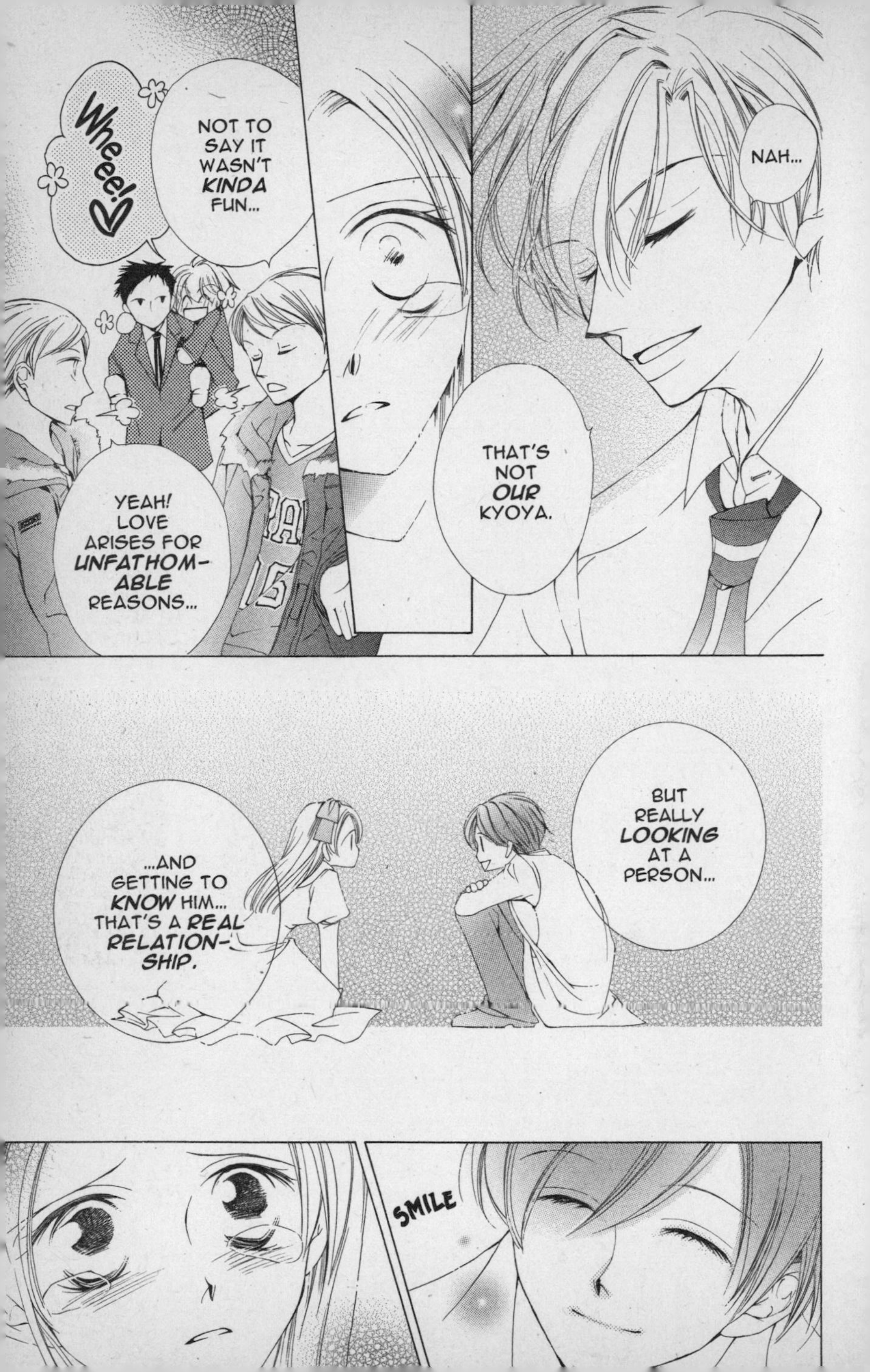
NAH...
THAT'S NOT OUR KYOYA.
NOT TO SAY IT WASN'T KINDA FUN...
Wheee!♥
YEAH! LOVE ARISES FOR UNFATHOM-ABLE REASONS...
BUT REALLY LOOKING AT A PERSON...
...AND GETTING TO KNOW HIM... THAT'S A REAL RELATION-SHIP.
SMILE

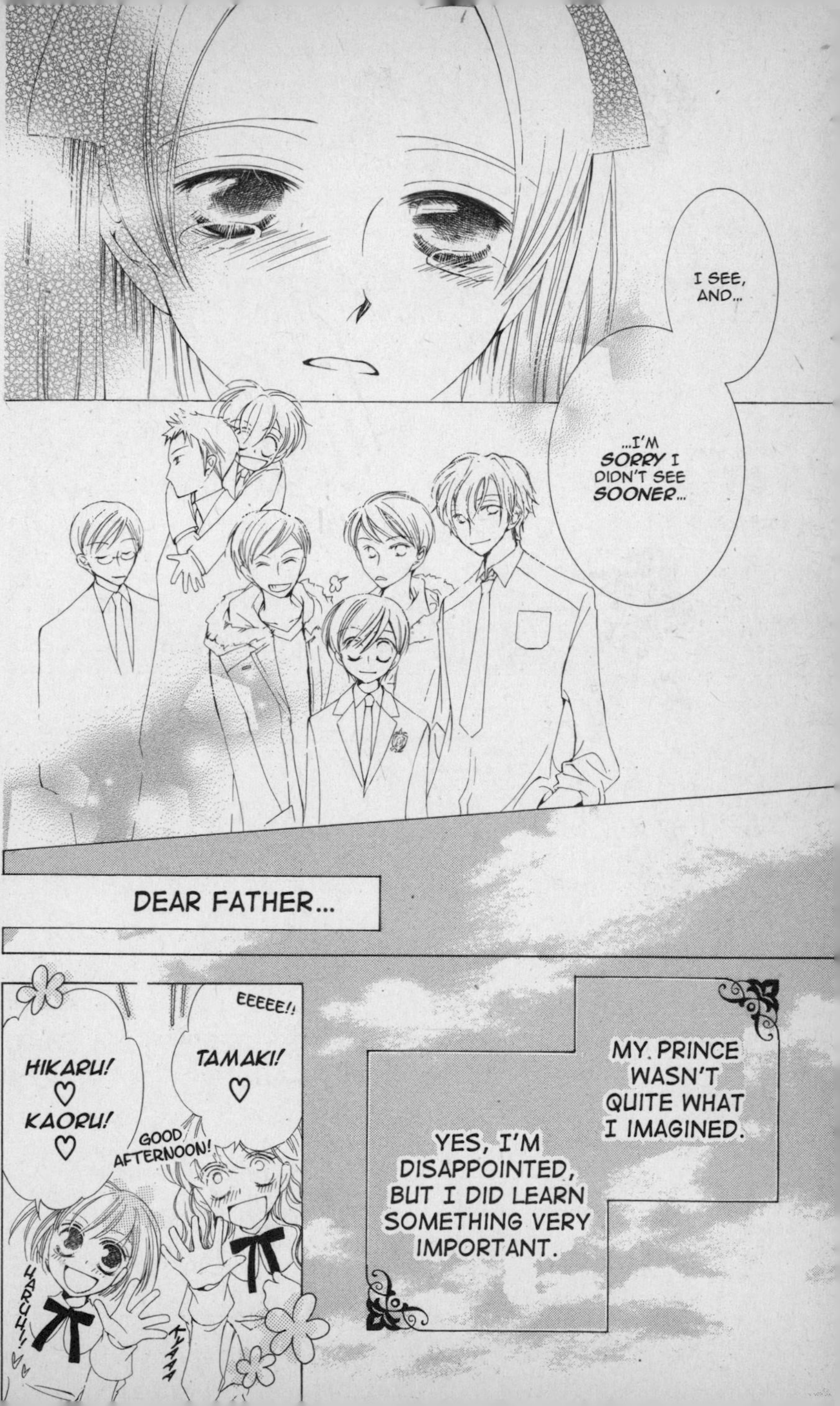
I SEE, AND...
...I'M SORRY I DIDN'T SEE SOONER...
DEAR FATHER...
MY PRINCE WASN'T QUITE WHAT I IMAGINED.
YES, I'M DISAPPOINTED, BUT I DID LEARN SOMETHING VERY IMPORTANT.
EEEEE!!
TAMAKI! ♡
HIKARU! ♡ KAORU! ♡
GOOD AFTERNOON!
HARUHI! ♡
KYAAA

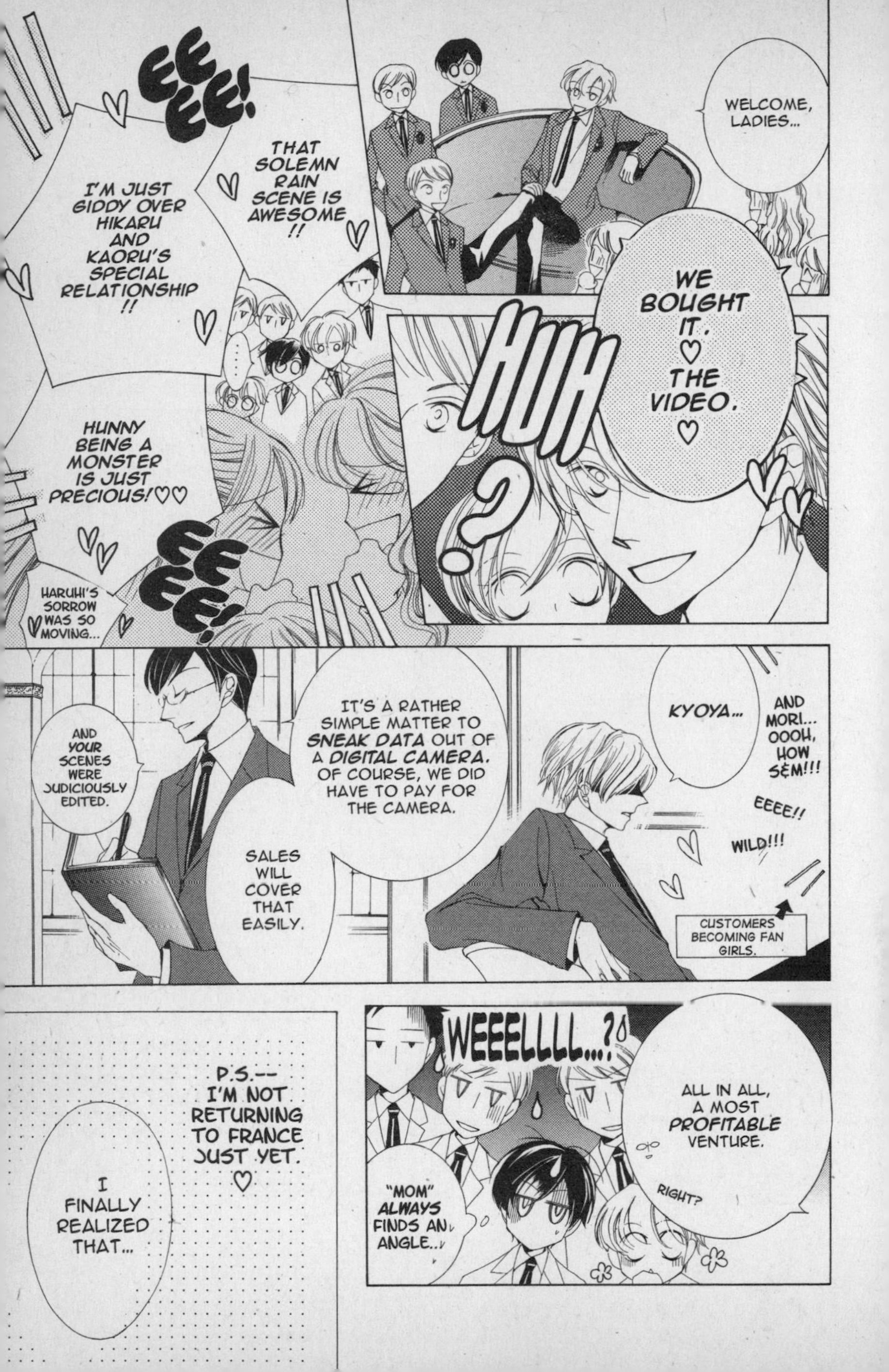
WELCOME, LADIES...
WE BOUGHT IT. ♡ THE VIDEO. ♡
HUH?
EEEEEE!
THAT SOLEMN RAIN SCENE IS AWESOME!!
I'M JUST GIDDY OVER HIKARU AND KAORU'S SPECIAL RELATIONSHIP!!
...
HUNNY BEING A MONSTER IS JUST PRECIOUS! ♡♡
EEEEEE!
HARUHI'S SORROW WAS SO MOVING...
KYOYA...
AND MORI... OOOH, HOW S&M!!!
EEEE!!
WILD!!!
CUSTOMERS BECOMING FAN GIRLS.
IT'S A RATHER SIMPLE MATTER TO SNEAK DATA OUT OF A DIGITAL CAMERA. OF COURSE, WE DID HAVE TO PAY FOR THE CAMERA.
SALES WILL COVER THAT EASILY.
AND YOUR SCENES WERE JUDICIOUSLY EDITED.
WEEELLLL...?
ALL IN ALL, A MOST PROFITABLE VENTURE.
RIGHT?
"MOM" ALWAYS FINDS AN ANGLE...
P.S.-- I'M NOT RETURNING TO FRANCE JUST YET. ♡
I FINALLY REALIZED THAT...

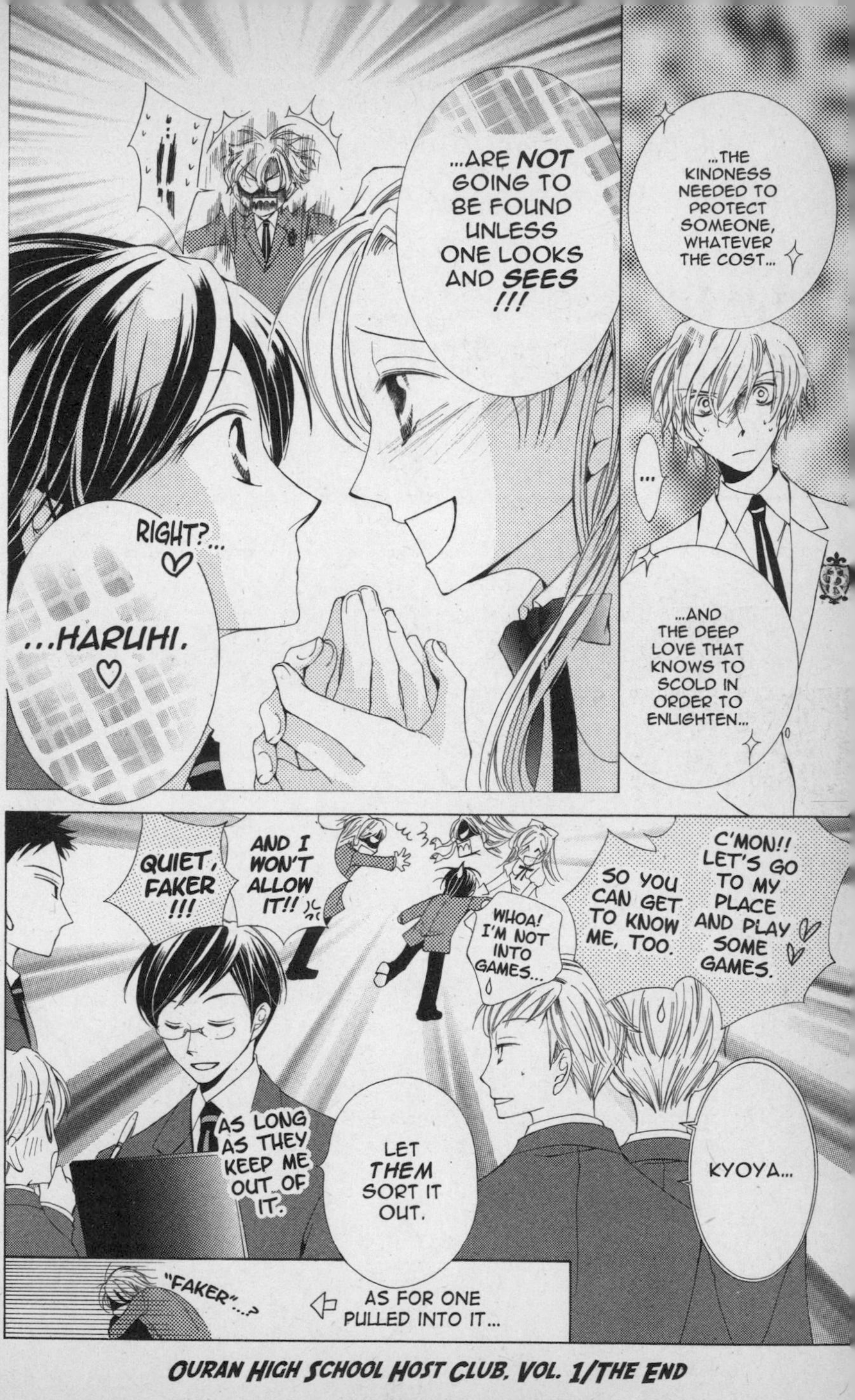
...THE KINDNESS NEEDED TO PROTECT SOMEONE, WHATEVER THE COST...
...
...AND THE DEEP LOVE THAT KNOWS TO SCOLD IN ORDER TO ENLIGHTEN...
...ARE NOT GOING TO BE FOUND UNLESS ONE LOOKS AND SEES!!!
!!
RIGHT?... ♥
...HARUHI. ♥
C'MON!! LET'S GO TO MY PLACE AND PLAY SOME GAMES.
SO YOU CAN GET TO KNOW ME, TOO.
WHOA! I'M NOT INTO GAMES...
AND I WON'T ALLOW IT!!
QUIET, FAKER!!!
KYOYA...
LET THEM SORT IT OUT.
AS LONG AS THEY KEEP ME OUT OF IT.
AS FOR ONE PULLED INTO IT...
"FAKER"...?

OURAN HIGH SCHOOL HOST CLUB. VOL. 1/THE END

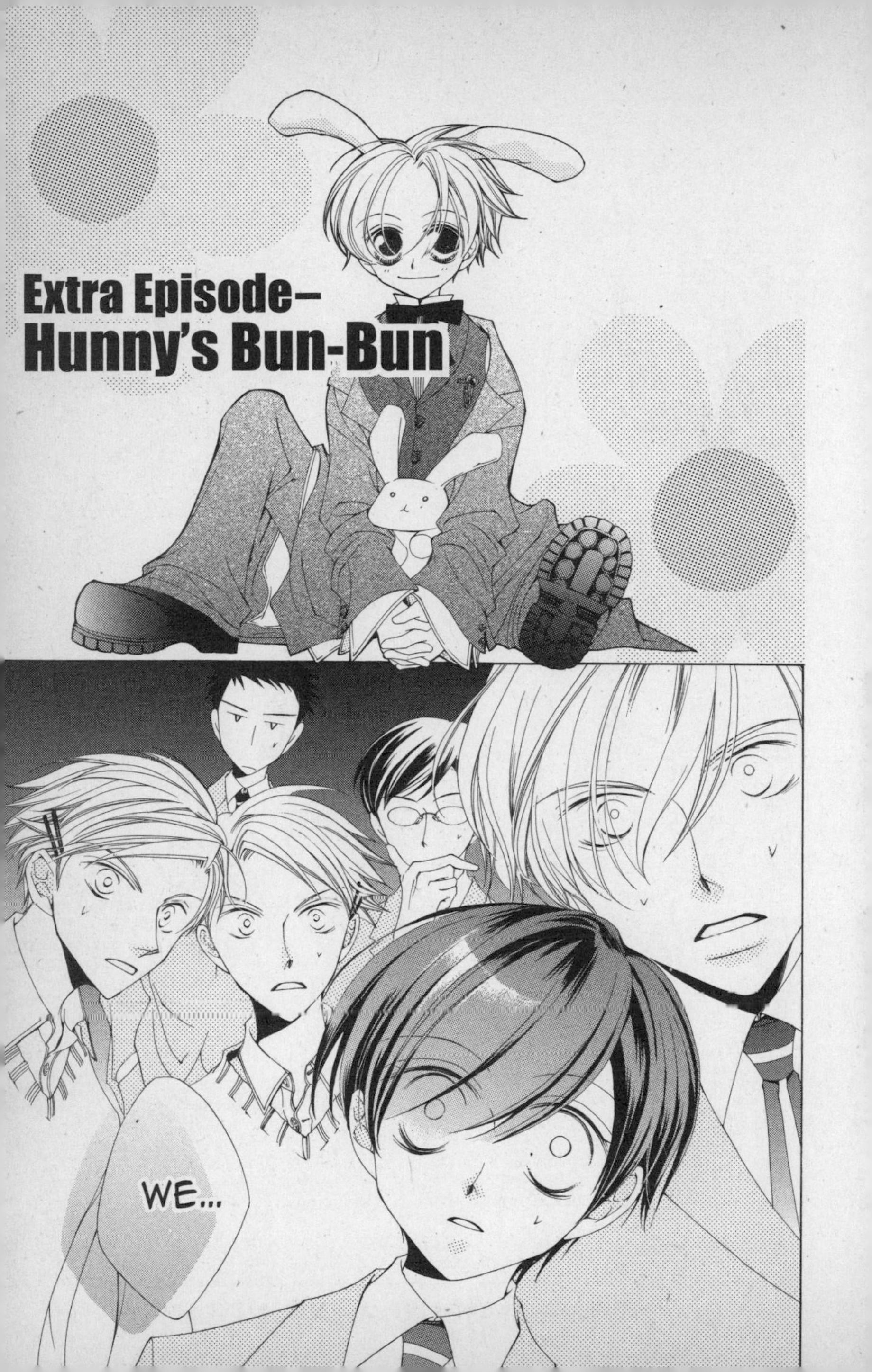
Extra Episode—
Hunny's Bun-Bun
WE...

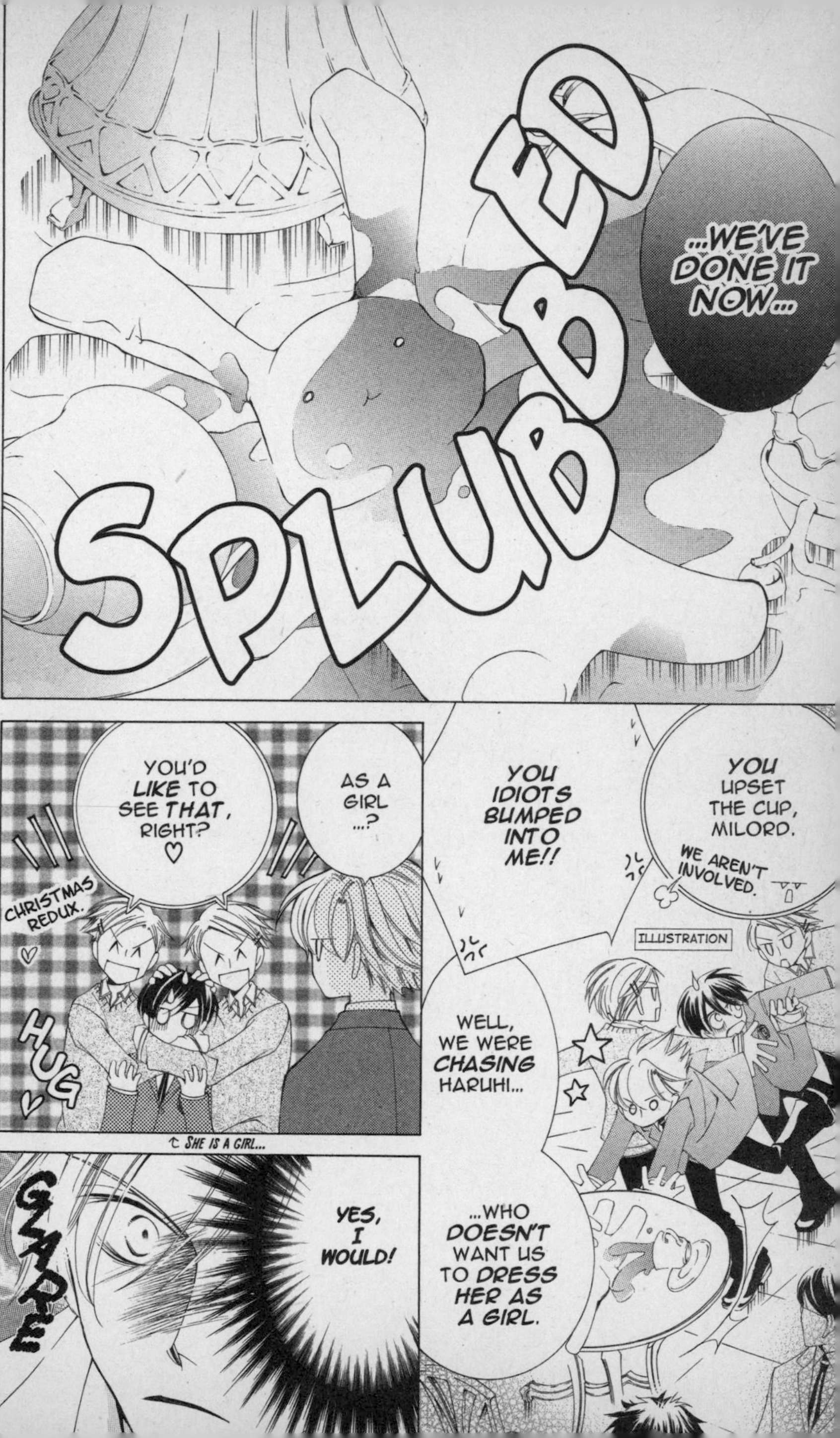
SPLUBBED
...WE'VE DONE IT NOW...
YOU UPSET THE CUP, MILORD.
WE AREN'T INVOLVED.
YOU IDIOTS BUMPED INTO ME!!
ILLUSTRATION
WELL, WE WERE CHASING HARUHI...
...WHO DOESN'T WANT US TO DRESS HER AS A GIRL.
AS A GIRL ...?
YOU'D LIKE TO SEE THAT, RIGHT? ♡
CHRISTMAS REDUX.
HUG
SHE IS A GIRL...
YES, I WOULD!
GLARE

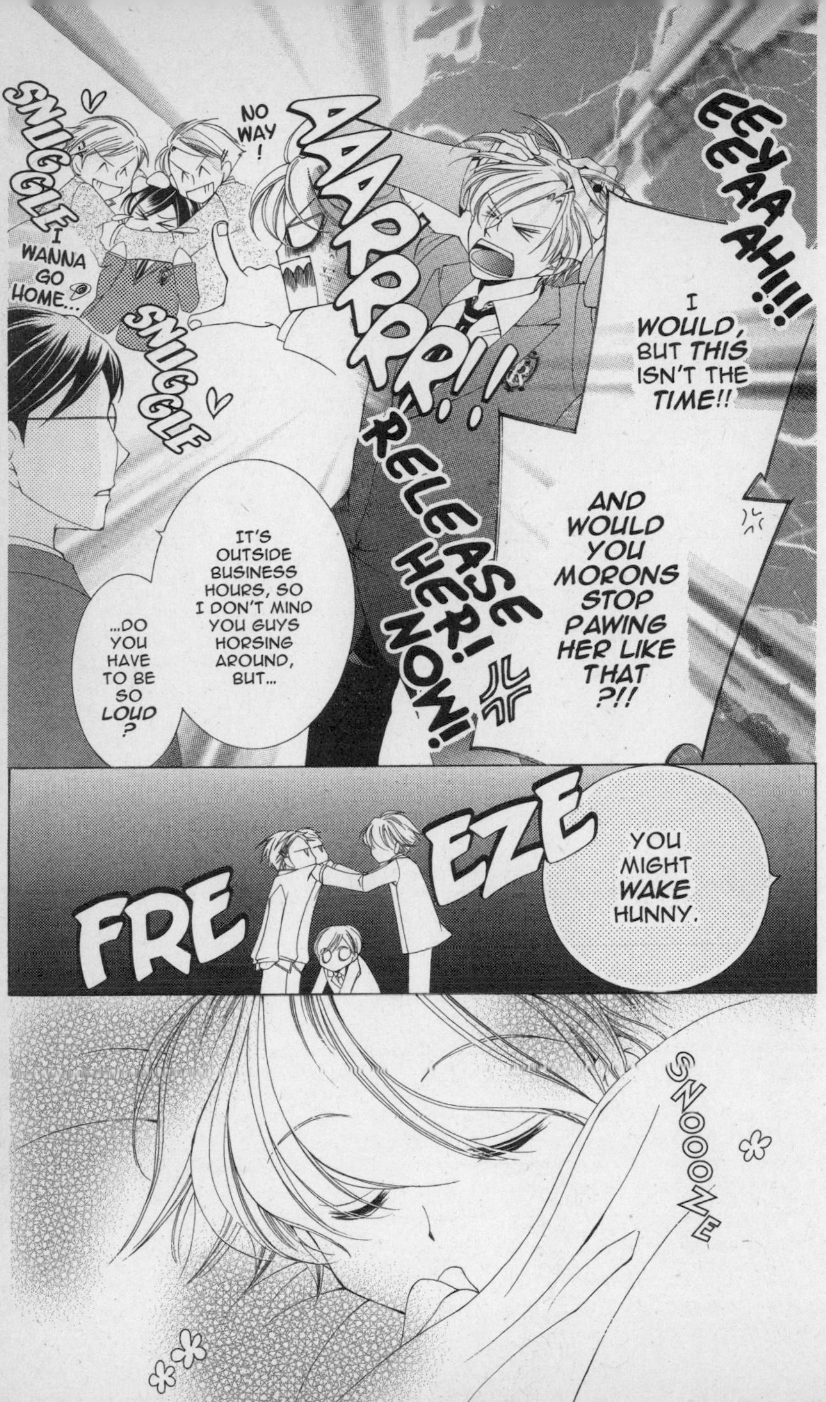
EEYAEEAAAH!!!!
I WOULD, BUT THIS ISN'T THE TIME!!
AND WOULD YOU MORONS STOP PAWING HER LIKE THAT?!!
RELEASE HER! NOW!
AAARRR!!
NO WAY!
SNIGGLE
I WANNA GO HOME...
SNIGGLE
IT'S OUTSIDE BUSINESS HOURS, SO I DON'T MIND YOU GUYS HORSING AROUND, BUT...
...DO YOU HAVE TO BE SO LOUD?
YOU MIGHT WAKE HUNNY.
FREEZE
SNOOZE

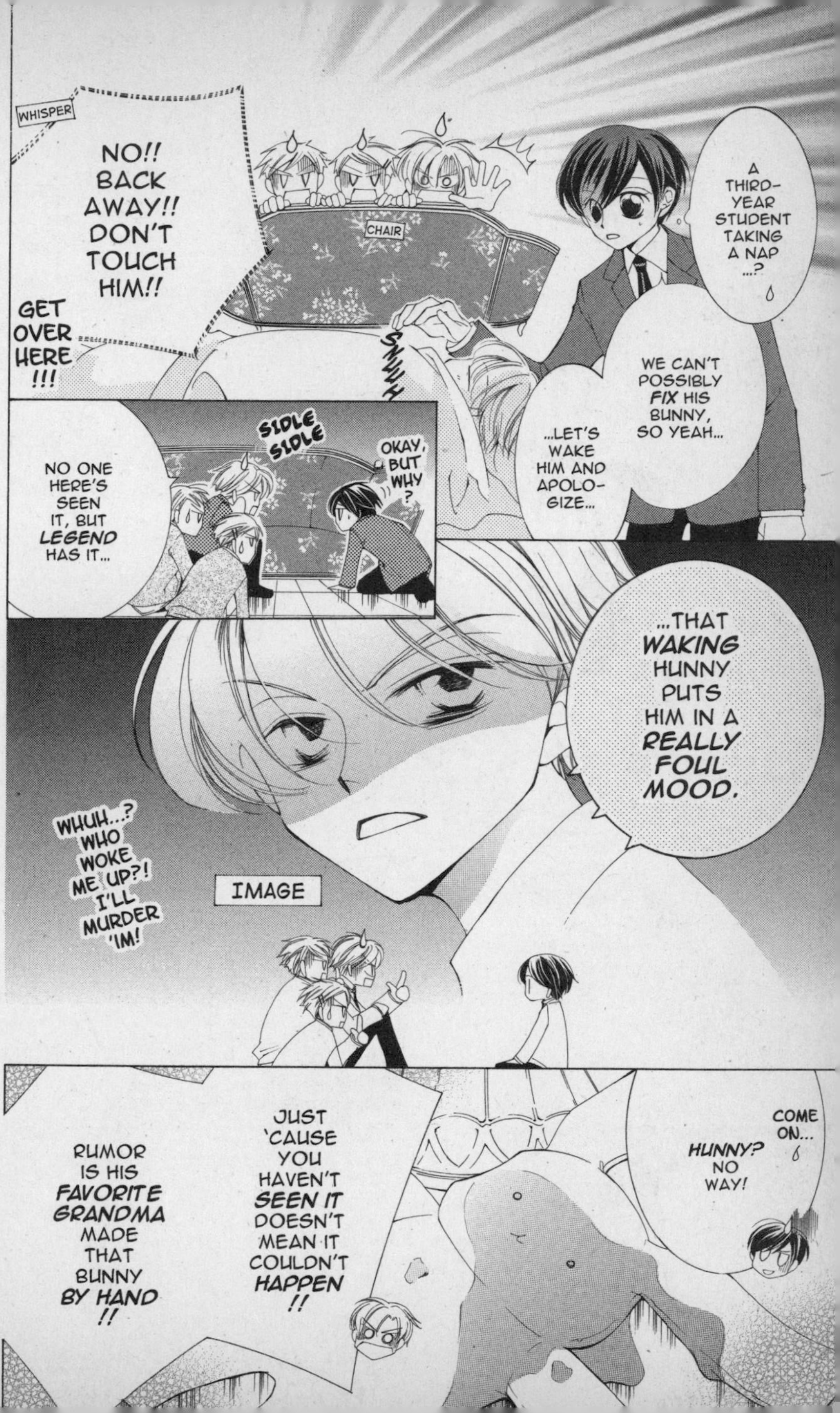
A THIRD-YEAR STUDENT TAKING A NAP ...?
WE CAN'T POSSIBLY FIX HIS BUNNY, SO YEAH...
...LET'S WAKE HIM AND APOLOGIZE...
SNUH
CHAIR
WHISPER
NO!! BACK AWAY!! DON'T TOUCH HIM!!
GET OVER HERE !!!
OKAY, BUT WHY?
SIDLE SIDLE
NO ONE HERE'S SEEN IT, BUT LEGEND HAS IT...
...THAT WAKING HUNNY PUTS HIM IN A REALLY FOUL MOOD.
WHUH...? WHO WOKE ME UP?! I'LL MURDER 'IM!
IMAGE
COME ON... HUNNY? NO WAY!
JUST 'CAUSE YOU HAVEN'T SEEN IT DOESN'T MEAN IT COULDN'T HAPPEN !!
RUMOR IS HIS FAVORITE GRANDMA MADE THAT BUNNY BY HAND !!

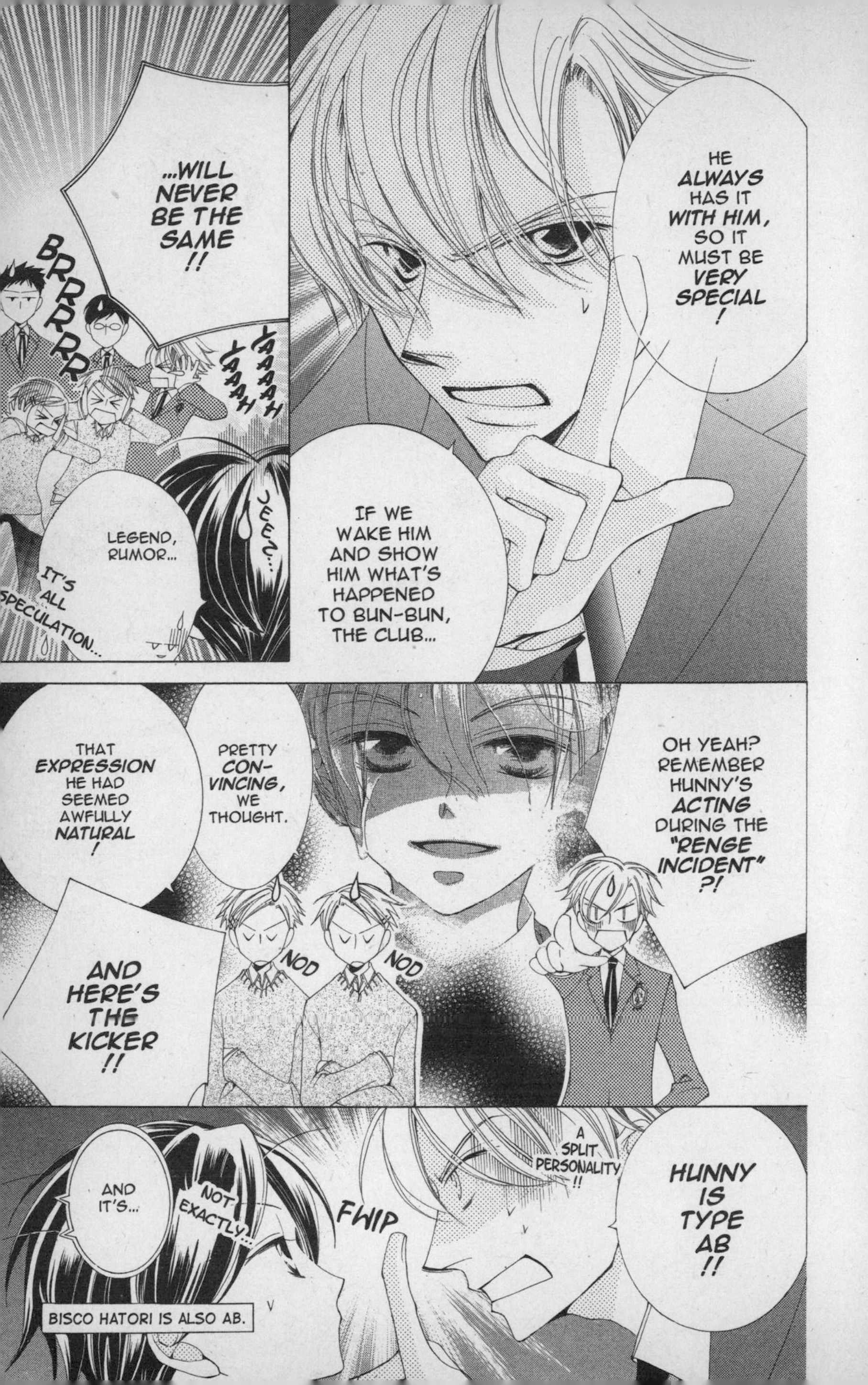
HE ALWAYS HAS IT WITH HIM, SO IT MUST BE VERY SPECIAL!
IF WE WAKE HIM AND SHOW HIM WHAT'S HAPPENED TO BUN-BUN, THE CLUB...
...WILL NEVER BE THE SAME!!
BRRRRRR
YAAAAAH YAAAAH
JEEE...
LEGEND, RUMOR...
IT'S ALL SPECULATION...
OH YEAH? REMEMBER HUNNY'S ACTING DURING THE "RENGE INCIDENT"?!
PRETTY CONVINCING, WE THOUGHT.
THAT EXPRESSION HE HAD SEEMED AWFULLY NATURAL!
NOD
NOD
AND HERE'S THE KICKER!!
HUNNY IS TYPE AB!!
A SPLIT PERSONALITY!!
FWIP
NOT EXACTLY...
AND IT'S...
BISCO HATORI IS ALSO AB.

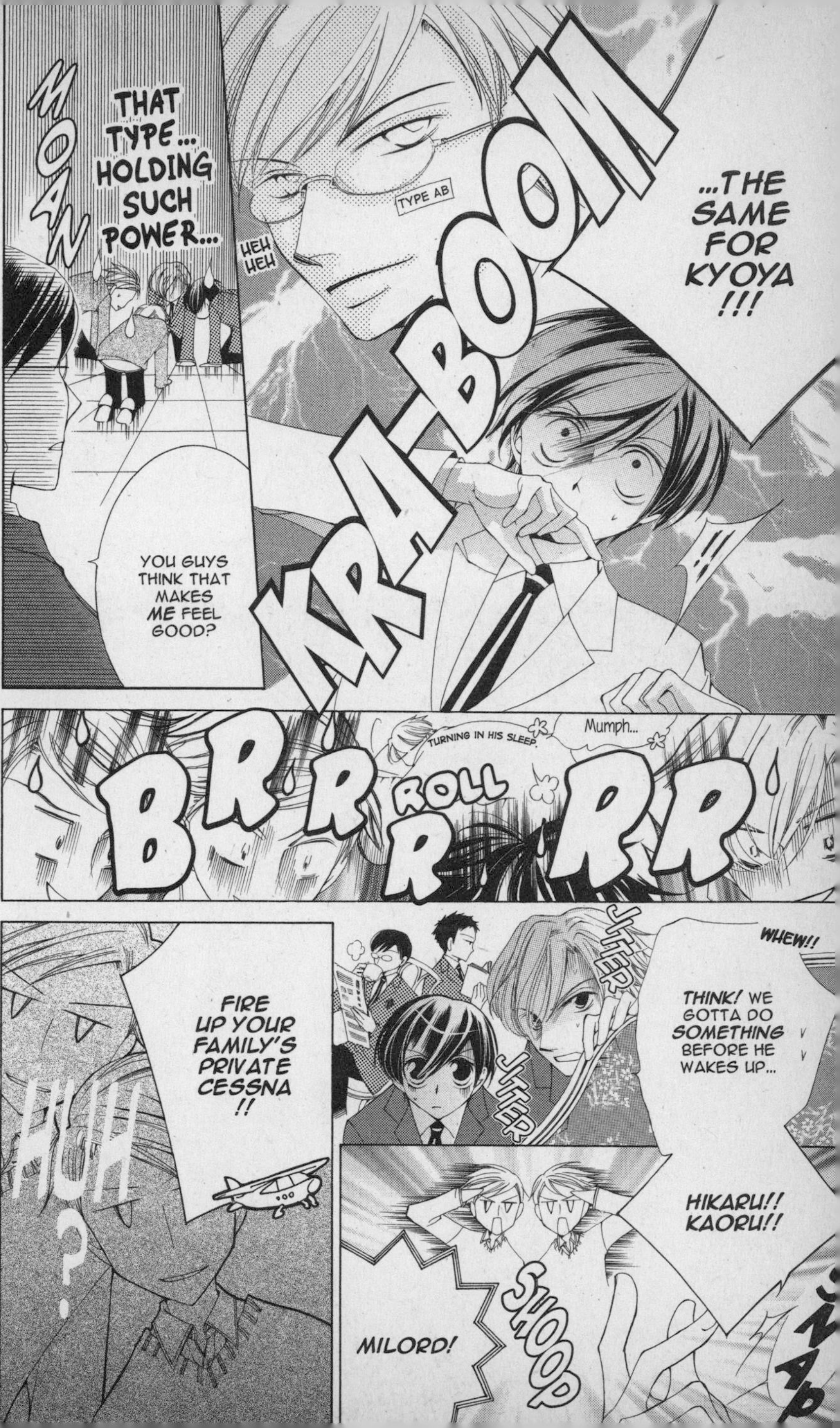
...THE SAME FOR KYOYA!!!
KRA-BOOM
TYPE AB
HEH HEH
!!
THAT TYPE... HOLDING SUCH POWER...
MOAN
YOU GUYS THINK THAT MAKES ME FEEL GOOD?
Mumph...
TURNING IN HIS SLEEP.
BRRR ROLL RRRR
WHEW!!
THINK! WE GOTTA DO SOMETHING BEFORE HE WAKES UP...
JITTER
JITTER
HIKARU!! KAORU!!
SNAP
SHOOP
MILORD!
FIRE UP YOUR FAMILY'S PRIVATE CESSNA!!
HUH?

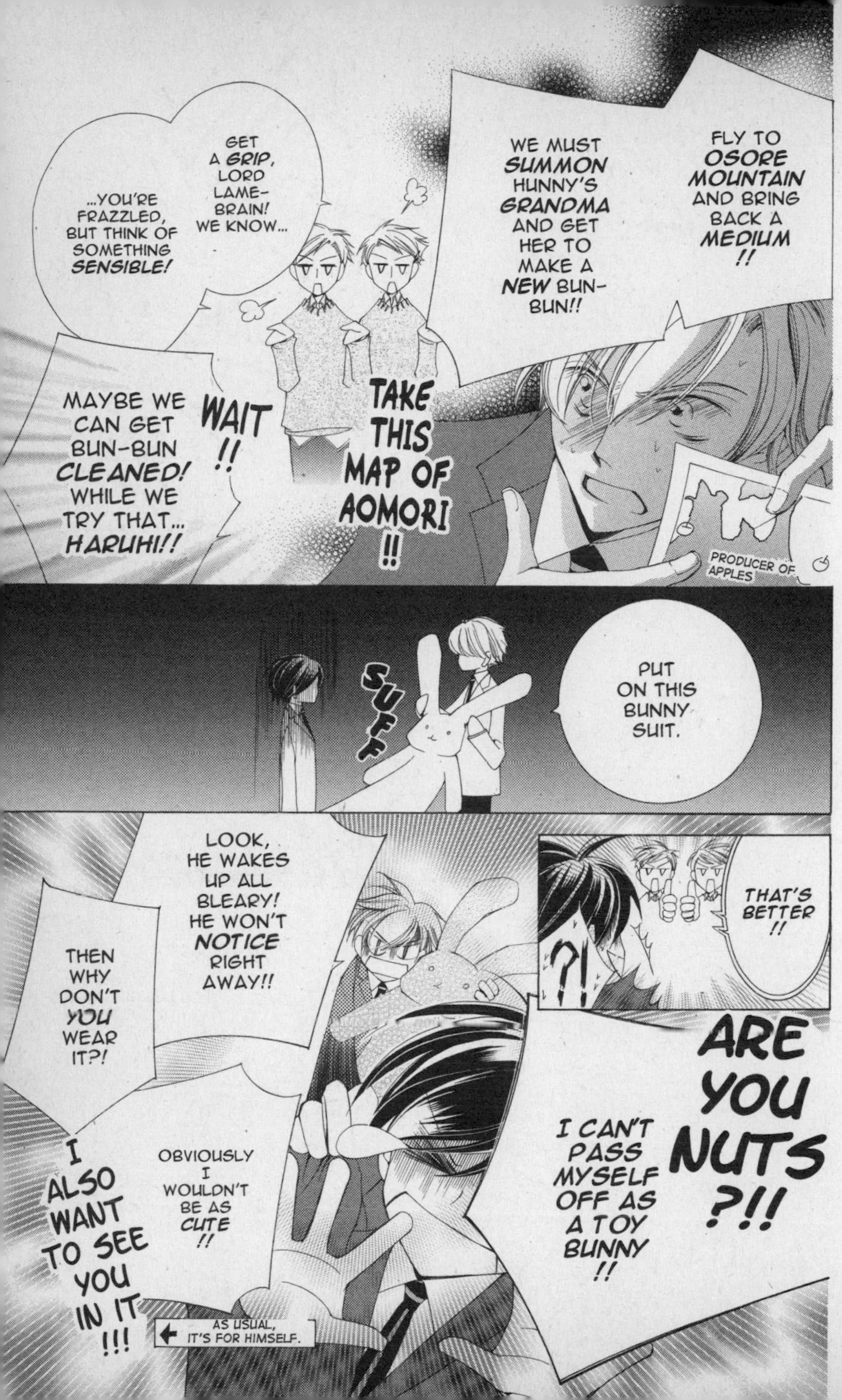
FLY TO OSORE MOUNTAIN AND BRING BACK A MEDIUM!!
WE MUST SUMMON HUNNY'S GRANDMA AND GET HER TO MAKE A NEW BUN-BUN!!
GET A GRIP, LORD LAME-BRAIN! WE KNOW...
...YOU'RE FRAZZLED, BUT THINK OF SOMETHING SENSIBLE!
TAKE THIS MAP OF AOMORI!!
PRODUCER OF APPLES
WAIT!!
MAYBE WE CAN GET BUN-BUN CLEANED! WHILE WE TRY THAT... HARUHI!!
PUT ON THIS BUNNY SUIT.
SUFF
THAT'S BETTER!!
?!
ARE YOU NUTS?!!
I CAN'T PASS MYSELF OFF AS A TOY BUNNY!!
LOOK, HE WAKES UP ALL BLEARY! HE WON'T NOTICE RIGHT AWAY!!
THEN WHY DON'T YOU WEAR IT?!
OBVIOUSLY I WOULDN'T BE AS CUTE!!
I ALSO WANT TO SEE YOU IN IT!!!
AS USUAL, IT'S FOR HIMSELF.

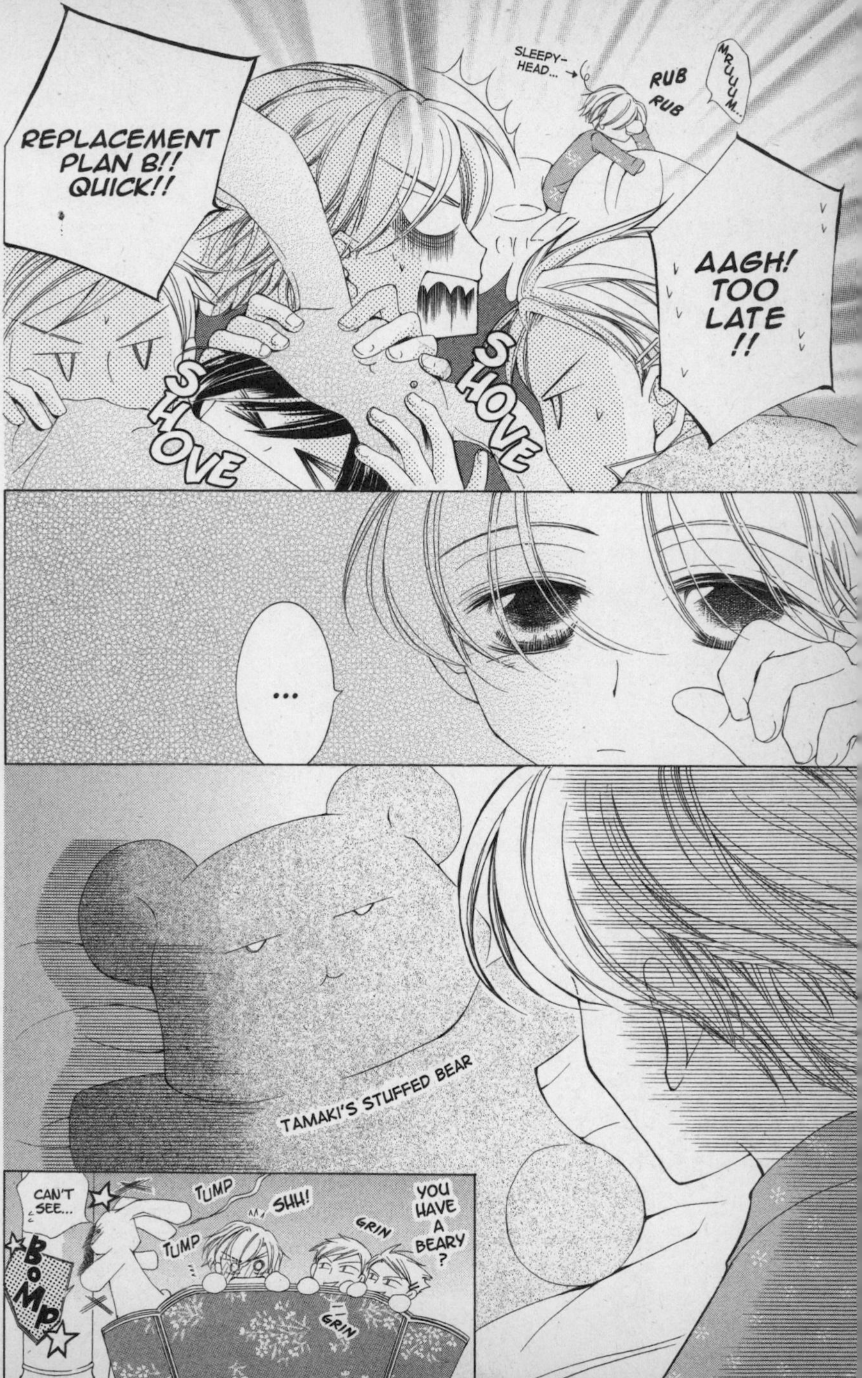
MRUUUM...
RUB RUB
SLEEPY-HEAD...
AAGH! TOO LATE!!
SHOVE
SHOVE
REPLACEMENT PLAN B!! QUICK!!
...
TAMAKI'S STUFFED BEAR
YOU HAVE A BEARY?
GRIN
GRIN
SHH!
TUMP
TUMP
CAN'T SEE...
BOMP

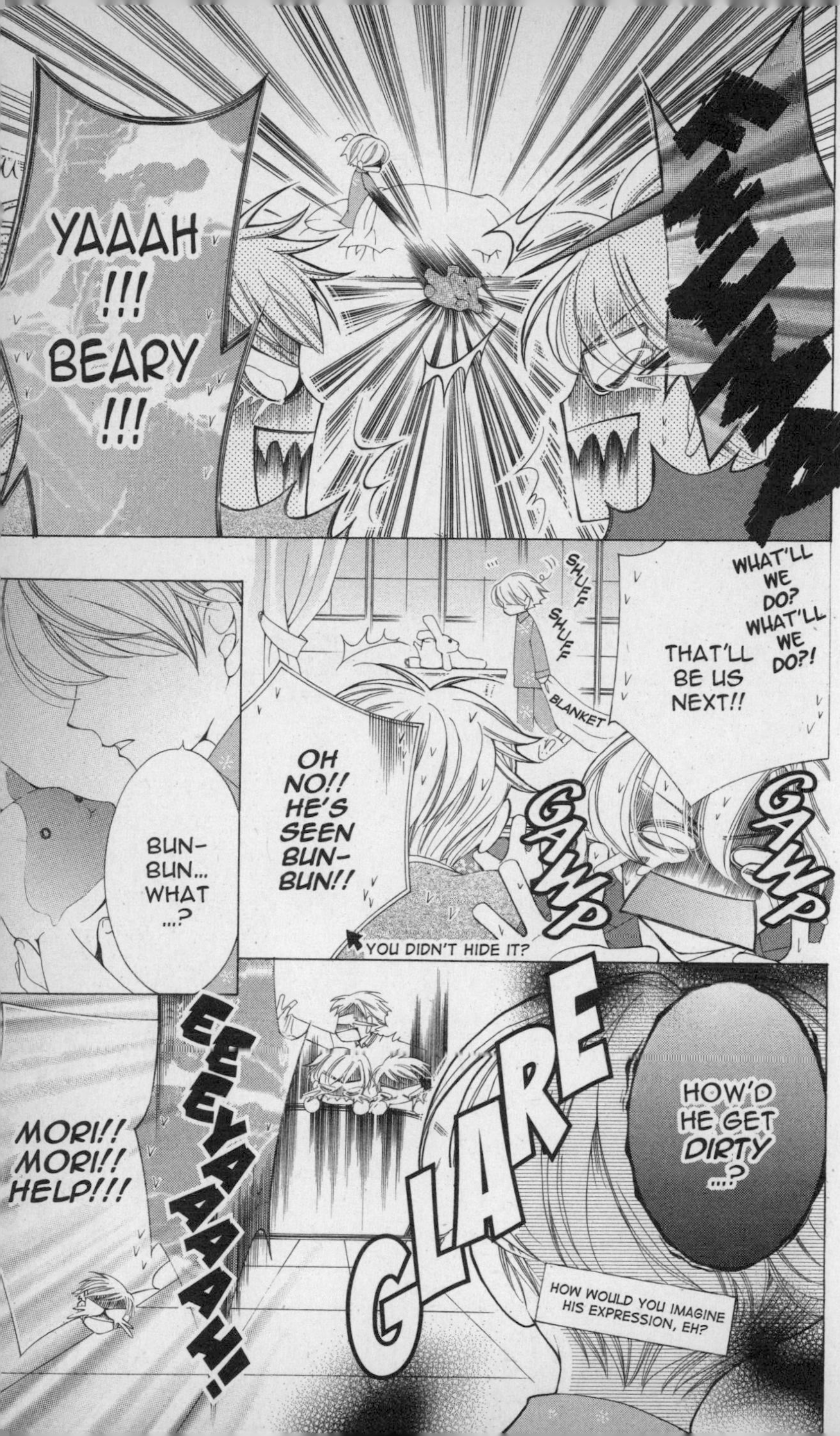
THWUMP
YAAAH!!! BEARY!!!
WHAT'LL WE DO? WHAT'LL WE DO?!
THAT'LL BE US NEXT!!
SHUFF SHUFF
BLANKET
GAWP GAWP
OH NO!! HE'S SEEN BUN-BUN!!
YOU DIDN'T HIDE IT?
BUN-BUN... WHAT ...?
HOW'D HE GET DIRTY ...?
GLARE
HOW WOULD YOU IMAGINE HIS EXPRESSION, EH?
EEEYAAAAAH!
MORI!! MORI!! HELP!!!

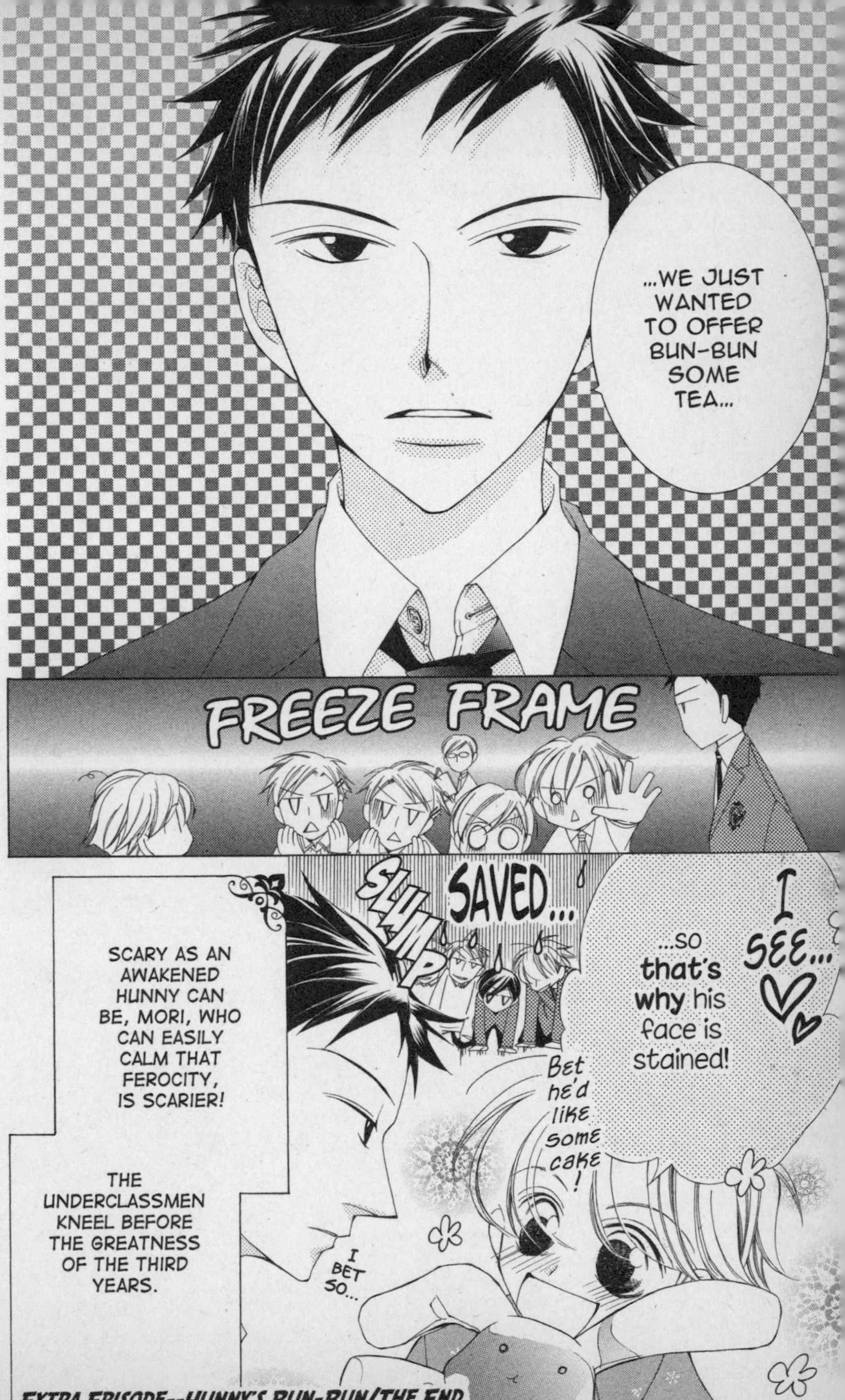
...WE JUST WANTED TO OFFER BUN-BUN SOME TEA...
FREEZE FRAME
I SEE...
...so that's why his face is stained!
SAVED...
SLUMP
Bet he'd like some cake!
I BET SO...
SCARY AS AN AWAKENED HUNNY CAN BE, MORI, WHO CAN EASILY CALM THAT FEROCITY, IS SCARIER!
THE UNDERCLASSMEN KNEEL BEFORE THE GREATNESS OF THE THIRD YEARS.

EXTRA EPISODE--HUNNY'S BUN-BUN/THE END

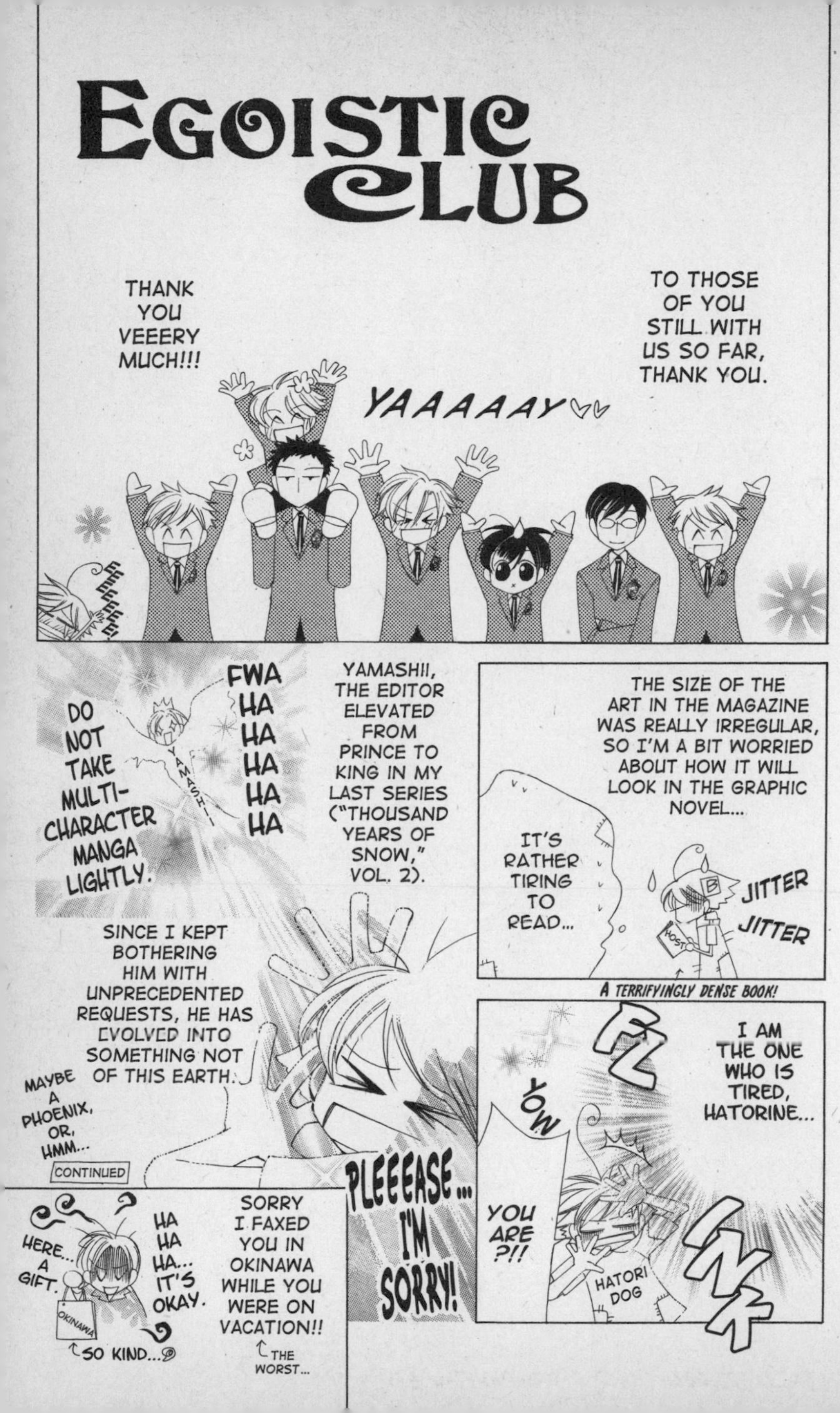
EGOISTIC CLUB
TO THOSE OF YOU STILL WITH US SO FAR, THANK YOU.
YAAAAAY
THANK YOU VEEERY MUCH!!!
EEEEEEEE!
THE SIZE OF THE ART IN THE MAGAZINE WAS REALLY IRREGULAR, SO I'M A BIT WORRIED ABOUT HOW IT WILL LOOK IN THE GRAPHIC NOVEL...
IT'S RATHER TIRING TO READ...
JITTER
JITTER
B
HOST
A TERRIFYINGLY DENSE BOOK!
I AM THE ONE WHO IS TIRED, HATORINE...
FL
INK
YOW
YOU ARE ?!!
HATORI DOG
YAMASHII, THE EDITOR ELEVATED FROM PRINCE TO KING IN MY LAST SERIES ("THOUSAND YEARS OF SNOW," VOL. 2).
FWA HA HA HA HA HA
DO NOT TAKE MULTI-CHARACTER MANGA LIGHTLY.
YAMASHII
SINCE I KEPT BOTHERING HIM WITH UNPRECEDENTED REQUESTS, HE HAS EVOLVED INTO SOMETHING NOT OF THIS EARTH.
MAYBE A PHOENIX, OR, HMM...
CONTINUED
PLEEEASE... I'M SORRY!
SORRY I FAXED YOU IN OKINAWA WHILE YOU WERE ON VACATION!!
THE WORST...
HA HA HA... IT'S OKAY.
HERE... A GIFT.
OKINAWA
SO KIND...

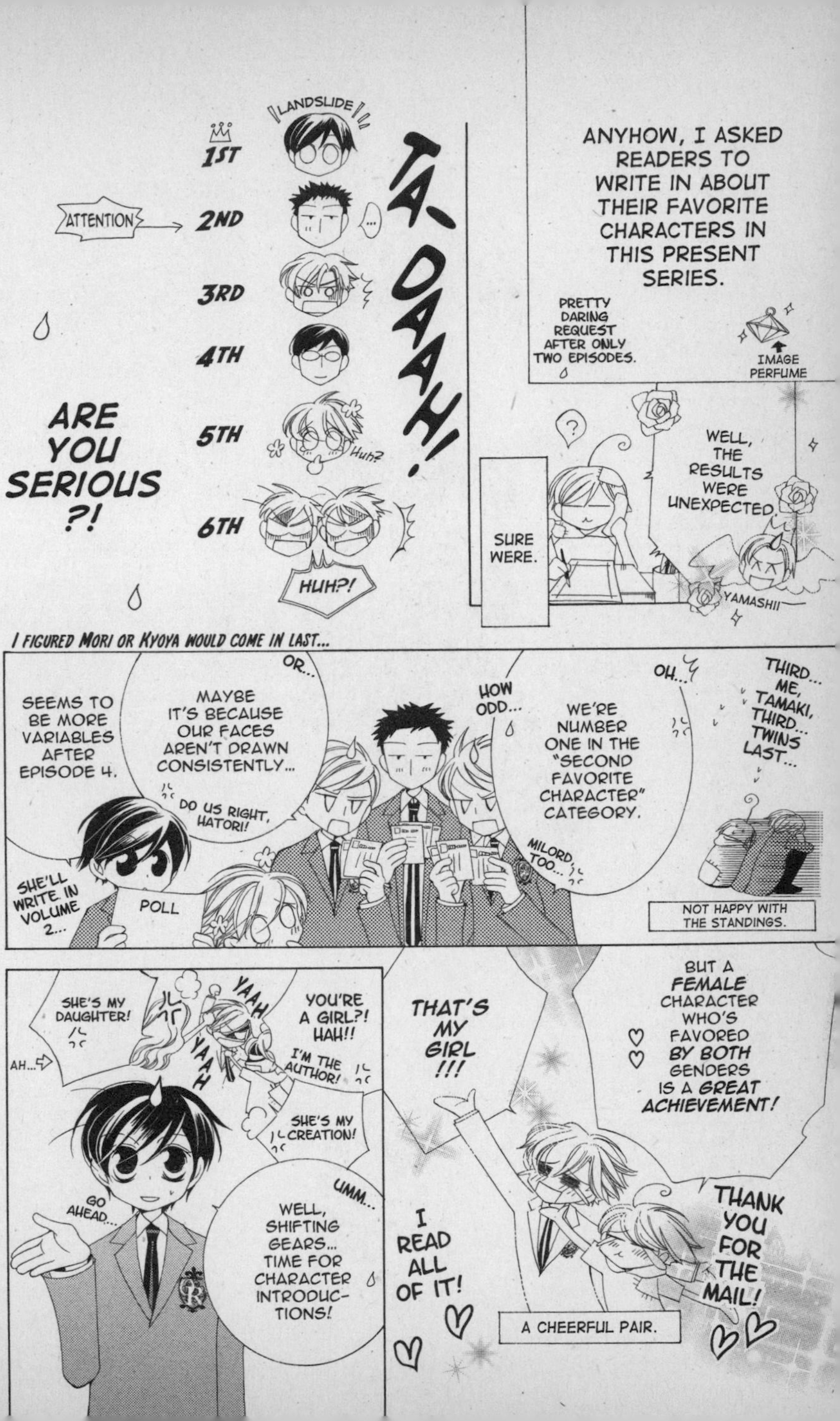
ANYHOW, I ASKED READERS TO WRITE IN ABOUT THEIR FAVORITE CHARACTERS IN THIS PRESENT SERIES.
IMAGE PERFUME
PRETTY DARING REQUEST AFTER ONLY TWO EPISODES.
WELL, THE RESULTS WERE UNEXPECTED.
YAMASHII
SURE WERE.
LANDSLIDE
1ST
ATTENTION
2ND
...
3RD
4TH
TA-DAAAH!!
5TH
Huh?
ARE YOU SERIOUS?!
6TH
HUH?!
I FIGURED MORI OR KYOYA WOULD COME IN LAST...
THIRD... ME, TAMAKI, THIRD... TWINS LAST...
NOT HAPPY WITH THE STANDINGS.
OH...
WE'RE NUMBER ONE IN THE "SECOND FAVORITE CHARACTER" CATEGORY.
HOW ODD...
MILORD, TOO...
OR...
MAYBE IT'S BECAUSE OUR FACES AREN'T DRAWN CONSISTENTLY...
DO US RIGHT, HATORI!
SEEMS TO BE MORE VARIABLES AFTER EPISODE 4.
SHE'LL WRITE IN VOLUME 2...
POLL
BUT A FEMALE CHARACTER WHO'S FAVORED BY BOTH GENDERS IS A GREAT ACHIEVEMENT!
THANK YOU FOR THE MAIL!
A CHEERFUL PAIR.
THAT'S MY GIRL!!!
I READ ALL OF IT!
YOU'RE A GIRL?! HAH!!
YAAH
YAAH
I'M THE AUTHOR!
SHE'S MY DAUGHTER!
SHE'S MY CREATION!
AH...
UMM...
WELL, SHIFTING GEARS... TIME FOR CHARACTER INTRODUCTIONS!
GO AHEAD...

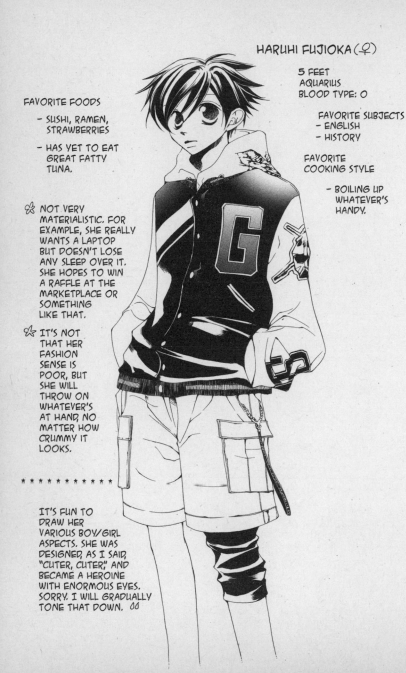

HARUHI FUJIOKA (♀)

5 FEET
AQUARIUS
BLOOD TYPE: O

FAVORITE SUBJECTS
- ENGLISH
- HISTORY

FAVORITE COOKING STYLE
- BOILING UP WHATEVER'S HANDY.

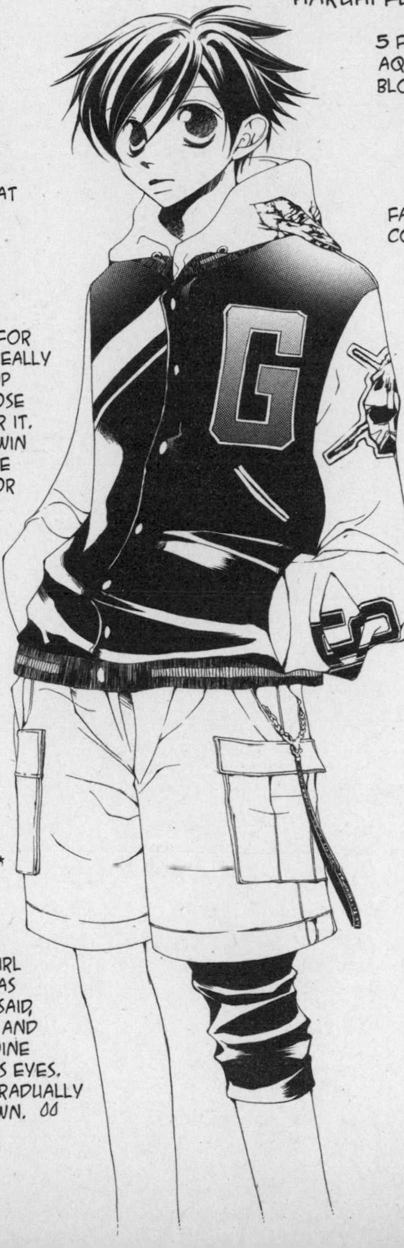

G
S

FAVORITE FOODS
- SUSHI, RAMEN, STRAWBERRIES
- HAS YET TO EAT GREAT FATTY TUNA.

✿ NOT VERY MATERIALISTIC. FOR EXAMPLE, SHE REALLY WANTS A LAPTOP BUT DOESN'T LOSE ANY SLEEP OVER IT. SHE HOPES TO WIN A RAFFLE AT THE MARKETPLACE OR SOMETHING LIKE THAT.

✿ IT'S NOT THAT HER FASHION SENSE IS POOR, BUT SHE WILL THROW ON WHATEVER'S AT HAND, NO MATTER HOW CRUMMY IT LOOKS.

* * * * * * * * * * * *

IT'S FUN TO DRAW HER VARIOUS BOY/GIRL ASPECTS. SHE WAS DESIGNED, AS I SAID, "CUTER, CUTER," AND BECAME A HEROINE WITH ENORMOUS EYES. SORRY. I WILL GRADUALLY TONE THAT DOWN.

TAMAKI SUOH

HOST CLUB KING
6 FEET
ARIES
BLOOD TYPE A

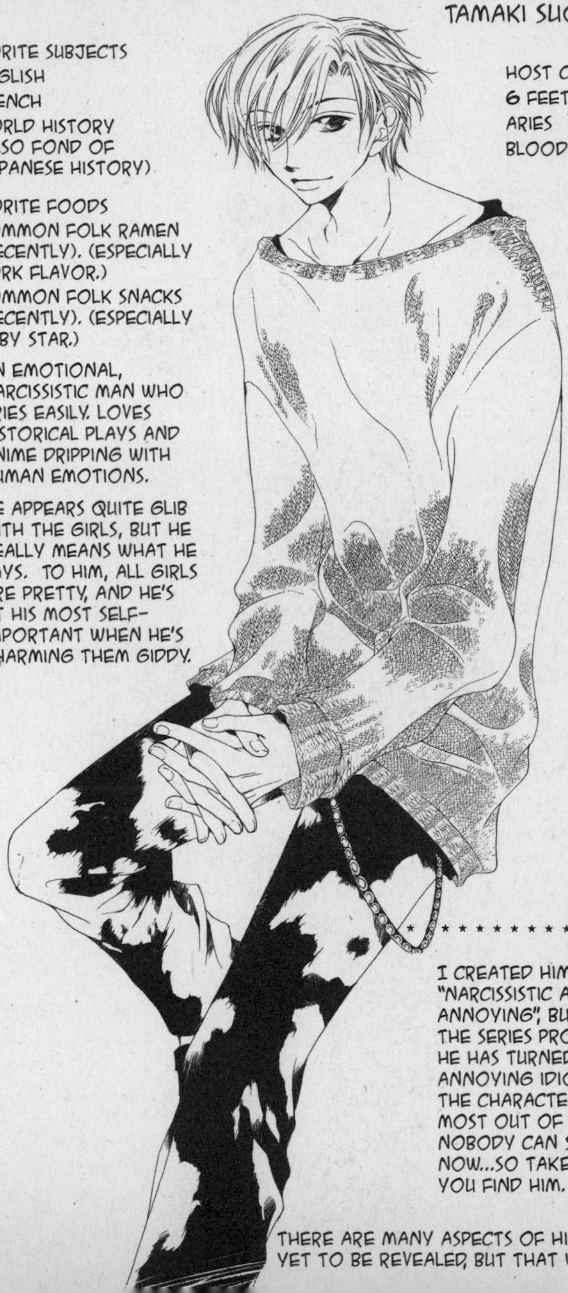

FAVORITE SUBJECTS
- ENGLISH
- FRENCH
- WORLD HISTORY (ALSO FOND OF JAPANESE HISTORY)

FAVORITE FOODS
- COMMON FOLK RAMEN (RECENTLY). (ESPECIALLY PORK FLAVOR.)
- COMMON FOLK SNACKS (RECENTLY). (ESPECIALLY BABY STAR.)

✿ AN EMOTIONAL, NARCISSISTIC MAN WHO CRIES EASILY. LOVES HISTORICAL PLAYS AND ANIME DRIPPING WITH HUMAN EMOTIONS.

✿ HE APPEARS QUITE GLIB WITH THE GIRLS, BUT HE REALLY MEANS WHAT HE SAYS. TO HIM, ALL GIRLS ARE PRETTY, AND HE'S AT HIS MOST SELF-IMPORTANT WHEN HE'S CHARMING THEM GIDDY.

* *

I CREATED HIM TO BE "NARCISSISTIC AND ANNOYING", BUT AS THE SERIES PROGRESSED HE HAS TURNED INTO AN ANNOYING IDIOT. HE IS THE CHARACTER WHO'S MOST OUT OF CONTROL. NOBODY CAN STOP HIM NOW...SO TAKE HIM AS YOU FIND HIM.

THERE ARE MANY ASPECTS OF HIM THAT HAVE YET TO BE REVEALED, BUT THAT WILL COME LATER.

KYOYA OHTORI

HOST CLUB VICE PRESIDENT
5 FEET 10 INCHES
CANCER
BLOOD TYPE AB

FAVORITE SUBJECTS
- ENGLISH
- GERMAN
- PHYSICS

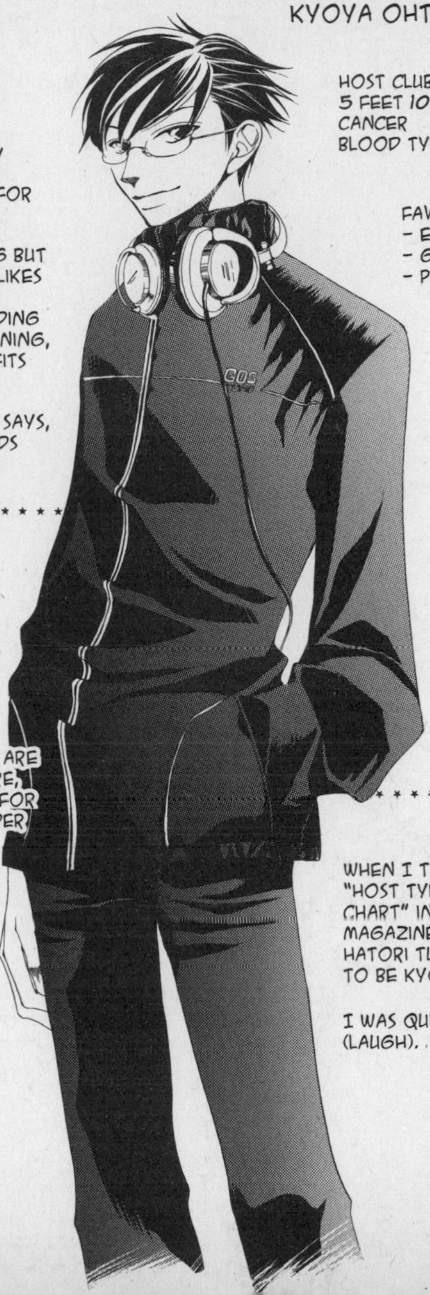

✿ FAVORITE FOODS
- ANYTHING SPICY

※ DOESN'T CARE FOR SWEET THINGS.

✿ HE IS CALCULATING BUT NOT GREEDY. HE LIKES TO MOVE THINGS FORWARD ACCORDING TO CAREFUL PLANNING, COLLECTING PROFITS ALONG THE WAY.

DESPITE WHAT HE SAYS, HE'S GOOD FRIENDS WITH TAMAKI.

* * * * * * * * * * * * * * * * * * *

IF "HOST CLUB"'S FIRST EPISODE HAD BEEN 40 PAGES INSTEAD OF 50, HE MIGHT HAVE BEEN CUT FROM THE CAST. (YIKES!)

SINCE THE REST OF THE MEMBERS ARE THE WAY THEY ARE, HE IS INVALUABLE FOR MAINTAINING ORDER AND OFFERING EXPLANATIONS. GOOD THING IT WAS 50 PAGES, KYOYA... ✦ (I MEAN FOR ME!)

HIS FASHION SENSE IS NOT "INTELLECTUAL" AT ALL.

* * * * * * * * * * * * * * * *

WHEN I TRIED THE "HOST TYPE HOROSCOPE CHART" IN THE MONTHLY MAGAZINE "LALA," HATORI TURNED OUT TO BE KYOYA...

I WAS QUITE OFFENDED (LAUGH).

HIKARU HITACHIIN (OLDER)
KAORU HITACHIIN (YOUNGER)

5 FEET 9 INCHES
GEMINI
BLOOD TYPE B

FAVORITE SUBJECTS
HIKARU - MATH, PHYSICS, CHEMISTRY
KAORU - ENGLISH, MODERN LITERATURE

THE FOLLOWING ARE FOR BOTH TWINS:

FAVORITE FOODS
- ITALIAN
- ANYTHING SUPER SPICY

THEY'RE NOT REALLY PARTIAL TO SPICY FOODS, SO MUCH AS BEING CONTRARY BY EATING WHATEVER'S "SO FIERY THAT NOBODY ELSE DARES TRY IT." THEY DO LOVE MAPLE SYRUP, THOUGH. PERHAPS NOT THE MOST IDEAL DINING COMPANIONS.

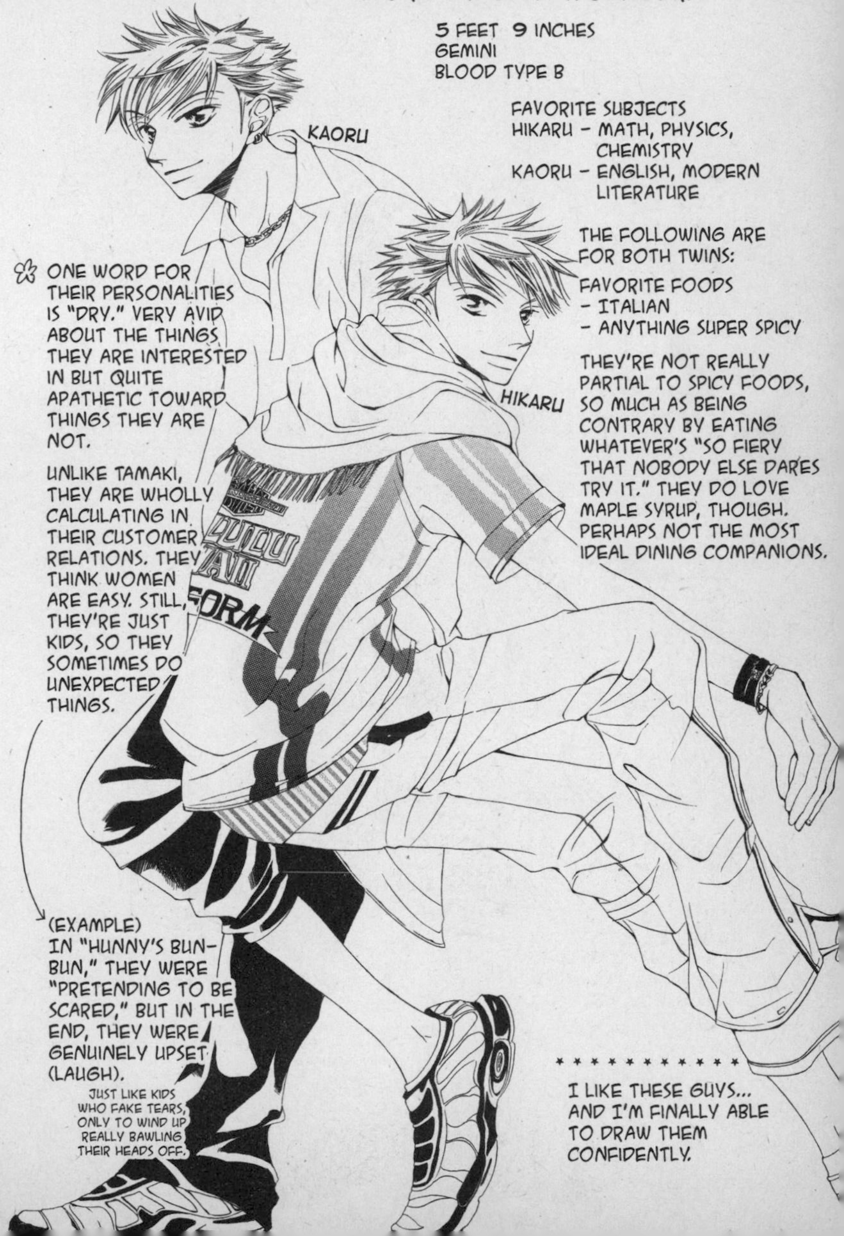
KAORU
HIKARU
FORM

✿ ONE WORD FOR THEIR PERSONALITIES IS "DRY." VERY AVID ABOUT THE THINGS THEY ARE INTERESTED IN BUT QUITE APATHETIC TOWARD THINGS THEY ARE NOT.

UNLIKE TAMAKI, THEY ARE WHOLLY CALCULATING IN THEIR CUSTOMER RELATIONS. THEY THINK WOMEN ARE EASY. STILL, THEY'RE JUST KIDS, SO THEY SOMETIMES DO UNEXPECTED THINGS.

(EXAMPLE)
IN "HUNNY'S BUN-BUN," THEY WERE "PRETENDING TO BE SCARED," BUT IN THE END, THEY WERE GENUINELY UPSET (LAUGH).

JUST LIKE KIDS WHO FAKE TEARS, ONLY TO WIND UP REALLY BAWLING THEIR HEADS OFF.

* * * * * * * * * * * *

I LIKE THESE GUYS... AND I'M FINALLY ABLE TO DRAW THEM CONFIDENTLY.

MITSUKUNI (HUNNY) HANINOZUKA

4 FEET 9 INCHES
(CAN SHRINK AT WILL). HA HA.
PISCES
BLOOD TYPE AB

FAVORITE SUBJECT
- MATH

FAVORITE FOODS
- CAKE, STRAWBERRIES
- WITH UNEXPECTED CRAVINGS FOR SPICY THINGS. (DOES NOT LIKE CARROTS.)

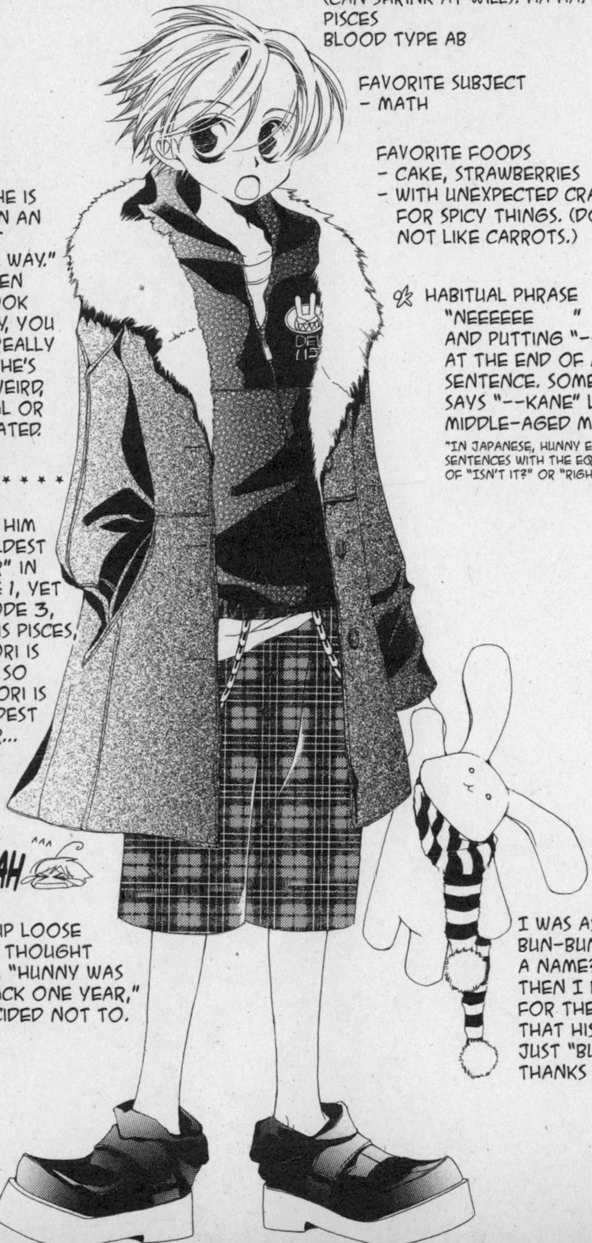

✿ HIS NICHE IS "CUTE IN AN ALMOST ILLEGAL WAY." BUT WHEN YOU LOOK CLOSELY, YOU CAN'T REALLY TELL IF HE'S CUTE, WEIRD, NATURAL OR CALCULATED.

✿ HABITUAL PHRASE
"NEEEEEE "
AND PUTTING "--NE" AT THE END OF A SENTENCE. SOMETIMES SAYS "--KANE" LIKE A MIDDLE-AGED MAN.*

*IN JAPANESE, HUNNY ENDS SENTENCES WITH THE EQUIVALENT OF "ISN'T IT?" OR "RIGHT?"

* * * * * * * * * * * * *

I MADE HIM "THE OLDEST MEMBER" IN EPISODE 1, YET IN EPISODE 3, HUNNY IS PISCES, AND MORI IS TAURUS, SO NOW MORI IS THE OLDEST MEMBER... SORRY ABOUT THAT.

WAAAAAH

TO TIE UP LOOSE ENDS, I THOUGHT I'D SAY, "HUNNY WAS HELD BACK ONE YEAR," BUT DECIDED NOT TO.

I WAS ASKED, "DOES BUN-BUN NOT HAVE A NAME?" THEN I REALIZED FOR THE FIRST TIME THAT HIS NAME IS JUST "BUN-BUN." THANKS (LAUGH).

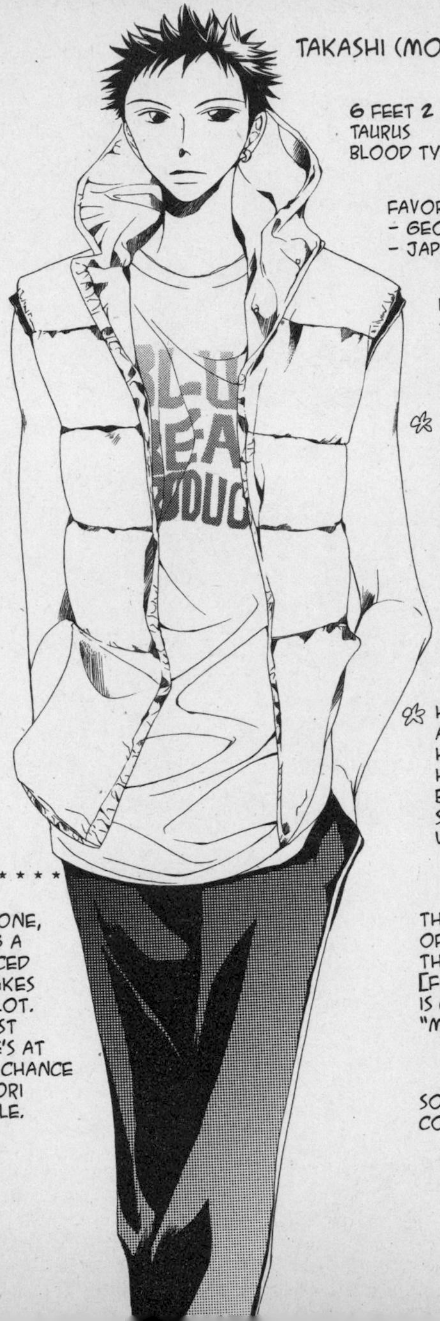

TAKASHI (MORI) MORINOZUKA

6 FEET 2 INCHES
TAURUS
BLOOD TYPE O

FAVORITE SUBJECTS
- GEOGRAPHY
- JAPANESE HISTORY

FAVORITE FOOD
- ORIENTAL (LIKE FERMENTED NATTO SOYBEANS)

"STRONG, YET KIND." PICTURE A SIBERIAN HUSKY... HE'S JUST LIKE ONE (LAUGH). BY THE WAY, HUNNY'S LIKE A POMERANIAN.

HE'S IN THE KENDO CLUB AND ONLY JOINED THE HOST CLUB BECAUSE HUNNY DID. HE SEEMS TO BE HAVING SOME FUN, SO I THINK HE'S OKAY WITH IT (LAUGH).

IF I LEAVE HIM ALONE, HE WINDS UP BEING A "QUIET, SOBER-FACED FELLOW," SO HE MAKES HATORI GROAN A LOT. BUT HIS LOVE IS VAST (LAUGH), SO THERE'S AT LEAST AN OUTSIDE CHANCE OF HARUHI AND MORI BECOMING A COUPLE.

THE PRONOUNCIATION OF "MORINOZUKA" IS THE SAME AS "MORI" [FOREST], BUT WHEN HE IS CALLED "MORI," THE "MO" IS EMPHASIZED.

SORRY FOR THE CONFUSION.

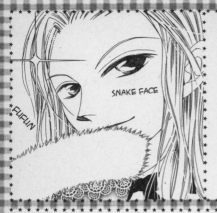

AYANOKOJI

A STEREOTYPICAL EVIL MISTRESS-TYPE CHARACTER. AS IT'S SO OBVIOUS, SHE SEEMS QUITE FRESH AND SOMEWHAT LIKABLE (LAUGH).

THROWING HARUHI'S BAG INTO A POND HERSELF, RATHER THAN LEAVING IT TO HER GOONS, ALSO MAKES HER A LITTLE MORE APPEALING (LAUGH).

SHE IS ACTUALLY A THIRD YEAR IN CLASS A. SINCE THE RECOUNTED INCIDENT, I FEEL SAD WHENEVER I THINK HOW SHE'S DOING IN HUNNY'S AND MORI'S CLASS...

SNAKE FACE
FUFUN

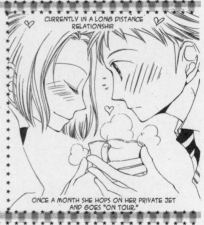

CURRENTLY IN A LONG DISTANCE RELATIONSHIP.
ONCE A MONTH SHE HOPS ON HER PRIVATE JET AND GOES "ON TOUR."

2-B KANAKO KASUGAZAKI
2-C TORU SUZUSHIMA

THE REASON TORU FEELS LESS THAN SUITABLE FOR KANAKO IS BECAUSE HE'S OF LOWER BIRTH. (THEY ARE BOTH FILTHY RICH, THOUGH.)

SHRUGGING OFF THE WARNING OF "TWO GUESTS IN THE SECOND EPISODE IS RECKLESS," IN THE END I DID 50 PAGES INVOLVING NINE CHARACTERS AND HIT ON THE CHRISTMAS PARTY IDEA IN A VERITABLE PANIC (BROUGHT UPON BY MYSELF...). I JUST COULDN'T THINK OF ANYTHING ELSE...

RENGE HOSHAKUJI

HATORI DOESN'T PLAY ANY GAMES, BUT SHE'S A REAL OTAKU! (HA! READ "FAN GIRL!") AH, GROUPIES ARE WONDERFUL... (LAUGH). I DID THIS EPISODE WANTING TO REASSURE AND AMUSE THOSE WHO MIGHT THINK THEY WERE OTAKU.

I INTEND HER AS A SEMI-REGULAR, BUT WHEN SHE APPEARS, THE STORY TENDS TO STRAY, SO I WILL RESTRICT HER TO OCCASIONAL VISITS. DRAWING BOTH OUT-OF-CONTROL CHARACTERS, TAMAKI AND RENGE, AT THE SAME TIME COULD BE DANGEROUS...

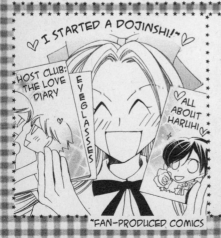

I STARTED A DOJINSHI!*
HOST CLUB: THE LOVE DIARY
EYEGLASSES
ALL ABOUT HARUHI

*FAN-PRODUCED COMICS

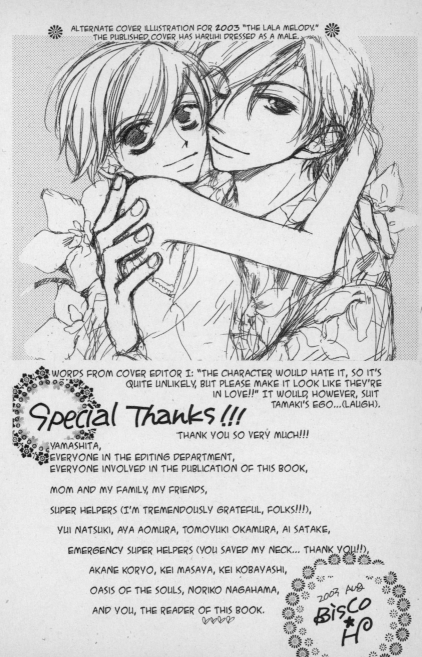

ALTERNATE COVER ILLUSTRATION FOR 2003 "THE LALA MELODY."
THE PUBLISHED COVER HAS HARUHI DRESSED AS A MALE.

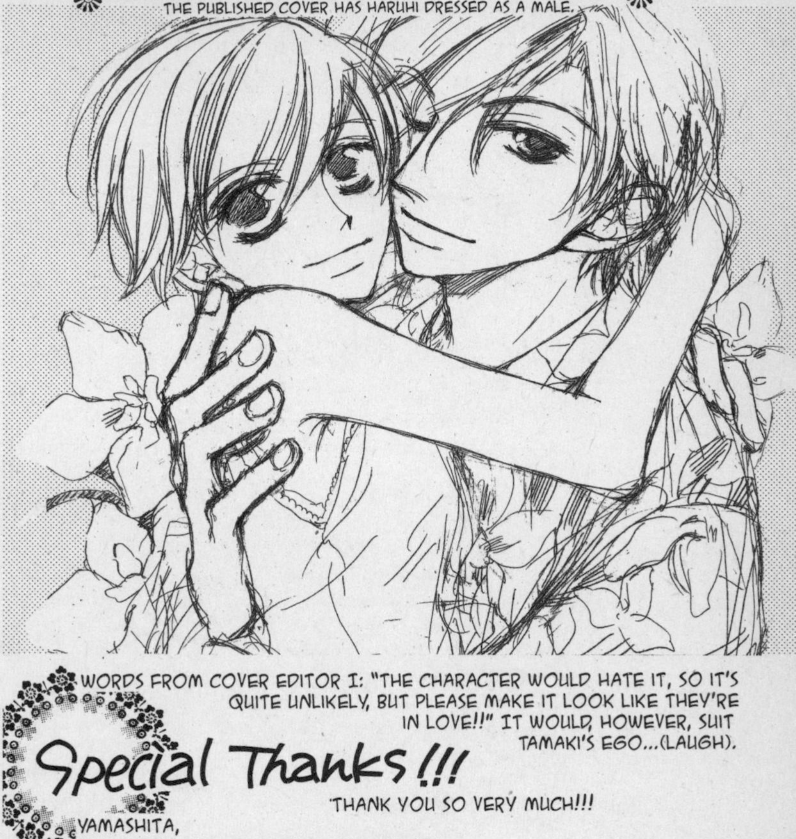

WORDS FROM COVER EDITOR I: "THE CHARACTER WOULD HATE IT, SO IT'S QUITE UNLIKELY, BUT PLEASE MAKE IT LOOK LIKE THEY'RE IN LOVE!!" IT WOULD, HOWEVER, SUIT TAMAKI'S EGO...(LAUGH).

Special Thanks!!!

THANK YOU SO VERY MUCH!!!

YAMASHITA,
EVERYONE IN THE EDITING DEPARTMENT,
EVERYONE INVOLVED IN THE PUBLICATION OF THIS BOOK,

MOM AND MY FAMILY, MY FRIENDS,

SUPER HELPERS (I'M TREMENDOUSLY GRATEFUL, FOLKS!!!),

YUI NATSUKI, AYA AOMURA, TOMOYUKI OKAMURA, AI SATAKE,

EMERGENCY SUPER HELPERS (YOU SAVED MY NECK... THANK YOU!!),

AKANE KORYO, KEI MASAYA, KEI KOBAYASHI,

OASIS OF THE SOULS, NORIKO NAGAHAMA,

AND YOU, THE READER OF THIS BOOK.

♡♡♡♡

2003 Aug
Bisco * H

EGOISTIC CLUB/THE END

Author Bio

Bisco Hatori made her manga debut with **Isshun kan no Romance (A Moment of Romance)** in **LaLa DX** magazine. The comedy **Ouran High School Host Club** is her breakout hit. When she's stuck thinking up characters' names, she gets inspired by loud, upbeat music (her radio is set to NACK5 FM). She enjoys reading all kinds of manga, but she's especially fond of the sci-fi drama **Please Save My Earth** and **Slam Dunk**, a basketball classic.

OURAN HIGH SCHOOL HOST CLUB
Vol. 1
The Shojo Beat Manga Edition

STORY AND ART BY BISCO HATORI

English Adaptation/Gary Leach
Translation/Kenichiro Yagi
Touch-up Art & Lettering/Curtis Yee
Graphic Design/Izumi Evers
Editor/Yuki Takagaki

Managing Editor/Megan Bates
Director of Production/Noboru Watanabe
Vice President of Publishing/Alvin Lu
Vice President & Editor in Chief/ Yumi Hoashi
Sr. Director of Acquisitions/Rika Inouye
Vice President of Sales & Marketing/Liza Coppola
Publisher/Hyoe Narita

Printed in the U.S.A.

Published by VIZ Media, LLC
P.O. Box 77010
San Francisco, CA 94107

Shojo Beat Manga Edition
10 9 8 7 6 5 4 3 2 1
First printing, June 2005

PARENTAL ADVISORY
OURAN HIGH SCHOOL HOST CLUB is rated
T for Teen. Contains some sexual themes.
Recommended for ages 13 and up.

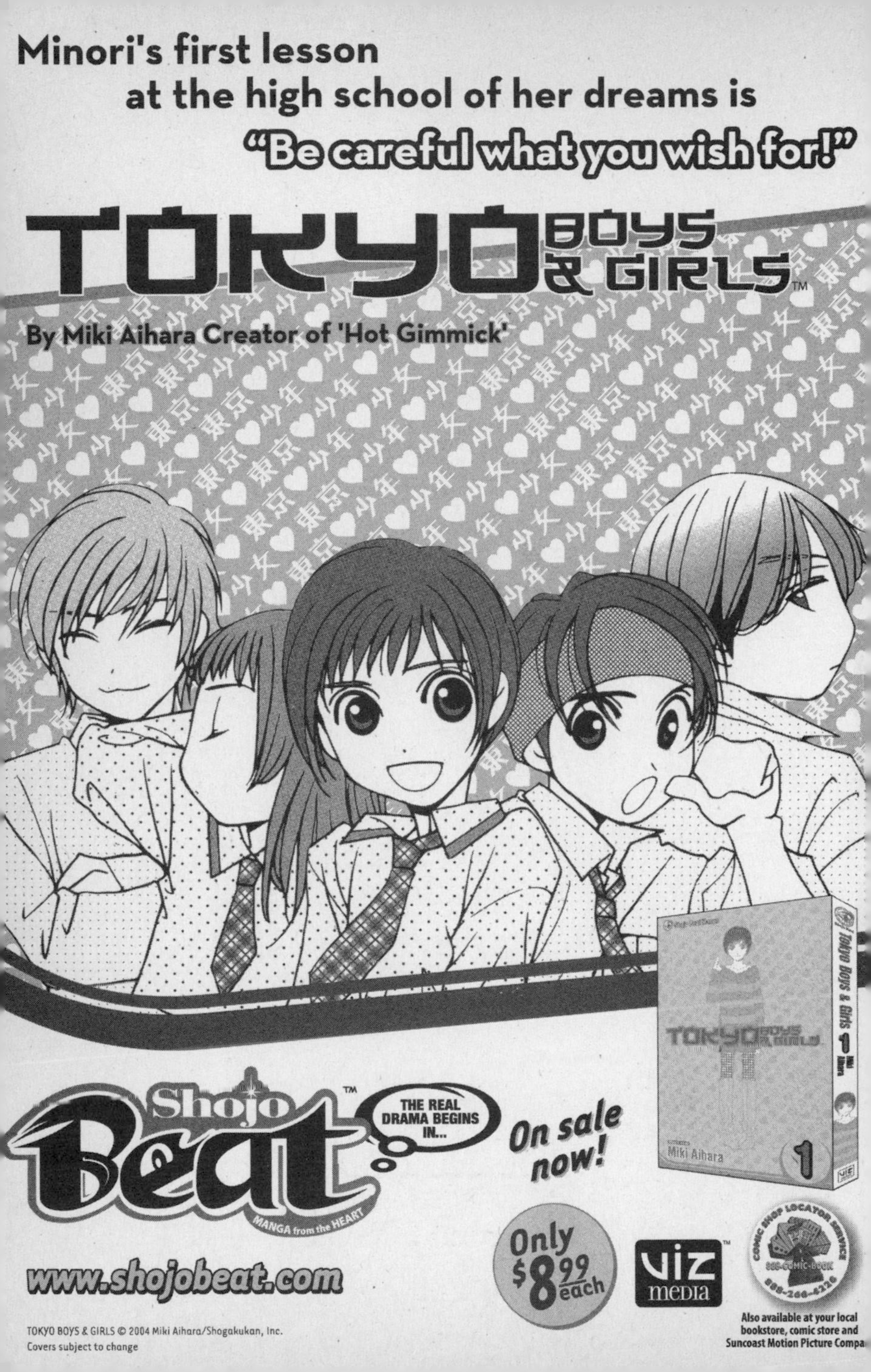
Minori's first lesson
at the high school of her dreams is
"Be careful what you wish for!"
TOKYO BOYS & GIRLS™
By Miki Aihara Creator of 'Hot Gimmick'
Shojo Beat™
MANGA from the HEART
THE REAL DRAMA BEGINS IN...
On sale now!
Only $8.99 each
www.shojobeat.com
VIZ media™
COMIC SHOP LOCATOR SERVICE
888-COMIC-BOOK
888-266-4226
Also available at your local bookstore, comic store and Suncoast Motion Picture Compa
TOKYO BOYS & GIRLS © 2004 Miki Aihara/Shogakukan, Inc.
Covers subject to change

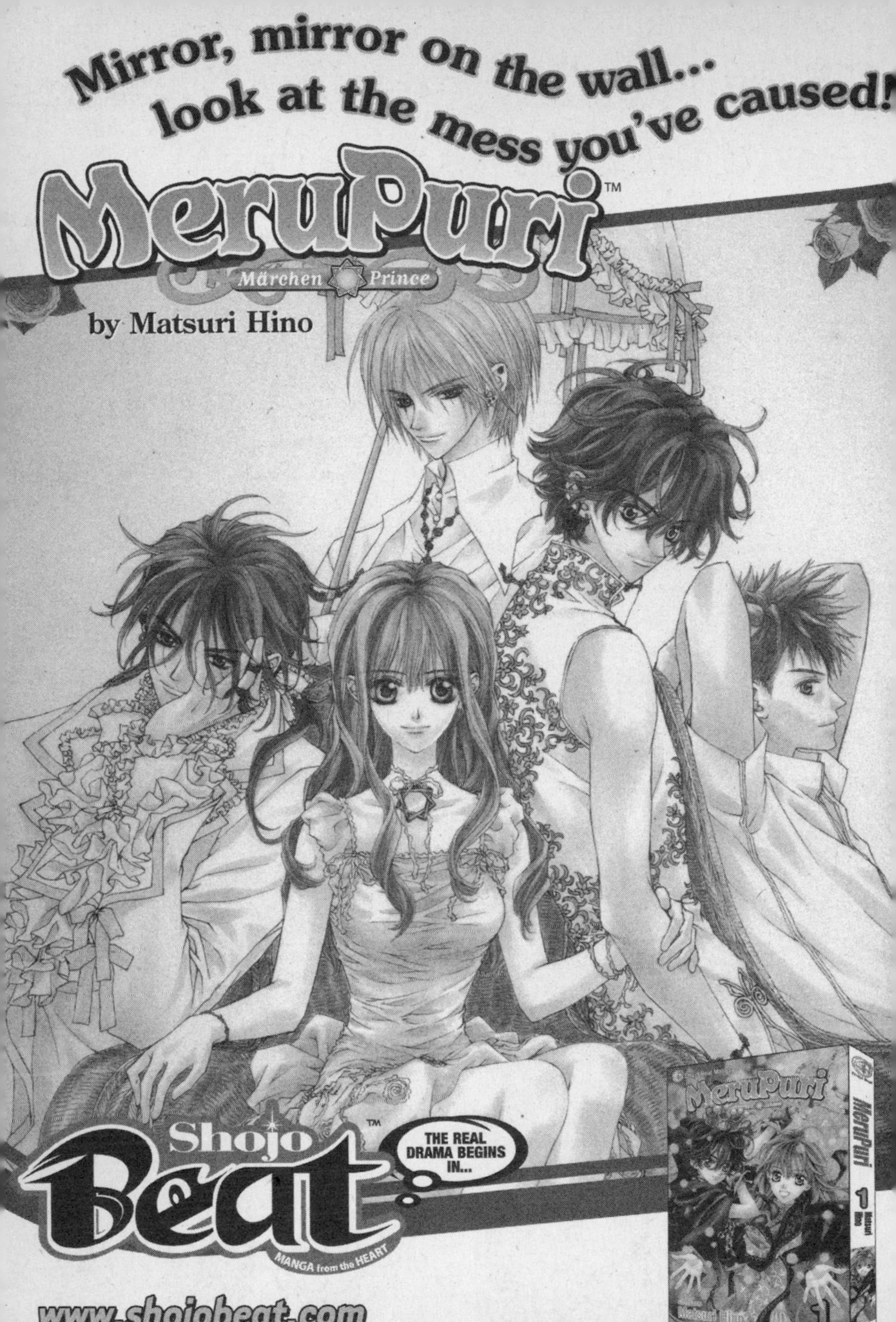
Mirror, mirror on the wall...
look at the mess you've caused!
MeruPuri™
Märchen Prince
by Matsuri Hino
Shojo Beat™
MANGA from the HEART
THE REAL DRAMA BEGINS IN...
www.shojobeat.com

Find the Beat online!
Check us out at
www.shojobeat.com!